Orbis Biblicus et Orientalis 125

Studies in the Iconography of Northwest Semitic Inscribed Seals

Proceedings of a symposium
held in Fribourg on April 17–20, 1991

edited by
Benjamin Sass and Christoph Uehlinger

University Press Fribourg Switzerland
Vandenhoeck & Ruprecht Göttingen

Die Deutsche Bibliothek – CIP-Einheitsaufnahme

Studies in the Iconography of Northwest Semitic Inscribed Seals.
Proceedings of a symposium held in Fribourg on April 17–20, 1991.
Edited by Benjamin Sass and Christoph Uehlinger. – Freiburg, Schweiz: Univ.-Verl.; Göttingen: Vandenhoeck & Ruprecht, 1993.
(Orbis biblicus et orientalis; 125)
ISBN 3-525-53760-3 (Vandenhoeck & Ruprecht)
ISBN 3-7278-0870-5 (Univ.-Verl.)
NE: Sass, Benjamin [Hrsg.]; Uehlinger, Christoph [Hrsg.]; GT

Publication subsidized by the Swiss Academy
of Humanities and Social Sciences, Berne

Die Druckvorlagen wurden von den Herausgebern
als reprofertige Dokumente zur Verfügung gestellt

Paulusdruckerei Freiburg Schweiz

ISBN 3-7278-0870-5 (Universitätsverlag)
ISBN 3-525-53760-3 (Vandenhoeck & Ruprecht)

CONTENTS

PREFACE

The present volume contains revised versions of the papers read at a symposium entitled "The Iconography of Northwest Semitic Inscribed Seals", held at the University of Fribourg (Switzerland) on April 17-20, 1991. The symposium was planned as part of a research project headed by Prof. Othmar Keel, with Benjamin Sass as associate, and sponsored by the Swiss National Fund for Scientific Research (project no. 12–26253.89: "Origin and effect of the biblical image ban as reflected in inscribed Hebrew seals of the 9th to 6th centuries BC"). It took place under the auspices of the Biblical Institute of the University of Fribourg and the Swiss Society for the Study of the Ancient Orient. Othmar Keel initiated the symposium, selected the topics, invited the contributors, and chaired the working sessions. Dr Dominique Collon (London, The British Museum) and Dr Felice Israel (Università degli Studi di Genova) participated as respondents. After three stimulating days of scholarly exchange, summaries of the papers and a synopsis of the symposium were presented at the spring meeting of the Swiss Society for the Study of the Ancient Orient.

We recall with gratitude the atmosphere of friendship and fruitful scholarly discussion engendered by the warmhearted hospitality of Hildi and Othmar Keel-Leu. Financial support was generously provided by the Swiss National Fund for Scientific Research, the Swiss Society for the Study of the Ancient Orient, the Jean Nordmann Foundation (Fribourg), and the Biblical Institute.

With the symposium's successful culmination, it was decided to publish the papers in the "Orbis Biblicus et Orientalis" series. Significant revisions have been made in some of the articles. Furthermore, the editors have added numerous cross-references which, together with the cumulative bibliography and the indices, should enhance the volume's utility for specialists and for scholars in neighbouring fields alike. The introduction and the concluding article have been written during the editorial preparation of the book, when it appeared that a synthesis, a review of some methodological issues and an outline of religio-historical perspectives would be a useful complement to the volume.

During the preparation of this book, we were fortunate to have the help of several people: Ines Haselbach and Andrea Jäkle assisted us with the assemblage and layout of figures and plates. (In order to facilitate the technical production of the volume and to lower costs, it was decided to present line drawings wherever possible. Note that these are not to a uniform scale.) Noga Z'evi, Hildi Keel-Leu, Ines Haselbach and Jürgen Rotner contributed numerous new drawings. To all of them, and to the authors, we express our sincere thanks. Othmar Keel, who relinquished the editorship of this volume because of other duties, nevertheless maintained a keen and encouraging interest in our editorial progress; it is with great pleasure that we acknowledge our gratitude to him.

Haifa and Fribourg,
October 1992

Benjamin Sass
Christoph Uehlinger

From left to right: Eric Gubel, Julia Asher Greve (guest), Hildi Keel-Leu, Pierre Bordreuil, Dominique Parayre, Stefan Timm, Andrea Jäkle, Felice Israel, Othmar Keel, Tallay Ornan, Dominique Collon, Benjamin Sass, Ulrich Hübner, André Lemaire.

INTRODUCTION: THE STATUS OF ICONOGRAPHY IN THE STUDY OF NORTHWEST SEMITIC INSCRIBED SEALS

Christoph UEHLINGER
Biblical Institute, Fribourg

I. Before Galling: episodic attention
II. Galling 1941: a landmark
III. The decade after Galling: limited, but promising response
IV. 1950-1975: no real progress
V. 1975-1990: growing interest
VI. The present *status quaestionis*

More than fifty years ago, in 1941, Kurt Galling published his article on the iconography of Northwest Semitic inscribed seals, a study breaking new ground in several respects. Half a century later, we still benefit from what remains even today an impressive synthesis. The following introductory remarks double thus as a tribute to the German scholar.[1]

I. BEFORE GALLING: EPISODIC ATTENTION

Earlier studies[2] had concentrated almost exclusively on the epigraphical aspects of Northwest Semitic inscribed seals, namely their palaeography and onomasticon, and confined the treatment of iconography to a mere description. True, a few of the pioneering authors in the field, such as M. de Vogüé (1868), had devoted some real interest and knowledge in trying to elucidate not only the meaning of the personal names attested in the inscriptions, but also the possible religious significance of the seals' figurative designs. The

1. I would like to thank Dr Helga Weippert (Heidelberg) who, in a letter of October 18, 1992, offered some important comments on Galling's scholarly work on seals (see below, section II). Thanks are due also to Othmar Keel and Benjamin Sass for their remarks, and to Stewart Watson for improving my English.

2. See Bordreuil 1992: 129-134 for a general history of research on Northwest Semitic inscribed seals.

case of Phoenician seals with their abundance of representations of Egyptian religious symbols seemed especially intriguing to de Vogüé, as it demonstrated a strong influence of Egyptian upon Phoenician religion long before hermetism (*ibid.*: 107f). And the presence of a striding bull on a Hebrew seal, to cite but one other example, attested to Israelite idolatry, namely the worship of Astarte (*ibid.*: 132).[3] But discussions like de Vogüé's remained episodic in the early days of Northwest Semitic glyptic research. Iconography and its bearing upon the study of the history of Levantine religions could not, at that time, be a subject of more serious scholarly attention.

As a matter of fact, the learned world was then chiefly impressed by the continuing progress in understanding the Egyptian hieroglyphs and language and the growing success in deciphering cuneiform. Philology offered completely new clues, avenues and horizons to the study of Ancient Near Eastern cultures, and consequently promised, for the first time, perspectives for an adequate understanding of Ancient Near Eastern religion as well. Philology was able to show, for instance, that the symbolical interpretation of Egyptian hieroglyphs, which had been current in Europe since the Renaissance, was in fact nothing but pure speculation. At the same time, as philology was in constant move and progress, *dies diem docet* became a recurring motto of 19th-century research on Ancient Near Eastern cultures.

Not surprisingly, the early study of Northwest Semitic inscribed seals also engaged almost exclusively in matters of philology, even if the number of Northwest Semitic inscriptions remained very limited when compared to the Egyptian records, and did not increase as quickly as the cuneiform documents. The state of Ancient Near Eastern studies in general gave more credit to philological than to iconographical research, leaving the latter, based on comparatively mute sources, to archaeologists, art historians and collectors, whose interests were mainly in realia[4] or aesthetical in nature.[5]

---

3. Cf. *infra*, p. 278, note 70.

4. See Keel 1992a: 361-369 on the use of iconography for the illustration of material culture, which rather bypassed Northwest Semitic inscribed seals but concentrated on Egyptian and Assyrian monumental art. Note that the following pages are designed as a summary introduction, and they follow only the main stream of research on Northwest Semitic inscribed seals along select publications of major importance for this field in particular. They do not aim at a comprehensive history of research, a task for which one would have to consider in detail numerous studies on individual seals, textbooks on "biblical archaeology", and collections of pictorial sources from the Ancient Near East such as H. Gressmann's "Altorientalische Bilder zum Alten Testament" (^{2}1927).

5. As one consequence of this state of affairs the study of Ancient Near Eastern iconography has been largely dominated by a pseudo-philological approach which confines itself to mere identification of motifs and figures and tends to interpret pictures exclusively according to what is known from literary sources. As a rule, however, pictures on seals – and elsewhere, even in books! – are not to be considered simple 'illustrations' to

Elucidating iconography was put on a coming generation's agenda. "Die Kenntniss um diese letztere[6] steht in der That noch auf der ersten Stufe der Kindheit, und wenn man dies eingesteht, wird man uns gewiss nicht tadeln, dass wir uns nicht in weitläufige Erklärungen über die Bedeutung der symbolischen Figuren auf unsern Denkmälern eingelassen haben", wrote M.A. Levy in the introduction to his "Siegel und Gemmen" (1869: III). To be sure, Levy actually considered "Rücksichtnahme auf die Kunst, Ausschmückung und symbolische Beigaben" to be useful, although never decisive, for the classification of the seals into various ethno-cultural sub-groups (*ibid.*: 3).[7] But, in contrast to his sometimes bold philological interpretations where he felt clearly more confident, he addressed the subject of iconography only in the most cautious and descriptive terms. The same holds true for the work of Ch. Clermont-Ganneau and M. Lidzbarski, to cite but two leading experts on Northwest Semitic inscribed seals of the 19th century. The prime interest of the seals – "ces petits monuments, qui constituent la menue monnaie de l'épigraphie sémitique archaïque" (Clermont-Ganneau 1883: 123) – was the fact that they were inscribed. More than half a century later, D. Diringer's corpus of 104 name-seals considered to be Hebrew (1934: chap. V) still offered no real alternative.

If the descriptions and many of the illustrations published by the aforementioned authors remain valuable and necessary references for modern students, their approach to a group of artifacts whose specific significance resides precisely in the combination of image *and* inscription, text *and* picture was clearly one-sided and has to be considered obsolete in this respect.

II. Galling 1941: a landmark

With Kurt Galling's 1941 article the study of Northwest Semitic inscribed seals entered a new era,[8] as it was now recognized at last that a truly archae-

---

texts (cf. Keel 1992b: chapter I), but may be interpreted in their own right. It goes without saying that a 'semantic' and 'syntactical' analysis of iconography is not opposed to, but presupposes the study of material, form, technique, style, etc.

6. In Levy's text, "diese letztere" refers to "semitische Archäologie" in general.

7. As usual at that time, Levy distinguished three: Aramaic, Hebrew, and Phoenician (cf. *ibid.*: 3f; de Vogüé 1868: 106).

8. Strictly iconographical studies of Northwest Semitic inscribed seals are as sparse before 1941 as after, and they do not make up a real line of research. However, some outstanding studies deserve special mention, such as G. Dalman's 1906 *editio princeps* of the seal *lʾlšmʿ bn gdlyhw* with its very sensitive interpretation of the iconography (cf. Sass, *infra*, p. 232ff with fig. 136), or I. Benzinger's balanced treatment of seals in the subsequent editions of his "Hebräische Archäologie" (1894: 257-261; 1907: 225-229; 1927: 223-229).

ological approach to decorated inscribed seals cannot ignore their iconography. The latter could prove helpful, if not occasionally indispensable, for the purpose of dating – a necessary prerequisite to any historical work. More important, Galling attempted to serialize groups of seals according to their treatment of selected iconographical motifs (griffin, sphinx, lion, bull, worshippers etc.) and style in order to distinguish workshops and possibly locate the respective areas of their activity. If the sub-title of his study placed all the decorated seals with Northwest Semitic inscriptions in the general orbit of Phoenician art,[9] his detailed discussion argued not only for workshops situated along the coast, but recognized others in inner Syria producing "dialectal variants" (*ibid.*: 170) of Phoenician art, and yet others in Palestine, i.e. Israel (especially at Megiddo and Samaria), Judah, Ammon, Moab, etc. Here he differenciated again between local workshops and privileged factories of Phoenician seal-cutters based in commercial colonies (cf. *ibid.*: 132-133 with a reference to 1 Kings 20:34).[10] This complex picture and the growing recognition of locally diverse glyptic trends and traditions resulted not only from Galling's refined analysis of the often unprovenanced inscribed seals, but also from his constant reference to excavated stamp seals, fairly numerous by then, that had been unearthed in the course of half a century of archaeological research in Palestine.[11]

Galling's work was an important step forward,[12] even if it had its own, deliberately set limits. These are to be understood against the background of the state of research fifty years ago. Aiming at complementary research in the formerly rather neglected area of iconography, Galling kept palaeographic discussions to a minimum. The divorce of epigraphy and art history, inherited from preceding generations, was thus not really challenged in his study. Galling clearly considered a seal's figurative decoration and its inscription as two separate things, the first being of primary importance for locating the area

9. Wherever possible, Galling draws on parallels from cognate artifacts such as decorated metal bowls, ivories or tridacna shells. Cf. Gubel, *infra*, pp. 107-108.

10. See already Diringer 1934: 159; and cf. Reifenberg 1950: 11. Lemaire has noted that the the presence of the seal of *pṭ's* (HD 41) at Samaria may be understood in this context: *pṭ's* is an Egypto-Phoenician name, and the palaeography points to Phoenicia (Lemaire 1980: 496; 1986a: 93-94), while the iconography (a sitting falcon-headed sphinx with sun-disk and debased uraeus) has correlates in Israelite glyptic (Lemaire 1990b: 100-101).

11. See already his 1937 article on seals for the first edition of his „Biblisches Reallexikon".

12. Reading Galling's 1941 article against the papers of the present volume, written fifty years later, one is struck by the many insights already formulated there in a necessarily seminal form. Compare Ornan's "preference for the depiction of mortals" (*infra*, pp. 52-73) with Galling's comment on the rarity of representations of gods or goddesses (1941: 168).

of manufacture.[13] Moreover, Galling chose not to enter into the discussion of the possible religious significance of the seals' iconography because he wanted his approach to remain strictly archaeological.[14]

This restraint was based on methodological considerations – it should not be interpreted in terms of the author's indifference or reluctance in principle to touch upon the field of religion and belief.[15] Even in his 1941 article, Galling marginally addressed the question of the religious meaning of specific motifs: Where a bull is represented on a seal, "wird man kaum an eine einfach naturalistische Wiedergabe zu denken haben. Das Tier stellt symbolisch die übermenschliche Kraft dar", or "kann man bei Löwe[16] und Stier[17] fragen, ob nicht eine Anspielung auf ein Göttertier vorliegt oder ein Hinweis auf die übermenschliche Mächtigkeit, die im Sinne magischer Kraftübertragung dem Siegelbesitzer gilt, so daß das Siegel in die Nähe des Amuletts rückt. Bei den Bildern des säugenden Muttertieres[18] dürfte eine Anspielung auf die *vis naturae* vorliegen" (*ibid.*: 138, 168). Galling considered the representation of various hybrid creatures ("Mischwesen") such as the griffin and the sphinx, the winged scarab, uraeus, and genii the most conspicuous and characteristic feature of "Phoenician" glyptic: "Man wird in diesen Mischwesen gute oder böse übermenschliche Mächte und Geister gesehen haben, die schützen und abwehren. So hat das Siegel zugleich eine apotropäische Kraft" (*ibid.*: 169). For the reasons mentioned, however, Galling limited himself to such cautious comments and did not explore further the significance of the iconic designs for the history of Syro-Palestinian religions of Iron Age II.

III. THE DECADE AFTER GALLING: LIMITED, BUT PROMISING RESPONSE

Galling's excellent article has been rightly acknowledged as a most competent and authoritative contribution to the study of Northwest Semitic inscribed seals. Curiously, however, it does not seem to have stimulated much

13. H. Weippert's observation; note already Galling 1928: 236. Cf. below, p. xx and note 44.

14. This limitation becomes more apparent when Galling's article is compared with the almost contemporary, very influential work on cylinder seals by H. Frankfort (1939). Most obviously, very different presuppositions on what archaeology – or, for that matter, iconography – can or cannot, should or should not do, are at work in Galling's, Frankfort's or Moortgat's catalogues (on the latter, see briefly below).

15. Note for instance the inclusion of decorated seals in his treatments of representations of goddesses (1937a, 1977).

16. Cf. Ornan, *infra*, p. 63; Sass, pp. 221-222.

17. Cf. Hübner, *infra*, pp. 136-138; Sass, p. 225.

18. Cf. Ornan, *infra*, p. 63; Bordreuil, pp. 77, fig. 6, and 97, fig. 36; Hübner, pp. 138 and 159, fig. 21; Timm, pp. 170 and 192, fig. 6.

further research on iconography. Galling himself never returned to the subject in his published work, except for a note on the seal of *ytm* from Tell el-Kheleifeh – which he considered, by the way, to have been produced by an eighth-century Jerusalem workshop in spite of its southern find-spot (1967: 132) – and some scattered general remarks.[19]

What were the reasons for the lack of response and initiative by other scholars? Of course, the article had appeared in the midst of the Second World War.[20] Moreover, one has to keep in mind that iconography as a discipline had no easy position in post-war Germany. In 1949, A. Moortgat published his mythological interpretation of Mesopotamian cylinder seals.[21] The book was rightly, but harshly criticised by the leading Assyriologists B. Landsberger and F.R. Kraus, who both claimed an absolute priority of texts for understanding Ancient Near Eastern cultures.[22] Their conjunct scholarly authority and skeptical stance to religio-historical research seem to have consolidated, for some time to come, the mutual alienation of philologists and iconographers. Even in France, Britain or the United States, where iconographical research continued under the guidance of H. Frankfort, E. Porada,[23] B. Buchanan, and P. Amiet, it had no immediate impact on the study of decorated Northwest Semitic name-seals.

As a matter of fact, Northwest Semitic glyptic research produced hardly more than a dozen strictly iconographical studies until the late seventies.[24] One of the most notable exceptions, which deserves special mention here, is

---

19. However, H. Weippert remarks that seals always remained an important subject in Galling's teaching. He was the supervisor of Welten's dissertation on the *lmlk* seal impressions, subsequently published as Welten 1969. (For a general appreciation of Galling's work, see M. Weippert's obituary in ZDPV 104, 1988, 190-194.)

20. Another study on Palestinian inscribed seals, much more limited in scope and method, was published in Dutch by J. Simons in 1943 but remained largely unnoticed. It included a brief presentation of the seals' form, function, and the possible significance of their iconography for the study of religious history, and discussed the problem of dating by provenance, palaeography, etc. Simons was unaware of Galling's research (even of his preliminary article of 1937) and did not consider the full potential of iconographical studies.

21. Tammuz. Der Unsterblichkeitsglaube in der altorientalischen Bildkunst, Berlin 1949.

22. See Keel 1992b: 18-23, for a short review of the positions involved.

23. See her treatment of Neo-Assyrian and Neo-Babylonian stamp seals, among them the seal of *ʾbgdh* (Porada's no. 790 = Ornan, *infra*, p. 69, fig. 74), in her catalogue of the Pierpont Morgan collection (1948: 96-100).

24. For some references see below, note 29. One should not disregard, however, that first editions of seals usually included at least a short description of the iconic decoration; but the latter was seldom thought worthy of an elaborate discussion of its own, and the question of meaning and significance of the iconographic motifs was rarely addressed.

A. Reifenberg's treatment of iconography in his brochure on "Ancient Hebrew Seals" (1950). Reifenberg not only discussed the origin of "Hebrew-Phoenician art" and various Egyptian or Mesopotamian influences on it, but also addressed the problem of reception and re-interpretation of foreign symbols by the Phoenician and Hebrew artists. In principle, he considered the borrowing of Egyptian motifs on Phoenician ivories to be "wholly archaistic, for the models have lost their significance and their religious symbolism has become meaningless" (*ibid.*: 18). With regard to the seals, this statement was somewhat attenuated, however: "here again these motifs are void of Egyptian religious symbolism and their new meaning *is not always clear*" (*ibid.*: 19, italics mine). But if Reifenberg possibly underestimated the Syro-Palestinian artists' understanding of the symbols they were creating and processing,[25] he nevertheless showed great interest in the iconography of the seals and handled the issue of its religious meaning and significance with remarkable balance. Not only did he identify, as others before him, the winged sphinx[26] with the biblical cherub or the winged uraeus[27] with the seraph, but he also tried to understand the overall preference of the seal-cutters for winged beings, reasoning that "these strange animals should be interpreted as mediators between heaven and earth, between God and men. They were at the same time protectors of holy places (Gen 3:24) and the wings had a protective influence on men, as is often stated in the Psalms..." (*ibid.*: 21).[28]

Suddenly, the seals opened new vistas on the biblical world and its religious symbolism, and the biblical texts could in turn give the modern student useful hints to understand what seals actually meant to their original owners.

IV. 1950-1975: NO REAL PROGRESS

Unfortunately, Reifenberg's sympathetic approach to iconography and its possible bearing on the history of religion and belief remained exceptional until the seventies.[29] S. Moscati (1951: chap. V), the first scholar to present a

25. Contrast the recent study by Hölbl (1989) who reaches totally different conclusions. As a matter of fact, however, the reception of symbols of foreign provenance always implies a process of creative re-interpretation by the receiving culture, and if Egyptian symbolism may be the general matrix of Phoenician symbolism, the latter has to be understood within its own cultural context, having its particular concepts and coherence.

26. Cf. Sass, *infra*, p. 226.

27. Cf. Sass, *infra*, pp. 212-213.

28. Compare the somewhat similar approach in GGG: §§ 148-153.

29. Strictly iconographical studies were generally authored by non-epigraphers, such as the Egyptologists R. Giveon (1961) and W.A. Ward (1968), or archaeologists as W.

new corpus of inscribed Hebrew seals since Diringer, simply referred to Galling, offering a synthetical list of motifs appearing on the seals he classified as Hebrew, and noting in passing the rarity, on Hebrew seals, of some motifs such as divine or human figures (*ibid.*: 47-50).[30] F. Vattioni's lists of Hebrew, Aramaic and Phoenician seals (VSE, VSA, VSF, 1969-1981) were primarily designed as a database for onomastic research and as a bibliographical tool. Useful as they are in this respect, they contributed further to limit the study of Northwest Semitic name-seals to pure philology, as the iconic designs present on more than half of the inscribed Northwest Semitic seals listed by Vattioni are not even mentioned in these catalogues.[31]

In 1979 appeared the well informed catalogue of inscribed seals from public collections in Israel by R. Hestrin and M. Dayagi-Mendels, a landmark in the study of Northwest Semitic inscribed seals as Hebrew, Ammonite, Moabite, Phoenician and Aramaic seals are clearly distinguished. This catalogue presents a photograph of each seal and/or impression; however, it still contains only short descriptions of the iconic designs represented on the seals, resembling in that respect 19th-century publications. There are general introductions on the use of seals in antiquity, seals of officials, seals of women, and on each of the 'ethnic' groups of seals included, but no separate chapter on iconography. If the authors admit that the original meaning of many of the designs had been religious or magic, they consider these motifs to be ornamental and simply decorative (see *ibid.*: esp. pp. 56-57),[32] falling somewhat behind Galling and Reifenberg. The statement that precisely "the seals which bear only inscriptions, without any decorative designs," should be considered worthy "of special interest" (*ibid.*: 9), comes as no surprise to the reader. To be sure: "Inscriptions reveal"[33] – but only inscriptions?

Culican (see his collected studies, 1986) and A.D. Tushingham (1970, 1971). See also P. Welten (1969: 10-33) on the origin and meaning of the winged sun-disk and the four-winged scarab on the *lmlk* jar handle impressions, and the Judaean rosette impressions.

30. Compare Sass, *infra*, pp. 228-238.

31. Obviously Vattioni's lists are today in bad need of revision. A new list of Hebrew seals has just been published as part of G.I. Davies' corpus of "Ancient Hebrew Inscriptions" (1991: 119-256; and note the synopsis with earlier collections at the end of the book). The author rightly admits that a number of seals mentioned there may not be Hebrew (*ibid.*: xi-xii). No mention is made of the seals' non-epigraphical characteristics, as the purpose of Davies' book is strictly philological. Yet another list, designed as an update of VSE, is being prepared by F. Israel, to be published in ZAH.

32. Such comments are produced in the chapter concerning Hebrew seals, whereas the iconography of Ammonite, Moabite, and Phoenician seals does not even receive more than one or two standard phrases each (cf. *ibid.*: pp. 123, 143, 151).

33. The title of a much appreciated special exhibition and its catalogue at the Israel Museum (1973).

V. 1975-1990: GROWING INTEREST

One *specific* aspect of decorated Northwest Semitic inscribed seals, the most important for our present concern, lies precisely in the simultaneous appearance of an inscription and one or several figurative designs, two complementary media of communication, on a single artifact. In principle, both media, picture and text, should be considered equally worthy of scholarly attention, as both may contribute not only to a better understanding of the religious history of Syria and Palestine, but of their social and cultural history in general.

After a century of philological one-sidedness, it is fortunate that one should note a clear increase in interest in iconography among Northwest Semitic epigraphers, an interest which has partly grown parallel to the recognition of the relative limits of palaeographical analysis for the classification and dating of Northwest Semitic seals. True, studies on palaeography,[34] onomasticon,[35] and linguistic aspects[36] of the inscriptions and their reference to titles and offices held in ancient society[37] continue to stand in the forefront of scholarly discussion on seals, and no one will dispute the need and value of such studies for the cultural history of the Northwest Semitic world (cf. Avigad 1985; 1987a; H. Weippert 1988: 674-678). At the same time, however, more and more publications address iconography as a topic in its own right and acknowledge its value for the adequate interpretation of Northwest Semitic inscribed seals.[38,39]

Thorough discussions of iconographical issues are found, for instance, in studies published by P. Bordreuil and A. Lemaire since the mid-seventies.

---

34. See, among others, Herr 1978, 1980a; Naveh 1970a, b, 1975, 1982, 1985; van der Kooij 1987; Timm 1989a: 277-302, and the discussion of Lemaire, *infra*, pp. 4-7.

35. See especially Jackson 1983b; Tigay 1986; Fowler 1988; Maraqten 1988; Zadok 1988; Israel 1989, 1991b, 1992.

36. E.g., Jackson 1983a; Israel 1979a, 1984; Davies 1991 (see note 30).

37. See the overviews, with references, of Avigad 1981, 1987a etc.; Hestrin 1983; Bordreuil 1992: 183ff.

38. That this growing interest parallels the progress of O. Keel's research on the iconography of Syro-Palestinian stamp seals in general (compare titles listed in the bibliography since 1977) is probably more than mere coincidence (cf. Lemaire 1988: 224 and n. 60; Parayre 1990a: 269). Much recent progress in the study of Phoenician iconography in particular is due to the late W. Culican (cf. his collected papers, 1986) and E. Gubel. Regarding the identification of styles and schools in ivory carvings, of crucial importance also for glyptic research, the work of G. Herrmann and studies by I.J. Winter have to be explicitly mentioned (see *infra*, p. 266, n. 37).

39. Faulty knowledge of iconography must lead to false results: in one particular instance, epigraphers have interpreted as an inscription what is clearly a figurative design (Uehlinger 1990).

Following up Galling's earlier project (and note the important update of Galling 1937 by Welten 1977c), the latter scholar has repeatedly chosen iconography as a starting point for workshop studies (e.g., Lemaire 1979; 1986a; 1990a; 1990b: 97-101), a line of research that is now further pursued by D. Parayre (1987; 1990a, b; see *infra*, pp. 28-51, and 259-260). P.R.S. Moorey has written informative introductions on typology and iconography of Iron Age stamp seals in the third volume of the Ashmolean Museum catalogue (Buchanan & Moorey 1988),[40] closely followed by H. Keel-Leu's publication of the stamp seal collection of the Biblical Institute in Fribourg (1991). R.W. Younker (1985, 1989) has discussed what he considers to be Ammonite, Israelite and Judaean royal iconography.[41] N. Avigad's catalogue of Hebrew bullae, which appeared in 1986, included a special section on iconography (pp. 118-119) despite the fact that only a slight minority of these bullae actually display iconic designs. In the same year, in an attempt to identify characteristic features of Philistine glyptic, G. Garbini, known for penetrating linguistic studies, even supported the opinion that "iconography is the best criterion for classifying seals, given the uncertainty of paleography and onomastics" (1986: esp. 444).

The latter statement might sound surprising in view of the history of research of the past 125 years.[42] The present writer could easily endorse it if "classification" were understood in the sense of workshop studies as pioneered by K. Galling. Obviously, it would then include the necessity of a combined study of inscribed and anepigraphic seals.[43] However, a *caveat* has to be raised immediately: As the iconic design and the inscription might well be

40. The Northwest Semitic inscribed seals are presented together on pp. 44-46, where A.R. Millard contributed the discussion of the inscriptions. Comparison with preceding "Phoenician" stamp seals shows that while the separate grouping of inscribed seals may be a matter of convenience, it cannot be justified on typological or iconographical grounds.

41. But see Moorey, *op. cit.*: 40-41; Hübner, *infra*, pp. 140-141; see also Sass, *infra*, pp. 214-217 for the relevant motif.

42. Garbini's own study seems to suffer from a certain confusion between iconographically founded workshop research and the aim for 'ethnic' classification on onomastic grounds: It starts from the identification of distinct iconographical features on a group of inscribed seals, namely (1) a four-winged scarab with drooping hind-wings (G 57-58, 60-63 and M 17-18), and (2) the combined representation of winged disk, uraeus and falcons (G 49, 52-55, and M 20) on seals that are usually classified as Phoenician (e.g. Parayre, *infra*, p. 43, fig. 5; Gubel, p. 117, figs. 33, 37, 39; B 11), Aramaic (e.g. Parayre, *infra*, p. 40, no. 8; Bordreuil, p. 89, fig. 27), and Hebrew (*nʿmʾl pʾrt*, Lemaire, *infra*, p. 18). Garbini then arrives at a "Philistine" classification of these seals mainly on the basis of rather general assumptions, namely Egyptian influence and mixed onomasticon. In practice, Garbini's conclusions are thus only partly based on strict iconographical arguments, and these are certainly open to discussion.

43. Cf. also Parayre, *infra*, p. 29; Gubel, pp. 110ff.

the product of different workshops separated from one another in time or place – or both (especially in the case, attested several times, of inscriptions being added to originally anepigraphic seals)[44] – iconography and inscription have first to be studied separately if one should avoid the pitfalls of circular reasoning (cf. *infra*, pp. 258-261). One may easily imagine an ancient Israelite acquire an anepigraphic Phoenician or North Syrian seal and have his name added later by an Israelite seal cutter (see Gubel, *infra*, p. 107; Sass, p. 228 with fig. 129; Uehlinger, pp. 261, 275-277 for some examples).

In the meantime, it has to be recognized that the iconographic argument is more and more used for the 'ethnic' classification of decorated seals,[45] a fact that certainly deserves some critical evaluation.[46] Not surprisingly, then, two recent authoritative reviews of the *status quaestionis* in Northwest Semitic glyptic studies both consider iconography to be an essential issue, which they declare not devoid of methodological pitfalls, but sadly neglected since Galling's pioneering article (Avigad 1988: 14-16; Lemaire 1988: 223-224; and see now Bordreuil 1992).[47]

VI. The present *status quaestionis*

As a matter of fact, the conditions for iconographical research are much better today than in the early fourties, when K. Galling had done his pioneering research. First, the number of decorated Northwest Semitic inscribed seals has grown considerably during the past fifty years,[48] and so has that of anepigraphic Iron Age stamp seals from Palestine/Israel and adjacent

---

44. To cite but one example, Lemaire has discussed this possibility for the seal *lʾbʿdn bt sdd* (or *srr*), where he argues for a fifth-century inscription having been added to an originally anepigraphic seventh-century seal (1990b: 106-109).

45. Cf. Bordreuil's catalogue of 1986, but also some more recent articles by Avigad (e.g., 1985, 1989a, 1992c).

46. Contrast Reifenberg's statement that "the problem of attribution (cannot) be solved by the pictorial representations, as the same motifs were used by all the peoples concerned" (1950: 17).

47. N. Avigad planned to return in detail to the iconography of Hebrew inscribed seals (1988: 16, n. 40). His passing away on January 28, 1992, regrettably leaves this project as an inheritance to other scholars.

48. Galling's article – limited to decorated seals with Northwest Semitic inscriptions – included 153 stamp seals. A rough estimate of the total number of seals known today, including those represented by impressions, amounts to ca. 1200; more than half of them bear iconic designs (Benjamin Sass, personal communication). These numbers may of course include a more or less important percentage of forgeries, on which see *infra*, pp. 270-271.

countries, albeit in somewhat more limited proportions.[49] Second, palaeography has seen tremendous progress since the early fifties. Today epigraphers are able not only to distinguish between the Aramaic, Phoenician and Hebrew scripts, but to differenciate various Transjordanian scripts which earlier had all been included in "Hebrew".[50] An ongoing debate on Northwest Semitic linguistics, especially the "Canaanite" branch, seems to evolve towards even greater refinement with the differenciation of central vs. fringe dialects, with the possible recognition of distinct features of such fringe dialects as "Gileadite". This state of affairs is of prime importance for glyptic research in general, and also for iconographers, as one is now reasonably entitled to compile hypothetical 'ethnic' or – with regard to Ammon, Israel, Judah, and Moab – 'national' glyptic corpora.[51] Do the decorated seals among these display specific and characteristic features which in turn could allow us to classify those inscribed seals that do not display any diagnostic letter forms?[52]

The possibility of establishing 'ethnic' or 'national' glyptic corpora could open the way to the compilation of corresponding 'national' iconographic repertoires.[53] On the other hand, the combination of iconographic and palaeographic studies may allow us to define the distribution – more or less regional or international – of specific motifs or clusters of motifs. What could such research tell us positively about cultural diffusion and interaction, and, as a related aspect, cultural identity of a certain people or 'nation'? May we detect

---

49. Consequently, studies on both categories, inscribed and anepigraphic, urgently need a respective corpus. The "Corpus of Northwest Semitic Seals" prepared by the late N. Avigad will be edited by Joseph Naveh and Benjamin Sass for the Israel Academy of Sciences and Humanities. Another catalogue by Pierre Bordreuil is in preparation. On a corpus of excavated – or, at least, clearly provenanced – stamp seals from Palestine/Israel, to be published by O. Keel, see *infra*, p. 269-270, note 50.

50. A progress that is largely due to studies of N. Avigad (1952, 1970a, 1977a, b etc.) and J. Naveh (1966, 1970b, 1982). See also Herr 1978, 1980a; van der Kooij 1987.

51. This has been attempted for the Ammonites by F. Israel (1987a), W.E. Aufrecht (CAI, 1989) and U. Hübner (see *infra*, pp. 130-160, esp. p. 131, n. 1), for the Moabites by Israel (1987b) and S. Timm (1989a: 159-264). Cf. Bordreuil 1992: 153-163.

52. W.E. Aufrecht acknowledges the lack of scholarly discussion and wonders whether one is entitled to speak about "Ammonite iconography" at all. He poses numerous questions: "(...) Did the artisans of Ammon employ distinctive and standard designs – ones not used by the designers of other nations (...)? Do the styles of animals, or even the choice of animals, give clues as to provenance? Can specific cultural influences ... or symbols ... tell us anything about Ammonite culture? And can the iconography contribute to dating of the inscriptions or complement the classification of the language which is inscribed with the picture?" without trying to look for an answer (pp. xxiv-xxvi). It is hoped that the present volume will offer at least some hints about how one could possibly deal with these problems.

53. But see *infra*, pp. 258-263, on the methodological principle of the separate study of epigraphy and iconography.

specific choices that conditioned 'ethnic' or 'national' repertoires at various periods? Could it even be possible to correlate such choices and the selective 'ethnic' or 'national' repertoires to the history of a people's or nation's cultural "symbolic system" – of which religious symbols are a significant part – so that the iconographical study of Northwest Semitic inscribed seals could lead us towards a "thicker description" and a better understanding of ancient Syro-Palestinian cultures, including their religions?[54] Methodological problems involved are complex and undoubtedly need thorough discussion. But time has come to put these questions on our agenda, and the Fribourg symposium was designed as a stimulus to that effect.

54. Both terms, "symbolic system" and "thick description" are concepts borrowed from Clifford Geertz's ethnographical and epistemological work on the interpretation of culture (Geertz 1973; cf. Rice 1980; Hofstee 1986).

LES CRITÈRES NON-ICONOGRAPHIQUES DE LA CLASSIFICATION DES SCEAUX NORD-OUEST SÉMITIQUES INSCRITS

André LEMAIRE
É.P.H.É., Paris

Un des problèmes fondamentaux de la sigillographie nord-ouest sémitique du Ier millénaire av. J.-C. est celui de la classification, du rattachement de chaque sceau à un royaume, une région ou une population précise, c'est-à-dire une "ethnie" du monde ouest-sémitique, le terme "ethnie" désignant ici simplement une population particulière avec ses traditions culturelles (langue, religion...), sociales et politiques propres, et vivant habituellement sur un certain territoire.

Une telle classification a l'intérêt de replacer chaque sceau dans son milieu humain et sa culture propre. Dépassant la simple description matérielle d'un objet, elle révèle comment celui-ci est "humanisé", réalisé et utilisé par des hommes d'une certaine époque. Finalement une telle classification représente une étape nécessaire pour réinsérer ces petits objets dans l'histoire.

Concrètement cette classification doit se baser sur certains critères. Avant de laisser à d'autres l'étude du critère iconographique, nous voudrions évoquer ici celui du lieu de la découverte et des caractéristiques matérielles; nous étudierons ensuite ceux directement liés à la présence d'une inscription: paléographie, disposition de la légende, langue et onomastique. Enfin quelques exemples concrets illustreront quelques conséquences de cette réflexion méthodologique.

I. Lieu de la découverte

On pourrait penser que la classification ethnico-géographique serait donnée avec la provenance archéologique et géographique du sceau. Cependant ce critère est souvent inutilisable du fait que la plupart des sceaux nord-ouest sémitiques inscrits proviennent du marché des antiquités. Ils sont donc, le plus souvent, sans indication d'origine ou, lorsqu'une indication d'origine est mentionnée par le marchand, celle-ci est évidemment sujette à caution: elle ne peut être utilisée, et encore de façon prudente, qu'après vérification soit de la source même de l'information, soit de la concordance de cette indication avec les caractéristiques particulières du sceau lui-même. Le même problème se pose d'ailleurs pour les bulles et estampilles sur vase, même si le pourcentage de bulles et surtout d'estampilles, essentiellement sur jarre, trouvées dans des fouilles régulières est heureusement plus important.

De toutes façons, le critère de l'origine, seul, ne peut être un critère suffisant pour préciser le rattachement ethnique d'un sceau, d'une bulle ou d'une estampille. Déjà dans l'antiquité, les sceaux pouvaient voyager, soit parce que leurs propriétaires eux-mêmes voyageaient de leur plein gré (commerce, diplomatie...) ou forcés (déportation, exil...), soit parce que, considérés comme des objets personnels relativement précieux, ils pouvaient être donnés en cadeau, transmis en héritage, ou même pillés et revendus.

Un problème similaire se pose pour les bulles, liées éventuellement à des lettres ou à des messages envoyés à des destinataires plus ou moins lointains, ou à des actes notariés que l'intéressé ou le successeur de l'intéressé pouvait emmener avec lui, comme le montrent, par exemple, les bulles des manuscrits araméens trouvés dans une grotte du Wadi Daliyeh mais provenant, en fait, de Samarie (bibliographie dans Lemaire 1990d: 65, n. 205). Il en est de même pour les jarres estampillées dont le contenu pouvait faire l'objet d'un certain commerce, éventuellement international, comme le montre le parallèle des jarres rhodiennes à l'époque hellénistique.

Un exemple récent permet d'illustrer la prudence avec laquelle il faut utiliser le critère de la provenance d'un sceau pour en déduire le rattachement ethnique. En 1982, lors du creusement des fondations d'une maison à Umm Udheinah, quartier ouest d'Amman, une tombe a été mise au jour contenant du matériel archéologique datant de la fin du VIIIe à la fin du Ve s. av. J.-C. Parmi ce matériel, on remarquait un scaraboïde inscrit *lplṭy bn mʾš hmzkr*, “à Palṭay fils de Maʾoš, le ‘hérault’” (**fig. 1**). Comme le fit remarquer F. Zayadine (1985b: 158), l'origine ammonite ne faisait apparemment aucun doute. Cependant un examen, même rapide, de la paléographie et de l'iconographie caractéristiques de ce sceau nous conduisit immédiatement à proposer de classer ce sceau comme moabite (*ibid.*: n. 25) et ce classement moabite a aussi été retenu par la plupart des autres commentateurs: M. Abu Taleb (1985), P. Bordreuil (La Voie royale: n° 170; 1987a: 285), F. Israel (1987b: n° XXV) et S. Timm (1989a: 217-219, n° 22; cf. *infra*, p. 184 et fig. 18), tandis que W.E. Aufrecht (1989) ne l'a pas inclus dans son *corpus* ammonite.

Cet exemple montre bien comment l'indication d'origine géographique et archéologique d'un sceau, quand elle existe, ne peut, à elle seule, et si utile qu'elle soit, déterminer son classement ethnique et son cadre spatio-temporel de fabrication et d'utilisation. Cette indication n'a de valeur que dans la mesure où elle est confirmée par les caractéristiques du sceau lui-même, en particulier, outre sa matière, sa forme et ses dimensions, son inscription et son iconographie.

II. CARACTÉRISTIQUES MATÉRIELLES

Le premier travail de classement des sceaux, en particulier de ceux dont l'origine est incertaine, consiste à préciser leur aspect matériel: forme, matière, dimensions. Ces caractéristiques peuvent déjà orienter vers une culture précise, voire un atelier particulier.

En effet, la forme du sceau (cylindre, scarabée, scaraboïde, conoïde, bouton, tampon, bague...) le rattache généralement à une certaine aire culturelle: le cylindre est plutôt caractéristique de la Mésopotamie ou de la Syrie du Nord, le scarabée de l'Égypte ou du monde phénico-punique, le scaraboïde de la Syrie-Palestine, le bouton du domaine hittite...

La matière des sceaux peut aussi aider à une classification en étant plus ou moins caractéristique d'une région ou d'un atelier donné. L'exemple le plus clair est celui de l'atelier de Tharros (Sardaigne) travaillant le jaspe vert provenant du Sud de la Sardaigne, essentiellement sous forme de scarabées, aux V-IVes s. av. J.-C. (Pisano 1978: 37-56; Moscati & Costa 1982: 203-210; Moscati 1987: 111-114). On connaît par ailleurs l'importance de la production des conoïdes octogonaux en calcédoine dits "néo-babyloniens" aux VII-Ves s. av. J.-C. Il s'agit là de deux exemples de pierre semi-précieuse pouvant faire l'objet d'un commerce international. Le lien entre la matière et le lieu de production était vraisemblablement plus fort pour les sceaux réalisés dans une matière commune comme le calcaire local (*mizzi*?) ou l'os, souvent utilisés dans les ateliers judéens aux VIII-VIes s. av. J.-C. (calcaire local: HD 51, 71, 73, 76-77, 80-81, 83-84; os: HD 34, 62, 91-96).

Les dimensions du sceau et le fait qu'il soit perforé ou non peuvent aussi orienter vers un certain classement car, dans un atelier, le travail en série devait avoir tendance à se faire sur des sceaux de dimensions similaires. On rattachera ainsi probablement à la même série, pour des raisons de matière et de dimensions (confirmées par l'iconographie), trois ou quatre gros scaraboïdes inscrits:

- *lš'l* : calcaire rouge-brun, 25 x 19 x 11 mm (Avigad 1954a: 236-237 = **fig. 2**),
- *lmnḥn* : calcaire jaune, 28 x 19 x 11 mm (VSE 182; Buchanan & Moorey 1988: n° 291 = **fig. 3**),
- *lmqn* : calcaire brun clair/rouge brique: 25 x 18 x 11 mm (Lemaire 1986: n° 2 = **fig. 4**),
- *lṣdqy* : schiste micacé: 20 x 14 x 9 mm (provisoirement Zuckerman 1987: 25-27 = **fig. 5**).

Ces quelques exemples suffisent à montrer l'intérêt des caractéristiques matérielles pour une classification des sceaux; en fait, l'utilisation de ce critère en sigillographie ouest-sémitique mériterait une étude spéciale utilisant toutes les données comparatives des sceaux inscrits, ainsi que des sceaux non-inscrits dont l'origine est certaine.

III. Paléographie

Le phénomène de la diversification de l'écriture alphabétique au début du Ier millénaire avant notre ère est de mieux en mieux connu. On distinguait, de manière classique, trois grandes écritures nord-ouest sémitiques: les écritures phénicienne, hébraïque et araméenne. Les recherches récentes ont mis en évidence un certain nombre de développements particuliers à l'écriture philistine (Naveh 1985) et aux écritures transjordaniennes (Naveh 1970b; Herr 1980a; van der Kooij 1987), en distinguant les écritures ammonite, moabite et édomite.

Les principales caractéristiques des écritures phénicienne, hébraïque et araméenne et leur évolution étant généralement assez bien connues (Peckham 1968; Naveh 1970a; 1982; Amadasi Guzzo 1987: 41-69), nous nous contenterons ici de quelques remarques sur les principales caractéristiques des écritures transjordaniennes et de l'écriture philistine:

- L'écriture *ammonite* est très proche de l'écriture araméenne, au point que J. Naveh (1982: 109-111) la considère comme une branche de l'écriture araméenne. En écriture sigillaire, l'ammonite se reconnaît généralement au caractère vertical ou quasi-vertical de ses hampes.
- L'écriture *moabite* semble avoir été très proche, au moins aux IX-VIIIes s. av. J.-C., de l'écriture hébraïque; elle se reconnaît assez facilement au caractère très incurvé de ses hampes, à ses têtes de *m* et de *n* à 3 ou 2 traits parallèles verticaux, ou quasi-verticaux, joints à la base par une barre horizontale, ainsi qu'à ses *ḥ* à deux barres horizontales et deux hampes verticales alternées, l'une vers le haut, l'autre vers le bas.

– L'écriture *édomite*, moins bien connue faute d'inscription monumentale, semble avoir d'abord été très proche de l'écriture moabite, avec, en particulier un *m* à large tête; elle paraît avoir subi ensuite l'influence des écritures phénicienne et araméenne (cf., en particulier, le *w*), ainsi que certains développements propres. L'un de ceux-ci est l'inversion du *d* de bas en haut, probablement afin de mieux le distinguer du *r* qui avait fondamentalement la même forme. Assez bizarrement, cette forme particulière de *d* ne semble avoir été relevée ni par L.G. Herr (1980a: 30), ni par J. Naveh (1982: 102-104), ni par G. Van der Kooij, ce dernier ayant confondu cette forme avec un *ṭ* ouvert (1987: 114). Bien plus, F. Israel, qui en avait signalé l'existence dès 1979 (1979b: 175-176), semble l'avoir ensuite considérée comme un trait moabite (1987b: 112, 120). Cependant l'apparition de ce type de *d* dans l'ostracon édomite de Khirbet Ghazzeh/Ḥorvat ʿOuzza (Beit-Arieh & Cresson 1985) en a confirmé et l'existence et le rattachement à la paléographie édomite (Lemaire 1987b: 69), tandis qu'un examen attentif de la bulle édomite *qwsg*[*br*] *mlk* ʾ[*dm*], trouvée à Umm el-Biyara (**fig. 6**; Herr 1978: 162-163), fait apparaître la forme d'un *d* inversé à la fin de la ligne 2 qu'on lit donc *mlk* ʾ*d̊*[*m*].

– L'écriture *philistine* reste encore assez mal connue. Certains traits semblent la rapprocher tantôt de l'écriture phénicienne, tantôt de l'écriture paléo-hébraïque. Mis à part quelques sceaux dont l'origine géographique est assurée et un scaraboïde portant probablement le nom d'un roi philistin (cf. Uehlinger, *infra*, p. 285, fig. 21), la classification des sceaux philistins reste encore très incertaine, comme le montre l'essai de G. Garbini (1986; cf. Uehlinger, *supra*, pp. XX, note 42).

Il faut souligner que l'analyse paléographique ne permet pas seulement un classement ethnique ou régional mais qu'elle donne aussi une indication chronologique même si celle-ci, surtout pour les sceaux, reste assez approximative.

Ce rapide rappel risque de donner l'impression que le rattachement d'un sceau à l'une des traditions scribales nationales est assez facile et évident. C'est vrai pour un certain nombre de sceaux; ce l'est beaucoup moins pour d'autres, en particulier lorsque la légende est courte et ne comporte aucune lettre caractéristique. En fait, sous une apparente simplicité, l'analyse paléographique des inscriptions sigillaires ouest-sémitiques comporte un certain nombre de *pièges* qu'il n'est pas inutile d'évoquer:

1. Les inscriptions sigillaires sont des inscriptions sur un matériau dur et sont généralement de type monumental, ce qui implique certaines tendances à formaliser, à archaïser et même parfois à déformer en fonction des limites de la place disponible.

2. La gravure de certaines légendes est très soignée tandis que celle d'autres peut être beaucoup plus négligée; cette différence de style n'a pas de valeur chronologique.

3. A la fin du IXe, dans la première moitié du VIIIe et, en partie, jusque vers la fin du VIIIe s., la paléographie araméenne est très peu différenciée de la paléographie phénicienne. On peut donc assez souvent parler d'une écriture phénico-araméenne, en y incluant d'ailleurs l'ammonite.

4. Vers la même époque, fin du IXe-VIIIe s. av. J.-C., les écritures moabites et hébraïques restent très proches.

5. Certaines formes, parfois considérées comme exclusivement ammonites, peuvent être aussi attestées dans d'autres écritures. Ainsi en est-il du *ʿayin* carré qui apparaît aussi en araméen (cf. le sceau *lʾlhʿm*: **fig. 7** et *infra*, p. 17), en hébreu (cf. le sceau *lmqnyw ʿbd yhwh*: **fig. 8**; Cross 1983), et en moabite (Israel 1987b: n° III, XXVIII; 1991a: 231).

6. Certaines formes parfois considérées comme exclusivement moabites peuvent aussi être attestée en écriture paléo-hébraïque, voire en édomite. C'est le cas:

- du *m* et, surtout, du *n* avec tête à trois et deux traits verticaux parallèles et base horizontale, forme que l'on retrouve aussi sur des sceaux hébreux du VIIIe s. (*lmqnyw ʿbd yhwh*: **fig. 8**; *lšmryhw bn pdyhw*: **fig. 9**, Bordreuil & Lemaire 1976: n° 5 = VSE 363; [*l*]*żkryw khn dʾr*: **fig. 10**, Avigad 1975a; *lʿzʾ bn bʿlḥnn*: **fig. 11**, B 50, cf. Avigad 1987a: 197; *lšmʿ bn ywstr*: B 55) et des estampilles judéennes de la fin du VIIIe s. av. J.-C. (HD 14-18, 21, 25) ou même un peu plus tardives (A 77, 83, 89, 95-96, 103, 114-116, 161, 172);
- du *ḥ* à deux barres horizontales et hampes alternées vers le haut et vers le bas. En fait, ce type de *ḥ* apparaît aussi sur des sceaux israélites (*lʿzʾ bn bʿlḥnn*: **fig. 11**; *lʿzʾ bn ḥts*: **fig. 12**, Avigad 1954a: 237; Herr 1978: 135, n° 126; malgré Israel 1991a: 229), sur des estampilles judéennes (HD 15, 20; A 80, 153) et probablement en écriture édomite (Beit-Arieh & Cresson 1985: 100).[1]

7. Enfin la paléographie de certaines bulles judéennes post-exiliques révèle parfois une sorte d'écriture mixte araméo-hébraïque (Avigad 1976a) qui se rapproche de celle des sceaux classés généralement comme ammonites (CAI 89 [= **fig. 15**], 90).

---

1. Nous hésitons donc à accepter comme moabites les sceaux *lklkl mnḥm* (Avigad 1979: n° 9; Timm 1989a: 203) et *lḥmlk* (Timm 1989a: 199-200, n° 14 = Sass, *infra*, p. 227, fig. 125) qui peuvent être tout aussi bien hébreux.

Au-delà même du rattachement ethnique, il semble parfois possible que l'analyse paléographique permette l'identification d'un atelier (voire d'un graveur?) grâce à des formes particulières de lettres. Ce pourrait être le cas du *q* à tête en forme de demi-cercle et base quasi-horizontale légèrement brisée, forme qui apparaît sur les sceaux *lʿšyw bn ywqm* (**fig. 13**; D 38 = Sass, *infra*, p. 203, fig. 32, pl. I:1) et *yḥzq* (**fig. 14**; D 83); ce dernier, provenant de Naplouse selon les indications de Clermont-Ganneau (1883: n° 7) pourrait révéler une tradition particulière d'un atelier du royaume d'Israël (Garbini 1982: 165, 176) situé à Sichem ou Samarie.

Il faut d'ailleurs réfléchir à la signification du rattachement paléographique de l'inscription par rapport au processus de fabrication d'un sceau inscrit et donc à son classement: la paléographie caractérise-t-elle la tradition scribale du graveur/vendeur de sceaux ou celle de l'acquéreur? Cette question peut paraître futile puisque, le plus souvent, ces deux traditions scribales devaient être identiques. Cependant, dans certains cas, vendeur et acheteur pouvaient se rattacher à des ethnies et à des traditions scribales différentes, en particulier lorsque l'acheteur ou le vendeur était un étranger de passage ou en résidence provisoire dans un autre pays. Dans ce cas-là, la paléographie du sceau reflète-t-elle la tradition scribale du graveur ou celle de l'acheteur qui pourrait avoir fourni lui-même le modèle de la légende à graver? Cette dernière possibilité ne peut être absolument exclue, cependant l'existence de sceaux avec début d'abécédaires, sceaux sur lesquels le graveur s'est apparemment entraîné à graver à l'envers les premières lettres de l'alphabet pour qu'elles apparaissent à l'endroit sur l'empreinte (Lemaire 1978a: 226-227; 1985b: 47; B 116, 120[2]) semblent révéler que la paléographie de la légende correspond plutôt à la tradition scribale du graveur qu'à celle de l'acheteur.

IV. Disposition de la légende

La disposition de la légende est souvent liée à l'arrangement iconographique, s'il s'agit de sceaux iconiques; c'est donc un critère se situant souvent à la limite de l'étude iconographique. Nous nous contenterons ici de trois remarques sur la disposition de la légende des sceaux ammonites, moabites et édomites:

1. Un certain nombre de sceaux ammonites présentent une iconographie centrale (quadrupède ou sphinx marchant ou galopant, scarabée aux quatre ailes déployées, soleil ailé, bucrâne flanqué de deux oiseaux...) située entre deux lignes d'écriture (CAI 9, 19, 30, 52, 68, 79, 89 [= **fig. 15**], 99, 106,

2. A l'examen direct, l'authenticité de ce sceau paraît douteuse: il pourrait s'agir d'une copie moderne, maladroite, de n° 116.

114, 126, 129, 140; cf. Hübner, *infra*, pp. 157-159, figs. 1, 7, 14, 16, 23-24). Une des variantes de cette disposition situe une ou deux lettres (souvent *bn*) dans le champ médian, éventuellement de part et d'autre du motif iconographique central (CAI 1, 3, 5, 23, 42, 85, 118, 129, 131-133, 135, 141; cf. Hübner, *infra*, figs. 4, 8, 16, 19, 25). Cette disposition en trois registres, le champ médian étant occupé par l'iconographie, se retrouve sur la bulle édomite *qwsg*[*br*] *mlk* *ʾḋ*[*m*] (**fig. 6**) mais semble absente de la glyptique moabite.

2. Une autre disposition, qui peut aussi se retrouver sur certains sceaux araméens et hébreux, semble avoir été assez répandue en sigillographie ammonite: une légende disposée verticalement, soit d'un seul côté, soit de part et d'autre d'un motif iconographique central disposé verticalement (personnage debout, oiseau dressé, Horus assis sur une fleur...: CAI 14-15, 17-18, 24, 28, 46, 60, 82-83, 96, 102-103, 105, 111, 128, 143; cf. Hübner, *infra*, figs. 3, 5, 9-11; Sass, pp. 201-202, figs. 13, 20).

3. Ces deux dispositions semblent absentes de la sigillographie moabite, au moins à ce jour. A l'inverse, la disposition de la légende sur, au moins, trois lignes d'écriture, le sceau étant disposé dans le sens de la hauteur, disposition attestée sur le sceau moabite *lplṭy bn mʾš hmzkr* (**fig. 1**) évoqué plus haut, semble absente dans la sigillographie ammonite,[3] alors qu'elle est attestée en moabite, édomite, hébreu, philistin et phénicien.

V. Langue

Etant donné la brièveté habituelle des légendes sigillaires, il est évident que l'utilisation du critère linguistique risque fort de rester assez limité. De fait, un certain nombre d'inscriptions sigillaires ne comportent que le nom du propriétaire, éventuellement précédé du *l* d'appartenance commun à tout le nord-ouest sémitique et qui ne peut servir pour une classification. D'autres, apparemment plus souvent en hébreu et en ammonite qu'en phénicien, araméen ou moabite (Dion 1989: 75), mentionnent aussi le patronyme, soit en l'adjoignant directement, soit en le faisant précéder d'un terme indiquant la filiation. L'indication d'un titre, d'une fonction ou d'un métier reste beaucoup plus rare, de même que la mention du grand-père.[4] L'appartenance linguistique apparaît donc essentiellement:

---

3. CAI 56 pose un problème particulier car il participe probablement aux deux cultures: ammonite et phénicienne.

4. Il faut mettre à part deux sceaux votifs: le sceau phénicien de "Baʿalyaton" (BM 48507), peut-être à lire *lbʿlytn ʾšʾl mʾš lmlqrt ṙṡṗ* ou *ḃṩṙ* (Lemaire 1991a: 115) et le sceau d'"Abinadab" (BN, Coll. de Luynes, N 3316) ...]*ʾbndb ʾš ndr l ʿšt bṣdn tbrkh* (CAI 56).

- soit lors de l'emploi du terme de filiation: *bn* / *bt* (dialecte "cananéen") ou *br* / *brt* (araméen);
- soit lors de l'adjonction d'un titre de fonction impliquant l'emploi du relatif (cf. hébreu *ʾšr ʿl hbyt*, *ʾšr ʿl hms*) et/ou l'emploi de l'article préposé *h-* (en "cananéen") ou de l'état emphatique postposé *-ʾ* (en araméen): ainsi, par exemple, "le scribe" écrit *hspr* ou *sprʾ*.

De toutes façons, l'emploi du terme de filiation, de l'article ou de l'état emphatique permet seulement de distinguer l'araméen des dialectes "cananéens" (Israel 1984; Garr 1985) sans permettre, pour ces derniers, de préciser s'il s'agit du phénicien, de l'hébreu, du philistin, de l'ammonite, du moabite ou de l'édomite.

Cependant, malgré ces limites, ce critère linguistique ne peut être négligé. En fait, il permet de préciser un rattachement ethnique là où le critère paléographique est pratiquement inutilisable, en particulier lorsqu'il s'agit de distinguer les sceaux ammonites des sceaux araméens. En effet, la paléographie ammonite étant très semblable sinon identique à la paléographie araméenne (*supra*), l'emploi de *bn* au lieu de *br* devient dès lors un bon indicateur d'un éventuel rattachement au domaine ammonite.

Outre ces deux différences linguistiques faciles à discerner, on peut aussi éventuellement, mais avec beaucoup plus de nuances, utiliser des critères d'usage qui restent plus incertains:

- Il semble que l'article préposé ait été moins usité en ammonite que dans les autres dialectes cananéens (Israel 1979a: 156), comme le montre, en particulier, le syntagme *ʿbd mlk* au lieu de *ʿbd hmlk* (Avigad 1977a: n° 1).
- La relation d'une épouse à son mari semble exprimée par l'état construit *ʾšt*, "femme de", en sigillographie hébraïque, phénicienne (cf. *lʾḥtmlk ʾšt yšʿ* : G 41) et, probablement, édomite (cf. *lmnḥmt ʾšt ṗdmlk*, cf. *infra*, p. 16 et **fig. 23**), tandis que la tradition sigillaire ammonite (CAI 36, 44) et probablement araméenne (Avigad 1976a: n° 14; Lemaire 1990d: 34-35) utilisait plutôt l'état construit *ʾmt*, "servante de" (Lipiński 1985: 165; 1986: 450; cf. l'emploi de *aššatum* et de *amtum* en accadien: Kienast 1984: 94-100).
- Dans la tradition sigillaire araméenne, la légende commence parfois par désigner le sceau lui-même: *ḥtm*. Cet emploi initial de *ḥtm*, à distinguer de l'emploi de la finale *hḥtm z* sur deux sceaux phénico-louvites (Lemaire 1977a: 34), se retrouve aussi sur trois sceaux classés souvent comme ammonites (CAI 55 [= **fig. 16**], 57, 61); cependant, selon J. Naveh (1988: 115), le premier se rattache plutôt au domaine araméen tandis que l'authenticité des deux autres reste discutée (Garbini 1967; 1968; Naveh & Tadmor 1968; Bordreuil 1973a: 183; Avigad 1985: 5, n. 24; Hübner 1989b: 223).

Au total, l'utilisation du critère linguistique, théoriquement très important, reste très limitée dans la pratique, d'autant plus limitée qu'elle ne fournit pas, jusqu'à maintenant, d'indication temporelle, l'évolution de chacune des langues étant très lente et pratiquement insensible au niveau du vocabulaire attesté sur les sceaux. De plus, il faut ajouter que ce critère linguistique doit être manié avec beaucoup de précautions pour les époques tardives à cause du rôle de plus en plus grand joué par l'écriture et la langue araméennes. Après la disparition des royaumes d'Israël, de Juda, d'Ammon, de Moab et d'Edom, les dialectes cananéens de ces ethnies ont été peu à peu remplacés, au moins au niveau de la langue écrite, par l'araméen. L'emploi de l'araméen sur des sceaux ou estampilles judéennes post-exiliques est un phénomène bien connu (Avigad 1965: 231-232; 1976a: n° 5, 14). Il faut noter qu'un phénomène similaire semble s'être produit dans l'ancien territoire ammonite comme le montrent deux sceaux provenant probablement du même atelier: le conoïde *lzkʾ br mlkmʿz* (**fig. 17**; B 84; Bordreuil 1987a: 284; CAI 136); et le conoïde *ltmkʾl br mlkm* (**fig. 18**; CAI 1; cf. Hübner, *infra*, p. 159, fig. 26).[5] Ces deux conoïdes sont clairement d'écriture et de langue araméennes même si leur onomastique (*infra*) est non moins clairement ammonite. On pourrait dès lors proposer de les appeler *ammonito-araméens*, en parallèle à l'appellation reçue "judéo-araméen". Au-delà de l'écriture et de la langue, ils révèlent l'importance de l'onomastique pour un classement "ethnique".

VI. Onomastique

L'information essentielle donnée par la légende sigillaire est généralement de type onomastique: elle précise le nom du propriétaire, éventuellement complété par son patronyme ou son titre. On sait que l'exploitation de l'onomastique pour préciser un rattachement ethnique ne peut se faire sans certaines précautions, spécialement aux époques d'important brassage des populations, ou lorsque la région ou l'ethnie fait partie d'un empire plus vaste tel que l'empire perse, ou, plus tard, l'empire romain. Cependant l'onomastique qui apparaît sur les sceaux est une information directement liée au propriétaire du sceau et peut donc nous révéler le milieu, l'"ethnie" dans laquelle ce sceau inscrit a été utilisé.

L'exploitation ethnique de l'onomastique varie suivant l'époque et suivant le type d'onomastique; celle-ci peut être plus ou moins caractéristique d'une

5. La lecture de ce sceau a été très discutée: on a proposé de lire [ʿ]*bd mlkm* (Cross 1973: 127-128, n. 6; Israel 1987a: 143) ou *bdmlkm* (Avigad 1985: 5, n. 25). Cependant, après examen de ce sceau, il semble assez clair qu'il n'y a pas de place pour la restitution d'un *ʿayin* avant le *b* (Cross 1983: 61, n. 36; Tigay 1987: 187, n. 66) et que c'est la lecture *br mlkm* qui s'impose (B 84; Lemaire 1989: 88, n. 4).

"ethnie", ou, au contraire, commune au monde ouest-sémitique. On distinguera donc:

1. Les noms théophores comportant un théonyme caractéristique d'une culture, d'un royaume, d'une ethnie. Ainsi:

- Milqart, ʿAshtart ou Eshmoun pour l'onomastique phénicienne;
- Yahvé pour l'onomastique hébraïque, en distinguant la finale yahviste écrite habituellement *-yw* dans le royaume du Nord (Israël) et *-yhw* en Juda (cf. Sass, *infra*, p. 199);
- Milkom pour l'onomastique ammonite (cf. Hübner, *infra*, p. 132);
- Kamosh pour l'onomastique moabite (Timm 1989a: 159; cf. *infra*, pp. 161ss.);
- Qôs pour l'onomastique édomite;
- et probablement Hadad (*hdd*) et *ʿtr* pour l'onomastique araméenne.

On remarquera que "El" et "Baʿal" n'apparaissent pas dans cette liste de théonymes caractéristiques d'une ethnie. En effet:

- "El" est pratiquement attesté dans toute l'onomastique ouest-sémitique et même dans toute l'onomastique sémitique en général, incluant l'accadien, le nord- et le sud-arabe. De façon plus précise, "El" est attesté en phénicien, où il reste relativement rare,[6] en hébreu (Fowler 1988: 38-44), en araméen (Maraqten 1988: 44-45, 223), en ammonite, où il est très fréquent (Tigay 1987: 171, 187; Aufrecht 1989: 357-358), en moabite (Israel 1987b: n° III, XXXII), en édomite[7] et en épigraphie philistine (Naveh 1985: 9, 17, 18). El peut désigner soit le dieu "El", soit la divinité, "dieu", en général. L'araméen semble permettre de distinguer ce dernier sens avec la graphie *ʾlh*, caractéristique de l'onomastique araméenne (Maraqten 1988: 45; Lemaire 1990a: 17).
- Même si "Baʿal" était surtout populaire dans l'onomastique phénico-punique (Benz 1972: 288-290), ce théonyme était pratiquement commun à tout le domaine ouest-sémitique. Il était attesté en hébreu (Fowler 1988: 54-63; Avigad 1988: 8-9) et, plus rarement, en araméen (Maraqten 1988: 48-49), en ammonite (CAI 58, 129), en moabite (Israel 1987b: n° XVI),[8] en édomite[9] et en épigraphie philistine (Naveh 1985: 11, n° 1).

---

6. La liste de F.L. Benz (1972: 266) inclut plusieurs sceaux hébreux ou ammonites.

7. Cf. *ʿdʾl* (*infra*, pp. 16-17, et Israel 1979b: n° 2), *šmʿʾl* (Herr 1978: 165, n° 5), *bʿżrʾl* (Driver 1945: 82; Herr 1978: 166, n° 7; cf. *infra*, note 9).

8. Pour ce sceau *bʿlntn*, on pourrait quelque peu hésiter entre un rattachement à l'épigraphie moabite et un rattachement à l'épigraphie hébraïque de la deuxième moitié du VIIIᵉ s. av. J.-C.

9. Cf. le sceau *lbʿżrʾl ʿbdḣbʿl* acheté à Pétra en 1940 (*supra*, n. 7; Millard 1983a: 193, n. 20). P. Bordreuil (1986d) et F. Israel (1987a: 142; 1987d: 338) ont proposé de lire *lbʿzrʾl ʿbd hbʿl* et de classer ce sceau comme ammonite; cependant, ni l'origine, ni la

– Enfin "Shamash" est, au moins, commun à l'onomastique araméenne (cf., par ex. *šmšʿdry* : CIS II, 87; B 111; *šmšʿzr* : Avigad 1986b: 53) et phénico-punique (Lemaire 1990a: 19-20).

2. En dehors des noms théophores, certains noms peuvent être linguistiquement caractéristiques d'une langue précise.

– De ce point de vue, l'onomastique araméenne mériterait une étude détaillée (provisoirement Silverman 1969; Kornfeld 1978; Maraqten 1988). Parmi les éléments caractéristiques de cette onomastique, outre *ʾlh* (*supra*), on peut noter *br*, "fils" (cf. *brhdd, brrkb, brṣr, brgʾyh...*), *mrʾ*, "maître", *ʿdr*, "aider" (versus *ʿzr* en araméen ancien et en cananéen), *yhb*, "donner", *mtʿ*, "sauver", *rqy*, "aimer, se complaire" (versus *rṣy/h* en cananéen), auxquels on peut ajouter les participes haphʿel avec préformante *h*, ainsi: *mᵉhēyṭabʾēl* (Fowler 1988: 127). De plus, on notera que l'onomastique araméenne comporte assez souvent trois éléments, se terminant par le suffixe personnel de la première personne du singulier: ainsi *ʾlhly, ʾlnwry, ʾlsmky, bytʾldlny, bytʾlʿšny, grmʾlhy, hdysʿy, yhwpdny, ssnwry* etc. (Maraqten 1988: 105-106).

Dans le domaine cananéen, il est difficile de proposer des caractéristiques propres à tel ou tel dialecte. Même si tel élément est particulièrement populaire dans une onomastique spécifique, il est nécessaire de rester prudent:

– *tmk* est très bien attesté dans l'onomastique ammonite (CAI, pp. 375-376; cf. **fig. 18**), cependant le verbe *tmk* est aussi attesté en hébreu et en phénicien (KAI 24 I,13; Israel 1979a: 153).

– *bqš* est bien attesté dans l'onomastique ammonite (CAI 37, 137.7[10], 140); cependant le verbe *bqš* est aussi attesté en hébreu tandis que le nom *bqšt* est attesté sur un sceau (**fig. 19** = BM 113200) à paléographie hébraïque mais à iconographie et onomastique ammonites (Prideaux 1877; Clermont-Ganneau 1883: n° 22; Bordreuil & Lemaire 1979: 83, note 7; Lemaire 1986: 319; cf. Ornan, *infra*, p. 59, fig. 16).

---

paléographie, ni la disposition, ni l'onomastique, ni l'iconographie ne semblent justifier cette classification. L'écriture étant très aramaïsante, il semble préférable d'interpréter *ʿbdhbʿl* comme un anthroponyme, soit avec une sorte de *h compaginis*, variante en quelque sorte vocalisée de *ʿbdbʿl* (Naveh 1979: n° 45,7), soit comme une sorte de transcription de l'article arabe *h(n)-* (Knauf 1988a: 70s., n. 334) comme, peut-être, *ʿbdʾbʿly* dans un ostracon de Béérshéba (Naveh 1979: n° 34, verso 3, n° 35,1), en parallèle à l'onomastique nabatéenne: *ʿbdʾlbʿly* ou *ʿbdʾlg(y)ʾ/w* (cf. Cantineau 1932: II, 125). Cf. aussi la bulle *lmlklbʿ ʿbd hmlk*, vraisemblablement à lire *lmlkbʿl ʿbd hmlk* (Lemaire 1975; Bennett 1983: 11; pour deux autres essais d'interprétation, cf. Puech 1977: 12; Layton 1991).

10. A la la suite de F.M. Cross, W. Aufrecht lit *ṗṙš* mais un examen attentif révèle que ce qui a été lu *ṗṙ* est plutôt un *q* (cf. déjà Puech 1991: 231, n. 46 proposant de lire [ʿ]*qš*); dès lors la restitution [*b*]*qṡ* semble très probable.

- L'élément *ndb* est aussi très populaire dans l'onomastique ammonite (Aufrecht 1989: 369); cependant il est aussi attesté dans l'onomastique hébraïque et dans l'onomastique moabite (cf. le roi moabite *Kamusunadbi* sous Sennachérib: ARAB II, § 239).
- *mšʿ* est probablement aussi à placer dans ce groupe. Il est bien attesté pour le roi moabite du IXe s. av. J.-C., cependant il a peut-être été aussi utilisé dans une onomastique voisine, en particulier en Edom (*infra*, p. 16).
- La finale *-w* des noms propres semble nous faire sortir du domaine ouest-sémitique car elle est assez caractéristique de l'onomastique nord-arabe ancienne (cf. en nabatéen).[11]

3. La prudence est encore plus nécessaire lorsqu'il s'agit de noms attestés dans tout le domaine ouest-sémitique tels que *mnḥm*, *šlm* ...

Tout en permettant, avec nuances, de proposer assez souvent un rattachement ethnique ou régional, le critère onomastique paraît difficile à utiliser pour une datation, même approximative. En effet, l'évolution des usages onomastiques paraît avoir été souvent assez lente et quasi-imperceptible sur une durée de deux ou trois siècles. On notera, cependant, que l'onomastique d'époque royale semble comporter de plus en plus de noms yahvistes au fur et à mesure que l'on approche de la chute de Jérusalem en 587. Cette évolution statistique peut malheureusement difficilement être exploitée au niveau de l'onomastique d'un sceau car les premiers noms yahvistes remontent probablement déjà au XIIIe s. av. J.-C. (Lemaire 1990e: 239-240). Une évolution similaire a pu se produire dans le royaume ammonite puisque toutes les attestations actuellement connues du théonyme "Milkom" dans l'onomastique ammonite (CAI 1 [= **fig. 18**], 127, 129, 136 [= **fig. 17**], 147) semblent dater du VIe s. av. J.-C. Cependant il paraît quelque peu prématuré d'en déduire un critère possible de datation de l'onomastique ammonite.

Par ailleurs, l'utilisation du critère onomastique dans la classification "ethnique" nécessite une très grande prudence lorsqu'il s'agit d'identifier un personnage d'un sceau avec un homonyme attesté ailleurs, dans la tradition littéraire (biblique, assyrienne ou autre) ou en épigraphie. Ce problème a déjà été abordé par N. Avigad à propos de l'épigraphie paléo-hébraïque et de la Bible (1987b; cf. Herr 1980b; Elayi 1986; Schneider 1988; 1991).

- En ce qui concerne les noms de rois d'Israël et de Juda, N. Avigad ne retient que ceux qui sont clairement attestés comme rois parce que, sur les sceaux ou sur les bulles, leur nom est précédé de *ʿbd*, "serviteur/ministre".

11. La lecture de *plṭẇ* (B 70; CAI 75) est à corriger en *plṭ.̇* (Lemaire 1985b: 42, n. 76; Aufrecht 1989: 196-197; Puech 1989: 590) tandis que nous ne comprenons pas la lecture *-šʿw* pour VSE 117:1, proposée par F. Israel (1989: 93-94, n. 16): après le *ʿayin*, il y a une fleur de lotus (CAI 38).

Sont ainsi nommés le roi d'Israël Jéroboam (II) et les rois de Juda: Ozias, Achaz et Ezéchias.

– Pour les autres personnages, il est nécessaire d'avoir au moins le même anthroponyme et le même patronyme; c'est encore mieux si s'y ajoute l'identité d'un qualificatif, d'un titre ou d'une fonction (Avigad 1978c) ou encore du nom du grand-père. De toutes façons, il faut qu'il y ait une bonne correspondance chronologique. Dès lors, outre cette correspondance chronologique, l'identité de deux éléments semble nécessaire pour que l'identification puisse être considérée comme probable et celle d'un troisième élément pour qu'elle puisse être considérée comme pratiquement sûre. Cette prudence méthodologique peut être généralisée à l'identification de personnages mentionnés sur les autres sceaux nord-ouest sémitiques.

VII. HARMONIES OU CONTRADICTIONS DES DIFFÉRENTS CRITÈRES: EXEMPLES

Le plus souvent, les résultats de l'analyse paléographique, linguistique et onomastique ne font que confirmer l'indication de l'origine, si elle est connue, ainsi que le rattachement iconographique étudié dans ce symposium. La convergence de ces différents indicateurs conduit évidemment à un rattachement clair et sans hésitation qui pourra servir de référence pour les cas moins évidents. A ce sujet, on peut rappeler que les premiers essais de classification des sceaux nord-ouest sémitiques inscrits se sont souvent faits en utilisant les deux critères les plus évidents, lorsqu'ils existent: d'une part, l'origine, d'autre part, une onomastique comportant un théonyme national. C'est seulement à partir de ces premières identifications que s'est précisé, peu à peu, le critère paléographique. Ainsi en a-t-il été pour les sceaux hébreux et moabites dès le XIXe s., et pour les sceaux ammonites depuis 1946 (Avigad 1946; 1952).

Dans les faits, il est rare que l'analyse de chacun des critères conduise à une conclusion précise totalement assurée; elle n'aboutit souvent qu'à une certaine probabilité. Cependant, pour aboutir à un résultat relativement certain, il suffit qu'un seul des critères utilisés soit caractéristique et que les autres ne s'opposent pas à ce résultat. C'est en tenant compte de ce principe que nous voudrions proposer quelques corrections de classification:

1. Le sceau *lʿbdḥwrn* (**fig. 20**; B 2) a généralement été classé comme phénicien; cependant P. Bordreuil a noté, à juste titre, que "l'écriture rappelle surtout celle de Mésha". Dès lors, avec M.G. Amadasi Guzzo (1989), on peut mettre sérieusement en doute la classification phénicienne à cause de la paléographie: le *ḥ* à deux barres horizontales attesté dans ce sceau est pratiquement inconnu en paléographie phénicienne (Herr 1978: 18); le *ḥ* phénicien

a, en effet, trois barres; bien plus, l'incurvation assez prononcée de la hampe du *n* ne paraît pas phénicienne. Ces deux caractéristiques indiquent plutôt une paléographie moabite ou hébraïque.

Le classement de l'onomastique semble plus difficile. Comme le théonyme "Ḥôron" ne semble attesté qu'ici dans toute l'onomastique nord-ouest sémitique du Ier millénaire av. J.-C. (Benz 1972: 309; Xella 1988: 57),[12] il est malaisé de prendre position. Le culte de Ḥôron est bien attesté en punique, à Antas en Sardaigne (Sznycer 1969; Uberti 1978), mais les deux toponymes bibliques "Beyt-Ḥôron" et "Ḥôronayim" (= "Ḥôronên) montrent que ce culte n'était probablement pas inconnu en Palestine ni, peut-être, en Moab. Si l'onomastique semble de rattachement incertain, il faut noter l'orthographe particulière de ce nom: "Ḥôron" est écrit *ḥwrn*, avec un *w mater lectionis*, ce qui paraît contraire à l'orthographe phénicienne (Puech 1989: 592) et à l'orthographe philistine, puisque, aussi bien à Antas que dans l'ostracon de Tell Qasilé, Ḥôron est écrit *ḥrn* (Amadasi Guzzo 1989: 147). Par contre, la présence d'un *w* n'étonnerait pas dans une inscription moabite puisque le toponyme "Ḥôronên" est écrit *ḥwrnn* dans la stèle de Mésha (lignes 31, 32?). Comme l'iconographie précise de ce sceau est unique (Gubel 1987b: 247-249), il est difficile d'en situer l'atelier de gravure, mais on peut dire que la légende de ce sceau est très probablement moabite et qu'il s'agit même vraisemblablement du plus ancien sceau moabite inscrit connu à ce jour, à peu près contemporain de la stèle de Mésha (fin du IXe s. av. J.-C.: Gubel 1987b: 247).

2. Le sceau de *ydlʾ* (**fig. 21**; B 3; cf. Timm, *infra*, pp. 173-174 et fig. 9) a été publié comme phénicien. Cependant sa paléographie, en particulier la forme du *ʾaleph* pratiquement en étoile, autoriserait tout aussi bien un rattachement à la paléographie moabite. Le nom *ydlʾ* semble, jusqu'à maintenant, inconnu, aussi bien en phénicien qu'en moabite; il en est de même du verbe *dlh*. Dès lors, ici, c'est probablement l'iconographie qui fera éventuellement pencher la balance du côté moabite car ce type de griffon stylisé est déjà bien attesté en glyptique moabite (cf. Timm, *infra*, p. 192, figs. 7, 10), spécialement avec aigrettes (Timm, fig. 8).

3. Le sceau *lmṣry* (**fig. 22**; B 65; cf. Gubel, *infra*, p. 119, fig. 48) a été récemment classé comme moabite, mais, avec J. Naveh (1988) et S. Timm (1989a: 251, n. 147), cette nouvelle classification ne paraît pas convaincante. Paléographiquement, selon J. Naveh, "Such a *ṣade* does not exist in the script of the Moabites. It may be Aramaic or Phoenician, or perhaps Ammonite" (1988: 115) et on note que P. Bordreuil avait déjà rapproché les formes des lettres de ce sceau de celles des inscriptions phéniciennes de Karatépé. Le nom *mṣry*, très probablement "Égyptien", est bien attesté en phénico-punique

12. Cependant il pourrait être attesté dans le nom sabéen *ʿbdḫrn* (Garbini 1976: 302, 307).

(Benz 1972: 142), en particulier dans la fameuse stèle de *mṣry* ancêtre, à 16 générations, d'un Carthaginois (CIS I, 3778; Xella 1990: 211). On le rencontre aussi à Ougarit (Gröndahl 1967: 161, 401), probablement en paléo-hébreu (A 108; Timm 1989a: 250, n. 145), en araméen (Maraqten 1988: 88, 181)[13] et en néo-assyrien (Tallqvist 1914: 140) où il est, en particulier, attesté pour un roi de Moab à l'époque d'Assarhaddon et d'Assurbanipal (ANET: pp. 291, 294) et probablement pour un autre roi de Syrie-Palestine de cette époque (Timm 1989a: 312, 314, n. 24).[14] Etant donné que la paléographie de ce sceau n'est pas moabite, il ne semble y avoir aucune raison de privilégier la mention d'un roi du même nom comme roi de Moab et de proposer de l'identifier avec le propriétaire de ce sceau comme cela a été fait récemment (Bordreuil 1985: 25-26, n° 3; 1986a: n° 65; 1986d; 1986e: 133, n° 171; 1986f: 120; 1987a; 1991: 464; Israel 1987b: n° XXIII; Gubel 1991a: 915; cf. *infra*, pp. 109, 121). En fait, l'onomastique semble plutôt confirmer les indications de la paléographie en faveur d'un rattachement probable au domaine phénicien comme l'avaient proposé auparavant la plupart des épigraphistes.

4. F. Israel a proposé de classer comme moabites deux sceaux: *lmšʿ ʿdʾl* et *lmnḥmt ʾšt ṗdmlk*[15] (**fig. 23**; Israel 1987b: n° XXVI, malgré Israel 1979a: n° 15 le classant comme édomite) qui présentent un *d* inversé de bas en haut. Or cette forme de lettre n'est attestée sûrement qu'en édomite (*supra*, p. 5); les autres lettres ne s'opposeraient pas à un rattachement à la paléographie édomite; au contraire, la forme du *k* de la fin de la ligne 1 semble inconnue en moabite. On proposera donc plutôt de rattacher paléographiquement ces deux légendes à l'édomite (pour la face anépigraphe de ce sceau, cf. Ornan, *infra*, p. 66, fig. 52).

5. Pour ce qui est du sceau *lmšʿ ʿdʾl* (Israel 1987b: n° VI; CAI 31), N. Avigad (1951: 34) avait, le premier, proposé de reconnaître dans la deuxième lettre un *m* de forme particulière avec une hampe de droite vers le haut et une hampe de gauche vers le bas. Ce type de *m* apparaît aussi sur le sceau *lmš* (**fig. 24**; Israel 1987b: n° X), comme l'avait bien vu Avigad (1970a: 291-292), ainsi que sur le sceau *lḥkš* (**fig. 25**; B 67; Israel 1987b: n° XV; Timm 1989a: 197-198, n° 13), en fait à lire *lḥkṁ* comme l'avait bien vu L.G. Herr (1978: 51, n° 109; cf. Timm, *infra*, p. 181-182). Ce type de *m* existe donc

---

13. On peut proposer de lire *ḥtm ṁṣry* sur un sceau-cylindre phénicien ou, plutôt, araméen provenant de Cilicie que A. Dupont-Sommer (1950: 43-45) proposait de lire *ḥtm š ṣry*. Malheureusement aucune photographie n'en a été publiée et nous ne savons où il est.

14. Cependant, malgré Timm 1989a: 250, n. 145, *Mu-ṣu-r(i)* ne semble pas avoir été roi de Gaza.

15. Paléographiquement, la lecture *ṗdmlk* semble préférable à *gdmlk*. Le nom *ṗdmlk* est déjà attesté sur un sceau moabite (Israel 1987b: n° XIII).

vraiment[16] et, au moins, à trois exemplaires.[17] F. Israel avait classé les trois sceaux comme moabites; cependant puisque ce type de *m* apparaît au moins une fois en compagnie d'un *d* édomite, inversé de bas en haut, on songera plutôt à rattacher ce type de *m*, et donc ces trois sceaux, à la sigillographie édomite.

6. Le sceau *lʾlhʿm* (**fig. 7**; CAI 10) avait été classé comme ammonite par L.G. Herr (1978: 70-71, n° 35) et nous avions nous-mêmes souligné la forme carrée du *ʿayin* (Bordreuil & Lemaire 1979: 83) et celle du *h* apparemment à deux barres horizontales. Cependant un examen plus minutieux de l'empreinte de ce sceau révèle que ce *h* présente, en fait, une troisième barre un peu décalée vers la gauche, entre la barre supérieure et la barre inférieure. Paléographiquement l'écriture de ce sceau est donc plutôt araméenne. La disposition de la légende vers le milieu du champ et son iconographie ne sont pas attestés jusqu'ici sur des sceaux ammonites.[18] Le nom comporte l'élément *ʾlh* assez nettement araméen (cf. déjà Israel 1987a: 144). Ce sceau se rattache donc plutôt à la sigillographie araméenne.

7. Le conoïde *lmnḥm* (CAI 29) peut, paléographiquement, être aussi bien araméen (B 108) qu'ammonite (Israel 1987a: 145). L'onomastique est commune au monde ouest-sémitique, même si elle est populaire en ammonite; l'iconographie néo-babylonienne (cf. Ornan, *infra*, p. 65, fig. 41) n'a rien de typiquement ammonite. Nous hésiterions donc, aujourd'hui encore plus qu'en 1985 (cf. Lemaire 1985b: 46-47), à classer ce sceau comme ammonite.

8. Le sceau de *ʿšnʾl* (**fig. 26**; CAI 6) avait été classé comme ammonite par L.G. Herr (1978: 72, n° 39) à cause de la forme carrée du *ʿayin*. Cependant cette forme est aussi attestée en paléographie hébraïque du VIIIᵉ s. av. J.-C. (*supra*, p. 6). Le nom *ʿšnʾl* ne semble attesté qu'ici en nord-ouest sémitique; il pourrait se rattacher au verbe *ʿWŠ* attesté dans l'onomastique hébraïque (Fowler 1988: 84, 106, 131, 354). Dès lors, on retiendra plutôt la proposition de G. Garbini (1982: 176; Israel 1987a: 144) d'y voir un sceau israélite du royaume de Samarie où une iconographie similaire du lion rugissant (Lemaire 1990a: 13-16; Avigad 1992c) et du scarabée volant à deux ailes est bien attestée (cf. Sass, *infra*, pp. 214, 221-222, motifs B2.2. et D1).

9. Récemment N. Avigad (1989a: n° 19) a hésité à rattacher le sceau *lšlmʾl* (cf. Uehlinger, *infra*, p. 264, fig. 6) à l'épigraphie moabite. En fait, aucune

---

16. Malgré Timm 1989a: 293 qui doute de l'authenticité des sceaux *lmš* et *lmšʿ ʿdʾl*.

17. Un autre exemplaire semble assez clairement attesté à la fin de la ligne 1 d'un sceau du marché des antiquités où on pourrait proposer de lire, de façon conjecturale: *q̇ẇṡʾm* (Wolfe & Sternberg 1989: n° 24, classé comme moabite). On notera, à droite du registre médian, sur une espèce de cube, la présence possible d'un *d* inversé.

18. Le sceau *lšmʿ* (Israel 1987a: 145 = CAI 63) n'est probablement pas ammonite.

des lettres, et surtout pas le *m*, ne semble moabite. Le nom *šlmʾl* n'est pas attesté en moabite alors qu'on le trouve sur un conoïde pouvant provenir de la région d'Ashdod (Herr 1978: 21), ainsi qu'en hébreu biblique (Nb 1,6; 2,12 etc.). Comme l'iconographie (cf. Keel 1977: 288-308; GGG: § 178; Sass, *infra*, p. 234; Uehlinger, pp. 264-265) n'est pas attestée jusqu'à maintenant sur des sceaux moabites, il ne semble y avoir aucune raison de rattacher ce sceau à la sigillographie moabite.

Ces quelques exemples révèlent diverses nuances de certitude ou de probabilité dans la classification ethnique, même lorsqu'il y a une certaine convergence minimale. Cependant, pour un certain nombre de sceaux inscrits, cette convergence minimale (non-contradiction des critères) n'existe pas: il y a une apparente *contradiction* entre la provenance, les caractéristiques matérielles, la disposition de la légende, les résultats de l'analyse paléographique, linguistique, onomastique et iconographique.

1. La contradiction entre la *provenance* et les autres caractéristiques du sceau, dont nous avons vu un exemple plus haut, peut assez facilement s'expliquer par le fait que ce sceau, avec ou sans son propriétaire, avait pu voyager dès l'antiquité. C'est ainsi qu'on peut facilement expliquer la découverte d'un certain nombre de sceaux inscrits nord-ouest sémitiques dans des fouilles mésopotamiennes, pensant particulièrement aux déportations, mais sans écarter totalement le commerce et la diplomatie. C'est le cas du sceau *lšbʾl bn ʾlyšʿ* (CAI 45), des sceaux de *kmšntn* (Israel 1987b: n° VIII), provenant d'Ur, de *ʿbdbʿl* (B 8) et de *rpty* provenant de Khorsabad (B 89; cf. Bordreuil, *infra*, p. 87 et fig. 17), de *bʿlntn* provenant de Tello (B 61; cf. Gubel, *infra*, p. 123 et fig. 65; Timm, pp. 175-178), ainsi que des bulles *ʿtrʿzr* provenant de Ninive (CIS II, 52).[19]

On notera aussi que deux sceaux paléo-hébreux, au moins, datant du VIIIe s. et probablement israélites, ont été trouvés sur la côte de la Méditerranée occidentale: le sceau *lywʾb*, trouvé à Carthage dans une tombe du IV-IIIe s. av. J.-C. (D 9; cf. Sass, *infra*, p. 235 et fig. 140), ainsi que le sceau *lnʿmʾl pʾrt*, provenant de Puerta de Tierra (Cadix) (Lemaire 1985b: n° 17[20]). On pourrait éventuellement songer ici à la participation d'Israélites au commerce international des Phéniciens (cf. Lemaire 1984: 137-138).

---

19. On pourrait aussi mentionner, avec réserve, deux sceaux dits provenir de Bagdad: *lgbrt mrḥd* (G 88) et *lšʿl bn ʾlyšʿ* (G 28 = CAI 30), ainsi qu'un sceau dit provenir de Mésopotamie: le conoïde *lbqšt bt ʿbdyrḥ* (*supra*, p. 12).

20. On notera que le petit personnage debout, de face, sur ce sceau peut être rapproché d'une représentation similaire sur un sceau anépigraphe inédit, probablement palestinien (collection privée), comportant ce motif entouré d'une bordure cablée à l'intérieur d'une guirlande de grenades (pour ce motif, cf. Sass, *infra*, p. 207, fig. 52).

Enfin on remarquera que, entre deux pays voisins, les échanges ont pu naturellement être assez nombreux (*supra*: le sceau *lplṭy bn mʾš hmzkr*, **fig. 1**). A titre d'exemple, on rappellera que trois sceaux paléo-hébreux, au moins, ont été trouvés en Transjordanie: le sceau *lšlm bn mnḥm* provenant de Tell Ṣafūt (Bordreuil & Lemaire 1976: 51, n. 15; Weippert 1979; 1980); le sceau *lʾlšmʿ pll* (**fig. 27**), provenant de ʿAïn el-Basha dans la Buqéia (Jordanie centrale), publié comme ammonite (Puech 1976) mais à la paléographie et à l'iconographie clairement hébraïques (Bordreuil & Lemaire 1976: 63; CAI 95, pp. 247, 250); ainsi que le sceau *lgʾlyhw ʿbd hmlk*, provenant d'Umm el-Qanafid, près de Naʿur (Fulco 1979).

2. Les contradictions, *sur le sceau lui-même*, entre la paléographie, la langue, l'onomastique et l'iconographie, paraissent plus difficiles à expliquer. Pour essayer de les comprendre, il peut être utile de rappeler les principales étapes de la fabrication des sceaux. Assez schématiquement, on peut distinguer:

- le choix du matériau par le graveur (pierre commune, semi-précieuse ou autre),
- la première mise en forme du sceau: scarabée, scaraboïde, conoïde, cylindre dans une dimension précise,
- la gravure de l'iconographie,
- la gravure de l'inscription.

Il est vraisemblable que le même atelier de graveur pouvait souvent assurer toutes les étapes de cette fabrication. Cependant, outre le commerce du matériau à l'état brut, il semble y avoir eu un certain commerce de sceaux "nus", simplement mis en forme et non encore gravés, ainsi que de sceaux gravés en série ne comportant que l'iconographie. Il semble même vraisemblable que, pour la plupart des sceaux inscrits comportant une iconographie importante, cette iconographie ait été préparée à l'avance, en série, avec éventuellement, mais pas toujours (Dion 1989: 75), une place réservée pour l'inscription, celle-ci ne pouvant être gravée qu'au moment de l'achat du sceau ou après. Cette pratique semble confirmée par le fait que, lorsque l'acheteur ne demandait pas à faire graver son nom (et ne voulait pas payer pour cela), le graveur se contentait habituellement de remplir la place réservée pour l'inscription par une simple ligne brisée, en zig-zag, ou un autre motif de remplissage, comme l'attestent un certain nombre de sceaux anépigraphes comportant la même iconographie que les sceaux inscrits.

Dès lors, les contradictions apparentes entre l'iconographie et l'inscription peuvent s'expliquer:

- soit par le fait d'une grande diffusion d'une série iconographique à partir d'un même atelier dans divers ateliers régionaux secondaires où on les vendait en y ajoutant éventuellement l'inscription,

– soit par le fait, plus rare, que la gravure du nom du propriétaire ait pu être rajoutée après coup, éventuellement assez longtemps après (Lemaire 1990b: 109).

3. En ce qui concerne les contradictions possibles entre les diverses caractéristiques de *l'inscription* elle-même (paléographie, disposition, langue et onomastique), il faut mettre à part le problème onomastique posé par l'adoption habituelle de certains noms étrangers dans une ethnie au point que le commun du peuple ne devait plus sentir ce nom comme étranger. L'exemple classique de cette acculturation onomastique est *pšḥr*, "Pashḥour", nom d'origine égyptienne, mais très bien attesté en hébreu biblique (Jr 20,1.2.3...) et épigraphique, en particulier en sigillographie (A 151-153; Avigad 1989b: 94-95, n° 4; cf. Sass, *infra*, p. 201 fig. 2, p. 211 fig. 61).

Il faut aussi mettre à part des groupes de sceaux liés à un contexte politico-culturel particulier. Ainsi:

– les noms asianiques (louvites ou autres) apparaissant sur des sceaux phéniciens (Lemaire 1977a; 1991b: n. 6) ou phénico-araméens (Lemaire 1985b: 32-33; cf. B 122) du VIII-VIIe s. av. J.-C;
– l'emploi quasi-général de l'araméen par les diverses ethnies de l'empire perse;
– un certain nombre de légendes avec une paléographie originale (aramaïsante?) sur des conoïdes de la fin du VIIe et du VIe s. av. J.-C., période marquée par le développement de l'emploi de l'écriture araméenne. Ainsi, outre les sceaux ammonito-araméens mentionnés plus haut:
  • le conoïde octogonal *lḥwnn bn y'znyh* (D 21),
  • le conoïde octogonal *l'bdyhw bn šḥrḥr* (D 35; B 56),
  • le conoïde octogonal *lšḥrḥr bn ṣpnyhw* (D 39),
  • le conoïde *lntnyhw bn 'bdyhw* (D 32; B 49; cf. Sass, *infra*, p. 202 fig. 30, p. 223 fig. 117),[21]
  • le conoïde *lsryh bn bnsmrnr* (D 33),
  • le conoïde octogonal *lbqšt bt 'bdyrḥ* (**fig. 19**) à l'écriture hébraïsante et l'iconographie et l'onomastique probablement ammonites ou araméennes (cf. *supra*, p. 12).[22]

A ces conoïdes, on peut proposer d'ajouter quelques scaraboïdes qui semblent dater de cette période de transition:
  • le scaraboïde *lḥnnyh bn wryh* (CAI 4) dont la langue est "cananéenne" et la paléographie araméenne ou ammonite;

21. L'ouverture du *'ayin* sur ce sceau semble plutôt indiquer une datation vers la fin du VIIe s. av. J.-C. (Puech 1989: 590).

22. Cette particularité pourrait s'expliquer par le fait que le graveur ait pu être un Israélite ou un Judéen (résidant en Ammon ou Juda, ou même déporté en Mésopotamie?).

- le scaraboïde *lyhwyšmʿ bt šwššrʾṣr*[23] (Avigad 1965: 228-230; B 54) avec une graphie hébraïque à la première ligne et une graphie araméenne à la seconde;
- le scaraboïde *lnḥmyhw bn mykyhw* (**fig. 28**; D 30) qui présente un *k* à tête en triangle, inconnu par ailleurs, semble-t-il, en paléo-hébreu, mais bien attesté en ammonite.

Evoquons enfin le problème posé par le conoïde *ḥtm mngʾnrt brk lmlkm*[24], "sceau de Mannu-ki-Inurta, béni par Milkom"[25] (**fig. 16**). La mention de Milkom l'a fait classer généralement comme ammonite (B 76; Israel 1987a: 142; CAI 55; H 90); cependant, l'exemple du sceau ...] *ʾbndb š ndr l ʿšt bṣdn tbrkh*, classé aussi souvent comme ammonite (CAI 56), semble montrer que l'invocation du dieu Milkom n'est peut-être pas un critère suffisant: selon J. Naveh (1988: 115): "The seal of Mannu-ki-Inurta is definitely Aramaic". En fait, paléographiquement l'inscription peut être aussi bien araméenne qu'ammonite. La formule *ḥtm* ... oriente normalement vers la sigillographie araméenne. Le nom propre, *Mannu-ki-Inurta*, est assyrien. L'iconographie (cf. Ornan, *infra*, figs. 1+71) paraît assyrianisante mais est bien attestée sur des sceaux ammonites (Aufrecht 1989: 352). On peut donc hésiter entre une classification "assyro-araméenne", "araméenne" et "ammonito-araméenne".

L'évocation de ces derniers sceaux révèle, semble-t-il, les limites de notre effort de classification des sceaux nord-ouest sémitiques inscrits: la rigueur méthodologique doit aussi tenir compte des particularismes et des originalités liées à des conjonctures originales, ici, à la rencontre de deux personnalités: le graveur et le propriétaire/acheteur. Plus encore que l'iconographie, qui semble d'abord l'œuvre du graveur, l'acheteur n'ayant plus qu'à la choisir après coup, l'inscription porte inévitablement la marque de l'originalité de ces deux personnages marqués culturellement. Les contradictions entre les différentes caractéristiques de l'inscription peuvent donc éventuellement révéler que le graveur/vendeur et l'acheteur se rattachaient à deux cultures différentes, ou même que, chacun de leur côté, le graveur/vendeur et/ou l'acheteur participaient de deux cultures différentes.

---

23. Pour la lecture du *w* à la deuxième ligne cf. Naveh 1988: 116; Puech 1989: 590; Dion 1989: 76.

24. La lecture *br klmlkm* (Naʾaman & Zadok 1988: 45s., n. 51) est paléographiquement possible mais reste très conjecturale dans l'attente d'une attestation claire d'un tel anthroponyme.

25. Malgré Bordreuil 1986a: 68-69, cette traduction s'impose (cf. CAI 55; Bunnens 1989: 174; Dion 1989: 76).

LISTE DES ILLUSTRATIONS

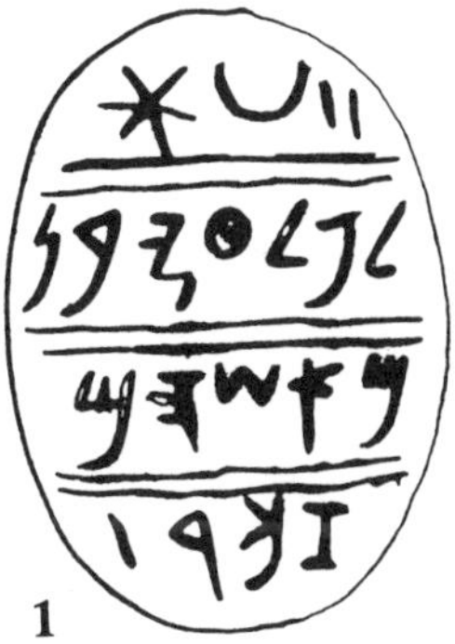

1

2

3

4

5

6

7

8

9

10

11

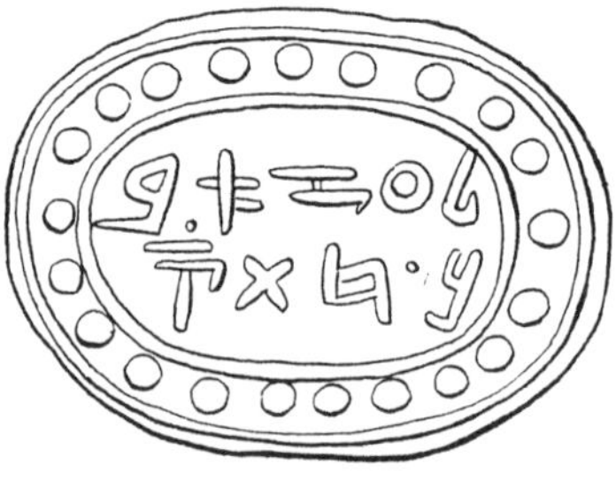

12

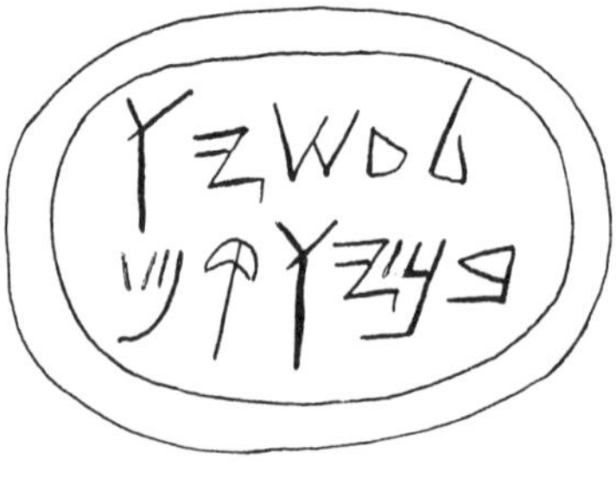

13

14

15

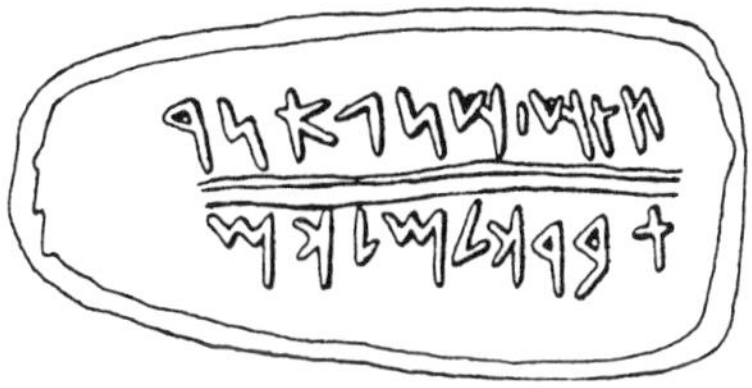

16

17

18

19

20

21

22

23

24

25

26

27

28

À PROPOS DES SCEAUX OUEST-SÉMITIQUES: LE RÔLE DE L'ICONOGRAPHIE DANS L'ATTRIBUTION D'UN SCEAU À UNE AIRE CULTURELLE ET À UN ATELIER

Dominique PARAYRE
Université de Lille III

L'idée directrice de notre contribution à ce recueil consacré à l'iconographie des sceaux ouest-sémitiques est simple: il s'agit d'une réflexion méthodologique sur le rôle de l'iconographie dans le classement des sceaux en général et de la glyptique ouest-sémitique en particulier. Cela par rapport au rôle plus traditionnel des critères épigraphiques, dont André Lemaire nous propose une analyse critique dans l'article précédent. Ce choix est très réducteur par rapport à la richesse potentielle de l'iconographie. Nous nous bornons ici à un travail de classification des données, à la fois géographique et chronologique, ce qui est en fait le fondement même de la démarche du spécialiste: intégrer le document au contexte qui l'a produit avant de l'interroger dans telle ou telle perspective.

Pour éviter toute généralisation facile, nous avons choisi de fonder cette réflexion sur l'étude d'un motif figuratif précis auquel nous avons consacré récemment un article publié dans la revue *Syria* (Parayre 1990a). Le motif choisi était en réalité un symbole, celui du disque solaire ailé. Ce symbole est une création de l'Egypte et non de l'Orient; et l'Orient lui-même ne l'aurait sans doute pas créé, parce qu'il associe deux éléments de nature radicalement différente, une composante astrale (le soleil) et une composante empruntée au règne animal, plus précisément à celui des oiseaux (les ailes du "faucon pèlerin" à l'origine). Il est arrivé d'Egypte à l'époque du Bronze Moyen, avec une configuration toute particulière et une symbolique très forte, à la fois solaire et royale. Cette image est doublement idéale pour notre propos. En effet, elle combine les apports de l'Egypte et de l'Orient, ce qui est précisément la marque des terres ouest-sémitiques. De plus, elle est quasi omniprésente et très malléable, ce qui en fait une excellente pierre de touche pour distinguer les différents centres de production de ce vaste domaine, du Taurus jusqu'à l'Arabie et de la Méditerranée orientale jusqu'à la Mésopotamie; cela, à la fois pour la période pré-achéménide (IXe-VIe siècles) et pour la période de la domination perse (VIe-IVe siècles).

Il n'est pas possible de chiffrer avec exactitude la proportion de sceaux qui arborent le symbole solaire par rapport au total actuellement accessible; on peut simplement dire qu'il s'agissait d'une image fréquente, ce qui est naturel pour des régions entourées de tous côtés par des empires et des royaumes où elle surabondait. Par contre, *pour ce qui est des documents dont le répertoire comporte un disque ailé*, nous pouvons proposer une répartition provisoire entre cachets inscrits et cachets anépigraphiques au sein de chaque ensemble culturel. Sont inscrits:

- 80% des cachets phéniciens antérieurs à la conquête perse, contre seulement 8% pour l'époque achéménide;
- 55% des cachets israélites et 45% des cachets araméens;
- presque 100% des sceaux judéens, qui se limitent à quelques exceptions près aux fameuses "empreintes royales" de Juda;
- 100% des sceaux ammonites et moabites.

La morphologie du symbole solaire est la même, que le sceau comporte ou non une légende. L'article publié dans *Syria* était pour l'essentiel une typologie, qui proposait un classement des différentes variantes de l'image dans l'espace et dans le temps. Nous nous proposons ici de le compléter, de corriger certains points, et surtout d'en dégager une méthode de travail, méthode qui est déjà pratique courante en iconographie orientale, mais qu'il importait de préciser pour le monde ouest-sémitique, où la prédominance de l'épigraphie a très longtemps relégué toute autre approche des sceaux à une place secondaire.

Quelques impératifs méthodologiques simples et évidents se sont ainsi imposés d'emblée à tous les participants au colloque de Fribourg.

Sur le plan de l'analyse et de la reproduction graphique des données, il nous a semblé indispensable d'étudier puis de dessiner l'image choisie de la façon la plus précise et la plus exacte possible: en effet, souvent seul un détail infime permet de préciser l'origine et la date d'un document. Il est tout aussi nécessaire d'harmoniser le rendu des différentes images du corpus étudié, et de respecter l'échelle, afin de permettre un travail de comparaison correct.

Sur le plan de la méthode de recherche *lato sensu*, il est apparu essentiel de travailler constamment dans un cadre contextuel, selon un certain nombre de principes:

- éviter d'isoler les sceaux de l'ensemble de la culture matérielle. Il est capital de les comparer aux autres productions accessibles, quel que soit le matériau et quelles que soient les dimensions. Ainsi avons-nous utilisé à la fois l'art monumental et les "arts mineurs" comme les ivoires, les coquillages, les petits objets en pierre, les monnaies... Le seul ancrage sûr est bien entendu l'art monumental, et nous disposons malheureusement de bien peu de repères dans le monde ouest-sémitique: citons Zincirli, Karatepe et Tell Halaf dans le monde araméen.
- éviter d'isoler les sceaux livrés par les fouilles des sceaux conservés dans les divers musées et collections, les premiers étant naturellement la pierre de touche pour classer les seconds. Quelles que soient les réserves émises judicieusement par André Lemaire, et malgré la rareté des données stratifiées dans le domaine des sceaux ouest-sémitiques, les objets mis au jour dans les chantiers de fouilles sont fondamentaux, ce qui justifie d'ailleurs le projet mis en œuvre à Fribourg par le Professeur Othmar Keel lui-même.
- éviter d'isoler les sceaux inscrits des sceaux anépigraphes. D'une part l'étude de détail prouve que les mêmes ateliers fabriquent indifféremment les uns et les autres dans de nombreux cas, et que seule une approche globale de la production est pertinente. Ce principe est capital pour travailler sur les rapports entre demande et production, et distinguer les sceaux gravés à l'avance auxquels on rajoute le nom du propriétaire (travail en série) des sceaux de commande, où la légende est prévue dès le départ (travail à la demande ou au coup par coup).
- éviter d'isoler image et écriture. Entre les sceaux aniconiques et les sceaux purement figuratifs, une masse de documents combinent de multiples façons légende et représentation figurée, les uns associant plusieurs images à la légende, les autres se limitant à une image isolée.[1] Ce n'est qu'en analysant les diverses façons dont cette combinaison s'est opérée que l'on peut espérer dégager les séries significatives.
- éviter d'isoler les images les unes des autres, et notamment d'isoler le disque ailé de son contexte figuré. Là-aussi seul un travail sur les associations récurrentes et sur les exclusions permet de repérer les séries significatives, maître-mot de toute recherche iconographique pertinente.
- éviter d'isoler le travail de gravure à proprement parler des autres données intrinsèques: la forme, le matériau, les dimensions de l'objet.

1. Il faut mettre à part les cachets bifaces, où le jeu entre image et écriture est plus subtil.

Ces considérations générales une fois posées, nous allons présenter maintenant l'essentiel des résultats de notre enquête, en trois points:

- l'espace: image et aires culturelles, soit une approche globale.[2] Ou comment l'étude du disque ailé permet de mettre en lumière les caractéristiques majeures du répertoire et du style des différentes aires culturelles qui se côtoient ou se recoupent dans l'Orient ouest-sémitique des IXe-VIe siècles.
- l'espace: image et ateliers, soit une approche ponctuelle.[3] Ou comment l'étude du disque ailé permet d'identifier et de localiser les fabriques sur le terrain.
- le temps: image et événement, soit une recherche sur l'impact d'un changement politique sur les arts figurés. Ou comment l'étude du disque ailé permet d'appréhender la conquête perse et ses conséquences sous l'angle des permanences et des nouveautés.

I. L'ESPACE: IMAGE ET AIRES CULTURELLES (IXe-VIe SIECLES)

L'enquête engagée dans une perspective globale aboutit à une constatation majeure. Nous avons affaire à des éléments hétérogènes de nature et d'origine diverses: d'un côté, des traditions figuratives qui remontent à l'Age du Bronze (éléments endogènes); de l'autre, les traditions figuratives des grandes puissances du Ier millénaire, d'autant plus pourvoyeuses d'images qu'elles furent des puissances conquérantes (éléments exogènes).

1. Eléments endogènes

L'analyse permet d'abord de repérer ce que les arts figurés des régions étudiées perpétuent de l'imagerie des siècles antérieurs, problème qui naturellement ne se pose pas avec l'écriture.

On peut classer dans cette catégorie *les empennages*. L'adjonction d'une queue d'oiseau au disque ailé remonte à la Mésopotamie du Bronze Récent. Elle devient courante à partir du début de l'Age du Fer (XIIe-XIe siècles), si bien que les disques ailés et empennés sont la norme au Ier millénaire: il y a là un phénomène de quasi-cannibalisme figuratif par rapport à l'oiseau éployé, qui du même coup se raréfie considérablement dans le répertoire oriental. Les empennages sont naturalistes en Mésopotamie et dans les royaumes louvites (**fig. 1**), stylisés au Levant (**figs. 2-3**). Les empennages doubles sont exclusivement levantins (**fig. 3**).

On peut également classer dans cette catégorie des éléments particuliers: notamment certains modes de remplissage des ailes, par exemple les ailes à

2. Ou macro-analyse ou contexte au sens large.

3. Ou micro-analyse ou contexte au sens restreint.

rebord frangé de plumes (**fig. 4**), ou encore la tradition ajourée dont une des racines est la Syrie du Bronze Moyen (**fig. 1**).[4] Sans oublier des associations figuratives, dont celle du soleil et du croissant de lune, combinaison qui va prendre des formes particulières au Ier millénaire (**figs. 4-6**).

Nous avons constaté avec intérêt qu'Eric Gubel est parvenu à une hypothèse analogue à propos des sceaux phéniciens, pour lesquels il évoque à plusieurs reprises la résurgence des scarabées "Hyksos" du Bronze Moyen. Il est fort possible en effet que les symboles solaires et le répertoire de ces scarabées aient été une des sources d'inspiration des graveurs levantins, à côté naturellement des objets contemporains.

2. Eléments exogènes

L'analyse globale permet aussi de repérer ce que les arts figurés des régions étudiées ont emprunté aux grandes puissances voisines du Ier millénaire. Problème qui là non plus ne se pose pas pour l'épigraphiste. Ces sources d'inspiration sont au nombre de trois: à l'Ouest, l'Egypte; au Nord, le monde anatolien, c'est-à-dire les principautés louvites qui perpétuent les traditions du Grand Empire hittite; à l'Est, la Mésopotamie assyro-babylonienne.

D'*Egypte* viennent le disque vide, les cobras ou uraeï; les modèles ornithomorphiques complexes de l'art monumental, et les nombreuses séries simplifiées des scarabées, en particulier une série aux ailes ajourées des XXIIe-XXVIe dynasties, possible racine égyptienne de cette tradition figurative (**fig. 7**).[5]

Du *monde anatolien* viennent les ailes à volutes, qu'elles se présentent sous la forme de spires véritables ou de simples crochets (**figs. 8-9**): c'est une caractéristique très pertinente depuis le Bronze Récent. C'est là aussi qu'a sa source un tracé particulier de l'aile, à ligne supérieure en double courbure et extrémité retroussée (**fig. 10**).[6]

La *Mésopotamie assyro-babylonienne* (l'Assyrie jusqu'en 612 av. J.-C., puis la Babylonie jusqu'en 539 av. J.-C.) fut aussi une grande pourvoyeuse d'images et de techniques. C'est d'elle que viennent les quelques disques ailés anthropomorphes du répertoire ouest-sémitique (**fig. 12**): ils sont à l'origine une création de l'Assyrie du IXe siècle. C'est d'elle que viennent aussi quelques types ou éléments caractéristiques. Il est exceptionnel qu'un modèle

---

4. Cf. par exemple certains documents d'Alalaḫ, très caractéristiques à cet égard (cf. Collon 1982: figs. 105, 106, 108).

5. L'Egypte a aussi fourni un très riche répertoire figuré, ainsi que la façon de placer le disque ailé au-dessus d'un cartouche.

6. D'Anatolie viennent aussi des formes de sceaux (cachets cylindriques à bélière, cachets-boutons…), l'hématite (?), des éléments du répertoire figuré (rosette, guilloche…), certains modes de répartition des images (zones concentriques; disque ailé au-dessus d'une inscription).

de disque ailé assyro-babylonien transite tel quel (**fig. 11**). Il s'agit d'ordinaire d'emprunts sélectifs, c'est-à-dire de détails figuratifs ou techniques, notamment: des ailes plutôt rectilignes, faites de plumes longitudinales (**fig. 13**) ou de simples encoches·dans la pierre du sceau (**figs. 14-15**); un empennage inférieur naturaliste (**fig. 13**) ou réduit à une encoche (**fig. 15**); des appendices fourchus empruntés au Style Modelé de la glyptique assyrienne (**fig. 16**); l'usage de la bouterolle pour les empennages (**fig. 17**) ou pour les appendices (**fig. 18**).[7]

C'est la combinaison multiforme de ces éléments endogènes et exogènes qui suscite précisément les types et variantes de disques ailés que nous avons présentés dans l'article publié dans *Syria*. Ces éléments, modèle global de disque ailé ou simple détail, se combinent suivant des modalités diverses en fonction des lieux et des époques.

3. Combinaison des éléments: les types caractéristiques d'une aire culturelle

L'impact des modèles égyptiens est à l'origine des *types égyptisants* (Parayre 1990a: pl. II-VI), qui comportent une majorité de modèles aux ailes ajourées (complexes ou simplifiées) et une minorité de modèles aux ailes naturalistes. Ils caractérisent avant tout la côte, comme à l'Age du Bronze. L'aire de prédilection des premiers est la Phénicie et le royaume d'Israël, parenté culturelle tout à fait significative.

L'impact des autres zones d'influence est à l'origine des autres types, dont la combinaison caractérise d'abord les terres de l'intérieur:

– les types *orientaux sans volutes* (Parayre 1990a: pl. VII-X), répartis entre 5 groupes aux séries caractéristiques (royaumes araméens, Juda et Ammon, Moab et Edom);

– les disques ailés *orientaux à volutes* (*ibid.*, pl. XI), dont l'aire de prédilection est le Nord phénico- et araméo-louvite, du royaume de Que à l'Ouest jusqu'à Tell Halaf à l'Est. Les ailes en double courbure et à extrémité retroussée sont quant à elles très fréquentes dans les royaumes araméens, ainsi qu'en Juda et Ammon.

– les disques ailés *anthropomorphes* (*ibid.*, pl. XI), avant tout moabites et édomites (cf. Ornan, *infra*, p. 66, figs. 52, 55). Les cachets inscrits en araméen et porteurs de ce motif posent problème, dans la mesure où il est encore très difficile de préciser avec certitude leur zone de production (Mésopotamie

7. Des empires mésopotamiens proviennent de même des formes de sceaux (cylindres, cachet pyramidal, conoïde) et des images (héros maître du lion, atlante, personnages debout face à face).

elle-même ou royaumes araméens): ainsi avons-nous préféré rester à cet égard dans l'expectative.[8]

Ajoutons que la mise en place de l'image par rapport à l'écriture apporte un élément complémentaire essentiel dans la définition de ces vocabulaires et de ces syntaxes figuratifs propres à des aires culturelles.[9]

Deux constatations s'imposent. D'une part, nous avons affaire à un ensemble géographique très vaste et très disparate, où toutes les régions ne sont pas sur le même plan. Il y a d'un côté des aires culturelles relativement homogènes, qui témoignent d'une forte personnalité sur le plan des arts figurés: c'est le cas de la Phénicie et sans doute du royaume d'Israël, la Phénicie conservant cette forte "idiosyncrasie" par-delà la conquête perse. De l'autre, des terres qui se définissent d'abord et avant tout par le caractère composite et hétérogène de leur arts figurés. C'est le cas du répertoire des royaumes de l'intérieur, et notamment des terres araméennes et du pays de Moab. Parler d'aire culturelle ne se justifie alors que par référence à la langue et à l'écriture, puisque la part des emprunts et de leur combinaison est autrement prédominante. Dans ce contexte, l'étude du disque ailé met en lumière les "phénomènes de frontière" qui expliquent les fortes influences égyptiennes, anatoliennes et mésopotamiennes à l'Ouest, au Nord et à l'Est. Elle permet également de repérer des affinités culturelles entre les royaumes araméens, Juda et Ammon d'une part;[10] les royaumes araméens, Ammon et Moab de l'autre, soit une sorte de mouvance orientale au sein de la zone étudiée.[11] Ammon est bien en position intermédiaire entre les traditions judéennes (ailes à la mode hittite, sceaux purement symboliques, disque ailé en position médiane) et les traditions de la mouvance orientale (double empennage asymétrique).

D'autre part, il ne faudrait pas croire que les types d'images que nous avons distingués sont stables, et ne se contaminent pas. Bien au contraire, on observe une extraordinaire mobilité des images créées par les ateliers, quelles qu'aient été les modalités pratiques de cette circulation d'images ou de parties d'images. Transferts de modèles qui ont sans doute leur répondant dans le

8. La plupart des cylindres présentés par Pierre Bordreuil lors de sa communication ont été fabriqués par des ateliers mésopotamiens. Par contre, certains cachets qui arborent un dieu dans le disque ailé (cf. Ornan, *infra*, figs. 9-10, 12, 52 53, 55) sont sans doute de fabrication occidentale. Il y a là encore à faire un difficile travail de répartition des données.

9. Cf. Parayre 1990a: 286-288, pl. XII-XIII, suivant que le disque ailé est en haut, au milieu ou en bas du champ de la représentation, inséré dans un registre ou non.

10. Ailes en double courbure et à extrémité retroussée; double empennage *symétrique* (araméen et judéen); disque ailé dans un registre au milieu du champ (judéen et ammonite).

11. Empennages *asymétriques*; forte "assyrianisation" de la glyptique (araméen et moabite).

domaine épigraphique, et il serait intéressant à cet égard de comparer les apports respectifs des deux disciplines.

Nous constatons d'une part des *emprunts* d'une aire culturelle à l'autre, ce qu'en termes d'ethnologie on appelle les "occurrences extérieures" d'un type. Il peut s'agir de l'emprunt d'un type global: par exemple, l'emprunt d'un disque ailé égyptisant ajouré peut dénoter une influence de la Phénicie ou du royaume d'Israël (**fig. 30**). Il peut s'agir de l'emprunt d'une série (disque ailé et contexte): par exemple, des scaraboïdes en pâte de verre de Zincirli transposent une série israélite contemporaine (**fig. 31**).

Nous constatons d'autre part des *phénomènes de métissage*, pour employer de nouveau le vocabulaire de l'ethnologie: soit l'interférence et la contamination des types, qui échangent des éléments caractéristiques. Citons l'adaptation des empennages stylisés caractéristiques des disques ailés égyptisants à d'autres types d'ailes (**figs. 13-17, 36**). Citons l'adaptation du tracé ajouré à des ailes non égyptisantes (**figs. 8-9**).[12] Citons à l'inverse l'adaptation de tracés d'origine anatolienne à des ailes égyptisantes (double courbure et extrémité retroussée: **fig. 30**; ailes tangentes au disque et secteur de couverture en pseudo-volute: **fig. 31**). Ces phénomènes de contamination sont largement dus au fait qu'à chaque emprunt d'une culture à l'autre, l'image qui circule est transformée en fonction des particularités de l'idiome figuratif de la culture d'accueil.

Ce double phénomène connexe d'emprunts de types et de métissages figuratifs complique l'analyse, et impose de descendre au niveau des ateliers.

II. L'ESPACE: IMAGE ET ATELIERS (IXe-VIe SIECLES)

L'impératif majeur pour repérer les fabriques sur le terrain est une analyse très fine: comme nous l'avons souligné en introduction, parfois seul un détail infime au premier regard permet de repérer un atelier.[13] Nous avons choisi de présenter quelques cas particulièrement pertinents.

1. Premier exemple: les ateliers du royaume d'Israël

Il s'agit de disques ailés égyptisants de tracé ajouré. Rappelons que ces types sont caractéristiques de la Phénicie et du royaume d'Israël.

L'orientation des ailes semble déterminante. Les ailes horizontales au milieu du champ seraient proprement israélites, et elles se répartissent entre deux

---

12. Ce tracé caractéristique peut d'ailleurs se limiter à l'empennage (**figs. 33, 36**). Sans oublier qu'il existe aussi une racine orientale de ce mode de remplissage.

13. La recherche de la nature de l'atelier, atelier de palais, de temple ou de quartier urbain n'est pas ici en cause, ni le problème de la clientèle.

séries, la série type Jezebel (**fig. 19**) et une série à registres superposés (**fig. 20**); le seul repère sur le terrain est un scarabée fragmentaire de Megiddo, ce qui est bien peu de chose (Megiddo I: pl. 67:7; cf. GGG: fig. 259a). Les ailes orientées vers le bas seraient de tradition proprement phénicienne, qu'il s'agisse d'objets fabriquées en Phénicie même ou d'objets fabriqués dans cette veine en Israël.

C'est là qu'intervient un second critère, celui de *la forme* de l'aile. Les cachets phéniciens semblent privilégier les ailes cintrées (**fig. 21**); les cachets israélites inscrits ou anépigraphes (arbre, scarabée, sphinx, griffon, oudjat...), les ailes en double courbure (**figs. 22-25**). Plusieurs de ces derniers proviennent des fouilles de Samarie et de Sichem, et pourraient donc caractériser des ateliers locaux. De même, il serait possible de rattacher à ces fabriques deux modes parfois combinées: les bordures perlées (**figs. 22** (?), **23-24**) et la façon de disposer symétriquement deux disques ailés aux deux extrémités du champ (**figs. 23-24**). Ces deux modes sont attestés l'une et l'autre sur des documents issus précisément des fouilles de Samarie et Sichem (**figs. 23-24**). Peut-être enfin faut-il considérer comme des avatars plus tardifs de ces ateliers, marqués par une nette tendance à l'aniconisme, deux cachets qui semblent de la même main (**figs. 26-27**).[14] Le travail précieux de Benjamin Sass sur les séries de cachets inscrits sera déterminant dans ce difficile domaine de recherche.

Il est possible de repérer les "occurrences extérieures" de la production de ces ateliers israélites. L'exemple le plus net est celui d'un scarabée araméen au nom de Barᶜatar (**fig. 30**), qui dédouble justement le symbole solaire de part et d'autre d'un griffon, et qui transpose à la mode syrienne les ailes rectilignes horizontales des documents israélites. Leur tracé en double courbure est en effet caractéristique: c'est ce détail infime de contour qui trahit sur le plan figuratif l'origine araméenne de l'objet.

Nous avons tenté la même recherche ponctuelle d'ateliers avec les cachets à disques aux ailes horizontales placés en exergue, mais sans les mêmes résultats. Seuls deux cachets ainsi gravés pourraient provenir de la même fabrique (**figs. 28-29**), sans qu'il soit possible de proposer une localisation: sur l'un des deux documents, un scarabée est substitué en exergue au symbole solaire, qui est placé en position médiane (**fig. 29**), mais l'analogie des contextes (deux Horus symétriques de part et d'autre d'un élément médian) et l'analogie de facture (traitement schématique et hachures grossières) semblent déterminantes.

---

14. Même type de disque ailé, même association de motifs (disque ailé, oudjat, serpent), même facture schématique.

2. Deuxième exemple: les ateliers du royaume de Samʾal

Le cas des ateliers de Zincirli et des centres apparentés, entre le pays de Que et la boucle de l'Euphrate, est particulièrement intéressant. L'art figuratif de cette zone de contacts est un creuset de toutes les traditions; c'est aussi le lieu par excellence de résurgence des traditions de l'Age du Bronze (royaumes de Yamḫad et de Mukiš); c'est enfin l'un des rares endroits où l'on peut utiliser l'art monumental à des fins de comparaison.

Ainsi avons-nous pu attribuer à cette zone de production les séries suivantes, qui sont toutes attestées dans les fouilles de Zincirli ou des sites localisés dans la mouvance de la grande capitale du royaume de Samʾal:

– des scaraboïdes anépigraphes en pâte de verre aux disques ailés caractéristiques, version locale d'une série israélite particulière (**fig. 31**), et traités à la manière des orthostates du site. Les disques ailés présentent des éléments hittites indéniables (cf. plus haut, p. 34: ailes tangentes au disque et secteur de couverture en pseudo-volute). Le contexte figuré est répétitif: *ʿankh* et uraeï; sphinx et griffons; génies ailés tétraptères; faucon éployé; exergue quadrillé. La facture en à-plats est celle des orthostates locaux.

– des cachets aux disques ailés "assyrianisants", apanage des milieux de cour, et d'abord des rois (**fig. 32**, empreinte du sceau de Bar-Rākib; **fig. 33**). Ils évoquent aussi en miniature certaines dalles du site, aux symboles empruntés à l'Assyrie: c'est le cas sur l'orthostate au nom de Kilamuwa (**fig. a**), qui s'inspire directement de l'Obélisque Noir de Salmanazar III.

– le groupe dit du "Joueur de Lyre", qui comporte de très nombreux scaraboïdes anépigraphes aux disques ailés de formes diverses mais de tracé toujours ajouré (**fig. 34**).

– des disques ailés à double empennage *symétrique* (propres aux pays araméens et à Juda). Seul un exemplaire provient de Zincirli elle-même, mais il est plausible qu une partie des sceaux et des petits objets ainsi décorés aient été fabriqués là (**fig. 35**).

– des disques ailés à double empennage *asymétrique* (**fig. 36**). Certes, aucun document de ce type ne provient des fouilles de la zone étudiée, et ce type de symbole solaire semble plutôt propre à la mouvance orientale des royaumes ouest-sémitiques: terres araméennes, Ammon et Moab). Mais il n'est pas impossible qu'une partie de ces images aient été faites aussi plus au Nord, comme en témoignent notamment les analogies remarquables entre deux coquillages publiés par Stucky (**figs. b-c**), ainsi que les affinités septentrionales de la palette en calcaire publiée par Barag (**fig. d**).[15]

15. L'empennage en pans coupés évoque le disque ailé de l'orthostate ancien de Kilamuwa (**fig. a**), et les volutes en crochets évoquent les disques ailés d'un orthostate de Tell Halaf (Orthmann 1971: pl. 12b).

– enfin des disques ailés à volutes et *double empennage*, à ce point caractéristiques du site qu'ils apparaissent sur tous les supports (**fig. e**; art monumental; ivoires, métal, cylindres et cachets). Si l'on regarde ce groupe de sceaux en détail, il est clair qu'il provient de plusieurs ateliers, ou à tout le moins d'un atelier aux traditions composites. En effet, les *supports* sont différents, supports de tradition anatolienne (cachet cylindrique à bélière et cachet circulaire à tenon), de tradition égyptienne et levantine (scarabées) et de tradition mésopotamienne (cylindre). Les *matériaux* sont différents: hématite pour les sceaux de tradition hittite et l'un des scarabées, autres pierres dures pour le reste. Les *thématiques* sont différentes: copie du système du "cartouche royal" hittite sur le cylindre (**fig. 38**), animaux en zone concentrique à la hittite sur le cachet cylindrique (**fig. 39**); pour le reste, indifféremment, atlante et héros "assyrianisants" (**figs. 37, 40**), animaux ou hybrides confrontés et/ou superposés (**figs. 41-42**). Les *disques ailés* enfin sont différents: les uns présentent des ailes naturalistes de tradition mésopotamienne et anatolienne (**figs. 38-39**), les autres des ailes ajourées de tradition phénicienne (**figs. 37, 40-42**), et ils pourraient donc avoir été fabriqués plutôt dans la zone phénico-louvite de Que, particulièrement sensible aux apports de cette culture phénicienne.

Certes, aucun de ces documents ne provient de Zincirli à proprement parler, mais l'analogie avec les dalles sculptées du site est frappante. De plus, le scarabée (**fig. 41**) provient du cimetière de Yunus près de Carchémish. Enfin, l'onomastique est elle aussi probante: le nom *nnz* du propriétaire du scarabée en quartzite (**fig. 42**) est de tradition anatolienne, et les noms de personne en *-ṣur* sont attestés dans le royaume de Samʾal. Il est donc très probable qu'une partie de cette belle série provient de Zincirli elle-même; le sceau de "Aḥiṣur" (**fig. 37**) pourrait avoir été celui d'un grand personnage de la cour royale, chez lequel l'"assyrianisation" s'est traduite par le choix non point du disque ailé, ancré dans la tradition locale, mais du personnage principal, l'atlante à genou qui soulève l'astre solaire.

3. *Troisième exemple: vers la définition d'une koinè tardive (fin VIIe-VIe siècles)*

Peut-être assiste-t-on à la fin du VIIe et au début du VIe siècles, dans les décennies qui précèdent la conquête perse, et dans les zones de l'intérieur, à une sorte d'unification du répertoire figuratif, avec une forme de *koinè* où prévaudraient des disques ailés "assyrianisants" plus ou moins schématisés, dans un contexte désormais purement symbolique ou simplement inscrit. A l'inverse de la démarche précédente, nous n'allons plus à la recherche des spécificités locales, mais bien à la recherche d'un "idiome" commun propre à une période.

Nous avons retenu six documents significatifs: dans le domaine araméen, un scaraboïde en cornaline, qui inverse le schéma des ateliers de Samʾal (**fig. 43**, disque ailé au dessous de l'inscription) et un scaraboïde anépigraphe en calcaire de l'Ashmolean Museum (**fig. 44**, soleil, croissant, rhombe et quatre boules); un scaraboïde en calcaire de l'ex-royaume de Samarie (?) avec une bordure perlée et, de part et d'autre d'une ligne de séparation également perlée, un croissant et un disque ailé (**fig. 45**); une empreinte de sceau de l'ex-royaume de Juda, découverte à En-Gedi, où le disque ailé est placé là aussi au-dessous de l'inscription (**fig. 46**); un cachet moabite ou édomite (**fig. 47**); des avatars sud-arabiques aux symboles dédoublés (**fig. 48**).

Peut-être faudrait-il vérifier si ce phénomène de généralisation tardive de formules minimales très simples, souvent d'allure assyrienne au niveau du disque ailé, a son répondant au niveau des écritures.

III. Histoire et culture matérielle: la conquête perse, permanences et nouveautés

Nous posons là le problème du rapport entre période historique et période archéologique. La conquête perse unifie en quelque décennies l'Orient ancien d'une extrémité à l'autre sous une domination politico-militaire nouvelle.

Sur le territoire des ex-royaumes ouest-sémitiques, des changements majeurs s'opèrent. Sur le plan épigraphique, l'époque achéménide est marquée par l'expansion généralisée de l'écriture araméenne: il est désormais bien difficile de distinguer des ateliers par la seule étude des légendes. Sur le plan iconographique, l'époque perse est marquée aussi par une double réduction: une réduction géographique (l'essentiel des documents provient désormais de la Phénicie) et une réduction figurative au profit d'un certain nombre de modèles "impériaux" qui se répandent dans toute l'étendue dominée par le Grand Roi, et notamment au profit des modèles égyptisants. C'est précisément le cas avec le disque ailé, dont la palette se simplifie singulièrement au profit des types égyptisants, qui sont d'ailleurs, sur place, une tradition séculaire. Ainsi l'étude précise des arts figurés de chaque satrapie montre-t-elle justement comment des éléments du passé se perpétuent à l'intérieur même d'un art de cour qui a tendance à s'uniformiser. L'analyse du disque ailé permet à cet égard de distinguer trois ensembles différents parmi les sceaux de Transeuphratène.

Parmi les *permanences*, il convient de citer les disques ailés ajourés, avec ou sans empennages stylisés, qui continuent directement les modèles préachéménides. Quelques innovations apparaissent: nouveautés de forme (larges ailes à convexités accentuées; extrémités arrondies ou en biseau); nouveautés de remplissage (limite entre secteur transversale et concave, et non plus longitudinale; ailes multipartites totalement ajourées; ailes tripartites à couvertures en écailles [**fig. 49**]). Désormais, la majorité des cachets sont des produits de fabrication rapide, avec des disques ailés simplifiés aux ailes monopartites. Beaucoup de ces petits objets sont alors faits en jaspe vert. On peut repérer des ateliers: c'est ainsi que les cachets **figs. 50** et **51** sont comparables non seulement par la forme du disque ailé, mais aussi par la thématique (thème isiaque, exergue quadrillé) et par la technique (marques de bouterolle).

Parmi les *nouveautés*, deux groupes se distinguent:

– d'une part, des cachets de série qui présentent des disques ailés très schématiques, aux petites ailes arrondies frangées de plumes. Ils sont placés au-dessus de thèmes levantins ou proprement perses (**fig. 52**). Ces cachets datent exclusivement des Ve-IVe siècles. Ils se répartissent entre plusieurs séries, dont une série de conoïdes en pâte de verre qui présentent le "héros perse" maître-des-animaux, et qui est attestée notamment à Sidon (De Clercq 1903: pl. III,57).

– d'autre part, des cachets en pierres dures, souvent de qualité, qui présentent des disques ailés composites, combinant des ailes égyptisantes et d'éventuels uraeï schématiques à un *empennage naturaliste* emprunté aux satrapies de l'intérieur. Variantes complexes qui sont l'équivalent miniature du symbole qui décorait le plafond du naos d'Amrit (**fig. f**). Elles présentent soit des ailes ajourées de tradition levantine (**figs. 53-54**), soit des ailes naturalistes plutôt conformes aux modèles des satrapies de l'intérieur (**figs. 55-56**). La thématique est double et correspond à deux traditions différentes. Il s'agit soit de thèmes levantins égyptisants traditionnels (Isis, Horus Harpocratès, Thot: **figs. 54-55**), cela d'ordinaire sur des scarabées. Soit de thèmes proprement perses, comme le "héros perse" maître-des-animaux (**fig. 53**), ou exceptionnellement l'orbe d'Ahura-Mazda (**fig. 56**)[16], cela sur des conoïdes ou des scaraboïdes. Le repérage des ateliers est bien difficile. Nous avons pu cependant attribuer à un artisan de Gezer deux scaraboïdes qui présentent un disque ailé analogue au-dessus d'un maître-des-animaux (lions et hybrides cornus), lui-même debout sur un animal ou un hybride (**figs. 57-58**). L'un des ces sceaux est inscrit au nom de *Pamin*.

Nous terminerons notre contribution par une question, une constatation et un souhait.

Une question. L'image est-elle plus pertinente que l'écriture pour identifier les ateliers et les localiser sur le terrain? L'écriture étant plus pertinente pour dater le matériel en finesse?

16. Dans un article à paraître dans la revue *Kadmos*, André Lemaire propose une origine lydienne pour le scaraboïde de **fig. 56**. Le répertoire figuré original concorde avec une telle attribution, excepté les ailes cintrées du disque solaire, inhabituelles sur les cachets de la satrapie de Lydie.

Une constatation. Dans l'état actuel des données, l'image semble particulièrement importante pour classer les documents du monde araméen, où l'épigraphie n'est pas aussi performante que pour les autres aires culturelles moins vastes et moins hétérogènes. De même, l'image nous paraît très utile pour classer les documents de la Transeuphratène achéménide.

Un souhait. Il paraît nécessaire à l'avenir pour les spécialistes du monde ouest-sémitique d'analyser de façon très précise d'autres images que le disque solaire ailé, et de replacer à chaque fois l'image étudiée dans son contexte figuré et inscrit pour essayer de repérer des séries, seules à même de faire avancer la recherche de façon sérieuse. C'est seulement à partir de là que l'on pourra enfin poser à ces images correctement classées des questions de fond sur la société et l'imaginaire des populations en question ainsi que sur les relations si complexes qu'entretenaient dans toute la glyptique orientale l'image et l'écriture.

CATALOGUE

[Note des éditeurs: Les dessins au trait des disques ailés seuls ont été exécutés par l'auteur. Les reproductions des sceaux proviennent des sources mentionnées ci-dessous, ce qui explique, lorsqu'il s'agit de dessins au trait, l'apparence occasionnelle de certains écarts entre les deux illustrations concernant un même objet. La numérotation de la deuxième colonne, entre parenthèses, renvoie à Parayre 1990a.]

1. (87.) Zincirli, empreinte de cachet circulaire araméen inscrit, sur une bulle, *lbrrkb br pnmw*, ca. 732-720 av. J.-C. (Sendschirli V: pl. 38,b).
2. (60.) Scarabée phénicien ou chypriote anépigraphe, V^{e}-IVe s. (Delaporte 1928: 54, pl. VII:2).
3. (38.) Scarabée phénicien ou chypriote anépigraphe, VIIe-VIe s. (Walters 1926: pl. 6:292).
4. (84.) Ḥuzirina, cylindre "assyrianisant" de style linéaire, IXe-VIIIe s. (Lloyd 1954: 108, 110; fig. 8:7).
5. (21.) Khorsabad, scaraboïde phénicien inscrit, *ʿbdbʿl*, VIIIe s. (G 55, B 8; dessin de Hildi Keel-Leu d'après B 8).
6. (116.) Cachet moabite inscrit, *lrʿš/ṣ* (?), VIIe s. (dessin de Hildi Keel-Leu d'après B 64; cf. Israel 1987b: n° XXXIV).
7. (4.) Kition, scarabée de la XXVIe dynastie (Clerc et al. 1976: 111-112).
8. (122.) Scaraboïde araméen inscrit, *ʾldlh*, fin VIIIe s. (Moscati 1951: 58-59, pl. 12: 8).
9. (124.) Scarabée araméen inscrit, *lnnz*, VIIIe s. (B 122).

10. (103.) Lachish, empreinte de cachet *lmlk*, ca. 701 av. J.-C. (Ussishkin 1976: 3, fig. 2).
11. (85.) Amrit, scarabée phénicien inscrit, *ḥb*, VIe-Ve s. (?) (G 104; B 9).
12. (125.) Scaraboïde moabite ou édomite (cf. Lemaire, *supra*, p. 16) inscrit, *lmnḥmt ʾšt pdmlk*, fin VIIIe-VIIe s. (D 64; G 82; Israel 1987b: n° XXVI = Ornan, *infra*, p. 66, fig. 52).
13. (112.) Scaraboïde moabite inscrit, *ʾmṣ hspr*, fin VIIIe-VIIe s. (D 74; G 122; HD 1; Israel 1987b: n° V; cf. Ornan, *infra*, p. 67, fig. 58; Timm, p. 193, fig. 14).
14. (115.) Scaraboïde moabite inscrit, *lkmšyḥy*, VIIe s. (G 71; B 66 = Timm, *infra*, p. 192, fig. 1).
15. (117.) Cachet (barillet tronqué) moabite inscrit, *lmlkyʿzr*, VIIe s. (B 63; Israel 1987b: n° XXVIII).
16. (99.) Scaraboïde allongé moabite (?) inscrit, *lmlkḥrm*, VIIe s. (B 7).
17. (119.) Scaraboïde ammonite inscrit, *lmnḥm bn mġrʾl*, fin VIIIe-VIIe s. (Bordreuil & Lemaire 1976: n° 33).
18. (89.) Cylindre araméen anépigraphe, VIIIe-VIIe s. (Wiseman 1958: n° 87).
19. (14.) Scaraboïde israélite inscrit, *yzbl*, ca. 850 av. J.-C.? (Keel 1977: 96, fig. 63 [corrigé], cf. HD 31).
20. (17.) Scaraboïde israélite (ou phénicien?), registre destiné à l'inscription laissé vide, VIIIe s. (Buchanan & Moorey 1988: n° 275).
21. (21.) Cf. fig. 5.
22. (19.) Sichem, scaraboïde israélite anépigraphe, IXe-VIIIe s. (GGG: fig. 258b, cf. Wright 1965: fig. 81).
23. (32_1.) Scaraboïde israélite inscrit, *lšbnyw ʿbd ʿzyw*, VIIIe s. (GGG: fig. 263b, cf. B 41).
24. (34.) Sichem, scaraboïde israélite anépigraphe, VIIIe s. (GGG: fig. 258c; cf. Rowe 1936: n° SO. 3).
25. (41.) Samarie, scarabée israélite anépigraphe, IXe-VIIIe s. (GGG: fig. 258a; cf. Reisner, Fisher & Lion 1924: pl. 56e:2).
26. (59.) Scaraboïde israélite inscrit, *lqnyw*, VIIIe-VIIe s. (?) (Welten 1977: 301, fig. 78:2; cf. Jakob-Rost 1975: n° 183).
27. (64.) Scaraboïde israélite inscrit, *šbnʾ*, VIIIe-VIIe s. (?) (dessin de Hildi Keel-Leu d'après Avigad 1954b: 146-148, pl. 4, fig. 6, n° 1).
28. (31.) Scaraboïde israélite inscrit, *lnʿmʾl pʾrt*, VIIIe s. (dessin de Hildi Keel-Leu d'après Lemaire 1985b: 39, figs. 6-7).
29. (47.) Scaraboïde israélite (?) inscrit, *ʿbdʾyw*, VIIIe s. (?) (dessin de E. Gubel d'après B 16; cf. *infra*, p. 117, fig. 37).
30. (18.) Scaraboïde inscrit en araméen, *brʿtr*, fin IXe-VIIIe s. (dessin de E. Gubel d'après B 93; cf. *infra*, p. 117, fig. 38).
31. (65.) Scaraboïde araméen anépigraphe, VIIIe-début VIIe s. (Vollenweider 1967: n° 142, pl. 59:1).
32. (87.) Cf. fig. 1.
33. (88.) Cachet circulaire araméen inscrit, *lssrʾl*, ca. 750-700 av. J.-C. (dessin de Hildi Keel-Leu d'après B 91).
34. (91.) Scaraboïde anépigraphe, VIIIe-début VIIe s. (Buchner & Boardman 1966: n° 160).
35. (106.) Til Barsip, tombe, cachet quadrangulaire araméen, anépigraphe, VIIe-VIe s. (Thureau-Dangin et al. 1936: 78, fig. 19).
36. (111.) Cylindre araméen inscrit, *lsrp/gd*, VIIIe s. (dessin de Hildi Keel-Leu d'après une photographie du British Museum; cf. Bordreuil, *infra*, p. 85, fig. 12).

37. (70.) Scarabée araméen inscrit, *ʾḥṣr*, VIIIe s. (dessin de Noga Z'evi d'après HD 130).
38. – Nimrud, temple de Ninurta, cylindre en lapis-lazuli (Parker 1962: pl. 12:1).
39. – Cachet cylindrique à bélière en hématite (Hogarth 1920: 70, fig. 72; BM 120242, photo reproduite avec l'aimable autorisation des Trustees of the British Museum).
40. – Cachet cylindrique en hématite (De Clercq 1903: pl. I:10).
41. – Scarabée en hématite (BM 103292, photo reproduite avec l'aimable autorisation des Trustees of the British Museum; cf. Boardman & Moorey 1986: n° 14).
42. – Scarabée en quartzite inscrit en araméen (?), *lnnz* (B 122).
43. – Cachet araméen en cornaline, inscrit *lwhbdh* (dessin de Hildi Keel-Leu d'après Avigad 1989a: n° 20).
44. – Scaraboïde araméen en calcaire, anépigraphe (Buchanan & Moorey 1988: n° 431).
45. – Scaraboïde en calcaire, ex-royaume d'Israël (?), anépigraphe (dessin de Hildi Keel-Leu d'après von der Osten 1934: n° 526).
46. – En Gedi, empreinte *lmrʾ*(?), ex-royaume de Juda, VIe s. (En Gedi: 34-35, fig. 12, pl. 26:1).
47. – Cachet moabite ou édomite inscrit *lmš*, faux (?) (dessin de Hildi Keel-Leu d'après HD 117; cf. Israel 1987b: n° X; Lemaire, *supra*, p. 16s.).
48. – Plaquette ovale sud-arabique inscrite *ḫmmhw* (dessin de Hildi Keel-Leu d'après photo Yale Babylonian Collection; cf. Sass 1991: fig. 37).
49. – Sidon, cachet en améthyste, V^e-IVe s. (Parrot, Chéhab & Moscati 1975: 110, fig. 115).
50. (57.) Scarabée phénicien ou chypriote anépigraphe, V^e-IVe s. (Harden 1962: p. 108:f).
51. (58.) Scarabée phénicien ou chypriote anépigraphe, Ve s. (?) (Vollenweider 1967: n° 155).
52. (77.) Conoïde phénicien anépigraphe, V^e-IVe s. (dessin de Hildi Keel-Leu d'après Vollenweiderl 1983: n° 41).
53. (44.) Conoïde phénicien anépigraphe, V^e-IVe s. (De Clercq 1903: pl. III:50).
54. (45.) Scarabée phénicien ou chypriote anépigraphe, V^e-IVe s. (dessin de Hildi Keel-Leu d'après Delaporte 1928: pl. VII:3).
55. (72.) Scarabée phénicien ou chypriote anépigraphe, V^e-IVe s. (dessin de Hildi Keel-Leu d'après Delaporte 1928: pl. VII:4).
56. (71.) Scaraboïde inscrit en araméen, *nḥm tnḥ[m]*, ou en lydien (A. Lemaire, cf. note 16), fin VIe-Ve s. (dessin de Hildi Keel-Leu d'après B 119).
57. (81.) Gezer, tombe dite "philistine", scaraboïde palestinien anépigraphe, Ve s. (Gezer II: 292, fig. 153).
58. (82.) Scaraboïde palestinien inscrit, *pmn*, Ve s. (dessin de Noga Z'evi; cf. Avigad 1954a: pl. 21B:3; Ornan, *infra*, p. 55, fig. 5).

a. – Zincirli, orthostate de Kilamuwa (Naveh 1982: fig. 45).
b. – Coquillage gravée (Stucky 1974: n° 7).
c. – Coquillage gravée (Stucky 1974: n° 69).
d. – Palette en calcaire (Barag 1985: 224, fig. 11).
e. – Orthostate de Zincirli (Orthmann 1971: 549, pl. 66:d).
f. – Naos d'Amrit (Wagner 1980: 8-10, n° 7, pl. 15:3).

1

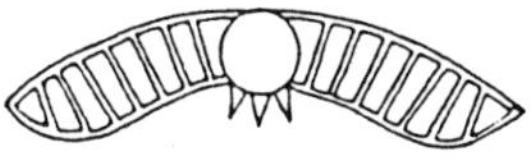

2

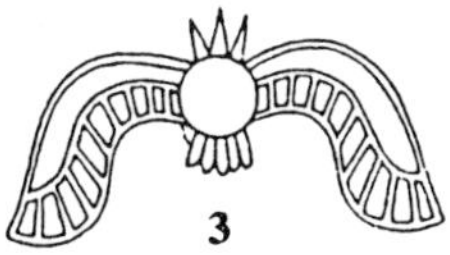

3

4

5

6

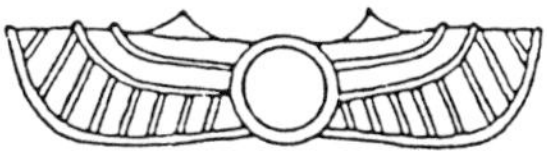

7

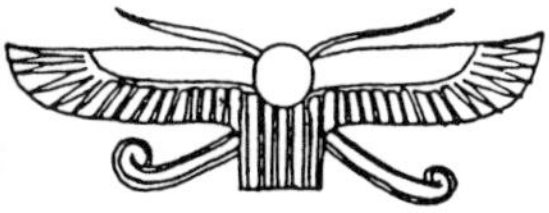

8

9

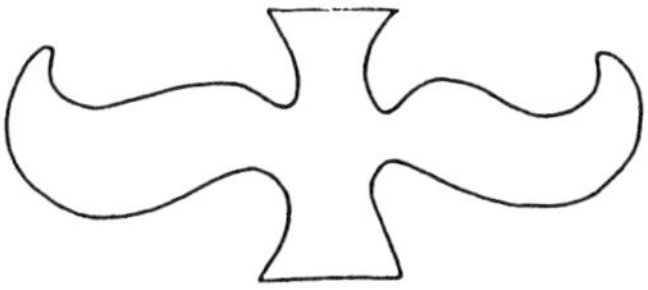

10

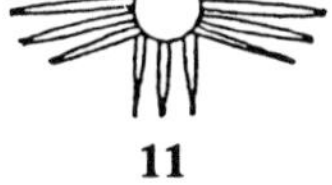

11

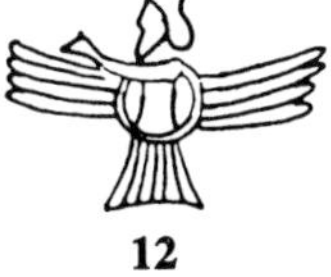

12

13

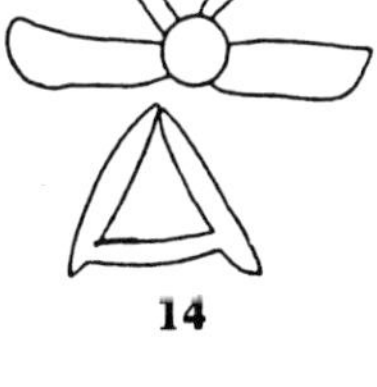

14

15

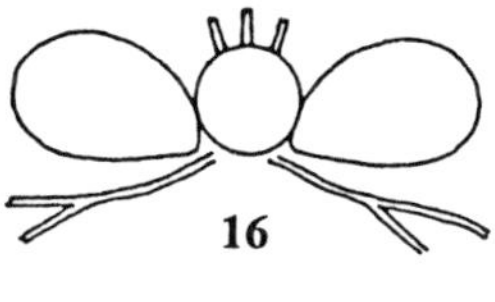

16

17

18

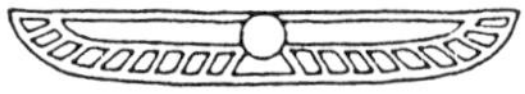

19–20

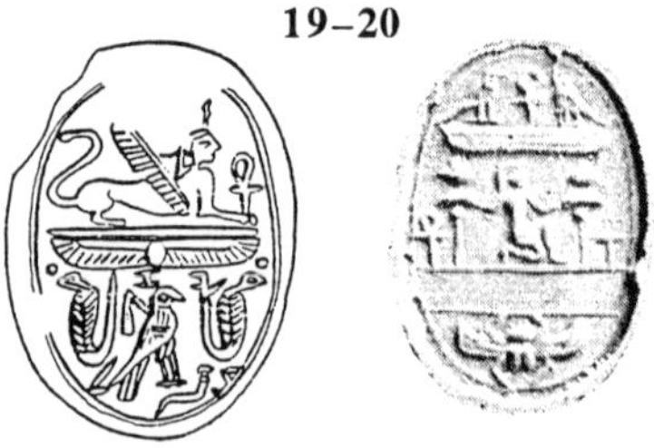

21

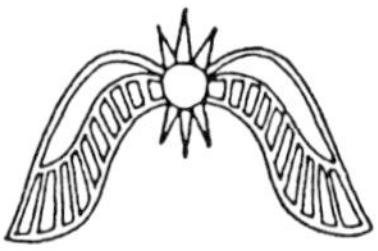

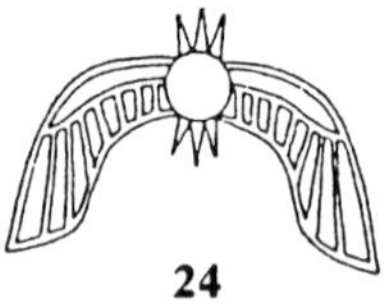

22 23 24

25

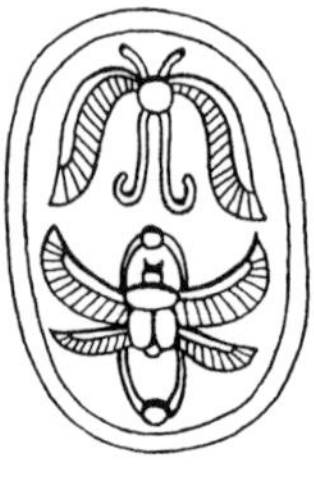

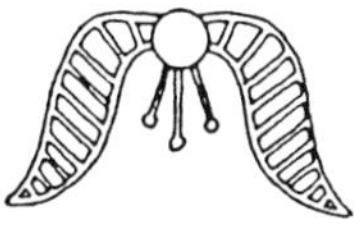

26

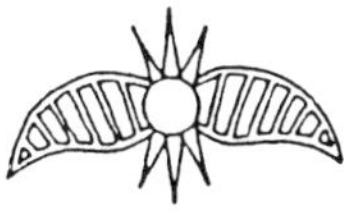

27

28

29

30

31

32

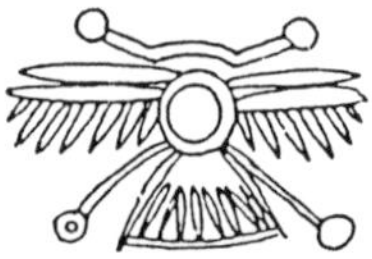
33

34

35

36

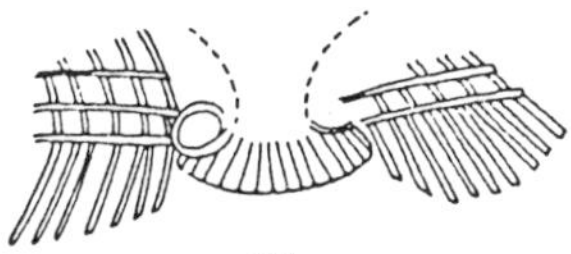

37

38

39

40

41

42

43

44

45

46

47

48

49

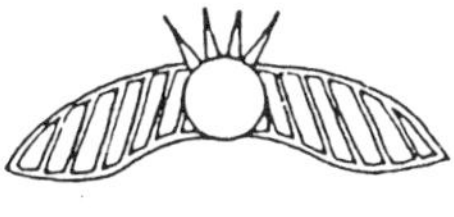

50–51

52

53–54

55

56

57–58

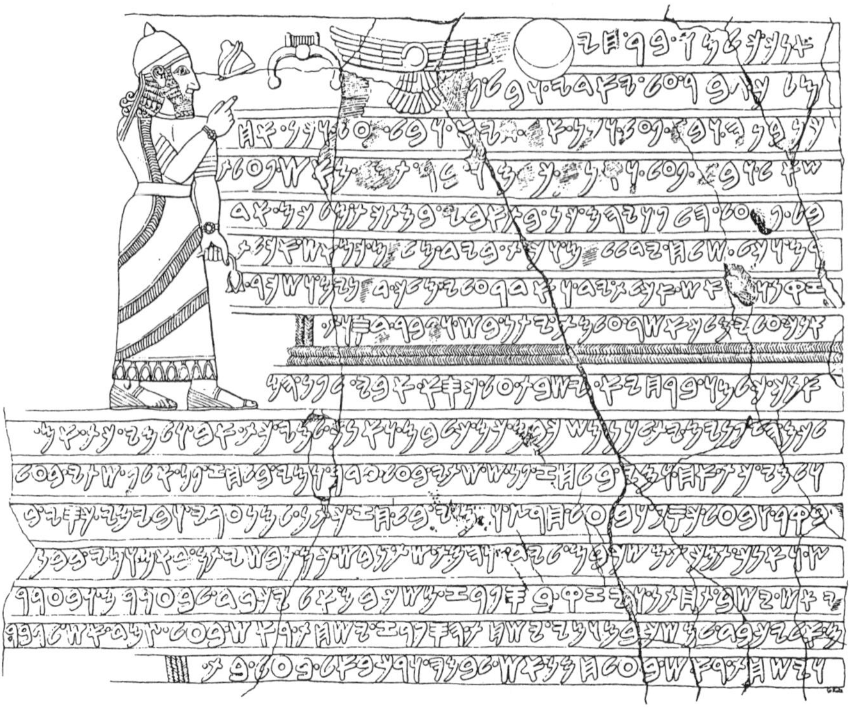

a

e

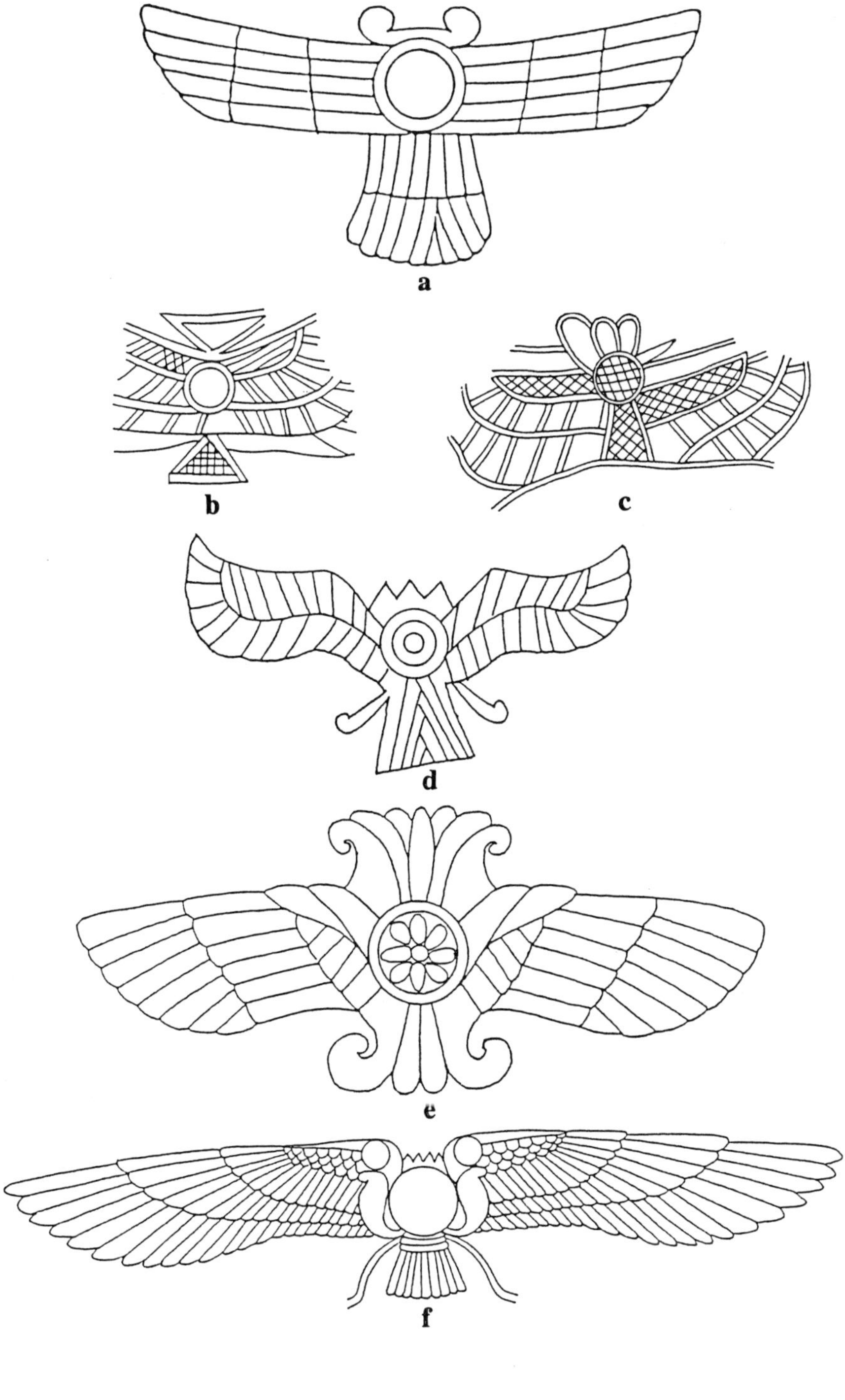
a
b
c
d
e
f

THE MESOPOTAMIAN INFLUENCE ON WEST SEMITIC INSCRIBED SEALS: A PREFERENCE FOR THE DEPICTION OF MORTALS

Tallay ORNAN
Israel Museum, Jerusalem

I. Preliminary Remarks

In dealing with the Mesopotamian influence on inscribed West Semitic seals a distinction between two main groups should be made. The first consists of Mesopotamian seals, both stamps and cylinders, inscribed almost entirely with Aramaic legends, the second of seals defined here as belonging to the West Semitic realm, whose inscriptions are not confined to Aramaic.

It is probable that the seals of the first group originated mainly in Mesopotamia and were used by the West Semitic population that lived in this region, or by Mesopotamians in the West. The seals of the second group probably originated in Syria, Palestine and Transjordan. It is the latter group, dated up to the end of the Neo-Babylonian period, which concerned me most.[1] The main question here is the choice of Mesopotamian-inspired com-

1. I would like to thank Benjamin Sass for placing at my disposal his documentation of West Semitic inscribed seals, and for his remarks on the manuscript.

positions and motifs used by the West Semitic seal cutter. Before proceeding with the examination of the seals themselves a number of remarks are in order.

As the pictorial prototype of the inscribed stamp seals is derived mainly from cylinder seals, one should note that this transition caused changes in the borrowed designs. This finds expression in the miniaturization of the original design and in the selection of specific elements from the cylinder. It is mainly these selected patterns that are dealt with here. The seals under discussion fall into two categories: those with complete scenes and those with selected motifs, arranged in compositions which are not necessarily Mesopotamian in character.

In determining whether the Mesopotamian motifs were selected deliberately, the relationship between picture and legend should be checked. There is a distinction between the seals of Mesopotamian shape and materials and Aramaic inscriptions, where the legend is cut haphazardly (e.g. **figs. 6, 7**), and those of the West Semitic realm, whose inscriptions tend to appear in a clear, pre-planned space (e.g. **figs. 48, 55**).

We can trace three main ways of combining legend and picture on these well-organized seals: 1. The exergual layout, popular mainly on seals depicting two antithetic human figures, where the text appears in one or two lines below the picture (**figs. 56-64**). 2. A composition in which the text is arranged vertically down one or both sides of the motif, typical of seals depicting a single human figure (**figs. 67-68, 70-79, 82**). The latter arrangement also occurs sometimes in the Aramaic-Mesopotamian group, but here the size of the letters and their relation to the picture indicate that the legend was squeezed in later (**figs. 36-39, 41-42**). 3. Picture and legend are totally separated, the picture on one side of the seal and the inscription on another. Here we find either bifacial scaraboids and plaques or rounded or faceted conoidal seals where the picture may appear on the base with the legend on the side, or vice versa (**figs. 28, 81**).

Shape should also be considered when seeking to establish Mesopotamian inspiration on inscribed West Semitic stamp seals. The Mesopotamian seals are generally of the rounded or faceted conoidal shape just mentioned, or duck-shaped, while scaraboids are typical of Palestine, Transjordan and, to a lesser extent, Syria (Buchanan & Moorey 1988: xiii-xiv). However, scaraboids decorated with Assyro-Babylonian elements were also found in the central cities of Mesopotamia (Jakob-Rost 1975: 45).

The Assyro-Babylonian inspiration is not equally noticed among the inscribed West Semitic seals. It is fairly frequent in Aramaic seals and seals attributed to Ammon and Moab, and less so in Hebrew glyptic. Mesopotamian motifs are rarely found on Phoenician seals.

II. ICONOGRAPHY

Scenes and motifs chosen to decorate the inscribed seals show the preference of the West Semitic seal-cutter.[2] Five main themes borrowed from Assyro-Babylonian iconography are found in the inscribed West Semitic stamp seals: combat; fantastic animals; semi-divine anthropomorphic figures; divine figures and symbols in various combinations; mortals as the main motif.

1. Combat

The combat scene is scarce among inscribed West Semitic seals, and when found, it is mostly accompanied by Aramaic legends (**figs. 1-5**).[3] The rarity of this composition on inscribed stamp seals stands in contrast to its popularity on cylinder seals with Aramaic inscriptions (G 155-160).[4] This may indicate a deliberate reservation for the royal Assyrian stamp seal (Sachs 1953).[5] The fact that the same contrast in the use of combat scenes seems also to exist between uninscribed stamp and cylinder seals, may confirm the above explanation (Buchanan & Moorey 1988: nos. 365, 368, 372-373; Delaporte 1923: pl. 91:18b, c).

This contrast is also evident in the Achaemenid Period, though here it is confined to inscribed seals (see Boardman 1970: 32-34). While numerous Aramaic cylinders depict combat between a king or a hero and animals/monsters (e.g. G 162, 163, 165, 168; B 129, 131, 135, 138), only a few examples of that theme appear on inscribed stamp seals (e.g. **fig. 5**).[6] The cylinders showing the king (Porada 1961: 68; and cf. Moorey 1978: 151-153) could have served the official administration, while the stamp seals were used by private people (Porada 1948: 101; Persepolis II: 47; Zettler 1979: 263, note 11).

Chariot scenes, popular on Assyrian cylinder seals (Porada 1948: nos. 659-663), are absent from West Semitic seals, both stamps and cylinders, though, imitating Assyrian prototypes, they are encountered among uninscribed stamp seals (e.g. a seal from Dan, Biran 1977: pl. 37c and an impression from Hazor, Hazor III-IV: pls. 196:27, 360:9). Such a distinction indicates a somewhat different repertoire for inscribed and uninscribed seals.

---

2. When possible, a distinction is made here between Assyrian and Babylonian inspiration.
3. Including the seal of *mngʾnrt* (figs. 1, 71), see CAI 143 with bibliography; cf. Lemaire, *supra*, p. 21; Hübner, *infra*, pp. 134, 140-141, 151.
4. Also on South Semitic cylinders, Sass 1991: nos. 21, 23-26.
5. Dominique Collon, personal communication.
6. A combat scene is also shown in the seal of *mnn*, Clermont-Ganneau 1883: no. 26, BM 102967.

1

2

3

4

5

6

The only examples of chariot scenes among the inscribed Semitic seals are found in the South Semitic group (Sass 1991: figs. 16, 35-36). The fact that the chariot scene, showing the king in hunt or battle (Porada 1948: 79), and probably of a secular character, does not occur on inscribed West Semitic seals, may imply a preference for religious subject-matter in the latter (see below, § 5, **fig. 66**).

2. Fantastic animals

The smallest group derived from Mesopotamian iconography is that of hybrid creatures. These beings appear on the seal with the Aramaic legend of *ʾlnwry*, on the Ammonite seal of *mlkmgd* (cf. Hübner, *infra*, p. 158, fig. 17) and on the South Semitic seal of *ʿgly* (Sass 1991: fig. 27). In the seal of *ʾlnwry* (**fig. 6**) it is a horned lion-dragon with a scorpion's tail (Seidl 1989: 184-187). In the other two seals Mesopotamian-type sphinxes are depicted (Avigad 1985: 5; Sass 1991: 50).

3. Semi-divine anthropomorphic figures

Among the seals discussed, more than a dozen show upright composite figures. On the base of the seal of *ʾbḥ* (**fig. 7**) a scorpion-man is depicted. On two examples, those of *šbʾl* and *ddbw* (**figs. 8-9**), we find the bull-man, though the wings of the *šbʾl* being could designate it as a different creature (Reade 1979: 41). The lion-headed figure appears three times, always on the side of the seal: on the seals of *šʾʿl*, *ʾbḥ* (**figs. 13-14**) and *klbydšmš*.[7]

These three beings can be identified. The figure with the scorpion tail is the *girtablullû* (Wiggermann 1992: 180-181), the bull-man with human head, arms and torso and a bull's hindquarters is identified with the *kusarikku* (Green 1983: 92; Wiggermann 1992: 174-179). The lion-headed figure, having a donkey-eared, bird-footed human body, is the *ugallu* (Green 1984: 83, 90-91; Wiggermann 1992: 170-172). As on Assyrian palace reliefs, he is shown (**fig. 13**) together with a smiting figure, the "house god" (*il bīti*) (ibid.: 82). This apotropaic pair is common on uninscribed stamp seals dating to the Neo-Babylonian Period (Green 1986: 165).[8] The *girtablullû*, the *kusarikku* and the *ugallu* belong to seven mythological "sages", the *apkallū*, who, guarding against evil spirits, appear on Assyrian palace reliefs and in clay figurines (Reade 1979: 39-40; Green 1983).

Two other animal-headed creatures are the winged bird-headed figure with human body in the seal of *ʾdnplṭ ʿbd ʿmndb* (**fig. 15**) and the winged, apparently ibex-headed figure on the seal of *bqšt bt ʿbdyrḥ* (**fig. 16**). The first

7. For a photograph of the latter see Green 1986: no. 145. G 120 shows only the base of this seal. The reading *klbydšmš* was proposed by P. Bordreuil during the symposium.

8. No. 141 in Green 1986 is the seal of *šʾʿl*.

7

8

9

10

11

12

13

14

can be confidently added to the *apkallū*, too, as he is attested in apotropaic function on Assyrian palace reliefs and in clay figurines (Reade 1979: 39; Green 1984: 82, ills. 6, 10b; cf. Wiggermann 1992: 75-76). By analogy, the ibex-headed figure on the seal of *bqšt bt ʿbdyrḥ*[9] might belong to the same group of semi-divine beings, as he shares several features of the *kusarikku*.

The three human-headed, winged figures depicted on the seals of *ʿzʾ* and *šgʾdd* (**figs. 18-19**) and perhaps *šbʾl* (reverse; **fig. 17**) probably belong to the *apkallū* too; they are also found as figurines and on Assyrian palace reliefs (Reade 1979: 35-36; Green 1984: 82) and may perhaps be identified with the *ūmu-apkallū* (cf. Wiggermann 1992: 73-75). In uninscribed cylinder seals these figures are shown mainly flanking a tree (Porada 1948: nos. 641, 734, 770-771; Moortgat 1940: no. 749). It seems that the two-winged male figures shown usually in profile with one hand raised in 'apotropaic' or 'greeting' gesture appear in all groups of the inscribed West Semitic seals but the Phoenician.[10] These figures should not be confused with various other winged male figures of purely Egyptianizing or mixed Egyptianizing and Syro-Mesopotamian appearance (e.g., Gubel, *infra*, p. 125, figs. 64-70).

A four-winged female in frontal position appears on the seals of *gʾl bn šʿl* (**fig. 20**; Lemaire 1990c) and *yklʾ* (**fig. 21**). Although this posture is known also in Egyptianized Phoenician seals, it has clear Mesopotamian connections, already known in Middle Assyrian glyptic (Keel 1977: 196-200; U. Winter 1983: figs. 171, 173-181).

In some of the seals mentioned above the semi-divine figures are part of a scene, always the atlantid scene (Frankfort 1939: 201), like the bull-man on the seal of *ddbw* (**fig. 9**; compare Buchanan & Moorey 1988: no. 367). The same scene is seen on the Aramaic seal of *šnḥṣr* (**fig. 10**), where the prototypal bull-men are replaced by human figures. In Aramaic cylinder seals (G 153; HD 136), the bull-men are more popular in this function than the *girtablullû*. However, the *girtablullû* with the upraised arms facing a worshipper on the seal of *ʾbḥ* (**fig. 7**) may be understood as a truncated Assyrian atlantid scene. While he usually holds a winged disk (e.g., Moortgat 1940: nos. 598-599; G 154), the figure on this particular seal supports a crescent.

The reason for the representation of the *girtablullû* and *kusarikku* in these scenes could be connected to the myth relating that after defeating the *apkallū*, the supporters of Tiamat in her battle against Marduk, the god set up their statues at the gate of his temple (Green 1984: 83). Presumably, then, what is

9. The latter has parallels in stamp seals in the Louvre (Black & Green 1992: fig. 14 bottom), in the Bibliothèque Nationale (Delaporte 1910: no. 535), and on a stamp seal from Gezer (Parayre, *supra*, p. 49, fig. 57).

10. The seal of *ʿzʾ* (**fig. 18**) should be regarded as Aramaic rather than Phoenician because of its *zayin*.

15

16

17

18

19

20

21

represented in the atlantid scenes is a view of the facade of the heavenly abode with its two caryatid-like creatures.

Another atlantid figure, depicted, albeit rarely, in the inscribed West Semitic seals, is the kneeling man. He is shown in the seals of *ʾḥṣr* and *šʾl* (**figs. 11-12**). This figure is known in first-millennium Mesopotamian seals (Collon 1987: nos. 352, 396) and has forerunners in the Old Babylonian and Middle Assyrian Periods and earlier (Matthews 1991: 108; Lambert 1985: 435-436, note 4, 447-448). In view of the above interpretation of the atlantid scenes with the bull- or scorpion-men, one tends to follow Mayer-Opificius (1984: 199) who suggests the identification of the kneeling figure with another *apkallu*, the *laḫmu*.

4. Anthropomorphic deities and divine symbols in various combinations

4.1. Anthropomorphic deities with mortals

All the seals depicting worshippers in front of divine figures, except the seal of *yh...* (**fig. 22**)[11] bear Aramaic inscriptions and belong to the group of Mesopotamian origin. The dominant scene in this group is a worshipper facing Sin in his crescent (**figs. 23-26**; Seidl 1989: 97-98), a motif popular from the seventh century (Parker 1955: 123, pl. 29:2; Buchanan & Moorey 1988: nos. 67, 358) to the Persian period. **Fig. 27** bears a rare depiction of Adad, standing on his bull, holding a lightning fork and wearing a Babylonian-type feathered crown (cf. Porada 1948: 94, no. 779). On the seal of *ʾsrʾdny* (**fig. 28**) the enthroned deity is seated on an animal, reminiscent of a theme seen on Assyrian cylinders and on reliefs from the end of the seventh century (Buchanan & Moorey 1988: 54). Unique on inscribed stamp seals is the goddess (Ishtar?) sitting on a star-studded throne on the seal of *hwdw sprʾ* (**fig. 29**; cf. Bordreuil, *infra*, p. 86 with fig. 14).[12]

4.2. Anthropomorphic deities alone

As in the previous group, almost all the seals showing an anthropomorphic deity as the sole element bear Aramaic legends and belong to the 'Meso-

---

11. The seal has Hebrew letters but the unusual representation of a winged god above an *aladlammû* ("*lamassu*") in front of a four-winged figure above a stylized Phoenician tree, makes it hard to attribute to one of the groups discussed here. Similar compositions are encountered in Urartian art, e.g. Merhav 1991: 85, no. 39; 112-113, nos. 79-80 (four-winged deity standing on a bull); 282, no. 10 (frontal-face fantastic animal); 314, no. 3 (two-winged deity on a lion). For a recent discussion, see GGG: 389 with fig. 331b and Sass, *infra*, pp. 236-237.

12. A worshipper facing Ishtar, but in her warrior aspect (cf. Porada 1948: no. 779), can be seen on a cylinder with a South Semitic inscription (Sass 1991: fig. 30) and an Aramaic one (B 85; cf. Bordreuil, *infra*, p. 77, fig. 5).

22

23

24

25

26

27

28

29

30

31

32

33

34

35

potamian' group. They depict Sin in his crescent (**figs. 30-33**), and, once, the enthroned Gula (**fig. 34**), sitting on a dog, her sacred animal, a theme popular in Neo-Babylonian glyptic (Seidl 1989: 142-143).

The only seal of the group under discussion which does not belong to the inscribed 'Mesopotamian' seals, is that of *ṣdyrk* (**fig. 35**). The name and script are considered Phoenician (Avigad 1968: 45, 48-49), while the iconography is more at home in Syria (cf. ANEP: nos. 500-501). The identification of this deity is difficult. On the one hand, it is usually the warrior Ishtar who stands on a lion (Seidl 1989: 139, 233; Porada 1948: 94; Jakob-Rost 1975: no. 188), but the *ṣdyrk* deity lacks her specific attributes, such as the bow and quivers. On the other hand, there are some cases in which a male deity stands on a lion, representing perhaps a storm god (ANEP: no. 486; Collon 1972: 131-133).

The rarity of the *ṣdyrk* theme emphasizes the West Semitic tendency of avoiding representations of anthropomorphic deities. The lion on which the god is standing may show in different light the West Semitic seals that have a lion as main motif or virtual scene (Lemaire 1979; 1990a), regarded usually as a symbol of royalty (Buchanan & Moorey 1988: 40). The few depictions in West Semitic seals of a deity on a lion (and its more frequent occurrence elsewhere), may hint that when on its own, it could stand for a deity. Another rare example of the same phenomenon is the suckling cow, a well-known theme on stamp seals, that is once, in the cylinder of *ʾlʾmr* (Teissier 1984: 172, fig. 236; cf. Bordreuil, *infra*, pp. 78-79 with fig. 6),[13] shown with a goddess on its back. A similar artistic convention, though with a longer and clearer iconographic history, is the image of the bull on Ammonite seals (e.g. B 69, 72-75; cf. Hübner, *infra*, pp. 137-148 with figs. 4, 13, 15, 22-23, 25), a non-anthropomorphic depiction of the storm god, who is shown elsewhere standing on the animal's back (Seidl 1989: 146; ANEP: nos. 531, 537; Frankfort 1939: 215, pl. 33f).[14] In the above examples we face the same phenomenon, the avoidance of the human-shaped deity and its substitution by its sacred animal: the lion, the suckling cow or the bull.

4.3. Divine symbols with mortals

This theme is encountered in both groups of inscribed West Semitic stamp seals. Its main manifestation is among the inscribed Aramaic 'Mesopotamian' seals, mostly those showing the popular Neo-Babylonian representation of a worshipper in front of the symbols of Marduk and Nabu (**figs. 36-46**),[15] and to a lesser extent the lamp of Nusku (**fig. 47**; Porada 1948: 98). The

13. Speleers 1943: 129, no. 1490 is similar.

14. I am grateful to Pirhiya Beck for discussing this with me.

15. See also D 92 (pl. 22:5). For the other two faces of this seal see figs. 12-13 above.

composition of these seals is, again, different from that of the Aramaic cylinder seals depicting the same theme, in that the latter frequently show a worshipper in front of an atlantid scene (G 149, 153-154, 161; cf. Porada 1948: 93, no. 772).

To the group of the West Semitic realm we can attribute several seals with a worshipper in front of divine symbols (**figs. 48-54**). In each of these, except the seals of *ddʿlh* and *šnsrṣr* (**figs. 53-54**), astral symbols appear as the focus of the scene. According to Avigad (1989a: nos. 17-18), two seals of this group, those of *mʾš* and *ʾmṣ* (**figs. 49-50**), are Moabite. The seal of *stmk* (**fig. 48**) has an "inscription akin to Hebrew" (ibid.: 18), while the seal of *ḥnn* (**fig. 51**) was classified as Phoenician (HD 123). The scenes on the seals of *mnḥmt ʾšt pdmlk* (**fig. 52**, Moabite or Edomite, cf. Lemaire, *supra*, p. 16) and *ddʿlh* (**fig. 53**, Aramaic) have clear Assyrian prototypes (e.g. Porada 1948: nos. 642-649). But in the case of *mnḥmt* the crescent and star (or sun) replace the Assyrian tree, while on the seal of *ddʿlh* one of the flanking figures is missing and the whole composition is off-center. The attribution of the seal of *šnsrṣr* is more complicated. The scenes on the base and side of the seal (**figs. 32, 45**) are clearly Babylonian in theme and style (the name is Babylonian too), and kneeling figures in adoration of a central symbol are found in Assyrian seals (e.g. Porada 1948: no. 641). But a boat as the central motif, as on the Hebrew seal of *ʾlšmʿ bn gdlyhw* (Sass, *infra*, pp. 232-234, 240 with fig. 155) and on some anepigraphic stamp seals (GGG: § 178), suggests Syro-Palestinian inspiration.

4.4. Divine symbols alone

The only divine symbols as main or sole elements in inscribed West Semitic seals are celestial bodies. These abound in Transjordanian seals, are less frequent among Aramaic seals, rare in Hebrew seals, and are missing from the Phoenician seals. However, the star and the crescent, so popular in the entire ancient Near East, cannot in the West Semitic realm be traced specifically to Mesopotamian inspiration.[16] As to the crescent on a pole, although it is known in Neo-Assyrian and earlier glyptic, it is regarded by some as Aramaean (Spycket 1973; but see Buchanan & Moorey 1988: 54).[17] Neither is the winged sun, except the anthropomorphic variant, an exclusively-Mesopotamian motif; most western occurrences of the winged sun are apparently local variants (cf. Parayre, *supra*, pp. 31-32 with fig. 11). A unique example of the anthropomorphic version as a sole pictorial element is

---

16. Cogan 1974: 85.

17. Also missing from the inscribed stamp seals are the Neo-Assyrian *sebetti*, and they appear only rarely on inscribed cylinder seals, e.g. the seal of *tbly mn ʾblny* (Bordreuil 1988a: 444-445).

36

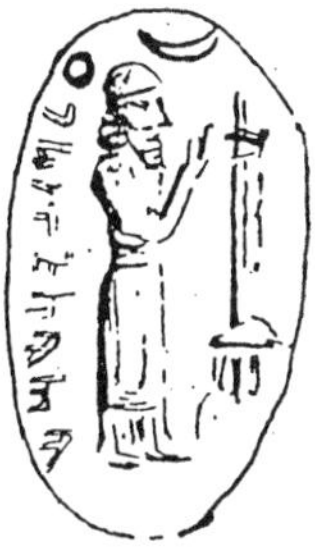
37

38

39

40

41

42

43

44

45

46

47

48

49

50

51

52

53

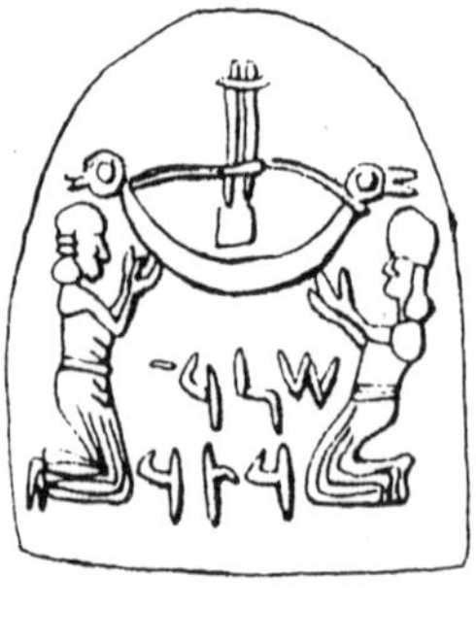

54

55

56

57

58

59

60

61

62

63

64

65

66

to be seen in the Moabite seal of *yḥṣ* (**fig. 55**). In an atlantid scene this motif is depicted in **figs. 9-11** (and with a worshipper in **figs. 52-53**; cf. Parayre 1990a: figs. 125-126; *supra*, p. 43, fig. 12).

5. Mortals as the main motif

Seals depicting mortals only are very rare on the inscribed West Semitic 'Mesopotamian' group. Of the seals shown here,[18] three (**figs. 65, 79, 81**) are regarded as Aramaic, three bear Hebrew inscriptions (**figs. 66-68**), and two are Hebrew or Moabite (**figs. 56, 69**). The rest are classified on onomastic, palaeographical and iconographical grounds as Ammonite or Moabite.[19] It should be noted that Phoenician seals are absent from this group.

The common denominator of the figures on these seals is their lack of any divine devices (headgear, costume, or attributes such as divine symbols or animals). Moreover, in their postures – their arms and palms in particular – they clearly imitate Mesopotamian worshippers (Tadmor & Tadmor 1967: 74; Naveh & Tadmor 1968: 451; Sass 1991: 52).

This group is divided into two: seals which depict two antithetic worshippers (**figs. 56-65**),[20] probably inspired by cylinders with two figures flanking a divine motif (e.g. Moortgat 1940: nos. 675, 679), and seals with a single worshipper (**figs. 67-82**). The 'one worshipper' seals might have been influenced either by Babylonian stamp seals (see above, 4.3.) depicting the adoration of symbols, or by worshippers in front of an anthropomorphic deity seen on cylinders (e.g. Moortgat 1940: nos. 596, 599, 601-605). In both cases it is clear that the West Semitic seal cutter singled out the mortal figure, omitting the divine figure or symbols.

These 'single-worshipper' and 'double-worshipper' seals can also be differentiated in their picture-legend relationship and their secondary elements:

a. Most 'two worshippers' seals are exergual,[21] while the legends in the 'one worshipper' group usually run vertically, along one or two sides of the figure (except the seals of *kpr*, *mngʾnrt*, *ʿbdwḥbn* and *nrglslm*,[22] i.e. **figs. 69, 71, 80, 81**).

---

18. Another example with the same motif, the unpublished bifacial seal of *bylʾnn*, is exhibited in the Hecht Museum, Haifa.

19. For the special status of the seal of *mngʾnrt* (fig. 71) see note 3.

20. This group is discussed by Keel (1990c), among others, who notes general Aramaean influence; with regard to Moabite classification, cf. Timm, *infra*, pp. 180-183.

21. As are the seals of *stmk*, *ʾmṣ*, and *mʾš* (figs. 48-50), similarly assigned to the West Semitic realm.

22. Ornan & Sass 1992.

67

68

69

70

71

72

73

74

75

76

77

78

79

80

81

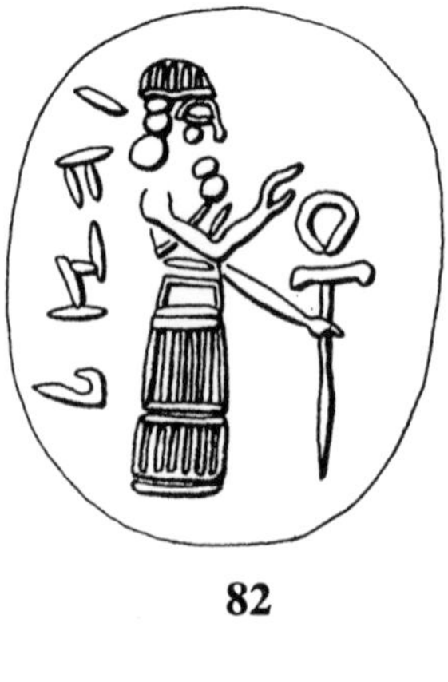

82

b. As to secondary motifs, in the 'one-worshipper' seals we sometimes find a plant and a bird (e.g. **figs. 73, 74**), and only seldom an astral symbol in front and above the worshipper, as in **fig. 78**, or a cult object, as in **fig. 80**. On the other hand, astral symbols, chiefly the crescent, and an object of cultic use, are frequent on the seals depicting two worshippers. Here cultic paraphernalia such as an offering(?) table (**fig. 65**), a candelabrum (**fig. 63**), a high stand or altar (**figs. 57-59, 64**) replace the Mesopotamian human-shaped deity or divine symbol. The arched central element in the seal of *ʾḥyḥy* (**fig. 62**) may have framed a symbol or an object used in cult, now effaced.[23]

Apart from the position of the worshippers' arms and hands it is the astral symbols seen as secondary elements and the object of cultic use which lend these seals their religious character. This character is emphasized by comparison with the *šrhʿr* secular scene, depicting two mortals with no cultic objects or divine symbols (**fig. 66**). The fact that the theme on the *šrhʿr* bullae is so far unique (Avigad 1986a: 30; cf. Sass, *infra*, p. 238, subject F11), reinforces the predominance of religious themes in the inscribed West Semitic seals (see II.1. above with regard to chariot scenes).

III. Conclusions

From the rich iconographic repertoire of Mesopotamia the West Semitic seal cutter chose only certain elements, most prominently that of the worshipper. Thus, one element of the original composition became a subject on its own. It seems that this process cannot be attributed simply to the technical/compositional changes following the transition from cylinder to stamp seals, but had deeper reasons.

Tha avoidance of the anthropomorphic deity is evident on seals throughout the West Semitic regions. It is differently represented among the seals of the subgroups of that realm, where its conspicuous manifestation is, of course, among Hebrew seals, most of which lack pictorial elements at all (cf. Sass, *infra*). But traces of this attitude are evident also in non-Hebrew seals, regarded as Aramaic, Ammonite and Moabite. As Mesopotamian inspiration is not so evident on Phoenician seals, we cannot include them in that iconographic trend. Uninscribed seals engraved with similar themes, found in Palestine and Transjordan, reinforce our evaluation that this iconographic

23. Such an arched element is seen on the cylinder of *mrbrk* (G 154; Bordreuil, *infra*, pp. 82-83 with fig. 11). While Bordreuil considers this to be a variant of the sacred tree, the *mrbrk* seal rather shows a niche in which a candelabrum is placed (cf. Galling 1941: 195), demonstrating that the arched element is not always the outline of a sacred tree.

preference had profound roots among certain elements in these regions (cf. further Uehlinger, *infra*, pp. 263-265).

At the same time, one should bear in mind that the tendency to avoid the depiction of anthropomorphic deities is not confined to the regions of Syria, Palestine and Transjordan. The typical Neo-Babylonian theme of a worshipper in front of divine emblems reflects the same phenomenon, but on a different level. The rejection of the human-shaped deity observed occasionally in Near Eastern art in the first millennium could have been expressed in different ways: substituting the god with his symbol or sacred animal; retaining only mortals; retaining only vegetal and geometric motifs or avoiding even those.

LIST OF FIGURES

Drawings are by Noga Z'evi unless indicated otherwise.

1. *mngʾnrt brk lmlkm*, after B 76.
2. *ʾlsmky*, after HD 132.
3. *bytʾlrʿy*, after B 126.
4. *ʾḥnry*, after Aimé-Giron 1939: pl. 3:116B.
5. *pmn*, after Avigad 1954a: pl. 21:3.
6. *ʾlnwry*, after G 12.
7. *ʾbḥ*, after B 117.
8. *šbʾl*, from A. Lemaire's impression.
9. *ddbw*, after Buchanan & Moorey 1988: no. 371, and an impression.
10. *šnḥṣr*, after B 98.
11. *ʾḥṣr*, after HD 130.
12. *šʾʿl* (*šʾʿn*?), Keel 1977: 212, Abb. 163.
13. *šʾʿl* (as fig. 12), D 92 (for third view, cf. Bordreuil, *infra*, p. 97, fig. 39).
14. *ʾbḥ*, see fig. 7.
15. *ʾdnplṭ ʿbd ʿmndb*, G 99.
16. *bqšt bt ʿbdyrḥ*, BM 113200.
17. *šbʾl*, see fig. 8.
18. *ʿzʾ*, G 98.
19. *šgʾdd*, after Sass 1991: fig. 29.
20. *gʾl bn šʿl*, after B 44.
21. *yklʾ*, Keel 1977: fig. 140.
22. *yh...*, after B 58.
23. *knbw*, G 113.
24. *ḥnky* (*ḥzk*), G 114a.
25. *ydʾḥ* (*ʾḥt*?), drawing Hildi Keel-Leu after B 114.
26. *pqd yhd*, after Bordreuil 1986b: fig. 9.
27. *nbwšgb*, after B 112.
28. *ʾsrʾdny* (*qsrʾdny*), G 112.
29. *hwdw sprʾ*, Welten 1977c: 305, fig. 78:18.
30. *šmšʿdry*, drawing Hildi Keel-Leu after B 111.
31. *brky*, drawing Hildi Keel-Leu after B 95.
32. *šnsrṣr*, after B 109.

33. *ʾkmʾ*, after B 115.
34. *nšk khn bn dgnbzy*(?), after Heltzer 1981: no. 108.
35. *ṣdyrk*, after Avigad 1968: 45.
36. *ʾḥymn*, G 118.
37. *klbydšmš*, G 120.
38. *hnmy*(?), G 119.
39. *nškn*ʾ*d*, after B 123.
40. *nškbr*, after B 110.
41. *mnḥm*, G 117.
42. *mnk*, G 116.
43. *blṭy*, after Heltzer 1981: no. 109.
44. *nšk khn bn dgnbzy*, see fig. 34.
45. *šnsrṣr*, see fig. 32.
46. *ʾšl*, Carchemish III: fig. 76.
47. *hml ddh*(?), Yassine 1988: 148.
48. *stmk*, after Avigad 1989a: no. 22.
49. *mʾš*, after Avigad 1989a: no. 18.
50. *ʾmṣ*, after Avigad 1989a: no. 17.
51. *ḥnn*, after HD 123.
52. *mnḥmt ʾšt pdmlk*, GGG: fig. 294; for other face, cf. Lemaire, *supra*, p. 26, fig. 23.
53. *ddʿlh*, IMJ 71.46.94.
54. *šnsrṣr*, Clermont-Ganneau 1883: no. 32 (see fig. 32).
55. *yḥṣ*, G 81.
56. *km...*, GGG: fig. 311a.
57. *ḥkš* (*ḥkm*), drawing Hildi Keel-Leu after B 67.
58. *ʾmṣ hspr*, Naveh 1982: 103, fig. 89.
59. *ʿzrʾ*, drawing Hildi Keel-Leu after Avigad 1977b: pl. 13:1.
60. *škr*, after Lemaire 1990b: no. 3.
61. *ʿy...*, drawing Hildi Keel-Leu after B 102.
62. *ʾḥyḥy*, drawing Hildi Keel-Leu after Lemaire 1983: no. 12.
63. *ylʾ*, drawing Hildi Keel-Leu after Bordreuil & Lemaire 1976: no. 24.
64. *ʾḥʾ*, GGG: fig. 311b.
65. *ʾḥlkn*, drawing Hildi Keel-Leu after B 97.
66. *šrhʿr*, A 10.
67. *yqmyhw bn nḥm*, A 77.
68. *šbnyw ʿbd ʿzyw*, GGG: fig. 263a.
69. *kpr*, from Ch. Uehlinger's impression, cf. NAAG 1991: no. 25.
70. *ʾlʿz bn mnḥm*, drawing Hildi Keel-Leu after Puech 1976: pl. 2.
71. *mngʾnrt brk lmlkm*, see fig. 1.
72. *ʾlšmʿ*, after B 77.
73. *ʾbgd*, after Bordreuil & Lemaire 1976: no. 25.
74. *ʾbgdh*, G 127.
75. *šr*, after Lemaire 1986: 315.
76. *ʾlrm*, after Lemaire 1985b: fig. 8.
77. *ʾlʾmṣ bn ʾlšʿ*, G 128.
78. *ʾlrm bn tmʾ*, G 126.
79. *hdrqy ʿbd hdbʿd*, G 129.
80. *ʿbdwḥbn*, G 124.
81. *nrglslm br ʾḥʾrs*, IMJ 73.19.41.
82. *hṣl*, BM 48499.

LE RÉPERTOIRE ICONOGRAPHIQUE DES SCEAUX ARAMÉENS INSCRITS ET SON ÉVOLUTION

Pierre BORDREUIL
CNRS, Paris

Il y a plus de cinquante ans, en des temps tragiques, paraissait un travail fondamental de Kurt Galling (1941) qui, rétrospectivement, fait aujourd'hui figure d'article-programme. En effet, pour la première fois, étaient rassemblés, classés dans le temps et dans l'espace, cent quatre-vingt trois cylindres et cachets porteurs à la fois d'iconographie et d'une inscription ouest-sémitique. Un commentaire substantiel était joint au catalogue et justifiait les classements épigraphiques et les datations proposées par l'auteur. Cet article reste encore aujourd'hui à la base de toute recherche sur le sujet, en mettant à part bien entendu les nombreux *ajouts* que les découvertes ultérieures de documents ont amené à opérer, les *relectures* rendues indispensables par le progrès des connaissances paléographiques, les *reclassements* qu'impose l'apparition de nouvelles provinces de l'épigraphie sémitique, les *datations* nouvelles obtenues par une meilleure connaissance soit du matériel associé, dans le cas de fouilles régulières, soit tout simplement de l'iconographie du Proche-Orient ancien. Le présent exposé souhaite s'inscrire dans la ligne de recherche inaugurée par ce savant sémitisant de Tübingen décédé en 1987.

On sait que le terme "araméen" recouvre une *langue*, attestée dès le IXe siècle, une *écriture*, née probablement en Mésopotamie, à laquelle le support des tablettes d'argile confèrera rapidement un caractère cursif bien reconnaissable, une *réalité collective* dont témoigne le Credo bien connu de Deut. 26,5: "Mon père était un araméen nomade..." et une *réalité politique*, c'est à dire une pléiade de royaumes syriens dont l'existence sera écourtée par les expéditions assyriennes dès la moitié du IXe siècle. A l'intérieur de ce cadre complexe, a-t-il existé une expression artistique araméenne spécifique et plus précisément, quelles sont les caractéristiques qui permettraient de dire qu'un sceau historié ou simplement décoré est araméen et que son titulaire devait être un araméen?

Ecartant de notre propos l'ensemble des sceaux araméens aniconiques, puis les sceaux historiés et décorés dont le caractère araméen se limite à l'écriture, on rassemblera les sceaux portant, en même temps qu'une scène ou un décor, une *inscription araméenne en langue araméenne* et on s'interrogera sur les caractéristiques éventuelles de leur répertoire iconographique, sur ses origines et son évolution.

I. CRITÈRES D'ÉLIMINATION

1. L'aniconisme

Sont particulièrement visées ici les bulles et estampilles araméennes découvertes en Palestine, qui remontent aux époques perse et hellénistique. Il s'agit là en effet d'une extension relativement tardive de la langue et de l'écriture araméenne à une région qui avait connu dans le passé une glyptique inscrite spécifique, israélite et judéenne. Porteurs le plus souvent d'anthroponymes yahwistes (Avigad 1976), ces sceaux d'écriture araméenne, mais dépourvus de toute scène figurée, sinon de tout décor (**fig. 1**), sont par conséquent extérieurs à notre propos. Il avait existé toutefois longtemps auparavant certains sceaux araméens aniconiques comme celui de *nrš*ʾ *ʿbd ʿtrsmk* aux environs de 800 av. J.-C., qui est pratiquement dépourvu de décor (**fig. 2**). Son caractère araméen peut difficilement être mis en doute puisqu'il a vraisemblablement appartenu à un ministre de Attaršumki, roi d'Arpad et père de Matiʿʾel, ce dernier étant lui-même partenaire du traité de Sfiré rédigé en araméen au milieu du VIIIe siècle.

2. L'onomastique personnelle

Elle est le critère déterminant et nous contraint à éliminer des documents importants porteurs d'inscription en écriture araméenne dont voici quelques exemples:

1. Noms persans: le sceau-cylindre inscrit *ḥtm pršndt br ʾrtdt* (CIS II, 100; G 163; VSA 75 [et 76!]), grand personnage de l'empire achéménide qui n'est pas encore identifié; le sceau-cylindre *lʾrtym*, transcription du nom *ʼΑρτίμας*, satrape de Cyrus le Jeune en fonction à la fin du Ve siècle qui est mentionné dans Xénophon (CIS II, 99; Bivar 1961; VSA 78 [et 157!]); un cylindre du IVe siècle, élément décoratif dont l'inscription, lisible directement sur la pierre, désigne son propriétaire comme "zarathoustrien" (*zrtštrš*, B 136).

2. Noms égyptiens: les cachets dont l'inscription porte *ḥr ḥby* : "Horus le hébite" (CIS II, 140; VSA 91); *npsy* : "Isis est bonne".[1]

3. Noms accadiens: L'élimination de noms accadiens est plus délicate à opérer car ils sont formés à partir de racines qui sont souvent communes au sémitique oriental et occidental et il faut veiller à ne pas écarter un anthroponyme en réalité araméen mais d'apparence accadienne. La présence de théophores n'est pas toujours un critère suffisant puisque, par exemple, le dieu Sin pouvait aussi bien être vénéré par un fidèle portant le nom accadien Sin-aḫa-uṣur (*šnḥṣr*; **fig. 3**) que par Sin-ab (*šn ʾb* ; **fig. 4**)[2] dont l'aspect est plus occidental. Aḫia-likin (*ʾḥlkn*, G 121; VSA 51; B 97) en revanche est un nom de structure tout à fait mésopotamienne, comme cela a été remarqué depuis longtemps; par conséquent on laissera de côté de tels sceaux portant des anthroponymes du type sujet-complément-verbe (p.ex. *plthdn* = Beltu-aḫa-iddin[3]), qui sont spécifiquement accadiens, de même que certains noms-mot.[4] Malgré son iconographie partiellement égyptisante, on laissera également de côté le cachet portant *trtn* qui est la transcription araméenne du titre assyrien *turtānu* (Bordreuil 1988a: 445).

Ailleurs, c'est l'orthographe du théophore qui est accadienne: le fait de transcrire en araméen Addou-nouri par *ʾdnr* (G 156; VSA 68; lecture B 96) reproduit l'usage mésopotamien; inversement, la graphie occidentale *hdtkl* (CIS II, 89; G 155; VSA 67) de Haddou-takal ne suffit pourtant pas à en faire un nom araméen puisque l'élément verbal *takal*: "Il est fiable" est typiquement accadien.

---

1. Euting 1883: 541ss.; Clermont-Ganneau 1890: 430s.; cf. Driver 1957: 52; Kornfeld 1978: 84.
2. La lecture de Herr (1978: 34, n° Ar 62) et de HD 125 (*šmʾb*) a été corrigée par J. Naveh (1980: 76).
3. CIS II, 80; G 153; VSA 65; Collon 1987: 106s., n° 464.
4. Le conoïde portant le nom accadien *tasmur* "Louange" (*tsmr*, G 147; VSA 59; B 121) fait partie de cette dernière catégorie.

1

2

3

4

5

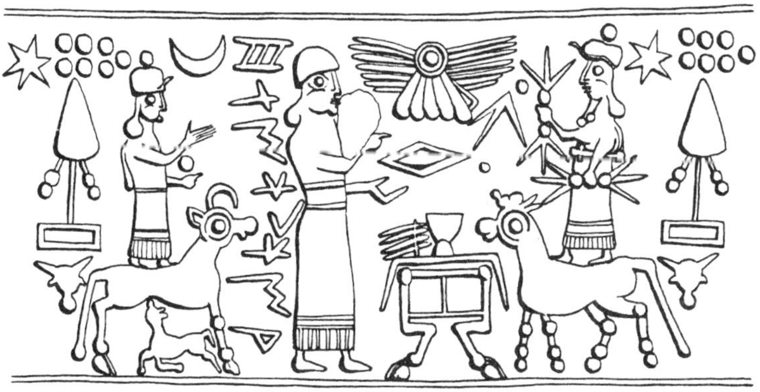

6

4. Noms incertains: *nbrb* (CIS II, 91; G 32; VSA 10; B 101) est-il la transcription d'un anthroponyme araméen Nabu-rab: "Nabou (est) grand", encore inconnu mais plausible, ou plutôt celle de l'accadien bien connu Nabu-iriba: "Nabou a remplacé"?

5. Noms mixtes: *mtrš* (CIS II, 101; G 169; VSA 81; B 128) vocalisé probablement Mitris: "le mithriaque" ne donne pas d'indication sur l'origine de son titulaire; le décor du cylindre est persan, mais le patronyme *šʿy* pourrait être araméen.

Il reste à examiner ceux qui peuvent être considérés à bon droit comme araméens, c'est à dire les sceaux historiés ou décorés dont le titulaire porte un nom relevant de la langue araméenne et/ou dénotant le culte d'une divinité araméenne.

II. L'ICONOGRAPHIE ASSYRIENNE OU ASSYRISANTE: SCÈNES MYTHOLOGIQUES

1. Le cylindre de Baraq serviteur de Atarshamin (*ḥtm brq ʿbd ʿtršmn*, VSA 142; B 85; **fig. 5**) est un document d'importance majeure qui doit dater de la fin du IXe siècle (ainsi Herr 1978: n° Ar 78), c'est à dire des débuts de l'écriture araméenne. Il représente à gauche "une déesse avançant à droite, vêtue d'un long habit fendu, un glaive au côté, coiffée d'un polos couronné de globules et surmonté d'un astre radié. Elle tient de la main gauche un anneau fait de globules, et elle lève la main droite; de sa tête, un fanon tombe jusqu'à hauteur de sa taille. Derrière elle, un bouquetin couché, un losange, un bucrane. Devant elle, une table d'offrande, chargée d'un vase à pied, d'un oiseau, et d'un autre objet. A droite, un personnage barbu, long vêtu, se tient dans l'attitude de la prière, les mains étendues avec la paume en l'air. Au-dessus de la scène, croissant et astre à huit rais" (Seyrig 1955: 42s.). L'inscription en lettres araméennes court verticalement de haut en bas sur deux lignes derrière le dos du personnage. Aussi bien le nom du titulaire, qui signifie "Foudre", que celui de sa Patronne, la déesse Atarshamin représentée vraisemblablement sur ce cylindre (voir Knauf ^{2}1989: 82s.), permettent de verser ce sceau au dossier de l'iconographie sigillaire araméenne.

2. Tout aussi important est le cylindre d'Elʾamar (*ḥtm ʾlʾmr*, Teissier 1984: n° 236; **fig. 6**) qui représente à droite de la scène une divinité masculine, long vêtue, de profil gauche, coiffée d'un polos surmonté d'un globe, la chevelure répartie en deux nattes sur les épaules et un chignon tombant dans le cou. Debout sur un taureau passant, le dieu tient dans sa main droite un double foudre vertical à six pointes et le même attribut horizontalement dans sa main gauche; à l'avant, un foudre à trois pointes est dirigé vers le centre de la scène. Ce dernier est occupé par une table d'offrande à pieds de ruminants,

recouverte d'une nappe, portant un vase à pied et un autre objet qui se trouve à la même place sur le cylindre de Baraq. Au-dessus de la table, un losange horizontal surmonté d'un disque solaire. Face à la table un personnage long vêtu, imberbe, tend la main gauche paume en l'air et la main droite paume vers le sol en direction de la table et de la divinité précitées. A gauche de la scène, c'est à dire derrière le personnage central, une divinité féminine, long vêtue, de profil droit, coiffée d'un polos surmonté d'un globe est debout sur un cervidé allaitant son petit. Dans sa main gauche on distingue un récipient et le geste esquissé par sa main droite est celui de Atarshamin sur le sceau précédent. Au dessus d'elle, flanqués par le croissant lunaire et par un astre à six rais, sept globes, représentant les Pléiades, surmontent un *marru* muni de pompons et fixé sur un socle. Sous ce dernier un bucrane. L'inscription d'une ligne en lettres araméennes court verticalement de haut en bas dans le dos du personnage; elle se lit sur l'original et non sur l'empreinte.

Les deux inscriptions diffèrent en raison de l'absence de la fonction d'El-ʾamar, omission qui est due peut-être à l'exiguïté du champ, mais formellement les lettres des deux inscriptions sont très proches et pratiquement contemporaines. D'autre part, on voit que l'iconographie du cylindre d'Elʾamar est voisine de celle du cylindre de Baraq. Or, dans la glyptique araméenne inscrite, la représentation d'un personnage debout sur un taureau est rare[5] et la divinité debout sur un cervidé n'est connue que sur ces deux cylindres. La comparaison entre le cylindre d'Elʾamar où la divinité féminine est debout sur le cervidé qui allaite son petit et le cylindre de Baraq où la divinité féminine, la main droite levée dans la même attitude que sur celui d'Elʾamar, est debout à terre devant le cervidé qui est accroupi, donne l'impression de deux scènes se succédant l'une à l'autre: dans la première, la déesse est debout sur le dos du cervidé et le dévot fait face au dieu qui est debout sur le dos du taureau; dans la seconde, la déesse a mis pied à terre pour agréer l'offrande du dévot qui s'est entre temps retourné et maintenant lui fait face, le dieu ayant disparu de la scène. Toutes les analogies qui ont été relevées donnent à penser que les deux documents proviennent du même atelier, sinon du même lapicide et on ne manquera pas de les comparer à deux cylindres anépigraphes de la Bibliothèque Nationale (Delaporte 1910: n°s 350, 360).

3. Un troisième cylindre, anépigraphe (Diehl 1965; Collon 1987: 136s., n° 573; **fig. 7**) appartient à un groupe homogène, contemporain du précédent, qui a été identifié par P.M. Pecorella (1980). Comme sur le cylindre d'El-ʾamar, on voit à droite une divinité masculine, long vêtue, de profil gauche, coiffée d'un polos surmonté d'un globe, la chevelure en chignon tombant dans le cou. Debout sur un taureau passant, le dieu, dépourvu ici d'attributs

5. On la retrouvera à la fin du VIIe siècle sur le conoïde de Nabušagab (*lnbwšgb*, B 112; cf. Ornan, *supra*, p. 61, fig. 27).

orageux mais tenant une hache dans sa main gauche, salue un personnage long vêtu, barbu, tendant la main gauche paume en l'air et la main droite paume vers le sol en direction de la divinité précitée. Ce personnage est figuré dans la même attitude que celui du cylindre d'Elʾamar et surmonté comme lui par un disque solaire, mais ici la table d'offrande et ses ustensiles sont absents; à leur place on distingue une sorte de récipient sur un support. A gauche de la scène, c'est à dire derrière le personnage central, une divinité féminine, long vêtue, de profil droit, coiffée d'un polos surmonté d'un globe, est debout sur une sorte d'estrade ressemblant à deux coussins empilés l'un sur l'autre. Comme sur le sceau de Baraq, de la main gauche elle tient un anneau fait de globules et de la main droite elle accomplit le même geste de salutation qu'Atarshamin. Comme sur le cylindre d'Elʾamar elle est surmontée par sept globes représentant les Pléiades et un *marru*, ici dépourvu de socle, est placé devant elle. Comme sur les deux autres cylindres, croissant lunaire et losange sont présents mais ici ils surmontent un poisson et une roue, prenant ainsi la place qui est occupée sur le cylindre de Baraq par l'inscription araméenne. Ce troisième cylindre est daté par de nombreux parallèles autour de 800 (Diehl 1965: 825s.). Bien qu'anépigraphe, il présente aussi le rare avantage d'avoir été découvert pendant une fouille régulière sur le sol d'une cella de l'Héraïon de Samos, en compagnie d'un cylindre inscrit en cunéiforme au nom de Bel-taklak, personnage qui pourrait avoir vécu dans le second quart du VIIIe siècle (*ibid.*: 827s.; Collon 1987: 137).

4. Tout à fait différente est la scène, elle aussi d'inspiration assyrienne, qui est représentée sur un cylindre portant l'inscription *ḥtm ypʿhd mpšr* : "Sceau de Yapaʿhaddou, l'interprète (des songes) (?)[6]" (G 160; **fig. 8**). L'anthroponyme signifie "Haddou a resplendi". A droite, un personnage debout, de profil gauche, vêtu d'une longue tunique, portant une coiffure hémisphérique et levant les mains devant lui. A gauche, un personnage, dont la taille plus élevée révèle le caractère divin, est debout le pied droit sur le dos, le pied gauche sur la corne d'un animal fantastique ailé. Derrière lui et devant lui trois et quatre étoiles forment les sept astres présents sur les cylindres dont on vient de parler. Portant une épée à la ceinture, il tire à l'arc en direction d'un lion ailé dressé sur ses pattes postérieures qui bondit à sa droite. L'inscription se lit de haut en bas: la première partie derrière le dieu, la seconde partie entre le lion dressé et le personnage de droite. L'ensemble n'évoque pas le début du VIIIe siècle (Galling 1941: 163s.) mais plutôt le IXe siècle d'après l'écriture. Cf. aussi le cylindre de Ninurta-bel-uṣur éponyme de 876 (Moortgat

6. Ce n'est pas la transcription de l'accadien *mupašširu (šūnāti)*, mais son équivalent araméen qui doit être vocalisé *m^{e}paššẹr* (cf. Dan. 5:16 où *piš^{ə}rẹh* signifie interprétation des songes).

7

8

9

1940: n° 595; cp. la scène dans Frankfort 1939: pl. XXXVb et dans Porada 1948: n° 689).

5. Sur un cylindre de la fin du VIIIe ou du VIIe siècle av. J.-C. récemment découvert (**fig. 9**), la scène se décrit ainsi: “Deux griffons, dressés sur leurs pattes de derrière, se tiennent de part et d'autre d'un personnage barbu, tourné vers la droite, qui saisit chacun par une patte. Les espaces entre les griffons et le personnage sont remplis en bas par deux petits singes accroupis, tournés vers le personnage et jouant de la flûte, en haut à gauche par un disque dans lequel est inscrit un croissant, et à droite par une étoile. La scène est terminée par un arbre stylisé qui est surmonté d'un disque ailé. Une inscription, qui se lit sur la pierre et non sur l'empreinte: *lšd/rh*, a été rajoutée derrière le singe de droite, peut-être à une date postérieure vu la forme des caractères araméens” (Collon 1986b: 425). La forme spécifique du *h* final évoque la graphie araméenne de Palestine de la seconde moitié du VIe siècle (voir Herr 1978: n^os^ Ar 26, 28, 35, 37) mais elle trouve des antécédents en Mésopotamie au début du VIIe siècle (*ibid.*: inscriptions n° 18 = CIS II, 17, 39).

6. Un autre cylindre (CIS II, 78; G 158; VSA 70; **fig. 10**) présente une scène composée d'un personnage anthropomorphe, barbu, vêtu d'une longue tunique et portant une coiffure hémisphérique, de profil droit, bras mi-tendus, tenant en mains les mains droites de deux créatures hybrides androcéphales ailés au corps de quadrupède, portant une coiffure hémisphérique. De part et d'autre du personnage central un losange et un poisson. A droite on lit dans le champ de haut en bas en écriture araméenne *lʾlyhb* qui signifie “Appartenant à Elyahab”, nom qui signifie “El a apporté”. On retrouve sur ce sceau losange et poisson comme sur le cylindre anépigraphe de l'héraïon de Samos dont il a été question tout à l'heure. Il est possible que la gravure de la scène aux environs de 700 av. J.-C.[7] soit ici plus ancienne que l'inscription. Cette dernière pourrait dater de la première moitié du VIIe siècle.

7. Enfin, un cylindre (G 154; Collon 1987: 79, n° 355; **fig. 11**) présente au centre un arbre sacré entouré d'une couronne de palmettes flanqué de part et d'autre par deux génies androcéphales à la coiffure hémisphérique à queue de scorpion et à l'arrière-train de rapace. De leurs bras dressés ils supportent un disque ailé d'où surgit le buste d'un personnage central tête barbue de profil gauche, coiffée d'une sorte de tiare, salué par deux acolytes à la coiffure hémisphérique qui le flanquent de part et d'autre.[8] De chaque côté de l'élément central, deux personnages opposés, debout de profil, élèvent une main. Celui de gauche, imberbe, vêtu d'une longue tunique et portant une coiffure hémisphérique, est immobile; celui de droite, barbu, vêtu à l'identique et portant une sorte de tiare, porte la jambe gauche vers l'avant. Derrière le per-

7. La date proposée par Herr (1978: 37, n° Ar 69) me paraît un peu trop haute.

8. On retrouvera cet élément central sur le cylindre de *tbly* (**fig. 34**); cf. G 153.

sonnage de droite, un personnage barbu, court vêtu, portant une coiffure hémisphérique, est représenté de face. Il enserre de ses mains deux cervidés dont les têtes, symétriques, sont dirigées vers l'extérieur. Dans le même mouvement il tient par l'arrière-train deux quadrupèdes plus petits qui sont des capridés ou des antilopinés. Derrière ce dernier est gravé de bas en haut en lettres araméennes le nom araméen *mrbrk* : "Le Seigneur a béni". On note qu'ici l'inscription a été gravée dans un espace demeuré libre dans le champ, ou qui avait même peut-être été prévu pour cette dernière. Au milieu de l'inscription on remarque un signe *ʿankh* de grande taille qui sépare le sujet et le prédicat. Cet élément iconographique d'origine occidentale a été gravé en même temps que l'inscription. Etant donné que la scène représentée ici trouve ses meilleurs parallèles entre 630 et 600 av. J.-C. (Collon 1987: 80) et qu'un *m* du même type est attesté vers 650 sur les épigraphes d'Assour (Herr 1978: 38s., n° 74), on proposera de dater l'ensemble de la première partie de la seconde moitié du VIIe siècle, soit vers 630.

III. L'ICONOGRAPHIE "SYRIENNE"

1. Scènes mythologiques

1. A la fin du IXe siècle, comme le cylindre de Baraq, appartient un cylindre (G 149, cf. p. 134; VSA 61; Collon 1987: 84s., n° 395; **fig. 12**) dont la gravure d'une rare qualité représente une scène dont le centre est formé par un arbuste. Ce dernier est surmonté d'un disque solaire ailé. A droite un sphinx ailé de profil est surmonté d'un disque et d'un croissant de lune; derrière lui un personnage debout immobile lève les deux mains dans un geste de bénédiction en direction du centre de la scène. A gauche, un capridé dressé sur ses pattes postérieures appuie ses pattes antérieures sur l'arbuste; un personnage symétrique du précédent avance en tenant une corne dans la main gauche et en levant la main droite en direction du centre de la scène dans un geste comparable à celui de son congénère. Entre le personnage et le capridé on lit verticalement de bas en haut: *lsrgd* "Appartenant à *srgd*".[9]

L'aspect syrien des deux personnages et la présence d'éléments égyptisants[10] tels que le sphinx sont incontestables, mais on peut se demander si la graphie *sr* est celle du théonyme mésopotamien *Aššur*[11], bien que *sr* puisse

9. Cette lecture me paraît préférable à *srpd* (adoptée par Herr 1978: 39, n° Ar 75) en raison du caractère anguleux de la tête de la lettre qui l'identifie à un *g* plutôt qu'à un *p* dont la tête est d'ordinaire plus arrondie.

10. Cf. Collon 1987: 83 qui le classe parmi les sceaux de Syrie et de Palestine.

11. Cf. la graphie *srgrnr* de Aššur-garûa-nēri, éponyme assyrien de 635 (Bordreuil 1973b: 100 et n. 3). F. Israel me signale que le nom araméen *sʿly* (G 22, cf. *infra*, n. 15), qui

aussi transcrire l'accadien *šarru* : "Roi", voire le théonyme égyptien Osiris. La forte connotation assyrienne que confèrerait à ce document la mention du dieu Assour n'est pourtant pas un élément décisif qui permettrait d'éliminer ce sceau de la glyptique araméenne. En effet, le second terme du nom du titulaire: *gd*, s'il est attesté dans l'onomastique mésopotamienne ancienne (Bottéro 1958: 56) où il désignait l'ancêtre divinisé, demeurera un élément caractéristique de l'onomastique araméenne du Ier millénaire.[12] D'autre part, la structure du nom lui-même, en forme de phrase nominale: "*sr* (est) *gd*", banale en araméen, ne correspond pas à la structure spécifique des anthroponymes accadiens dont on a parlé plus haut. Si les cylindres de Baraq et de Elʾamar d'une part attestent la contiguité entre une iconographie assyrisante et une onomastique araméenne, celui de *srgd* d'autre part atteste le phénomène inverse, à savoir une iconographie vraisemblablement syrienne accompagnant une onomastique assyrisante.

2. Un autre cylindre récemment découvert (**fig. 13**) présente "un génie casqué et doté de quatre ailes. Les griffons sont placés comme sur un plan incliné et penchent vers le génie; entre eux, à un niveau plus élevé, se trouve un motif égyptisant sur une ligne de base: deux personnages à tête de bélier surmontée de cornes et d'un disque, tendent les bras vers l'oeil *wedjat* audessous duquel se tient, sur une fleur de lotus, un faucon à tête de bélier, couronné de même. Au-dessus plane un disque ailé contenant le buste d'un dieu, tourné vers la droite et accompagné de deux petits dieux volants dont les corps se confondent avec les ailes du disque. A la droite de ce motif une inscription araméenne longe la fine ligne horizontale qui entoure le haut du cylindre: *ḥtm ʿbdkdʾh* 'Sceau de ʿAbd-Kadiah'. Les casques que portent les dieux et le génie sont munis de cornes vues de profil et d'une crête florale" (Collon 1986b: 425s.). Les costumes trouvent leurs meilleurs parallèles dans la glyptique des environs de 700 av. J.-C. et le motif égyptien indiquerait une facture phénicienne (*ibid.*: 426).

L'inscription, qui se lit sur la pierre et non sur l'empreinte, présente la même formulation que celle des cylindres de Baraq et d'Elʾamar: *ḥtm* + NP. L'identification du second élément de l'anthroponyme, qui est un nom divin présent parmi les dieux témoins du traité de Sfiré (Gibson 1975: 29, n° 7,36), est malaisée à établir. L'identification de *kdʾh* avec (Ishtar) "l'Akkadienne"[13] n'empêche pas le classement de ce document dans la glyptique syrienne. L'iconographie présente en effet plusieurs éléments d'origine occidentale et

---

est l'équivalent de *šʿly*, connu en ammonite (Israel 1987a: 146), pourrait provenir de la même région que l'inscription de Tell Fekheryé où ce phénomène a été relevé.

12. Par exemple *mlkmgd* sur un sceau ammonite d'époque achéménide (Avigad 1985: 4ss.; cf. Hübner, *infra*, p. 158, fig. 17).

13. Proposée par Fales 1990: 163 et n. 35: métathèse de *ʿbd ʾkdh* "serviteur de (Ishtar) l'Akkadienne".

10

11

12

14

13

cette divinité figure dans le traité araméen de Sfiré parmi des divinités mésopotamiennes et syro-araméennes.

3. Le scarabée de dimensions exceptionnelles (G 111; VSA 41; **fig. 14**), datant de la fin du VIIIe siècle (Herr 1978: 11s., n° Ar 2), qui est gravé au nom de “Houdou le scribe” (*lhwdw sprʾ*) présente une scène à deux personnages surmontés d'un astre à huit rais. Le premier debout de profil, barbu et coiffé à l'assyrienne, vêtu d'une longue tunique et représenté dans une attitude d'adoration devant une déesse (Ishtar?) qui lui fait face, assise sur un trône à haut dossier et portant un couvre-chef surmonté d'un globule, comparable à ceux des divinités des trois cylindres araméens présentés plus haut; entre les deux personnages un signe *ʿankh* vertical. La présence d'un *ʾaleph* postposé montre que ce sceau a été gravé à l'intention d'un fonctionnaire araméophone.

2. Personnages

1. Sur un scarabéoïde (G 129; VSA 55; Lemaire 1978b; **fig. 15**) dont l'inscription *lhdrqy ʿbd hdbʿd* fait le tour de la face gravée, un personnage est debout sur une simple ligne de sol, de profil droit, arborant un couvre-chef indéterminé, vêtu d'une longue tunique frangée à partir du genou et descendant à mi-mollets,[14] les bras étendus, le bras droit masquant le bras gauche, paume vers l'avant. Comme d'autres sceaux inscrits l'attestent (Bordreuil 1985), ce type de représentation caractérise les fonctionnaires d'autorité dont plusieurs, connus par les sources historiques, exerçaient leur charge à la fin du VIIIe et au début du VIIe siècle. Les noms du titulaire de ce sceau et de son patron sont encore inconnus et la datation paléographique situe ce document dans la première partie du VIIIe siècle (Herr 1978: 16, n° Ar 12).

2. Sur la base d'un conoïde octogonal (B 126; **fig. 16**) est gravée une scène mettant aux prises un personnage et un capridé. A gauche, l'homme de profil droit, long vêtu, barbu, dont la coiffure se confondant avec la chevelure pourrait être une perruque, tient de la main gauche la tête de l'animal dressé qui se détourne. La main droite est armée d'un glaive pendant le long du corps. Sous la simple ligne de sol, l'inscription *lbytʾlrʿy* est gravée sur deux lignes en boustrophédon. L'écriture est araméenne, de même que l'anthroponyme qui signifie “Bethel (est) berger”. L'ensemble du document est difficile à classer: le sceau conoïde est le support de prédilection des inscriptions sigillaires araméennes mésopotamiennes, mais l'aspect général du personnage est syrien. L'inscription trouve des analogies avec l'écriture araméenne d'Egypte, ainsi que le nom propre, attesté à Eléphantine (cf. Bordreuil 1986a: 98). En

---

14. On comparera la tunique de *hdrqy* à celle de son contemporain *šbnyw*, ministre du roi Ouziyaou (B 41; cf. Sass, *infra*, p. 233, fig. 132).

même temps, on se trouve ici devant la première inscription sigillaire sémitique en boustrophédon.

3. Animaux

1. Un scarabéoïde (G 20; VSA 6; B 89; **fig. 17**), daté des environs de 750 (Herr 1978: 43s., n° Ar 88), qui a été découvert pendant la fouille du palais de Sargon II à Khorsabad, porte l'inscription *rpty*, qui est peut-être un gentilice, gravée entre les pattes d'un lion de profil qui est lui-même surmonté d'un scarabée à deux ailes étendues. Ce dernier élément est égyptisant et, s'il émane du même lapicide que le lion, évoque nettement l'Occident, permettant ainsi de classer ce document parmi les sceaux araméens; en effet, la représentation du roi des animaux a elle-même connu une popularité trop universelle pour servir de critère. On note pourtant que la figuration de profil du lion rugissant semble avoir connu un regain de faveur pendant tout le VIIIe et au début du VIIe siècle, particulièrement en Syrie[15] et jusque dans le royaume de Samarie.[16] A la même époque, le propriétaire d'un cylindre d'iconographie assyrienne (G 157; VSA 69) porte même le nom *kpr* "lion",[17] gravé en écriture araméenne.

2. C'est aussi vers 700 (Herr 1978: 14, n° Ar 8) qu'est daté le cachet *lmrʾhd* "Appartenant à Marhaddou", nom signifiant "Haddou (est) Seigneur", qui est aujourd'hui égaré (G 44; VSA 14; **fig. 18**). Il porte un chameau passant à droite dont c'est l'unique représentation sur un sceau à inscription ouest-sémitique. Le titre *mrʾ* "Seigneur" est typiquement araméen comme l'est le théonyme Haddou. Mais, au contraire du cylindre de Addounouri évoqué plus haut (G 156; VSA 68; lecture B 96, cf. p. 76) où le nom divin est écrit *ʾd* selon l'usage mésopotamien, le nom divin est écrit ici *hd* à la manière syrienne (cf. le sceau de *hdrqy*, fig. 15).

Depuis l'*editio princeps* de ce dernier document qui est constituée par un dessin (Gesenius 1837: n° LXVIII), on admet que le tracé de l'avant-dernière lettre correspond à un *h* mais à partir d'une reproduction (de Vogüé 1868: 115, n° 15), on peut hésiter entre *h* et *ḥ*. Si cette dernière lecture devait être retenue, ce qui ne semble cependant guère possible au vu de la photo d'empreinte CIS II, 79, le théonyme ne serait pas *hd* mais pourrait être *ḥr* qui est la transcription ouest-sémitique habituelle du nom divin égyptien Horus. En toute hypothèse, cette alternative improbable n'affecterait nullement le caractère

15. G 18-24 (cf. Lemaire 1990a; Ornan, *supra*, p. 63). En particulier l'écriture du cachet G 22 (*lsʿly*, cf. n 11) est datée du VIIIe siècle (Naveh 1970a: 12).

16. Il s'agit du fameux cachet G 17, *lšmʿ ʿbd yrbʿm* "Appartenant à Shemaʿ, serviteur de Jéroboam" (II).

17. Cf. aussi le cachet moabite *lkpr* dans NAAG 1991: n° 25 (cf. Ornan, *supra*, p. 69, fig. 69).

araméen du document. De même, la représentation du chameau convient parfaitement à un sceau provenant de Syrie[18] ou d'Egypte.

4. Motifs astraux

1. L'empreinte de cachet circulaire *lbrrkb br pnmw* (**fig. 19**) qui est datée entre 732 et 720 av. J.-C. présente, surmontant l'inscription, un "disque ailé oriental sans volutes", relevant d'une iconographie assyrisante (VSA 129; cf. Parayre 1990a: 278ss., n° 87; *supra*, fig. 1, 32). Etant donné l'origine géographique bien établie de ce document, qui est le royaume de Samʾal en Syrie du Nord, ainsi que sa datation précise au VIIIe siècle grâce aux inscriptions monumentales des mêmes Bar Rakib et Panamou,[19] on le classera pourtant dans la glyptique syrienne.

2. Une ligne horizontale sépare en deux parties la face ellipsoïdale gravée d'un cachet (G 50; VSA 19; **fig. 20**). Celle-ci porte au registre supérieur l'inscription *yʿdrʾl*, nom qui signifie "El aide(ra)". Au registre inférieur un oiseau de profil gauche. Derrière lui astre à six rais, globe et croissant lunaire. La présence de *ʿdr*, qui a progressivement remplaçé *ʿzr* en araméen, suggère une datation à partir de la fin du VIIe siècle (voir B 111).

Pour d'autres documents présentant des combinaisons de motifs à caractère astral similaires, cf. *infra*, fig. 37-38.

IV. L'ICONOGRAPHIE ÉGYPTISANTE

1. Scènes mythologiques

1. Sur le cachet de *brʿtr* qui date de la fin du VIIIe siècle (B 93; **fig. 21**), le décor, essentiellement composé d'un sphinx hiéracocéphale et d'un disque solaire ailé, est égyptisant mais ce théophore de ʿAtar appartient au monde araméen.

2. De même, le scarabéoïde inscrit *lʾḥt brt nṣry* (Avigad 1958b; VSA 145; **fig. 22**), dont le disque solaire appartient au même type égyptisant que le précédent (cf. Parayre 1990a: n°s 18 [= *supra*, p. 45, fig. 30] et 40) et dont l'écriture est contemporaine,[20] est certainement araméen en raison de la présence de *brt* qui signifie "fille de" en araméen.

---

18. On se souvient qu'à la tête de mille chameaux, Gindibu l'arabe a participé à la bataille de Qarqar, quelque cent cinquante ans auparavant (ANET: p. 279).

19. *ʾnh brrkb br pnmw mlk šmʾl* ... (Gibson 1975: 89-93, n°s 15-17).

20. Herr (1978: 17, n° Ar 15) date l'inscription de la fin du VIIIe siècle.

15

16

17

18

19

20

21

22

23

24

25

26

27

2. Personnages

1. Sur le scarabéoïde inscrit *lgbrt mrḥr* (G 88; VSA 30; **fig. 23**) de datation incertaine, on distingue plusieurs éléments d'origine égyptienne, en particulier les deux égides à tête de chacal qui flanquent le personnage central. De plus dans le patronyme du titulaire, l'identité certaine de l'avant-dernière lettre, qui est un *ḥ*, amène à adopter la lecture *mrḥr* "Seigneur *ḥr*", comprenant donc le théonyme *ḥr* = Horus qui avait été écarté sur le sceau de *mrʾhd.*

2. La face inscrite d'un scarabée (B 92; **fig. 24**) présente, entourée d'une simple bordure, une femme de face, vêtue d'une jupe quadrillée et d'une sorte de blouse sur laquelle les seins sont marqués, cheveux retombant en boucles sur les épaules, tenant à bout de bras les tiges de deux éléments floraux. L'inscription *lmrʿly* "Appartenant à Marʿali" se lit dans le champ en commençant par la droite de haut en bas, puis à gauche de bas en haut. Le nom signifie "Le Seigneur (est) élevé". L'écriture de ce document le date de la fin du VIIIe siècle.

3. Motifs divers

1. Sur un scarabéoïde (G 57; VSA 22; **fig. 25**) l'inscription *lʿbdhdd* "Appartenant à ʿAbdhadad" qui est datable autour de 800 (Herr 1978: n° Ar 97) a été placée sous un scarabée à quatre ailes qui occupe la plus grande partie de la face gravée. La graphie *hdd* révèle l'origine syrienne, et donc araméenne, du théonyme, tandis que le scarabée tétraptère relève de l'iconographie sigillaire royale (Gubel 1991a: 919s.).

2. On trouve aussi le titre araméen *mr* "Seigneur" sur le scarabéoïde *lmrsmk* (G 61; VSA 23; **fig. 26**) "Appartenant à Marsamak", nom qui signifie "Le Seigneur a soutenu", qui est datable de la fin du VIIIe siècle (Herr 1978: 35, n° Ar 65). La face inscrite est divisée en trois registres superposés; aux registres supérieur et inférieur un fils d'Horus de profil gauche porteur du signe de Maʿat est flanqué de part et d'autre de signes *ʿankh* verticaux. Au registre médian, deux traits verticaux délimitent un rectangle central occupé par un scarabée à quatre ailes et par le début de l'inscription. De part et d'autre du rectangle, deux uraei verticaux sont tournés symétriquement vers l'extérieur. La disposition et le contenu des registres évoquent l'iconographie phénicienne du IXe siècle.[21]

3. On retrouve encore *mr* sur le scarabée "Appartenant à Marayišuʿa" (*lmrʾyšʿ* = "Le Seigneur a sauvé") (G 61a; VSA 24; **fig. 27**) qui est contem-

21. Ainsi que me le signale E. Gubel.

porain du précédent,[22] lui aussi d'iconographie égyptisante et de type comparable. Ici, les registres supérieur et inférieur sont subdivisés chacun par une ligne horizontale. Au registre supérieur on compte six éléments à la première ligne et neuf à la seconde ligne. Au registre inférieur l'inscription occupe la première ligne et la seconde ligne contient, symétriquement à la première ligne du registre supérieur, six éléments similaires. Dans le rectangle central, un scarabée à quatre ailes et de part et d'autre du rectangle, huit autres éléments sont répartis sur deux lignes. D'identification malaisée, ces derniers pourraient figurer des oiseaux stylisés[23] ou des uraei.

4. La répartition symétrique en cinq registres séparés par une double ligne est encore plus complexe sur le scarabée "Appartenant à Hadadʿezer" (*lhddʿzr* = Hadad a aidé) (G 103; VSA 36; **fig. 28**). Deux scarabées à deux ailes déployées occupent chacun l'un des registres extrêmes. Deux doubles traits verticaux séparent le registre médian en trois parties. A gauche et à droite, deux uraei sont dressés en direction du rectangle central qui est lui-même occupé par un buste de la déesse égyptienne Sekhmet. On compte sept signes *nefer* au registre intermédiaire inférieur et l'inscription occupe le registre intermédiaire supérieur. Découvert pendant la fouille régulière d'une tombe de Saqqarah, sa datation entre le VIIe et le VIe siècle (Galling 1941: 146) ne rend pas compte du caractère plus ancien que révèle l'inscription. Rassemblant des lettres de forme traditionnelle comme le *d* triangulaire, elle montre aussi un *z* caractéristique du VIIIe siècle et une datation vers 750 est plausible (Herr 1978: 11, n° Ar 1; cf. Naveh 1970a: 12).

En dépit des apparences, leur décor ne permet pas de considérer ces trois sceaux comme relevant de l'art égyptien mais plutôt d'un art égyptisant qui fleurissait sur les côtes du Levant au IXe et au VIIIe siècle av. J.-C. On s'attendrait alors à trouver ici une inscription phénicienne mais aucune lettre de ces sceaux ne présentant d'élément phénicien caractéristique, c'est le nom de leur titulaire comportant le titre araméen *mr* ou le théonyme syrien sous sa forme *hd* ou *hdd* qui permet de qualifier d'araméens ces trois derniers sceaux.

5. Le cachet de *ṣdqrmn* (G 16; VSA 3; **fig. 29**) présente deux registres séparés par un bandeau médian portant l'inscription. Au registre supérieur un sphinx ailé, de profil droit, couché, face à un élément encore indéterminé. Au registre inférieur un scarabée à quatre ailes étendues. L'ensemble des lettres amène à proposer une datation au VIIIe siècle (Naveh 1970a: 12) et plus précisément à la fin de ce siècle (Herr 1978: 43, n° Ar 87), mais ici encore c'est le nom du titulaire, évoquant le dieu "tonnant" (cf. Greenfield 1972), qui permet de classer ce document parmi les sceaux araméens.

22. Une datation à la fin du VIIIe siècle est en effet plus exacte que la datation au début du VIIe siècle proposée par Herr 1978: 19, n° Ar 20.

23. Suggestion d'E. Gubel.

6. Sur plusieurs bulles (G 62; VSA 25) découvertes sur le site de l'ancienne Ninive on trouve une disposition analogue, à savoir deux registres séparés par un bandeau médian portant l'inscription *lʿtrʿzr*, nom qui signifie "ʿAtar a aidé". Au registre supérieur, deux signes *ʿankh* verticaux flanquent un astre médian à six rais. Au registre inférieur qui occupe la moitié de la face inscrite un scarabée à quatre ailes étendues, comme sur le document précédent.

V. L'ICONOGRAPHIE PERSE: SCÈNES MYTHOLOGIQUES

1. Un scarabéoïde (G 83; VSA 27; B 119; **fig. 30**) datant approximativement de la fin du VIe siècle av. J.-C. "représente un disque solaire ailé qui porte une gloriole à croissant de lune, dans laquelle un personnage vêtu à l'iranienne tient une fleur de la main gauche et lève la main droite. En bas, deux lions rugissant, prêts à bondir, une patte antérieure levée, sont accroupis symétriquement vers l'extérieur, sur une double ligne de sol dans le champ à droite et à gauche". De part et d'autre de la gloriole, une inscription qui se lit *nḥm tnḥm*, à vocaliser "Nahum (fils de) Tanhum", livre deux noms bien connus dans l'onomastique ouest-sémitique; le nom du titulaire signifie "Consolé" et le patronyme signifie "Consolation".

2. Sur un conoïde octogonal de style achéménide (G 181, cf. p. 133; VSA 85; **fig. 31**) deux quadrupèdes léontocéphales ailés sont représentés debout, symétriquement affrontés, pattes gauches en contact, pattes droites croisées au dessus d'un arbuste médian. Entre leurs mufles, trois lettres araméennes forment le nom *ntn*. Dépourvu du *l* d'appartenance, ce dernier marque vraisemblablement l'étape ultime de la gravure de ce sceau. Bien qu'il ne soit pas caractéristique du vocabulaire araméen, Natan (en hébreu "Il [= Dieu] a donné") a pu être le nom d'un araméen ou d'un judéen de la diaspora (Galling 1941: 133 n. 4).

3. Sur un cylindre (B 129; **fig. 32**) est représenté un souverain achéménide, bras à l'horizontale, saisissant à l'encolure deux taureaux dressés symétriquement. Le taureau de droite est ailé. Le nom *ʿdry* qui signifie "(La divinité) a aidé" se lit de haut en bas dans le champ et l'ensemble se date vers 450 av. J.-C.

VI. ICONOGRAPHIE ET ÉPIGRAPHIE DANS LA GLYPTIQUE ARAMÉENNE

1. Anachronismes

Voici quelques exemples de sceaux historiés ou décorés dont l'écriture dénote certainement une réutilisation ultérieure. Il est évident que la modification d'un sceau anépigraphe historié ou décoré visant à le transformer en un

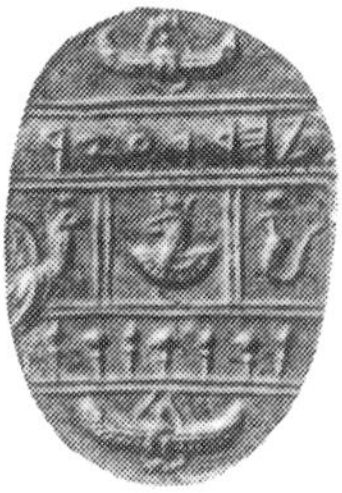

28

29

30

31

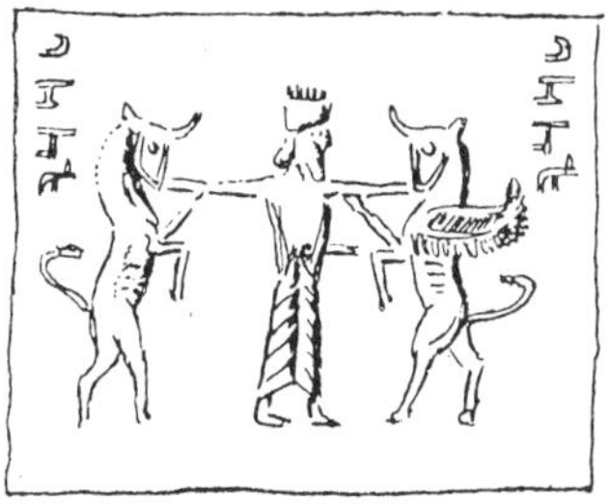

32

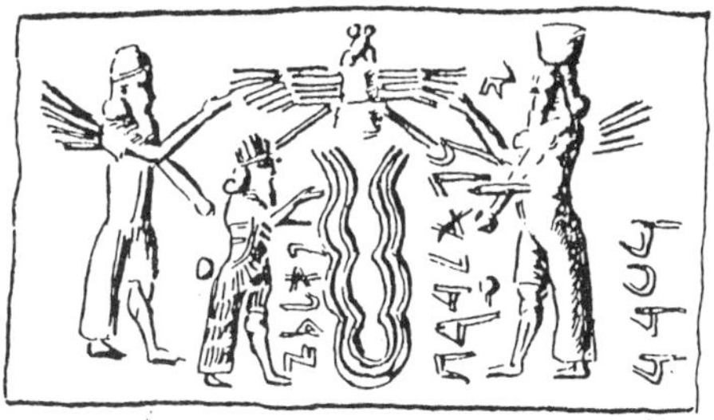

33

34

35

sceau personnel inscrit ne peut être perceptible que si le laps de temps, séculaire, voire multiséculaire, séparant iconographie et épigraphie est réellement mesurable. Or, de façon générale, nos connaissances incomplètes de l'iconographie proche-orientale et de l'épigraphie ouest-sémitique n'autorisent dans ce domaine ni certitude ni précision. Tout au plus peut-on souligner que l'inadaptation de l'inscription à son support révèle le caractère ultérieur de celle-ci.

Un bon exemple est donné par un cylindre relevant de la glyptique assyrienne (G 152; **fig. 33**)[24] qui a vraisemblablement été l'objet d'une élaboration en trois étapes. Il représente deux génies anthropomorphes ailés symétriques mais légèrement distincts l'un de l'autre par la taille et l'habillement. Ils se font face, les deux bras étendus vers l'avant dont le droit est dirigé vers le haut, c'est à dire en direction d'un disque ailé surmontant au milieu de la scène le foudre de Haddou vers lequel ils se dirigent tous deux. Entre le génie plaçé à gauche et le foudre médian, un personnage de taille plus réduite que les génies passe de profil droit, levant vers l'avant les mains, paumes ouvertes vers le haut. Entre ce dernier et le foudre on lit (de bas en haut) une première épigraphe donnant vraisemblablement le nom du propriétaire qui est en même temps représenté ici: *yrpʾl* (Galling 1941: 162, n. 10). Entre le génie de droite et le foudre médian on lit (de haut en bas) *yrpʾl br hdʿdr*. Les lettres de cette seconde épigraphe sont de taille supérieure à celles de la première et se lisent dans le sens inverse. Ne pouvant dater la scène avec précision on peut toutefois penser à une élaboration en plusieurs étapes. Ayant à sa disposition un cylindre gravé antérieurement dont la scène illustre le culte du dieu Haddou représenté par son foudre, *yrpʾl* entend s'identifier au dévot de Haddou en faisant graver son nom devant celui-ci, mais l'endroit est trop exigu pour permettre la gravure du patronyme. Dans un second temps, il affirme son identité complète: *yrpʾl br hdʿdr* en la faisant inscrire de part et d'autre du génie de droite. Cette seconde inscription le mettait davantage encore sous la protection de Haddou dont son patronyme est un théophore. L'écriture du nom patronymique situe la dernière étape de l'élaboration de ce sceau vers la fin du VIIe siècle,[25] ce qui correspond à ce qui a été dit plus haut de l'apparition de *ʿdr* en araméen.

2. *Maladresses*

Le cylindre de "Tubali d'Abilène" (*ltbly mn ʾblnh*, van den Branden & Naster 1981; **fig. 34**) qui relève de la glyptique assyrienne, présente au cen-

---

24. La datation proposée par Galling (1941: 162) va de la fin du IXe au début du VIIe siècle av. J.-C.

25. De ce point de vue la datation vers 700 proposée par Herr (1978: 38, n° Ar 73) paraît trop haute.

tre un arbre sacré entouré d'une couronne de palmettes flanqué de part et d'autre par deux génies androcéphales à la coiffure hémisphérique et à l'arrière-train de taureau. De leurs bras dressés ils supportent un disque ailé d'où surgit le buste d'un personnage central tête barbue de profil gauche, coiffée d'une sorte de tiare, salué par deux acolytes à la coiffure hémisphérique qui le flanquent de part et d'autre.[26] A gauche un personnage debout de profil, barbu, vêtu d'une longue tunique, élève la main vers l'élément central et, symétriquement à lui, un personnage recouvert d'un habit pisciforme, tenant une situle dans la main gauche, pratique l'aspersion de la main droite. Tournant le dos au personnage de gauche, un génie barbu et portant une coiffure hémisphérique, long vêtu, porte la jambe gauche vers l'avant et regarde vers l'arrière. Il tient dans la main droite une arme blanche et sous le bras gauche un quadrupède dont la tête est tournée vers l'arrière. Sous l'arrière-train de ce dernier, un personnage simiesque, de petite taille est accroupi vers la droite; au-dessus, sept astres à six rais.

Ce document appartient bien entendu au groupe des cylindres assyriens qui ont été examinés au début de ce travail. On l'a classé dans cette dernière partie car il permet d'illustrer le caractère parfois hétérogène des inscriptions par rapport aux décors, inadaptation que la maladresse de certains lapicides nous permet dans certains cas de reconnaître encore. La présence de la préposition *mn* aramaïse ici l'inscription de façon certaine mais l'ordre des deux lignes du texte est inversé puisque le sens de la lecture donne *mn ʾblnh ltbly* (Millard 1983b: 103 n. 20; Bordreuil 1988a: 444s.), alors qu'il convient de lire *ltbly mn ʾblnh*. Cela montre que l'inscription a été gravée après coup sur un cylindre d'origine mésopotamienne qui n'était pas destiné primitivement à la porter. Ici on ne peut pas parler d'anachronisme puisque l'iconographie et l'inscription datent toutes deux des environs de 650 av. J.-C. mais plutôt d'une indépendance foncière de l'une par rapport à l'autre. Le souhait exprimé par le titulaire de s'approprier la scène déjà gravée sur le cylindre a fait l'objet d'une réalisation trop rapide et le lapicide n'aura pas pris le temps de choisir le meilleur emplacement pour chacune des deux lignes.

3. Hétérogénéité

Le conoïde octogonal portant l'anthroponyme *šmšʿdry* (B 111; **fig. 35**) illustre un autre type d'inadéquation attestée sur un certain nombre de sceaux: celle qu'on peut observer entre le décor et le nom propre lui-même. En effet, la face inférieure présente le buste d'un dieu portant la tiare, l'épée et un bâton, émergeant main levée du croissant lunaire situé au dessus d'une plante. Derrière le dieu, la bêche de Mardouk et le stylet de Nabou sont dressés sur une estrade, mais l'inscription, gravée de haut en bas sur une face latérale,

26. Cf. *supra*, p. 82f, la description de l'élément central du cylindre de *mrbrk* (**fig. 11**).

porte un théophore de Shamash alors qu'aucun attribut de ce dernier n'est visible. L'iconographie, d'inspiration mésopotamienne, ne présente aucun élément susceptible de donner une indication chronologique précise mais l'inscription est datable de la fin du VIIe siècle et la réutilisation est patente. Il en va de même du cachet *lbrky* (B 95; cf. Ornan, *supra*, p. 62, fig. 31) qui présente une scène analogue mais ici, le dieu n'est pas identifiable au moyen d'attributs spécifiques et l'hypocoristique ne permet pas non plus de l'identifier avec précision avec une autre divinité.

VII. PEUT-ON PARLER D'UNE ICONOGRAPHIE DE LA GLYPTIQUE ARAMÉENNE INSCRITE?

Revenant au propos liminaire de ce travail, on doit admettre que des constantes iconographiques se laissent malaisément discerner dans la glyptique de langue et d'écriture araméennes. En effet, on a vu que la plupart des documents examinés amènent à l'évidence que les lapicides araméens ont puisé dans des répertoires préexistants d'une grande variété. Empruntant scènes complexes et éléments décoratifs à la *koinè* proche-orientale du Ier millénaire, leur centre d'intérêt pouvait osciller selon le cas entre la Perse, la Mésopotamie et l'Egypte via la Phénicie. Il s'ensuit que les caractères spécifiques éventuels d'une iconographie araméenne devront être recherchés en dehors de ces grandes provinces, relativement bien connues aujourd'hui, de l'art oriental.

Trois documents illustrent à des titres divers ce qui n'est pour l'instant qu'une piste de recherche[27]:

1. Un cylindre (G 150; VSA 62; **fig. 36**) présente une scène composée à gauche d'un quadrupède longiligne de profil droit, allaitant son petit et détournant la tête. A droite un disque ailé surmonte un losange et un poisson. Au milieu, l'inscription en écriture araméenne *lbʿlrgm* "Appartenant à Baʿalragam" se lit sur le sceau de bas en haut, flanquée en haut de part et d'autre par deux astres radiés, en bas à droite par une hampe, à gauche par un étendard de Sin surmontant un second losange.[28] Sur l'étendard de Sin, qui est certainement l'élément caractéristique de la scène, figurent de part et d'autre

27. Inaugurée dans une étude d'O. Keel (1990c); cf. GGG: chap. VIII, spéc. §§ 173-177, 182-188.

28. Ces éléments, présents à l'état isolé sur les trois cylindres assyrisants examinés plus haut, seraient-ils des yeux comme le propose Galling? Il s'agirait alors de représentations orientales apotropaïques destinées à combattre le "mauvais oeil"; leur équivalent occidental serait-il "l'œil de Min" des cachets hébreux et transjordaniens? Voir la liste dans Bordreuil 1992: 200.

36

37

38

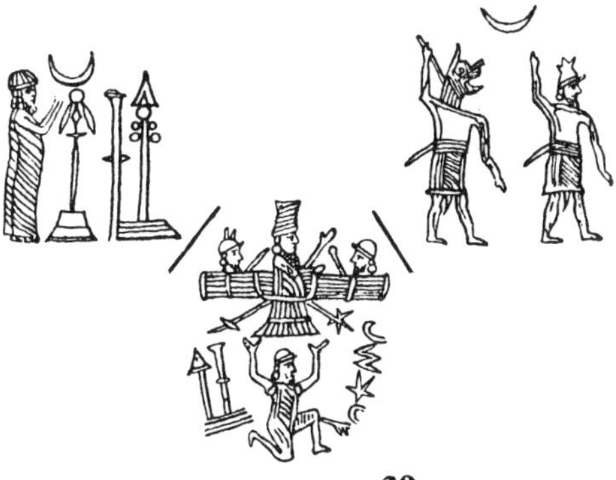

39

de la base du croissant deux objets de forme glandulaire.[29] Le document est daté peu avant 700 (Galling 1941: 162; Herr 1978: n° Ar 67: fin du VIIIe siècle). Ce type d'étendard de Sin est précisément représenté sur le relief du roi Barrakib de Zincirli cité plus haut, daté des environs de 730 av. J.-C. Sur ce relief le roi, représenté siégeant sur son trône, confesse dans l'inscription champlevée qu'on lit sur le côté: *mrʾy bʿl ḥrn* "Mon Seigneur (est) le Maître de Ḥarran". Or, le seul emblème divin représenté sur le relief est une lune

29. Illustré par un cachet inscrit *lʿwr* qui a été récemment publié (Lemaire 1990c: n° 4). Comme le propose l'éditeur, il s'agit certainement d'une transcription du néo-assyrien *A-u-i-ra-a* qu'on peut rapprocher de l'hébreu *ʿiwwēr* "aveugle" (ainsi Fales 1986: 258) auquel on ajoutera le syriaque. Pourtant, ce nom, absent de l'onomastique araméenne déjà connue, de même que le sceau qui le porte, ne peuvent être classés parmi les documents araméens proprement dits qui font l'objet de ce travail. Il me paraît vain de chercher avec F.M. Fales ce nom sur la tablette araméenne de 635 (*supra*, n. 13) car l'examen direct de l'objet, dont témoignait déjà la photo de l'*editio princeps*, montre une haste courte qui ne peut appartenir qu'à un *d* (cf. les hastes longues des *r*). La lecture *ʿwyd* et non * *ʿwyr* doit donc être maintenue; sur le nom *ʿwyd* voir Maraqten 1988: 196.

(croissant et disque imbriqués), supportée par une hampe et munie de glands. D'autre part à Ḥarran, ville distante de 200 km à l'est de Zincirli, ont été retrouvées plusieurs stèles des VIIIe et VIIe siècles montrant ce même emblème et l'inscription de Barrakib établit expressément l'identité entre l'emblème de Zincirli et le "Maître de Ḥarran". Si l'identité précise de ce dernier n'est pas indiquée sur le relief de Zincirli, elle est parfaitement établie par les inscriptions assyriennes de Ḥarran: il s'agit du dieu lunaire Sin.[30] Le caractère insolite de la juxtaposition d'un étendard de Sin et d'un théophore de Baʿal disparaît dès lors qu'on reporte dans cette inscription sigillaire l'équivalence établie par l'inscription de Barrakib entre l'emblème lunaire et l'appellatif divin Baʿal (= "Maître"). Sur le cylindre de Baʿalragam, c'est donc le dieu Sin, symbolisé par son étendard, qui est discernable sous le titre Baʿal.

2. Un cachet de base inscrite ovale, connu depuis quelques années (Avigad 1986b: 53; **fig. 37**) porte sur sa base plate entourée d'une simple bordure une inscription qui est vraisemblablement araméenne: *lšmšʿzr ʿbdšhr*. Entre les deux lignes: un signe *ʿankh* horizontal, un astre radié et un croissant de lune. Le nom du propriétaire qui signifie "Shamash a aidé" est évidemment de connotation solaire, mais ce personnage est aussi "serviteur (prêtre?) de Shahr" qui est un dieu lunaire. Il est dès lors tentant d'interpréter l'astre radié non pas comme l'étoile d'Ishtar mais comme le soleil (*šmš*) voisinant avec l'astre lunaire (*šhr*) (Bordreuil 1986g). L'écriture est difficile à localiser, car elle présente des caractéristiques araméennes et d'autres qui pourraient rappeler l'écriture hébraïque. La présence du dieu lunaire Shahr, connu à Neirab dans les inscriptions de ses prêtres Sin-zer-ibni et Siʾgabbar (Gibson 1975: n°s 18s.), nous oriente vers la région araméenne de Syrie septentrionale où plusieurs royaumes araméens ont coexisté durant le premier tiers du Ier millénaire. Se pose alors la question de la relation de Sin et de Shahr. Puisque les deux prêtres de ce dernier portent des noms théophores de Sin: accadien pour Sin-zer-ibni et araméen pour Siʾgabbar, il y a certainement une grande proximité voire une identification d'un dieu avec l'autre. En l'absence d'autres données, on peut se demander si la vénération du dieu-lune Sin sous le nom de Shahr n'était pas l'apanage de groupes aramaïsés d'origine arabe puisque *šhr*, attesté dans l'onomastique arabe ancienne (Knauf ^{2}1989: 5), deviendra en syriaque puis en arabe le nom générique du mois.

3. Le cylindre de *brkʾ br gdl br tblṭ* (G 94; **fig. 38**), est notable en raison de la place considérable prise par l'inscription qui énumère sur trois lignes le nom du titulaire, suivi par celui de son père et de manière tout à fait inusitée par celui de son grand-père. Ce dernier transcrit un anthroponyme accadien signifiant "Qu'Elle (la déesse) fasse vivre" mais les noms qui suivent relèvent de l'onomastique occidentale. On pourrait même dire que la succession du

30. Voir O. Keel, dans l'article cité *supra*, n. 27.

nom accadien de l'aïeul et des noms occidentaux de son fils (*br*) et de son petit-fils évoque une aramaïsation progressive. Le décor ici est de dimensions modestes mais on y observe une iconographie astrale plus complète qu'à l'ordinaire puisqu'un globe, qui doit être une planète, est joint à l'astre radié et au croissant lunaire. Comme sur le cachet précédent et sur celui de *ʿwr* (*supra*, n. 29), la présence du signe *ʿankh* permet de considérer que la composition dans son ensemble n'est pas mésopotamienne mais qu'elle pourrait, comme l'écriture de l'inscription, trouver son origine dans la Syrie peu avant 700.[31]

4. Sur la base du conoïde *lšʾʿn*! (G 107; **fig. 39**) un personnage, genou droite en terre, soutient un disque ailé androcéphale coiffé d'une tiare, bras dressé, flanqué de deux acolytes, bras dressé, têtes tournées vers le centre (cf. Ornan, *supra*, p. 57, fig. 12, p. 60). A gauche, la bêche de Mardouk et le stylet de Nabou, sont répétés sur l'une des faces latérales. Le nom *šʾʿn*: "Sin a répondu",[32] gravé dans l'espace disponible vraisemblablement dans un second temps, est indépendant de cette scène mais pas des deux autres puisque l'étendard de Sin a été rajouté sur la face latérale déjà mentionnée et que, sur l'autre face, le croissant de lune au-dessus des deux *apkallū* (pour lesquelles cf. Ornan, *supra*, pp. 56s. et fig. 13) montre que ce sceau a bien été 'sinisé' par un araméen.

Ayant écarté les types de décors d'origine étrangère que les lapicides araméens ont su mettre à la disposition de leurs clients, il reste que des représentations à ce point récurrentes du soleil, des étoiles et des planètes et surtout celle de l'astre des nuits (croissant et pleine lune) dans l'iconographie sigillaire des royaumes araméens, dénotent une faveur particulière, voire une véritable prédilection parmi des populations araméophones, fussent-elles d'origine mésopotamienne ou arabe et d'aramaïsation récente, pour des cultes astraux "syriens" encore largement méconnus aujourd'hui.

CATALOGUE ET SOURCES DES ILLUSTRATIONS

1. Estampille sur anse de jarre: *yhwd yhwʿzr pḥwʾ* (Avigad 1976a: pl. 17:7).
2. Cachet de Nouršiʾ serviteur de ʿAttaršumki, *lnršʾʿbd ʿtrsmk* (B 86).
3. Cachet conoïde octogonal de Sin-aḫa-uṣur, *lšnḥṣr* (dessin de Noga Z'evi d'après B 98; cf. Ornan, *supra*, p. 57, fig. 10).
4. Cachet de Sin-abi, *lšnʾb* (IMJ 71.46.84; Gubel 1991a: 921, fig. 4,d).

---

31. Herr 1978: 40, n° Ar 79. La date proposée par Galling (1941: 161) – début du VIe siècle – doit être révisée à la hausse.

32. Sur *šʾ* = Sin en araméen, voir l'interprétation de *šʾgbr* par Kaufmann 1970: 270s.; Gibson 1975: 97s., n° 19; sur *ʿn*, 3e p.m.s. de *ʿNY*, cp. *qn*, 3e p.m.s. du verbe *QNY* dans Kilamouwa II 1, Gibson 1982: 41, n° 14 et participe actif à Karatepe III 18, Bron 1979: 120.

5. Cylindre de Baraq serviteur de ʿAtarshamin, *ḥtm brq ʿbd ʿtršmn* (B 85).
6. Cylindre d'Elʾamar, *ḥtm ʾlʾmr* (collection privée, localisation actuelle inconnue; dessin de Jürgen Rotner d'après Teissier 1984: n° 236).
7. Cylindre anépigraphe des fouilles de Samos (dessin de Jürgen Rotner d'après Diehl 1965: fig. 1).
8. Cylindre de Yapaʿhaddou l'interprète (des songes), *ḥtm ypʿhd mpšr* (collection de l'Université de Iéna; dessin de Jürgen Rotner d'après Weber 1920: n° 311).
9. Cylindre de Sadah/Sarah, *lšdh* ou *lšrh* (collection privée, localisation actuelle inconnue; photographie de Dominique Collon).
10. Cylindre d'Elyahab, *lʾlyhb* (collection privée, localisation actuelle inconnue; CIS II: n° 78; cf. G 158).
11. Cylindre de Marbarak, *lmrbrk* (BM 102966; dessin Hildi Keel-Leu d'après photo du musée).
12. Cylindre d'Assourgad (?), *lsrgd* (BM 102964; dessin Hildi Keel-Leu d'après photo du musée).
13. Cylindre de ʿAbd-Kadiah, *ḥtm ʿbdkdʾh* (collection privée, localisation actuelle inconnue; photographie de Dominique Collon).
14. Scarabée de Houdou le scribe, *lhwdw sprʾ* (BM 48508; Welten 1977c: 305, fig. 78:18).
15. Cachet de Haddouraqi serviteur de Haddoubaʿadi, *lhdrqy ʿbd hdbʿd* (BM 48497; G 129).
16. Cachet de Bethelroʿy, *lbytʾlrʿy* (dessin NogaZ'evi d'après B 126; cf. Ornan, *supra*, p. 55, fig. 3).
17. Cachet de Rupti, *lrpty* (B 89).
18. Cachet de Marhaddou, *lmrʾhd* (localisation actuelle inconnue; G 44).
19. Empreinte sur une bulle du cachet de Barrakib fils de Panamou, *lbrrkb br pnmw* (Sendschirli V: pl. 38,b).
20. Cachet de *yʿdrʾl* (photographie de P. Bordreuil).
21. Cachet de Barʿatar, *lbrʿtr* (dessin de E. Gubel d'après B 93; cf. *infra*, p. 117, fig. 38).
22. Cachet d'Aḥat fille de Naṣri, *lʾḥt brt nṣry* (Haifa, Musée Hecht, H-1488; photographie du musée).
23. Cachet de *gbrt mrḥr* (localisation actuelle inconnue; G 88).
24. Cachet de Marʿali, *lmrʿly* (B 92).
25. Cachet de ʿAbdhadad, *lʿbdhdd* (jadis Berlin, VA 34, perdu pendant la guerre; G 57).
26. Cachet de Marsamak, *lmrsmk* (BM 48506; dessin de Hildi Keel-Leu d'après photo du musée).
27. Cachet de Marayišuʿa, *lmrʾyšʿ* (localisation actuelle inconnue; G 61a).
28. Cachet de Hadadʿezer, *lhddʿzr* (Le Caire, Musée d'Egypte?; CIS II: n° 124).
29. Cachet de Ṣadiqramman, *lṣdqrmn* (jadis collection P. Altmann, localisation actuelle inconnue).
30. Cachet de Naḥoum (fils de) Tanḥoum, *nḥm tnḥm* (dessin de Hildi Keel-Leu d'après B 119).
31. Cachet de Natan, *ntn* (localisation actuelle inconnue; G 181).
32. Cylindre de ʿAdri, *ʿdry* (G 164; cf. B 129).
33. Cylindre de Yeraphʾel fils de Haddouʿadar, *lyrpʾl br hdʿdr* (BM 102963; G 152).
34. Cylindre de Tubali d'Abilène, *ltbly mn ʾblnh* (collection M. de S.).
35. Cachet conoïde octogonal de Shamashʿadri, *lšmšʿdry* (dessin de Hildi Keel-Leu d'après B 111; cf. Ornan, *supra*, p. 62, fig. 30).
36. Cylindre de Baʿalragam, *lbʿlrgm* (Oxford, Ashmolean Museum, 1889.372; dessin de Hildi Keel-Leu d'après une photographie du musée).
37. Cachet de Shamashʿazar serviteur de Shahr, *lšmšʿzr ʿbdšhr* (Jérusalem, IMJ 85.15.21; dessin de Noga Z'evi d'après Avigad 1986b).
38. Cylindre de Barakaʾ fils de *gdl*, fils de Tuballiṭ, *brkʾ br gdl br tblṭ* (G 148, cf. B 94).
39. Cachet conoïde ellipsoïdal de Sinʿana, *lsʾʿn* (New York, Metropolitan Museum of Art n° 86-11-29; ESE II: 146s., G 107).

THE ICONOGRAPHY OF INSCRIBED PHOENICIAN GLYPTIC

Eric GUBEL
Bruxelles

I. SCOPE OF THE SUBJECT

Before proceeding to the present contribution's main subject, some questions as to its title should first be raised. Are we to deal with the glyptic evidence from *Phoenicia* properly, or, alternatively, with seals from the *Phoenician world*? However rhetorical this question may seem, its bearing on the geographical area as well as on the chronological range to be covered by the present survey is obvious. In both cases, the question of the chronological definition of the Phoenician civilization imposes itself.

A brief review of the *palaeo-Phoenician* period, which falls beyond the scope of the present colloquium's topic, may suffice here. In view of some anachronisms that turned up in the Phoenician period *sensu stricto*, it should be borne in mind that the palaeo-Phoenician material highlights the successive phases of cultural interaction Phoenicia has known. This phenomenon is illustrated by a seal in the Old Babylonian style from a tomb at Ruweise (Porada 1975-6), whereas Byblos has recently been tipped as the presumed origin of a group of mostly "green jasper" (rather green stone facies) cylinder and stamp seals of the "Egyptianizing Syrian" style (Collon 1986a; Keel 1989a). Growing international currents are also witnessed in the production of stamp seals, predominantly scarabs, from the early second millennium onwards. It is precisely to this period that we should turn our attention in order to establish the origin of the use of inscribed seals in the Phoenician realm.

II. The use of inscribed seals in second-millennium-BC Phoenicia

Three palaeo-Phoenician glyptic groups prefigure the use of inscribed seals on the Phoenician coast: scarabs and cylinder seals with names of rulers or officials written in Egyptian hieroglyphs, and cylinder seals with names of rulers written in cuneiform.[1]

1. Scarabs with names of rulers and officials written in Egyptian hieroglyphs

This group exemplifies the impact of the commercial traffic between Byblos and Egypt by the choice of the scarab, as well as by the fact that these seals were found in the homelands of both trade-partners alike. The examples represented here (**figs. 1-4**) show that the local rulers of Byblos transcribed their names in Egyptian hieroglyphs. Unlike the well-known pectoral of the Gyblite king Ibshemouabi (**fig. 5**) the outline of the scarabs' base apparently rendered unnecessary the addition of a cartouche. As illustrated by other examples, this royal practice was followed by officials working in the administration of the Egyptian overlords, or, later, acting for them as mayors of Byblos (Martin 1971: index, s.v. Jebail).

1. We may exclude from consideration an allegedly palaeo-Phoenician cylinder seal bearing a "Proto-Sinaitic" inscription presumed to mention a resident of Irqata, as this seal has been shown to be a forgery (Buchanan 1966: 213, no. 1072; Sass 1988: 99).

1

2

3

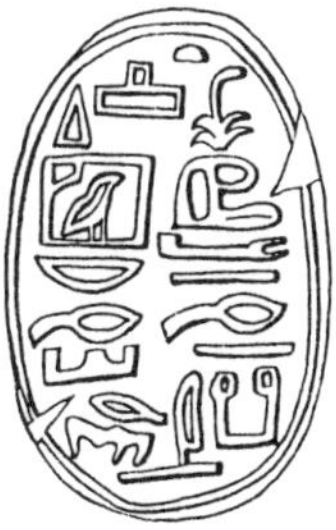

4

5

6

7

2. Cylinder seals with names of rulers and officials written in Egyptian hieroglyphs

Several cylinders, equally assigned to the production of Gyblite workshops, are by far more interesting owing to the combination of inscriptions and their iconographical context (Collon 1986a). Of special significance is the example of **fig. 6**, where the Egyptianizing trend is illustrated by elements of the scene and by the use of the cartouche, here containing the Amorite name *ḥndy*. The fact that this royal name equally occurs on scarabs, strengthens the assumption that a historical ruler was referred to (Ward 1976: 362-363). As illustrated by a beautiful hematite cylinder from Alalakh (**fig. 7**), the use of cartouches with Egyptian hieroglyphs was also adopted elsewhere on the Levantine coast (Collon 1982: 127-129; Keel 1989b: 257), albeit with decorative, rather than meaningful hieroglyphs.[2]

3. Cylinder seals with names of rulers written in cuneiform

On two more cylinders from Phoenicia the Egyptianizing style is maintained. The owners, Adummu and his son Annipi/Anniwi, were kings of Sidon in the 13th century. Following the example of their more illustrious counterparts at Alalakh or Ebla, they preferred their names to be written in cuneiform (**figs. 8-9**), albeit reversed in the father's case. Considering the lapse of time between the production of these seals, the Gyblite scarabs and, allegedly, the aforesaid cylinders as well, it would be unwise to draw any conclusions from the preference of script.

III. The Role of Inscribed Seals in Phoenician Glyptic

1. Ratio

The aim of the present colloquium being to further our appreciation of inscribed seals within the West Semitic glyptic production, some attention should first be paid to the percentual part they represent. Since the majority of Phoenician seals published thus far has not come to us via regular excavations, it remains an impossible task to express their number in absolute terms. As far as published examples of ascertained origin go, the following chart may give give an idea about the quantitative relationship between the inscribed and anepigraphic provenanced seals. The number of inscribed seals hardly nears 3% of the total excavated in the Phoenician East, and 0.3% in the West.

2. Compare also the "Green Jasper Workshop" example in Teissier 1984: no. 513 (see enlargement on p. 325, erroneously labelled no. 539).

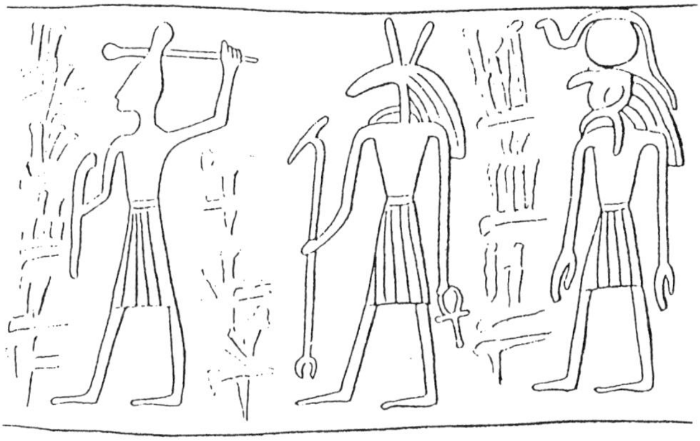

8

9

10

11

Site	Number of seals Uninscribed (estimated)	Inscribed (recorded)
Orient		
Tyre	48	3
Sidon	44	1
Byblos	121	6
Arwad	8	–
'Amrit' (Tartous)	253	5
total:	474	15
West		
Tharros	3000	4
Carthage	717	3
Ibiza	242	3
total:	3959	10

Chart I: Ratio of uninscribed and inscribed seals (sealings excluded) from five eastern and three western sites.[3]

2. *Chronology*

On the evidence of Bordreuil's 1986 catalogue (B 1-39), to which examples in Jerusalem (HD 30-31, 118-128) and Oxford (Buchanan & Moorey 1988: nos. 294, 299) may be added, the history of epigraphic Phoenician glyptic appears to span about six centuries, from the second half of the ninth till the early part of the third century in the East and till the first century BC in the West.

The carefully carved amethyst scaraboid of Ḥadi (**fig. 10**), now in the Louvre and assigned by Bordreuil to the last quarter of the ninth century on palaeographic grounds, is no doubt one of the most important examples of the early specimens. As this seal shows, both style and iconography of Phoenician gyptic had already gained a mature status before the end of the ninth century. The general posture, the details of both male persons' wigs and outfits as well as the particular type of the sceptre in their hands, are perfectly matched by a plaque (**fig. 11**) representative of what can henceforth safely

3. Sources: Tyre: Gubel 1983: pp. 37-44, 51-52; Gubel 1987b: 40 (n° 7), 60-61, pl. IV = B 26. Sidon: B 17. Byblos: VSF 59-63; Gubel 1991a: 914, fig. 1:a, 2. Amrit: VSF 18, 22, 23, 28, 31. Tharros: VSF 11, 13,14 (and possibly 8, 10, 93, 96-97). Carthage: VSF 39 (and possibly 67?); Vercoutter 1945: nos. 767-768, pp. 260-261, pl. XXI; and *infra*, pp. 114ff. Ibiza: VSF 45, 46, 52, 54.

12

13

14

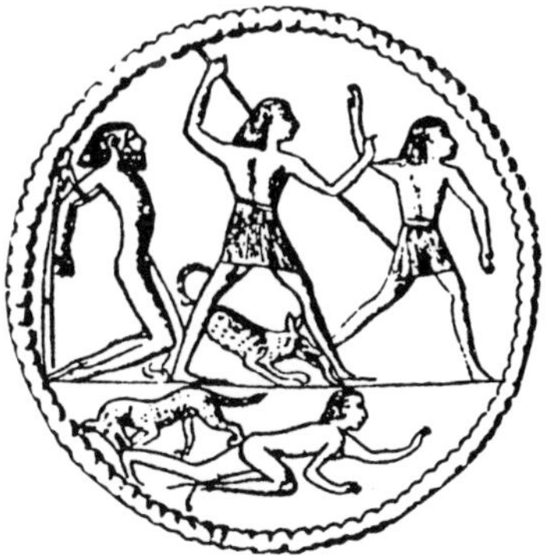

15

be regarded as one of the more archaic groups of Phoenician ivories found at Nimrud.

3. Seals and other media

Intimate links exist between the work of ivory carvers and seal cutters, which often prove helpful in locating the origin of the seals themselves. In this respect, the stylistic comparison between the limestone scaraboid eventually inscribed with the name of Yeqamyahu (**fig. 12**; cf. Sass, *infra*, p. 228, section F2) and a series of Phoenician ivories (**fig. 13**)[4] and bowls should be noted. The fact that the letters are squeezed in between the elements of the design indeed strengthens the assumption that the inscription was a later addition.

Quite a few other early Phoenician seals could be quoted as supplementary examples of the similarities between the work of seal cutters, ivory carvers and metal-workers. Thus, the motif of the brownish-red limestone scarab of Ṣûri, now in the Hecht Museum, Haifa (**fig. 14**), perfectly ties in with

4. Hermann 1986: pl. 19:85; cf. *ibid.*: pl. 19:86 for a plaque from the same workshop figuring a *winged* hero. The striding position of both antagonists on the seal contrasts with the more dynamic but less carefully executed figures on these ivories. The latter are undoubtedly Phoenician copies of the forerunners of this composition on the Curium Bowl (Frankfort 1970: fig. 393), represented by the ivories on Herrmann's pl. 17:79 and 81.

16

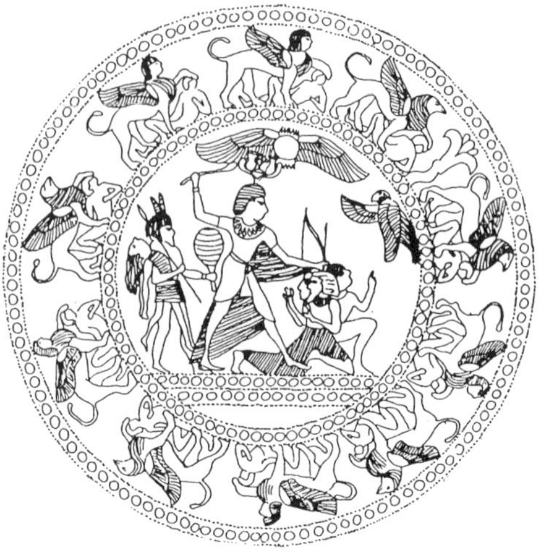

18

17

elaborations of the same theme elsewhere. Not only does it appear on Phoenician bowls as suggested by the debased version on an example from Praeneste (**fig. 15**) but, as pointed out by Avigad (1985: 6-7), it figures on an ivory from Samaria. On the seal of *ʾny* (**fig. 16**) the letters of the name are dispersed between the legs of a hieracocephalous sphinx *protecting* a seated man rather than trampling a defeated victim. Whereas this distinction is quite clear from other representations showing this heraldic hybrid protecting a winged snake for example (Herrmann 1986: pl. 28:119), exactly the same motif is met with on several Phoenician ivories (**fig. 17**) as well as on the Idalion bowl (**fig. 18**). The comparison, in fig. 17, which extends to the feather atop the wig of the recumbent male figure, suggests that the winged beetle was copied from a lower panel of similar composition. This would corroborate the opinion that the seal cutters' products were inspired by the more significant narrative friezes of bowls and ivory furniture inlays.

4. Distribution

Another question to be tackled in the context of this survey concerns the chrono-spatial distribution of inscribed Phoenician seals. In other words, is it possible to discern a pattern that could be explained in historical terms?

As for Phoenicia's immediate neighbours, the adoption of the icon of the striding "Pharaonic" figure or the four-winged beetle emblem on royal and official seals and sealings in early Ammonite, Israelite and Judaean glyptic clearly illustrates the cultural emanation of Phoenician art from the ninth until the early seventh century BC (e.g. Welten 1969; Lemaire 1981; Herr 1985; Younker 1985). One should of course add a few imported seals to these examples of cultural interaction, such as e.g. the seal showing a four-winged scarab from the well-known tomb of Adoninur at Amman (Harding 1953: pl. VI:2; cf. Hübner, *infra*, p. 159, fig. 19). Quite a few Aramaic seals bear witness to a similar impact of this phenomenon in the territories to the north and east of the Phoenician coastal strip (e.g. G 57, 60-62). The adoption of identical motifs and decorative devices on seals of officials in the West Semitic world of the day strongly reminds us of the "kings of the coast", an expression used by the Assyrian invaders to designate their adversaries in this part of the Near East. Besides its geographical relevance from the Assyrian point of view, the term is likely to have had an appropriate significance to the rulers concerned because of the apparent validity of its cultural connotation (cf. *infra*, pp. 118f).

Further north, where the gradual spread of Phoenician commercial interests is attested to since the ninth century by a series of well-known bilingual inscriptions, not a single inscribed Phoenician seal has been recovered in a controlled excavation. The pseudo-*ʿankh* and "Hyksos-angles" on one of the noteable exceptions allegedly from Cilicia (B 38) hardly need to be mentioned here, if Bordreuil is indeed correct in regarding this and similar seals (B 39) as fakes. Finally, I would like to remind that the seal of *mṣry* (**fig. 48**), perhaps to be identified as a Moabite king (but see Lemaire, *supra*, pp. 15-16), is said to have been acquired in Asia Minor. André Lemaire, in our symposium, has drawn our attention to the seal "of the Tyrian", an inscribed cylinder from Cilicia (VSF 68; Avigad 1985: note 36; but see Lemaire, *supra*, p. 16, note 13).

The few Phoenician seals found in Mesopotamia are traditionally linked with the Assyrian campaigns in the West, although, taking into account the many attestations of Phoenician trade activities in Mesopotamia, this view is undoubtedly one-sided. The examples in question include the late-eighth-century seal of ʿAbdbaʿal from Khorsabad (B 8), the agate scaraboid of Hanaʾ, allegedly from Baghdad (HD 126; VSF 70) and the sixth-century seal of ʿAbdmilk from Babylon (G 25). A brown-stone scaraboid from a cache in Nimrud's Nabu temple, attributed to the latter part of the seventh century by the excavators, should be added to this series even if it remains undecided whether the four alphabetic signs are Phoenician or Aramaic (Mallowan 1966: I, 259, no. 238).

The scarcity of inscribed Phoenician seals from Cyprus is surprising in view of the island's strong ties with the Phoenician mainland since the early Iron Age.[5] And, as a matter of fact, the same applies, for very much the same reasons, to the provenanced seals from Egypt, Phoenicia's traditional partner since the third millennium.[6]

5. Materials

Spot-checks in the major compilations of Phoenician seals suffice to establish that most of the stone varieties used were logically judged suitable for the addition of inscriptions. If one would really want to discern a pattern in the wide array of materials, the absence of glass is remarkable, for the hardness of the material ranges up to 6 on Moh's scale and would therefore have been appropriate for the engravers' purpose.

Soft stone varieties, on the other hand, are extremely rare and were obviously discarded in view of the practical function of inscribed seals. This might explain why the examples of individual groups of Phoenician seals such as the "Egyptian blue" production are invariably uninscribed. And if not entirely non-existant, inscriptions are exceptional within the Egyptianizing "steatite" groups as well, as already pointed out.

IV. Relationship between seal and inscription

1. Types of inscribed seals and sealings

The connection between inscriptions and seal-types is summarized in the chart appearing on the following page.

1.1. Scarabs and scaraboids

A Steatite scarabs

A1 The "pseudo-Hyksos" group

The first category of Phoenician seals includes steatite scarabs, the earliest examples of which are remarkably reminiscent in their style and iconography of "Hyksos"-age prototypes. Although the archaic phase of this category can be illustrated by a few dozen seals with common characteristics, solid dating evidence remains wanting. The fact that most of the items in question either

5. G 49, said to come from Cyprus, features a bird resting on the body of a uraeus, if not on the stem of a stylized plant, as on HD 127.

6. Amongst the notable exceptions is a dark-stone scarab formerly in the collection of the Rev. Dr. Ch. Murch, Luxor (Müller 1903) which we will republish with P. Bordreuil.

Glyptic Types	Inscriptions East	Inscriptions West
Scarabs	•	•
Scaraboids	•	•
Scaraboids, bifacial	•	
Scaraboids, pseudo-bifacial	•	
Cubical seals	•	
Sealings		
Bullae		•
Clay pellets	•	•
Jar impressions		
Stamped handles	•	•

Chart II: Seal-types and inscriptions

stem from illicit excavations in the Tyrian realm or from sites in northern Israel nonetheless suggests that their origin has to be sought in meridional, rather than in central or northern Phoenicia. Since the compositions and most of the decorative designs were obviously derived from Hyksos prototypes, I would suggest to name these seals the "pseudo-Hyksos group".

The group includes scarabs, a few of them inscribed with pseudo-hieroglyphs. This is for example the case of the scarab in **fig. 19**, as well as of some other unpublished seals from Tell Rechidiyeh in the Tyrian hinterland. As will be demonstrated in a separate contribution, eighth-century seals such as the steatite scarab of **fig. 20** with cartouches containing both apparently meaningless hieroglyphs and the owner's name ("Shemaryau" in Hebrew) probably represent the most recent output of the "pseudo-Hyksos" workshop(s) and their imitations in neighbouring countries. The striking resemblance in style and layout, as well as the use of meaningless hieroglyphs on several contemporary hardstone scarabs (cf. **fig. 60**), equally reflects the impact of that workshop.

A2 Persian Period steatite scarabs

For reasons remaining unexplained, steatite once more became fashionable during or shortly before the Persian period. Scarabs belonging to this last production phase have been studied by Hölbl (1986: 259), who assigned them to an oriental workshop (or workshops) active from the sixth to the fourth centuries. Although inscriptions on such seals are usually limited to meaningless hieroglyphs or Menkheperre cartouches, the one exception (**fig. 21**) is very remarkable indeed. As pointed out by Pernigotti (1983; cf. Uberti

19

20

21

22

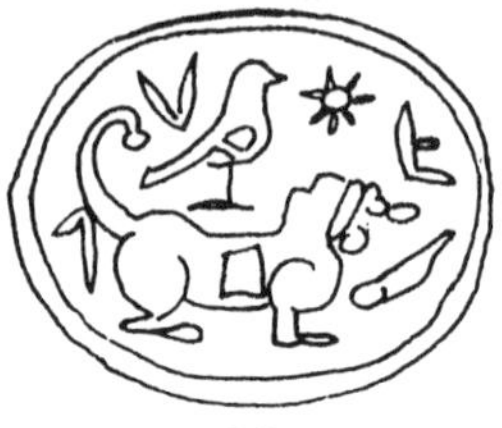

23

24

25

1977: 37, 39-42; VSF 93), the iconography of this large scarab (3.5 x 2.5 x 1.6 cm) found in Sardinia and belonging to *grʾšmn bn ḥmlk* according the positive Phoenician inscription, points to its origin in the Egyptian Delta. The material, dimensions, style and sum of details conform to the Egyptian norm and render the attribution of the present example to the late Phoenician "steatite group" very unlikely.

B Stone, mostly hardstone scarabs and scaraboids

Several seals featuring animals, both realistic and hybrid, contain secondary devices which were added to the compositions in an extremely off-hand way. These designs frequently bear a suspicious resemblance to Semitic letters, such as *šin* and *taw* on a steatite scarab from Acco (**fig. 22**) or *lamed*, *gimel* and *yod* on a stone scaraboid from Phoenicia (**fig. 23**). Both these and a few dozen others seem to represent summarized versions of the more complex compositions such as on a carnelian scarab now in Jerusalem's Hechal Shlomo Museum (Rahmani 1964: 181-184, pl. 41F-G).

C Zoomorphic scaraboids

These represent a yet rarely attested and apparently short-lived group of Phoenician seals. The main motif of the example in **fig. 24** (for the back see Sass, *infra*, pl. 1:5), a hawk on a *nwb* sign, and the use of hieroglyphic devices are all compatible with the iconography of several eighth-century scarabs. Palaeography points to a date about 700 BC. An eighth-century date for the group is also suggested by the palaeography of the seal of Bodbaʿal (**fig. 25**), which, to judge by the reliefed figure of the lion, could come from the same workshop. For reasons to be explained elsewhere, I would suggest to locate the activities of this workshop in the Tyrian area.

1.2. Cubical seal

Interestingly, only one cubical seal published to date bears an inscription (Rahmani 1964: 180-181, pl. 41A-E; on the group in general see Gubel 1987a). The legend contains the first four letters of the alphabet, and suggests an Ammonite source (Lemaire 1985b: 47). Perhaps this seal is a peripheral variation on the cubical type, but chances are nonetheless fair that its formal similarity to the latter is not intentional at all.

1.3. Sealings

A Bullae

Concentrations of clay bullae are generally thought to indicate the immediate vicinity of the archives where the documents they sealed were stored. Unfortunately, we do not have as yet enough inscriptions to guide our way through this still enigmatic field. The excavators of Phoenician occupation levels have met with uninscribed bullae at Tabbat al-Hamman on the Syrian coast (Braidwood 1940: fig. 7), in some Palestinian sites (references in Culican 1986: 218, notes 44-47), at Kition, Cyprus (Clerc et al. 1976: 114-116, nos. 516, 1072), at Selinus, Sicily (Hulot & Fougères 1910: 308) and at Carthage (Vercoutter 1945: 257-261; hundreds of other bullae – though none inscribed – have recently been discovered at Carthage, see T. Redissi apud Rakob 1990: 59-61). A small series of bullae with Egyptianizing and Oriental designs found in the area of ancient Acco (Culican 1986: 261-264, pl. 5, A-B; Giveon & Kertesz 1986: nos. 125, 173), as well as several contemporary examples from an unrecorded site in Lebanon (Culican 1986: 218-221; Gubel 1987b: 40-41, nos. 9, 61) should be added to this evidence. Whereas the bulk of this material belongs to the Persian period, the strongly Egyptianizing motifs of the bullae found in Palestine (Gezer, Lachish, Samaria) may be taken to illustrate the earlier phase (eighth century) of the Phoenician use of such sealings. Finally, we should mention some late bullae (**fig. 26**) from an archive in Delos bearing Phoenician or, at least, Semitic inscriptions (Bordreuil 1988b).

The Phoenician and/or Punic bullae found in the western Mediterranean may be passed over here, for eventual inscriptions are limited to cartouches bearing either "Menkheperre", the throne name of Tuthmosis III, or meaningless hieroglyphs (Vercoutter 1945: 257-261). Neither the Hellenistic nor the Egyptianizing motifs of the examples from Carthage or Selinus are combined with Semitic characters.

B Clay pellets

B1 Clay pellets from the East

The category of clay pellets, equally described as tesserae on account of their typological convergence with leaden equivalents (on the latter see Bordreuil 1987b: 81-82, fig. 3), is represented by a few examples from Phoenicia, invariably inscribed with the formula *ḥn*(*t*) *tmt*: "by grace(s) of Tanit" (Bordreuil 1987b: 82-84, figs. 1-2; 1988a: no. III. 4). A dolphin is found on two pellets under the inscription, and the so-called "Tanit sign" (**fig. 27**) appears in two others atop or to the left of the name *tmt*/Tanit. The fact that these pellets asociate two variant forms of the "pseudo-*ʿankh*" or "Tanit sign" with the name of the goddess in question, once more corroborates the identification of the sign. As for the dolphin, it should be remembered that representations of this animal do not necessarily suppose a specific association with the Tyrian Astarte (Bordreuil 1988a: no. III.5). Nonetheless, dozens of roughly contemporary female statuettes from Tyre and its vicinity feature similar signs, dolphins or combinations of both. A recently auctioned pellet (**fig. 28**) adds an interesting new instance of the correlation between script and image to the present series. The obverse of this bifacial pellet once again combines the image of the dolphin with the *ḥnt tmt* formula. The reverse does not represent a stylized Bes with flail (Wolfe & Sternberg 1989: no. 4), but a sun-disc flanked by two uraei. As with the other pellets, a date in the third–second centuries seems appropriate. On the typological level, there can be few doubts that they were derived from the impressions of the *ʿuśr* or "tithe" seals used by the fourth-century Tyrian administration in order to attest to the payment of taxes collected in the territories of Tyre and Sidon (Greenfield 1985).

Consequently, we may conclude that the correlation between script and image in this particular glyptic category is of a more intrinsic nature than in most other groups. This is perhaps to be explained by the suggested function of these items, which, very much like the Palmyrene tesserae (Bordreuil 1987b: 84), supposedly served as "tickets", allowing their owners to support certain religious events relative to the cult of the deity invoked in the inscriptions and symbolized by the depicted paraphernalia.

B2 Clay pellets from the West

To the best of my knowledge, only two such pellets are known from the Phoenician west, more precisely from the Dermech area of ancient Carthage. According to the excavators, both these examples were found with a group of clay bullae totaling over 150 items. If these documents indeed stem from a burnt library as maintained by current opinion, a comparison with the eastern Phoenician evidence suggests a multifunctional use of the pellet type, although "library" can of course easily be understood as "temple archive". Both

26

27

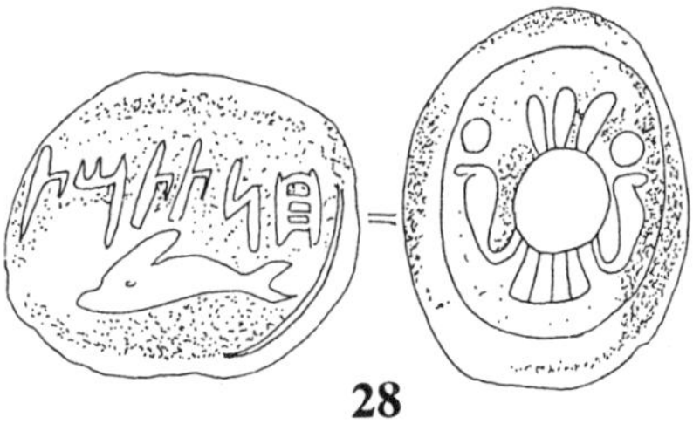
28

29

30

31

pellets in question are bifacial, the first featuring a cartouche with illegible signs flanked by a sphinx, a *mn* and a *nb* hieroglyph on the one, and an enthroned deity on the other side. The second **(fig. 29)** is even more interesting to this colloquium's topic, for it reads *lm* or *ln* on the obverse, and the reverse has a Harpocrates-like figure atop a *nb* sign, preceded by a huge uraeus. The *nb* links similar late-fourth-century pellets with the iconography of the eastern Persian Age production of steatite and faience scarabs discussed above (see Hölbl 1986: 202, 259, pl. 112:1; Moorey 1980: 116, fig. 19: 489, pl. II), corroborating the suggested dating of the former group.

C Jar impressions and stamped handles

C1 Jar impressions and stamped handles in the East

A few archaeological remnants from the late eighth–early seventh century bear witness to the fact that the rims of provision pithoi as well as the cylindrical necks of trade amphorae could occasionally be impressed with rather squarish and, presumably, wooden stamps (e.g. Keel 1977: fig. 153). Surprisingly, none of the latter contain inscriptions.

The impressing of jar handles was perpetuated in the Phoenician realm from at least the "Hyksos" period to the Greco-Roman Age. As shown by finds from recent excavations in northern Phoenicia, one or more handles of different types of jars were occasionally stamped with seals displaying animal and vegetal designs. Other handle impressions provide the name of the owner or producer of the jar's contents, often indicating capacity or weight (Bordreuil 1981). However, combinations of text and image are wanting as yet on Phoenician examples.

C2 Jar impressions and stamped handles in the West

Turning to the evidence from the western Phoenician realm, the situation is somewhat less disappointing. In this context it may suffice to remind of some examples: The excavations of the Tophet at Tharros, Sardinia, have yielded several examples of fourth–second-centuries jar handles with a stamped "Tanit sign" (**fig. 30**). Comparable finds were already reported at Carthage and Sicilian Eryx, Lilibeo, Heraclea Minoa and Selinus, occasionally combined with Punic characters (Falsone 1978: 139-140, note 12). Such a combination is also found on the handle of an early-second-century amphora from La Serreta (Cartagena), where a vase separates Punic *bet* and *nun* (**fig. 31**; cf. Amadasi Guzzo 1967: fig. 5, A1 from Malta).

2. Seal inscriptions and iconography

2.1. Phoenician inscriptions

Several distinct classes of Phoenician seals were judged suitable for the addition of inscriptions. For the sake of convenience, they are arranged and discussed by layout.

A In box layouts

A typical example from a Phoenician tomb in the cemetery of Khaldeh establishes that the production of seals with elaborate box-designs had already begun in the ninth century (Culican 1986: 385-390; Saidah 1983: 213-214). The stylistic evolution of this group can be traced in a few more examples, none of them inscribed, however. Inscriptions do occur on some of the more simplified versions of this group such as on the carnelian scaraboid of *zyʾ* (**fig. 32**) and related examples. The representative seals are characterized by a mixture of Egyptian, Egyptianizing and Oriental devices, with a marked preference for winged beetles, birds of prey with their wings spread in a protective gesture, sphinxes and griffins, not to mention *ʿankh*-signs or derivations thereof. Finally, the dispersed Aramaic letters on the seal of Marsamak for example (**fig. 33**), establish that such seals were also priced in neighbouring countries.

B In registral layouts

The seal with elaborate box design can perhaps be regarded as the progenitor of other glyptic series, each characterized by a different degree of simplification of the original layout. Closely affiliated is a series of rather large scaraboid seals (**figs. 34-36**, occasionally bifacial), where the subjects of the box-design class are arranged in a succession of horizontal friezes or registers. On the last of these, bearing the name Menaḥem, we find the four-winged genius which recurs on dozens of Phoenician artefacts (**fig. 36a**; cf.

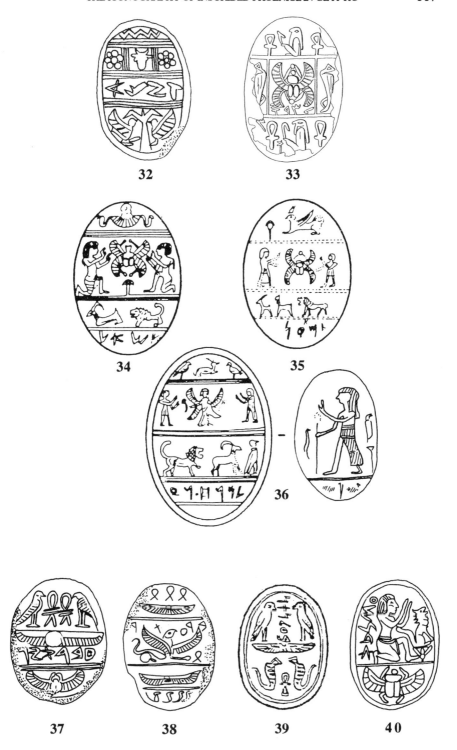

32

33

34

35

36

37

38

39

40

figs. 64-70). Of even greater importance to our topic is the presence of a simple, vertically arranged icon on this late-eighth-century seal's reverse (**fig. 36b**), the very presence of which betraying the chronological overlap of these glyptic trends.

One could distinguish half a dozen sub-groups within the production of seals with multi-registral compositions. During the eighth and early seventh centuries the largest sub-group consisted of a series of hardstone scaraboids decorated with confronted birds and winged beetles in their upper and lower registers. Other characteristic details include the use of winged sun-discs as field dividers as well as the repetition of Egyptianizing "good-luck" (?) signs. The links, in iconographical repertoire and style, with the box-design group are obvious. Many parallels, inscribed and uninscribed, can be quoted for compositions of the type here illustrated with the seal of ʿAbdayom (**fig. 37**; cf. Gubel 1988: 148-151). Both following examples (**figs. 38-39**) attest to the secondary use of such seals by Aramaeans and Hebrews alike.

If the sub-group just mentioned distinguishes itself by a rigid structuring of the field and by a severe stylization of the motifs which are almost reduced to mere pictographs, the bulged volume and the almost tangible, "fleshy" appearance of the figures must be cited as the distinct features of a class of late-ninth–eighth-centuries seals. In addition to the already mentioned seal of Ḥadi (**fig. 10**), these characteristics can be found on the seal of Adonishuaʿ (**fig. 40**) for example, in fact a link with the next group.

C In undivided, vertical layouts

The contemporaneity of seals with simple, vertically arranged compositions and the two former groups has already been pointed out. It is within the present group, which may be regarded as the direct predecessor of the "classical" Phoenician seal, that the major iconographical themes of these later, mostly (green) jasper and carnelian scarabs of the seventh–fifth centuries are to be found. Unfortunately, the accompanying inscriptions are of no help for the interpretation of the pictorial motifs. This is especially frustrating in the case of the seal of Gershed (**fig. 41**) for example, because we are still left in the dark as to the precise identity of the bearded god on the sphinx throne, an icon repeated on several Phoenician and Punic artefacts. Another seal, inscribed around 600 BC with the name Gerʿashtart (**fig. 42**), is typical of the so-called Phoenician "green jasper" series. The main importance, for our purpose, of the inscription lies in the fact that the inscription was obviously added later, establishing that the production of the typical "green jasper" series must have started *before* 600 BC.

As far as I know, there is only one sub-group of seals within this series where one could venture to postulate a correlation between text and image. This is a group of seals (**figs. 42-53**) reproducing, with a few minor vari-

41

42

43

44

45

46

47

48

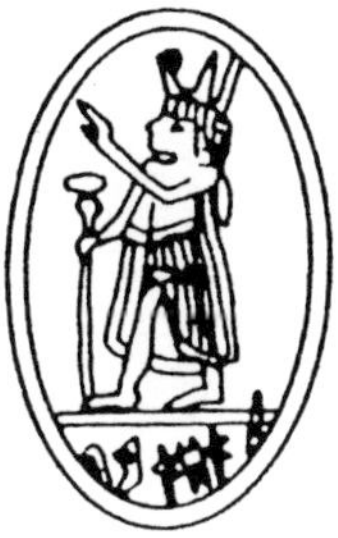

49

50

51

52

53

54

55

56

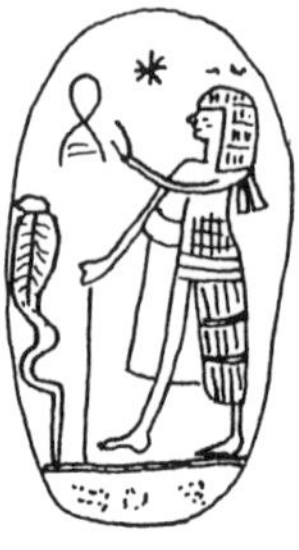

57

58

59

60

ants, the image of a king, as elucidated by parallels from other pictorial sources. Some of these examples possibly bear the names of contemporary kings mentioned as rulers of the coast in the Assyrian annals, as pointed out by both Bordreuil (1985) and myself (1990a; 1991a) in recent papers. New examples which became known since 1989 (**figs. 54-57**; and cf. Aufrecht 1992: no. 3), enhance the probability that such seals were once used by the high officials, if not by the kings of the Phoenician city-states themselves and, subsequently, by their counterparts in neighbouring countries (but cf. Lemaire, *supra*, pp. 15-16; Sass, *infra*, pp. 229-230).

D In undivided, horizontal layouts

Whereas the presentation of several types of combat scenes, for example, required a horizontal layout in later times, such an option was initially reserved almost exclusively for the representation of quadrupeds (e.g. Galling 1941: pl. 5). Two notable early exceptions are the agate scarab of Aḥatmilk, wife of Yashaʿ, now in Vienna (**fig. 58**) and a steatite scarab from the Acco region (**fig. 59**). The typological and compositional convergences between the two seals, extending on the iconographical level to the structural details of the throne-types (Gubel 1987b: 222-225, pl. 44), however, cast serious doubts on the palaeographical analysis, which places the former seal at the end of the ninth and the latter at the end of the eighth century. This situation is frequently met with elsewhere and calls for a more in-depth approach wherever the iconographical and palaeographical parameters can be combined.

2.2. Pseudo-hieroglyphic inscriptions

The adoption and use of Egyptian hieroglyphs as a means to transcribe West Semitic names was probably perpetuated at Byblos throughout the second millennium. From this center of the pseudo-hieroglyphic writing system stems the intriguing stamp seal of **fig. 53**, the inscription of which apparently combines all the scripts known to the seal cutter. The general composition is heralded by "pseudo-Hyksos" prototypes, at the same time linked with the scarabs and scaraboid seals of the royal glyptic iconography.

Whereas there is no point here in enumerating the many seals displaying apparently meaningless hieroglyphs as secondary decorative devices, it is not inappropriate to add that cartouches containing meaningless hieroglyphs recur in several series of seals, in some cases even as the trademark of a specific workshop. As illustrated here by the scaraboid seal of Yaḥzibaʿal (**fig. 60**), such decorative cartouches were smoothly combined with Semitic inscriptions, especially on seals closely linked with the multiple register group. One of the finest examples is the carnelian scaraboid, set in a silver mount, of Baʿalḥanan, on which a central cartouche with an alphabetic inscription is flanked by two others containing Egyptian and pseudo-Egyptian hieroglyphs (BM 134887; unpublished, see meanwhile Barnett 1967b).

Cartouches with meaningless hieroglyphs are still found on the "green jasper" series spanning the seventh–fifth centuries.

2.3. Non-Phoenician alphabetic inscriptions

Additional information on the relation between glyptic inscriptions and iconography in the Phoenician realm may be derived from external or secondary sources.

Several scarabs, scaraboids and bullae inscribed with Aramaean, Hebrew, Ammonite, Edomite and Moabite names show the heraldic figure of a four-winged beetle, illustrating the adoption of a divine symbol frequently found on Phoenician prototypes, and, eventually, even on the East Greek seal of Kreontidas (Boardman 1968: 73-74, pl. 11:A5). Because of the "international" use of this originally-Phoenician device, it is almost impossible to establish the precise origin of seals bearing it. However, Phoenician art has developed a number of variants, which were apparently unknown or judged too apocryphic beyond the boundaries of the coastal towns. The lapis lazuli scaraboid of *blth*, now in Péronne (**fig. 61**; cf. Sass, *infra*, p. 215, fig. 88), conveniently illustrates this point. As a short review of Iron II Phoenician art establishes, the female-headed beetle is already to be found, two-winged, on a Phoenician ivory from Nimrud (**fig. 63**), and the same motif (henceforth with four wings) recurs on the bowl from the Bernardini tomb (**fig. 62**), on a scarab from Cyprus mounted in silver (Vollenweider 1967: no. 151), on gold rings from Amrit and Carthage(?) (de Ridder 1911: 527, no. 2657 and note 6) and, finally, on one of three silver diadem elements from the Douïmes area in the same site (Delattre & Berger 1900: 224-225, pl. 32:5; cf. the – unacknowledged – review of oriental comparanda in Lancel 1991). This brief survey alone would justify a reconsideration of the theme of the four-winged scarab (cf. Uehlinger, *infra*, pp. 276-277).

2.4. Greco-Phoenician and Cypro-Phoenician seals

The inscription could have been added to a seal in a place other than its place of origin, and at a later time, even many years later.

The latter case is most conveniently illustrated by a blue chalcedony scaraboid representing Hermes with paraphernalia recurring on late-sixth-century seals (B 37; cf. Walters 1926: no. 316). The inscription was engraved three centuries after this seal had been cut. Another example to be quoted is a rock-crystal scarab with an archaic Greek motif and a Phoenician inscription reading *ʿbkʾ* (for *ʿbdmlkʾ*, "servant of the King"). Bordreuil (B 29), among others, had pointed out that Aramaic *mlkʾ* formed part of the protocol of the Persian king. In other words, here we have a most significant example from

61

62

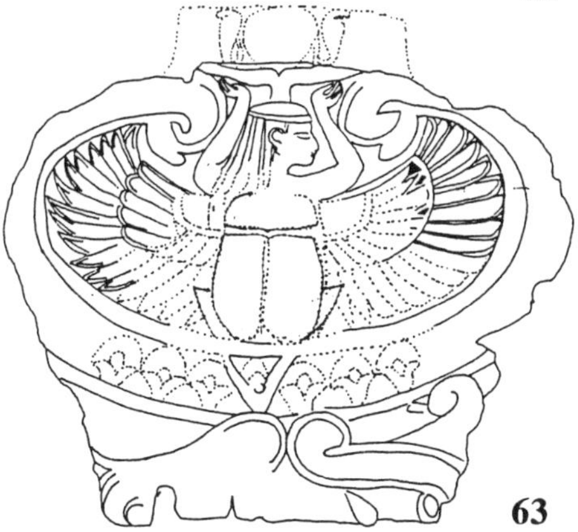

63

the glyptic medium which confirms the increasing impact of Greek art in Persian Age Phoenicia, a phenomenon also expressed in most other local media.

"Foreign" inscriptions on Phoenician seals can occasionally denote the close contacts between a Phoenician *koinè* and the local population. Several seals, paralleled by finds from the East or from the trading posts in the West, thus illustrate the solidity of Cypro-Phoenician relations. It may suffice to refer to a steatite scarab in Cambridge, inscribed with the name of *pi-lo-i* ("Philooi") above a heraldic merman inspired by the early Aradian coinage (Masson 1986: 162-163, pl. I:1; Gubel 1987c).

2.5. Inscriptions and workshops

The palaeographic analysis of inscriptions within a glyptic group representing the same subject may eventually lead to the identification of workshops, if combined with parameters of style and technique. Let us examine but one subject, the four-winged human figure. The recently-published seventh-century carnelian scaraboid bearing the Moabite name of Mepaʿah **(fig. 64)** can readily be compared with the variegated agate scaraboid from Tello of Baʿalnatan **(fig. 65)**, which is also identified as Moabite, about 750 BC (cf. Timm, *infra*, pp. 175-178 with fig. 11). The carving characterizing both seals (also found on the "royal series", B 100, cf. our schematic fig. 49), differs from the smoother versions on the scaraboid of ʿUzza from the

Dan area (**fig. 66**; cf. Timm, p. 178 with fig. 12) and on one Baʿalḥan's scarab now in the British Museum (**fig. 67**). The latter two depict straightforward Phoenician versions of motifs also met with on a Cypro-Phoenician bowl, ivories and a stamped jar rim (Keel 1977: 194-207; cf. GGG: § 121).

The stylistically interrelated and skilfully detailed seals of ʿUzza and Baʿalḥan show papyrus-like objects in the hands of the winged figure, which allow us to identify not only the clear-cut sceptres of figs. 43-44, 53, 55, but also the "astral sceptres" of the Phoenician royal iconography (figs. 45-47, 50-51, 54) as derivative forms of a floral (papyrus or lotus) sceptre. Together with the Phoenician seal of Batʾeshem (**fig. 68**, possibly depicting an actual cult statue), they represent the dress of the winged figure in a realistic way. These seals display the same multi-layered, *kaunakès*-like mantle-robe which constitutes another proprium of several "royal iconography" seals (esp. figs. 45, 53, 57). If the sum of details allows us to assign the seals of the "royal iconography" type, as well as figs. 66-68, depicting the four-winged figure, to individual workshops, the more schematic aspect of compositions such as our figs. 64-65 apparently betrays provincial or "outlandish" manufacture. The evident qualitative differences make it clear that, if Phoenicia should be regarded as the source of the motif in question, this does not necessarily mean that the production of the local workshops was uniform. The seals of Nuri (**fig. 69**) and Shatʾel (**fig. 70**; cf. Buchanan & Moorey 1988: no. 73) show similar, rather simplified versions of the motif.

As to the postulated Phoenician origin of the four-winged figure in its present form, it should be remembered that quite a few anepigraphic comparanda were recovered on the Phoenician coast. They include a carnelian scarab mentioned by de Ridder (1911: 559-560, no. 2786), a rock-crystal scaraboid from Konya (Buchanan & Moorey 1988: no. 273) and an early glass scaraboid from Tyre (unpublished). Since Phoenician art is the only West Semitic tradition perpetuating this icon all over the Mediterranean in variants such as two-winged (B 30) or kneeling four-winged figures (Borowski 1952: no. 18; NAAG 1987: nos. 36-37; Walters 1926: nos. 281, 268, to be compared with Hölbl 1979: 227, 283, pl. 84:2a-c), chances are fair that this civilisation was indeed the first as well to propagate the theme in the adjacent countries.

V. Conclusions

Several factors impede the definition of the exact ratio of epigraphic and anepigraphic seals in the Phoenician world. The palaeographical ambiguity of many a lapidary inscription, to name but one of these drawbacks, often renders impossible the identification of an inscription as positively Phoenician,

64

65

66

67

68

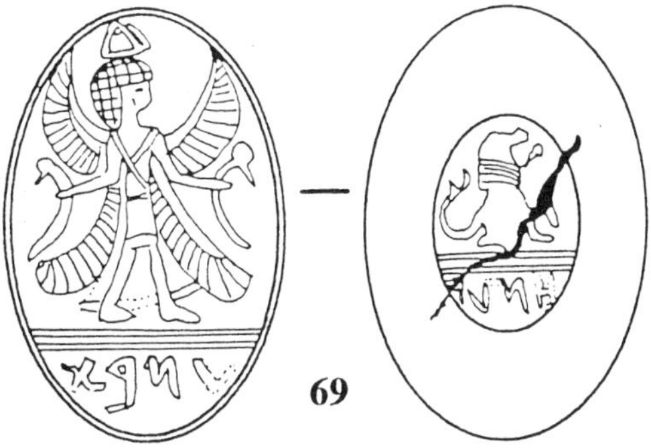

69

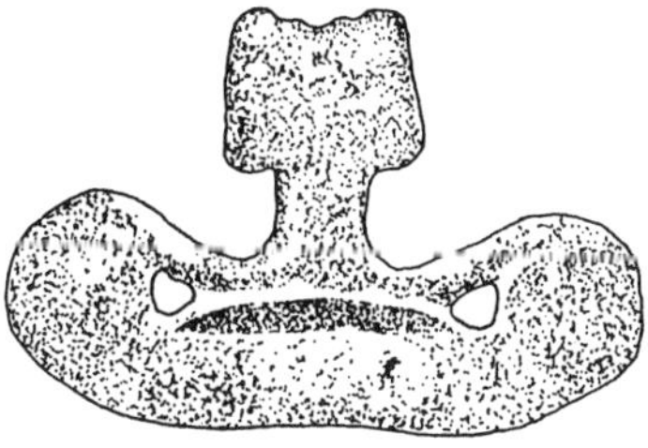

70

Aramaic or otherwise (see Lemaire, *supra*, pp. 4-7). The rapid propagation of Phoenician iconography in the wake of the expansion of the Phoenicians' mercantile activities and the reputed mobility of their craftsmen, not to mention the diffusion of the alphabet, confronts us with an additional problem. The aforesaid epigraphical drawbacks are indeed manifest whenever one tries to discern which Semitic entity was originally responsible for the concept, the development or the adaptation of a given glyptic motif.

Whilst it is clear that the ratio of inscribed and uninscribed Phoenician seals could not possibly be expressed in terms of absolute numbers, it seems reasonable to assume that less than 5% of the glyptic production was eventually inscribed. Are we therefore to conclude that only officials and, possibly, wealthy merchants possessed seals bearing private names? The declining number of Phoenician epigraphic seals from the later seventh century onwards could indeed be quoted in favour of this theory, especially so when one connects this phenomenon with the regression of Phoenicia's autonomy throughout the following centuries. One could also argue that, by and large, the inscriptions associated with the iconographical emblems of power, whether divine or profane, outnumber those associated with naturalistic themes.

A final remark in this context concerns the distinct preference for seals with Greek motifs during the latter half of the sixth to the outgoing fourth centuries (e.g. G 110a; B 29, 31-34; Lemaire 1986: no. 1). Since this period coincides with the incorporation of Phoenicia into the fifth Persian Satrapy, one wonders whether such a choice would not betray a political statement, a deliberate dissociation from the Achaemenid rule.

The foregoing review of some of the most remarkable aspects of Phoenician epigraphic seals has no doubt already elucidated that they did not form an independent group within the production as a whole. This point is illustrated by many examples, where the letters of the inscription were inserted in between the components of the design, occasionally even cutting their outlines (cf. **fig. 38**). This does not rule out that within the production of a specific series, room could be reserved for an inscription. The last point is illustrated by comparing a seal produced in what I would like to name the "*sebetti* workshop", where the artist reserved such a frieze for the inscription engraved about 700 BC (**fig. 32**), with uninscribed examples (cf. Buchanan & Moorey 1988: no. 289; Culican 1986: 197, pl. 36i). Instead of adding more examples, we may turn directly to the eighth-century seal of ʿAzem, servant of ʿAzorbaʿal (B 6), illustrating that at least certain inscribed seals were indeed carved upon commission. Finally, the orientation of the "positive" inscription on such as the early-seventh-century jasper scarab of Germilk (B 15), establishes that scarabs and scaraboids were not inscribed only in order to seal legal documents or personal belongings.

LIST OF FIGURES
All drawings by the author unless stated otherwise.

28. Clay pellet, Phoenicia, 3rd-2nd centuries (commerce; after Wolfe & Sternberg 1989: no. 4).
29. Bifacial clay pellet, Carthage, 4th cent. (after Vercoutter 1945: pl. XXI:767).
30. Stamped jar handle, Tharros, 4th-2nd centuries (Cagliari, Museo archeologico nazionale?; Manfredi 1986: pl. XIX:3-4).
31. Stamped handle of "Maña-C"-type amphora, late 3rd-first quarter 2nd cent. (Cartagena; Guerrero, Martín & Rodán 1988: fig. 1).
32. Carnelian scaraboid of *zyʾ*, Phoenicia, early 7th cent. (Paris, BN, 1972.1317.129; after B 13).
33. Rock-crystal scaraboid of Marsamak (London, BM 48506; drawing Hildi Keel-Leu after photo BM; cf. Bordreuil, *supra*, p. 89, fig. 26).
34. Scaraboid of Saul, c. 700 (Jerusalem, HU, Institute of Archaeology, no. 734; Gubel 1991a: fig. 3,f, after Lemaire 1986: fig. 2a).
35. Limestone scaraboid of Miqen, 8th cent. (private collection; Gubel 1991a: fig. 3e, after Lemaire 1986: fig. 2b).
36. Bifacial limestone scaraboid of Menaḥem, c. 700, bought in Aleppo (Oxford, Ashmolean Museum 1914.57; Gubel 1991a: fig. 3,d, after Lemaire 1986: fig. 2c).
37. Rock-crystal scaraboid of ʿAbdʾayom, early 7th cent. (Paris, BN M.5811; after B 16).
38. Agate scaraboid of Barʿatar, c. 700 (Paris, BN, 1972.1317.128; after B 93).
39. Chalcedony scaraboid of Baʿalnatan, bought in Istanbul (Jerusalem, Bible Lands Museum; G 54).
40. Jasperoid-agate scaraboid of Adonishuaʿ, second half 8th cent. (Paris, BN, M.8536; after B 5).
41. Red jasper scarab of Gershed, Tyre, early 6th cent. (Paris, BN, coll. De Clercq 2756; Keel 1977: 32, fig. 16, cf. B 26).
42. Green jasper scarab of Gerʿashtart, Tartous, early 6th cent. (Paris, BN, coll. De Clercq 2504; G 101, cf. B 25).
43. Banded agate scaraboid of Nûri, 8th cent. (Jerusalem, IMJ 69.20.661; after HD 122; Gubel 1991a: fig. 1:4).
44. Agate scaraboid of Yashda, 7th cent. (Paris, Louvre, AO 10882; after B 23; Gubel 1991a: fig. 1:6).
45. Bone scarab of Ragam, 7th cent. (Paris, BN, 1972.1317.139; B 22; Gubel 1991a: fig. 1:7).
46. Amethyst scaraboid of Shamaʿ, 7th cent. (Paris, BN, 1972.1317.124; B 21; Gubel 1991a: fig. 1:8).
47. Rock-crystal scaraboid of ʿAdy, 8th-7th cent. (Jerusalem, Bible Lands Museum; Muscarella 1981: no. 267; Gubel 1991a: fig. 1:9).
48. Carnelian scaraboid of Miṣri/Muṣuri, early 7th cent. (Paris, BN, coll. De Clercq 2515; drawing by Hildi Keel-Leu after B 65).
49. Carnelian scaraboid of Aḥʾabi, early 7th cent. (Paris, Louvre, AO 6006; B 100; Gubel 1991a: fig. 1:10).
50. Carnelian scaraboid of Abibaʿal, early 7th cent. (Firenze, Museo archeologico; Bordreuil 1985: 24, fig. 4; Gubel 1991a: figs. 1:11, 2,a).
51. Jasper scaraboid, bifacial, of *mksp* (< Milki-Asapa), early 7th cent. (London, BM 130667; Gubel 1991a: fig. 1:12).
52. Rock-crystal scaraboid of *šlmt* (Durham, Gulbenkian Museum of Oriental Art, N. 2307; Lambert 1979: no. 114; Gubel 1991a: fig. 1:13).
53. Carnelian scaraboid, legend illegible, Phoenician, 8th-7th cent. (Paris, BN, coll. F. Chandon de Briailles, no. 192; Gubel 1991a: fig. 1,a).

54. Limestone scaraboid of ʿAglaʾ, 8th-7th cent. (private collection; after Elayi 1990: pl. XVII:2).
55. Amethyst scaraboid of Ḥabli, 8th cent. (Haifa, Hecht Museum, H-2036; after Wolfe & Sternberg 1989: no. 2).
56. Rock-crystal scaraboid of ʿAzor, 8th cent. (commerce; after Wolfe & Sternberg 1990: no. 432).
57. Rock-crystal scaraboid of *ḥzt*, early 7th cent. (commerce; after Wolfe & Sternberg 1990: no. 433).
58. Banded agate scarab of Aḥatmilk, late 9th-early 8th cent. (photograph Vienna, Kunsthistorisches Museum, 2880).
59. Steatite scarab from Acco, late 9th-early 8th cent. (*lṣ...? ʾlw ʿzʾ*, inscribed later?) (Jerusalem, IAA 73-216; Giveon & Lemaire 1985: pl. 5B).
60. Quartz scarab of Yaḥzibaʿal, 8th cent. (Jerusalem, IMJ 65.11.6; after HD 118).
61. Lapis-lazuli (?) scarab of *blth*, 7th cent. (Péronne, Municipality collection; after Boardman 1971: no. 2, cf. G 63).
62. Silver bowl from Praeneste, c. 710-675, detail (Rome, Villa Giulia, 61574; Moscati 1966: 484, Abb. XXIII).
63. Ivory plaque, Fort Shalmaneser, Nimrud, 8th cent. (London, British School of Archaeology in Iraq; after Herrmann 1986: pl. 329:1265).
64. Carnelian scaraboid of Mepaʿah (Jerusalem, Bible Lands Museum; after Avigad 1990: pl. 6A).
65. Agate scaraboid of Baʿalnatan, Tello, c. 750 (Paris, Louvre, MNB 1500; after B 61).
66. Carnelian scaraboid of ʿUzza, Dan area, 8th cent. (Jerusalem, IAA 69-5530; Keel 1977: 202, fig. 152).
67. Scarab of Baʿalḥan, 7th cent. (London, BM 117908; Keel 1977: 202, fig. 151).
68. Marble scaraboid of Batʾeshem, 7th cent. (Jerusalem, IMJ, 69.58.144; Gubel 1991a: fig. 3,a).
69. Bifacial limestone scaraboid of Nûri, c. 650 (Paris, Louvre, AO 24413; after B 19).
70. Bronze seal of Shatʾel, end 7th cent. (Paris, BN, 1972.1317.143; after B 20).

DAS IKONOGRAPHISCHE REPERTOIRE DER AMMONITISCHEN SIEGEL UND SEINE ENTWICKLUNG

Ulrich HÜBNER
Universität Heidelberg

I. Die Anfänge der ammonitischen Siegel-Produktion

Um ca. 1200 v. Chr. brach das ostmediterrane und vorderasiatische Wirtschaftssystem zusammen, in seiner Folge auch die kanaanäischen Stadtstaaten des zentralen transjordanischen Hochplateaus wie ʿAmmān (Hübner 1992b), Saḥāb und Ḫirbet Umm ed-Danānīr (Hübner 1992a: Kap. 4.1). Die verbliebene kanaanäische Bevölkerung der Ammonitis entwickelte sich während der Eisen-I-Zeit in einem langen Prozeß kontinuierlich aus der Konkursmasse dieser spätbronzezeitlichen Stadtstaaten zu der vorstaatlichen, dörflich orientierten Tribalgesellschaft der Proto-Ammoniter, mit der sich dann später Jefta, Saul und David auseinanderzusetzen hatten (Hübner 1992a: Kap. 4.1-2).

Während dieser Zeit waren die spätbronzezeitlichen Skarabäen (z.B. Ward 1964: 50-52; Ward 1966: 5-14; Ibrahim 1983: Nr. 2f, 6b; McGovern et al. 1986: 284ff; Geraty 1988: 250f, Pl. 28) und Zylindersiegel (z.B. Ward 1964: 47-50; Ward 1966: 15f; Tournay 1967; McGovern et al. 1986: 290ff), seien es Importe oder lokale Imitationen, weiter in Gebrauch. Daneben traten aber auch neue, typisch früheisenzeitliche Stempelsiegel, wie sie z.B. in Saḥāb (Dajani 1970; Horn 1971; Ibrahim 1983: Nr. 4f, 6a, 8f), auf Ḫirbet el-Ḥaǧǧār (Thompson 1972: Nr. 22) oder am Rand der Buqēʿa (McGovern et al. 1986: 243) gut belegt sind. Aus der Eisen-I-Zeit sind – dem Befund im gesamten nordwestsemitischen Raum entsprechend – keine beschrifteten protoammonitischen Siegel oder Siegelabdrücke bekannt (zusammenfassend Hübner 1992a: Kap. 2.10.2; Keel 1990b: 384ff.419.421, Nr. 89, 99, 107-109; Shuval 1990: 158ff).

Zwischen der proto-ammonitischen Glyptik der Eisen-I-Zeit und den frühesten ammonitischen Siegeln bzw. Siegelabdrücken der Eisen-II-Zeit klafft eine Lücke von rund 250-350 Jahren, für die – bisher jedenfalls – keine ammonitischen Siegel oder Inschriften belegt sind (Hübner 1992a: Kap. 4.2-3). Die wahrscheinlich älteste ammonitische Inschrift überhaupt, die ʿAmmān-Zitadellen-Inschrift, stammt vom (Ende des 9. bzw.) Anfang des 8. Jhs. v. Chr. (CAI 59; Hübner 1992a: Kap. 2.1, Nr. 1). Am Ende dieser glyptischen Latenzzeit setzt dann in der Mitte des 8. Jhs. v. Chr. innerhalb weniger Jahrzehnte – geradezu explosionsartig – eine rege Siegelproduktion ein (H 38, 61, 68; CAI 119, 124, 121 = H 53, 91, 124) [1] Sie findet – wie die übrigen Inschriften allgemein – in ebenso kurzer Zeit innerhalb der ersten Hälfte des 6.

1. Ammonitische beschriftete Siegel werden im folgenden stets nach Hübner 1992a (= H) zitiert, wo sich die jüngste und bislang vollständigste Zusammenstellung findet. Die Nummern der entsprechenden Siegel im "Corpus of Ammonite Inscriptions" von W.E. Aufrecht (1989 = CAI; vgl. dazu die Rezension von Hübner & Knauf 1992) und in VSE, B usw. lassen sich, soweit es sich um Siegel mit ikonischem Dekor handelt, leicht der unten auf S. 154f gebotenen Konkordanz entnehmen.

Jhs. v. Chr. ein Ende (H 25, 34, 48, 153). Anfang und Ende der Siegelproduktion spiegeln, wie überhaupt die gesamte ammonitische Inschriften-Produktion, die politische und gesellschaftliche Entwicklung (Hübner 1992a: Kap. 5) innerhalb der eisen- und perserzeitlichen Ammonitis wieder.

II. Probleme einer ammonitischen Glyptographie

Aus der Eisen-II-Zeit, also aus der Zeit, in der die Ethnie bzw. Politie Ammon einen Territorialstaat bildete, der dann in der gleichnamigen neobabylonischen und achämenidischen Provinz aufging, sind bisher m.W. 160 *beschriftete* nordwestsemitische Siegel bzw. Siegelabdrücke bekannt, die jemals von verschiedenster Seite als ammonitisch eingeordnet worden sind. Davon können m.E. allenfalls 14 als sicher ammonitisch und etwa 58 als wahrscheinlich ammonitisch bestimmt werden, insgesamt also rund 70 beschriftete Siegel. Unter den übrigen Siegeln befinden sich eine Reihe von Exemplaren, bei denen eine ammonitische Herkunft nicht auszuschließen ist, aber eben auch nicht wahrscheinlich gemacht werden kann (vgl. insgesamt Herr 1978; Jackson 1983a; Israel 1987a; Aufrecht 1989; Hübner 1992a: Kap. 2.9; 1992c; Hübner & Knauf 1992).

Die Frage, welche Siegel als ammonitisch zu betrachten sind, ist stark umstritten. Die Kriterien, die angewandt wurden, um das hier vorausgesetzte Corpus sicher bzw. wahrscheinlich ammonitischer Siegel zusammenzustellen, sind:

1. der Gottesname Milkom,
2. die kanaanäische Sprache (wobei Aramäisch eine ammonitische Verfasserschaft nicht ausschließt),
3. die Schrift,
4. der – gesicherte – Fundort auf ammonitischem Territorium,
5. die Ikonographie,
6. das Onomastikon

[7. die (wahrscheinliche) Echtheit].

Außer dem Gottesnamen ist keines der Kriterien für sich allein ein klares Indiz oder gar ein Beweis für eine ammonitische Herkunft; je mehr Kriterien ineinandergreifen, desto größer ist ihre Beweiskraft (vgl. Lemaire, *supra*, S. 1-26). Die Einschätzung einzelner Inschriften bleibt immer in einem gewissen Maß subjektiv. Da ich relativ skeptisch bin, was die Möglichkeiten angeht, Siegel aufgrund der Schrift und/oder Ikonographie einigermaßen sicher einer *einzigen* Kultur zurechnen zu können, ist mein Corpus ammonitischer Siegel kleiner als das anderer Ammonitologen. Diese Skepsis hat aber m.E. den großen Vorteil, daß die als sicher und wahrscheinlich ammonitisch eingeordneten Siegel eine sicherere Basis für historische Schlußfolgerungen aller Art abgeben, als dies bei umfangreicheren Corpora der Fall ist, die Dutzende von Siegel aufnehmen, deren Herkunft und Authentizität letztlich unsicher und zweifelhaft ist.

Der naheliegende radikale Versuch, sich für die wissenschaftliche Arbeit nur auf Siegel aus kontrollierten archäologischen Projekten zu beziehen, ist allerdings minimalistisch und insofern problematisch: Weder läßt sich behaupten, alle Siegel aus dem Kunsthandel seien gefälscht, noch kann man davon ausgehen, daß sie alle echt seien. Bei Material aus dem Kunsthandel ist aber jedenfalls nicht einfach stillschweigend von der Echtheit auszugehen, sondern der Echtheitsnachweis konkret anzutreten – insbesondere bei der Erstveröffentlichung und sofern dies methodisch möglich ist (vgl. Sass, *infra*, S. 245-246; Uehlinger, S. 270-271).

III. Allgemeiner Überblick über die ammonitischen Siegel

Von den rund 70 beschrifteten ammonitischen Siegeln bzw. Siegelabdrücken sind nur bei neun die Fundorte gesichert, nämlich ʿAmmān (H 14, 17, 33, 96, 136) und Tell el-ʿUmēri (H 88, 142, 155f)[2]; bei den übrigen ist die Herkunft unsicher oder aber zumeist unbekannt. Mindestens vier Siegel sind als Fälschungen zu betrachten (vgl. Hübner 1989b; 1992a: Kap. 2. 10.1); weitere Fälschungen dürften in öffentlichen und privaten Sammlungen sowie im Kunsthandel häufiger vorhanden sein als allgemein angenommen wird; die Dunkelziffer ist wahrscheinlich sehr hoch.

Drei der rund 70 epigraphischen Siegel stammen von Frauen, der Rest von Männern. Nur eine dieser Frauen trägt einen Titel, nämlich *ʾmh* (H 127); alle Frauensiegel sind bezeichnenderweise rein epigraphische Siegel. Bei den Männern sind die Titel *ʿbd* (H 14f, 65, 88), *nʿr* (H 62, 116) und *h-nss* (H 138) belegt. Außer zwei mit Alphabetinschriften versehenen Siegeln (H 6, CAI 93 = H 8) sind alle beschrifteten ammonitischen Siegel Namenssiegel in des Wortes eigentlicher Bedeutung.

Dazu kommen ca. 20 bisher publizierte *anepigraphische* Siegel der Eisen-II-Zeit, die als sicher oder wahrscheinlich ammonitisch betrachtet werden können (Hübner 1992a: Kap. 2.10.2). Im Gegensatz zu den beschrifteten Siegeln ist ihre Herkunft zum größten Teil gesichert: Sie stammen vor allem aus ʿAmmān (Harding 1953: 54f, Nr. 4ff; angeblich aus ʿAmmān Ward 1968: Nr. 1), Ḫirbet el-Ḥaǧǧār (Thompson 1972: 53.59f.65f.69f, Nr. 5f, 29), Ḫirbet Ḫulde (Yassine 1988: 21f, Fig. 8:3-5), Umm Uḏaina (Hadidi 1987: 120, Fig. 12:6-9) und Ḫirbet Umm ed-Danānīr (McGovern 1989: 125,

2. Bei dem Siegel des *mṅnʾl bn ʾẇrʾ* vom Tell Dēr ʿAllā (CAI 106 = H 109; s.u. IV. 1.1.A, 1.3) ist zwar der Herkunftsort gesichert, m.E. aber keineswegs die Zuweisung an Ammon, da die Buchstaben schlecht erhalten sind (und ihre Lesung unsicher ist).

Fig. 4:3). Die Bildmotive 'Skorpion', 'Herr der Tiere' und 'Capriden am Lebensbaum' (s.u. IV.1.1.E, 1.5., 3.1. mit **Abb. 33-35**) sind in Ammon bislang nur auf anepigraphischen Stempel- und Zylindersiegeln belegt. Der Befund entspricht dem der nordwestsemitischen beschrifteten Siegel allgemein, auf denen diese Motive – wenn überhaupt – äußerst selten vorkommen.

Daneben sind eine Reihe von *nicht ammonitischen* Siegeln aus der eisen-II-zeitlichen und achämenidischen Ammonitis bekannt (Hübner 1992a: Kap. 2.10.3), vor allem drei beschriftete judäische Siegel (VSE 352, 373; Fulco 1979), ein moabitisches Siegel aus Umm Uḏaina (H 132; vgl. Lemaire, *supra*, S. 2f mit Fig. 1; Timm, *infra*, S. 184 mit Abb. 18) und eine ganze Reihe neoassyrischer bzw. neobabylonischer und achämenidischer Stempelsiegel (**Abb. 29f, 33-36**); bei letzteren ist nicht immer klar, ob es sich um Importe (Dajani 1962: 124f, Pl. 4:8; Harding 1950: 46, Nr. 33; sowie **Abb. 29-32**) oder um lokale Imitationen handelt (Yassine 1988: 21f, Fig. 8:3-5, vgl. **Abb. 33-34**; Porada 1989). Gelegentlich konnte auch ein anepigraphisches Stempelsiegel aus Mesopotamien importiert und dann vor Ort mit einer ammonitischen Inschrift, einem ammonitischen bzw. assyrischen Personennamen und/oder einem lokalen Bildmotiv versehen werden, wie es bei dem Siegel des *šbʾl* (H 136; vgl. Ornan, *supra*, S. 57, Fig. 8, und 59, Fig. 17), dem des **Mannu-ki-Inurta* (**Abb. 18**) und dem des *ʾdnplṭ ʿbd ʿmndb* (**Abb. 3**)[3] und wohl auch – der Siegel-Form nach – bei dem anikonischen, entenförmigen Stempelsiegel des *ʾmrʾl bn ynḥm* (H 59) der Fall war.

Insgesamt können m.E. ca. 30 mehr oder weniger rein epigraphische, knapp 20 anepigraphische Siegel sowie knapp 40 Siegel, die gleichzeitig beschriftet und 'bebildert' sind, für ammonitisch gehalten werden, insgesamt also etwa 90 Siegel bzw. Siegelabdrücke der Eisen-II-Zeit. Rechnet man die lokalen Imitationen neoassyrischer bzw. -babylonischer und achämenidischer Siegel dazu, erhöht sich die Gesamtsumme noch etwas.

Ihrer *Form* nach sind fast alle der rund 70 ammonitischen Namenssiegel der Eisen-II-Zeit Skaraboïde bzw. runde, ovale oder linsenförmige Platten. Vier Siegel sind Konoïde (H 80 [= **Abb. 15**], 87, 90 [= **Abb. 18**], 110). Ein Stempelsiegel hat zylindrische Form, ohne ein Rollsiegel zu sein (H 33), ein anderes die Form einer Ente mit zurückgelegtem Kopf (s.o.). Eisen-II- bzw. perserzeitliche Zylindersiegel sind – typisch für diese Epoche – nur in drei Exemplaren belegt, nämlich auf Tell el-ʿUmēri (Porada 1989; **Abb. 35-36**) und in Meqābelēn (Harding 1950: 46, Pl. 15:10). Das Siegel des *ʾdnnr ʿbd ʿmndb* (**Abb. 2**) ist in einem Silberring gefaßt. Bei dem Siegel des *mkmʾl* (H 87) haben sich Reste eines goldenen Drahtes erhalten, der durch die Durchbohrung gezogen ist.

---

3. Vgl. zu diesen drei Siegeln Lemaire, *supra*, S. 21; Ornan, Fig. 8+17, 1+71, 15.

Über das *Material* bzw. die Gesteinsarten, aus dem die ammonitischen Siegel gefertigt wurden, ist meist nur Unsicheres bekannt; die Angaben wurden häufig nicht von Fachleuten, also Mineralogen, und die entsprechenden Farbangaben fast immer rein subjektiv statt nach dem Munsell'schen Prinzip o.ä. gemacht. Klar ist dennoch, daß eine Minderheit der Siegel aus weichen Gesteinen wie Serpentin oder Kalkstein oder harten wie Granit, die Mehrheit aber aus (importierten) kieselsauren Quarzsteinen wie Achat, Chalzedon oder Amethyst hergestellt wurden.

Rund die Hälfte der ca. 70 beschrifteten ammonitischen Siegel sind nahezu weitgehend rein epigraphische Siegel (s.o.).

Von diesen 70 Siegeln weisen knapp 40 Siegel zwei, 19 Siegel drei und nur ein Siegel vier horizontale Register auf (**Abb. 26**, wobei hier die Register durch zwei einfache und eine Doppellinie voneinander getrennt sind). Auf den bislang publizierten anepigraphischen Stempelsiegeln der Ammoniter wird die Siegelfläche nicht in Register eingeteilt.

Sofern die Siegelflächen der Siegel in *zwei* horizontale Register eingeteilt sind, werden sie meist durch eine Doppellinie voneinander getrennt (z.B. **Abb. 2**); bei den rein epigraphischen Siegeln ist dies fast immer der Fall. Nur ausnahmsweise werden die beiden Register durch eine einfache gerade (H 136, 142) oder kordelähnliche Linie (H 48) oder aber durch eine Doppellinie getrennt, die in der Mitte mit einer Scheibe verziert ist (H 25, 37, 62 [= **Abb. 12**]).

Sofern die Siegelflächen in *drei* horizontale Register eingeteilt sind, werden sie in 12 Fällen durch zwei Doppellinien (**Abb. 1, 8, 14, 16, 22f, 24f** sowie H 30, 33, 113, 130) und auf 7 Siegeln durch zwei einfache Linien voneinander getrennt (**Abb. 4, 15, 17, 19** sowie H 72, 77).

Auf den bebilderten Siegelflächen, die in zwei horizontale Register eingeteilt sind, ist die 'Ikone' fast immer im oberen, größeren Register und die Inschrift im unteren eingraviert (**Abb. 6, 20** sowie H 39, 70, 130, 136, 150).

Auf den Siegelflächen, die in drei horizontale Register eingeteilt sind, ist im oberen stets der Beginn der Inschrift mit dem Namen des Siegelbesitzers angebracht. Im zentralen mittleren Register, das immer auch das größte der drei Register ist, ist stets die 'Ikone' eingraviert, die nicht selten von der Filiation *bn* (**Abb. 4, 8, 22, 25** sowie H 72, 113), einem Titel (**Abb. 16**) oder Teilen davon begleitet oder flankiert wird. Im unteren Register folgt fast immer der Rest der Inschrift, also meist der Filiation das Patronym oder der Titulatur ein Königsname; nur auf dem Siegel des *plṭ* (H 130) folgt eine weitere 'Ikone' (Astralsymbole), auf dem Siegel des *mlkmgd* (**Abb. 17**) blieb das untere Register frei (unvollendet?). Diese Reihenfolge von Schrift und Bild ist auf den ersten drei Registern des Siegels des *tmkʾl bṙ mlkm* die gleiche, auf dem vierten Register unten folgt dann eine weitere, eher ornamentale 'Ikone' (**Abb. 26**).

Zweiseitig gravierte Namenssiegel aus Ammon sind eher selten: Auf dem Siegel des *byd᾽l ᶜbd pd᾽l* (**Abb. 13**) wird auf der einen Seite 'Harpokrates auf dem Lotus' rechts und links von der Inschrift gerahmt, auf der anderen Seite ein schreitender Stier von einem eigens ausgearbeiteten Schriftband umrahmt, in dem sich die gleiche Inschrift wiederholt. Auf dem Siegel des *᾽lšmᶜ bn bᶜr᾽* (H 55) und dem des *᾽lybr bn mnḥm* (**Abb. 6**) sind die flachen Siegelflächen jeweils mit einer zweizeiligen Inschrift versehen (die offizielle Seite?), die bombierte dagegen im unteren Register mit der Kurzfassung der Inschrift, also ohne Filiation und Patronym, beschriftet und im oberen Register mit einer 'Ikone' (Flügelsonne bzw. Mischwesen) bebildert (die 'private' Seite?, vgl. z.B. Avigad 1980b: 171f). Auf dem Siegel des *᾽l᾽mṣ bn tmk᾽l* vom Tell el-ᶜUmēri (H 155) ist auf der einen Seite über einem im Zentrum der Siegelfläche befindlichen Widderkopf *en face* die Inschrift *l-᾽l᾽mṣ* eingraviert, auf der anderen ein Vogel (Falke?) auf einer Lotus(?)-Blüte, der von der Inschrift *᾽l᾽mṣ bn tmk᾽l* umrandet wird. Auf dem Siegel des *bd᾽l bn ndb᾽l* (**Abb. 11**) ist die flache Siegelfläche mit einer auf zwei horizontale Register verteilten, zweizeiligen Inschrift versehen, die bombierte mit einer frontal dargestellten *dea nutrix* bebildert, die an beiden Seiten von der gleichen Inschrift gerahmt wird.

IV. Das ikonographische Repertoire der ammonitischen Siegel

Im folgenden versuche ich, das ikonographische Repertoire der sicher oder wahrscheinlich ammonitischen Siegel und seine Entwicklung anhand einer repräsentativen *Auswahl* der beschrifteten und unbeschrifteten Siegel der Eisen-II- und der Perser-Zeit darzustellen.

1. Tiere

1.1. Bovine und Capride

A Widder- oder Stierkopf *en face*: Ein frontal dargestellter Tierkopf (der von zwei Vögeln flankiert werden kann, s.u. 1.5.) ist auf Siegeln mit drei horizontalen Registern mehrfach bezeugt:

Ein Widderkopf *en face* ist auf dem Siegel des *plṭ* (H 130), dem des *᾽l᾽mṣ bn tmk᾽l* vom Tell el-ᶜUmēri (H 155) und auf einem Siegel mit einer Alphabetinschrift (**Abb. 1**) belegt, ein Stierkopf *en face* nur auf dem Siegel des *᾽lyšᶜ bn grgṙ* (**Abb. 7**).

Sowohl die Widder- als auch die Stier-Köpfe dürften ähnliche symbolische Bedeutungen (*pars pro toto*-Funktion) haben wie die Abbildungen der vollständig dargestellten Species (s.u.).

Parallelen solcher Tierköpfe *en face* sind schon auf bronzezeitlichen Zylindersiegeln Syriens (z.B. Porada 1948: 968; Keel 1984: Abb. 98) und dann häufig auf nordwestsemitischen Stempelsiegeln des 1. Jts. v. Chr. nachweisbar, z.B. auf dem (gileaditischen?) Siegel des *ṁtnʾl bn ʾẇrʾ* (CAI 106 = H 109) vom Tell Dēr ʿAllā (Widderkopf *en face*), auf dem israelitischen (?) Siegel des *ʾšʾ* (CAI 78a = H 60) (Widderkopf *en face*), auf einem aramäischen Siegelabdruck aus Ḥamā, der zwei Capriden- und zwei Boviden-Köpfe *en face* sowie einen Bovidenkopf im Profil zeigt (Riis & Buhl 1990: 90, Fig. 47:159), auf dem phönizischen Siegel des *zyʾ* (B 13; vgl. Gubel, *supra*, S. 117, Fig. 32) (Bovide *en face*), auf dem anepigraphischen edomitischen (oder judäischen?) Stempelsiegel aus Aroër im Negeb (Biran & Cohen 1981: 263, Fig. 10:9, Pl. 48:4) (Stierkopf *en face*), auf anepigraphischen Stempelsiegeln vom Tell Ǧemme (Petrie 1928: 11, Pl. 20:5) (Capriden-Kopf *en face*) sowie auf dem Siegel des *ʾlḥnn* (CAI 19 = H 27) (Widderkopf *en face*).

In ganzer Gestalt dargestellte Bovinen und Capriden sind in verschiedenen Formen belegt:

B Das Motiv des angreifenden Stiers mit aufgestemmten Vorderbeinen und gesenktem Kopf ist auf ammonitischen Stempelsiegeln mit jeweils drei Registern mehrfach bezeugt: Auf dem Siegel des *ʾyʾ bn tmkʾl* (**Abb. 4**), dem des *tmkʾ bn mqnmlk* (**Abb. 25**), auf dem des *ṣnr bn ʾlʾmṣ* (**Abb. 22**), auf dem des *šʿl bn ʾlyšʿ* (**Abb. 24**) und auf dem des *ynḥm* (**Abb. 15**). Auf dem Siegel des *ʾlrm bn bdʾl* (H 48) dürfte es sich um einen laufenden (angreifenden?) Stier handeln. Eine Parallele zum Motiv des 'angreifenden Stieres' bietet z.B. das Siegel des *yšʿʾl* (CAI 11 = H 84).

Auf dem Siegel des *tmkʾl bṙ mlkm* (**Abb. 26**) und wohl auch auf dem des *zkʾ br mlkmʾz̈* (H 72; cf. Lemaire, *supra*, S. 25, Fig. 17) ist ein schreitender Stier zu sehen. Auf dem Siegel des *bydʾl ʿbd pdʾl* (**Abb. 13**)[4], einem zweiseitig gravierten Stempelsiegel unbekannter Herkunft, sind die gleiche Inschrift zweimal und zwei verschiedene ikonographische Motive, schreitender Stier und 'Harpokrates', je einmal eingeschnitten.

Stiere sind Attribut- bzw. Postament-Tiere einer bzw. der Wettergottheit (vgl. Ebeling 1928a; Hahn 1981; Weippert 1961; Seidl, Hrouda & Krecher 1971: 494; Seidl 1989: 146; Welten 1977a: 99ff); in Ammon dürfte damit meist der Staats- bzw. Nationalgott Milkom gemeint gewesen sein, der seinem Wesen nach eine lokale Erscheinungsform des syro-palästinischen Wettergottes vom 'Hadad-Typ' gewesen ist (Hübner 1992a: Kap. 6).

Parallelen zum Motiv des 'schreitenden Stieres' sind im nordwestsemitischen Bereich vor allem auf transjordanischen und aramäischen Siegeln mehrfach bezeugt, z.B. auf dem Siegel des *mnḥm bn brkʾl* (CAI 133 = H 95) und

---

4. Der *pdʾl* des Siegels ist wegen des Titels *ʿbd* und wegen der Datierung wahrscheinlich der *P/Buduilu* der Inschriften Sanheribs, Asarhaddons und Assurbanipals, also **Pȧdāʾil*.

denen des *ʾdnlrm* und des *ʾlʾn* aus Ḥamā (Riis & Buhl 1990: 90.276.279, Fig. 46:158; 47:159, AramSig1f).

C Auf dem Siegel des *mnr* (**Abb. 20**) ist im oberen Register ein springender Capride eingraviert. Parallelen dazu sind auf nordwestsemitischen Siegeln mehrfach nachweisbar, z.B. auf dem Siegel des/der *yʿ.* oder dem des *yšʿʾl* (CAI 11; Avigad 1989a: Nr. 23 = H 82, 84). Capriden sind Attribut-Tiere verschiedener Gottheiten, vor allem von Wettergottheiten (vgl. Seidl, Hrouda & Krecher 1971: 494). Parallelen sind auf nordwestsemitischen Siegeln mehrfach bezeugt (z.B. Bennett 1966: 396, Pl. 24a).

Die angreifenden bzw. schreitendenen Stiere und springenden Capriden sind sowohl Symbol von Virilität und Fruchtbarkeit als auch Attribut-Tiere einer/der Wettergottheit.

D Das singuläre Motiv des liegenden Widders, flankiert von zwei Pflanzen, ist nur auf dem Siegel des *ḥnʾ bn bydʾl* (H 77) im mittleren von drei Registern belegt. Parallelen auf nordwestsemitischen Siegeln sind mir nicht bekannt.

E Das Kompositionsmotiv antithetisch angeordneter Capriden an einer stilisierten Palme (zum Motiv 'Lebensbaum' vgl. z.B. Ebeling 1928b; York 1975: 269-282; Winter 1986; Keel 1986a: 107ff u.ö.; Schroer 1987a: 19ff) ist auf einem anepigraphischen perserzeitlichen Stempelsiegel aus Ḫirbet Ḫulde belegt (**Abb. 33**). Auf einem der lokal hergestellten Zylindersiegel vom Tell el-ʿUmēri ist das Capriden-Lebensbaum-Motiv in einer eher provinziell anmutenden Variante ebenfalls abgebildet (**Abb. 35**). Parallelen sind auf unbeschrifteten levantinischen Siegeln häufig nachweisbar (vgl. etwa GGG: Abb. 222a-c; Pritchard 1985: 87, Fig. 173:2 = ANEP² Fig. 860).

F Das Motiv eines Muttertiers, das ein Jungtier säugt, ist innerhalb der ammonitischen Glyptik auch belegt (Bovine), allerdings nur auf dem Siegel des *plṭy* (**Abb. 21**), wo es zusätzlich mit einer Mondsichel und zwei bis drei Scheiben verziert ist.

Das säugende Muttertier symbolisiert sowohl den Bereich neuen Lebens und der Lebenslust als auch die Göttin ʿAnat und/oder ʿAstarte selbst (zum Motiv Keel 1980; Keel 1985: 33ff; Knauf 1988b). Parallelen sind auf nordwestsemitischen Siegeln öfters nachweisbar, z.B. auf dem Siegel des *ʾḥndb* (CAI 16 = H 19), des *ʿzy* (CAI 2 = H 121) und des *ʾbgd.* (CAI 54a = H 2), auf einem anepigraphischen Siegelabdruck aus dem edomitischen Buṣēra (Bennett 1975: 14f, Fig. 8:10) und auf einem moabitischen (?) Stempelsiegel (Timm, *infra*, S. 192, Abb. 6; vgl. auch die Malereien von Kuntilet ʿAǧrūd).

1.2. Schwein

Auf einem anepigraphischen Stempelsiegel aus dem Grab des *ʾdnnr* in ʿAmmān ist ein Schwein (oder Flußpferd?) eingraviert (**Abb. 27**), beide im Altertum als Wildtiere in Palästina belegt (vgl. Hübner 1989a). Wirkliche Parallelen sind mir nicht bekannt. Schweine sind auf aramäischen Siegeln der Achämeniden-Zeit recht häufig bezeugt (z.B. VSA 14).

1.3. Vögel

Ebenfalls häufig ist das Motiv eines oder mehrerer stilisierter Vögel (Taube/n oder Falke/n?) belegt, nämlich auf dem Siegel des *ʾlʾr bn ʾlzkr* (H 25), dem des *ʾlḥnn bn mnḥ* (H 29), dem des *ʾlʾmṣ bn tmkʾl* (H 155) und dem des *btʾl* (H 70). Hierzu ist auch das Motiv der zwei Vögel zu rechnen, die einen frontal dargestellten Tierkopf flankieren, das auf einem Alphabetsiegel (**Abb. 1**), auf dem Siegel des *ʾlyšʿ bn grgṙ* (**Abb. 7**) und auf dem des *plṭ* (H 130) erscheint (vgl. das Siegel des *ṁtnʾl bn ʾẇrʾ* aus dem gileaditischen Tell Dēr ʿAllā, CAI 106 = H 109).

Vögel, vor allem Tauben, symbolisieren (als Krönungs-, Sieges- und Liebesboten) eine weibliche Gottheit, z.B. ʿAstarte (Seyrig 1960: 233ff; Keel & Winter 1977; Keel 1984: 53ff), in Mesopotamien aber auch Papsukkal (Seyrig 1960: 233ff; Seidl 1989: 148-150), der Falke den Gott Horus.

Parallelen sind auf bronzezeitlichen syrischen Zylindersiegeln (z.B. Porada 1948: Nr. 964f; Jericho II: 658f, Fig. 304:3) und nordwestsemitischen Siegeln des 1. Jts. v. Chr. mehrfach nachweisbar, z.B. auf den Siegel des *ʾlʿz bn ʿzrʾl* (CAI 46 = H 46), auf dem Siegel mit der Inschrift *ʾbgdh* (CAI 24 = H 4), auf dem israelitischen (?) Siegel des *ʿkbry bn ʾmṣʾ* (CAI 112 = H 123), auf den phönizischen Siegeln des *ʾl* (VSF 80) und des/der *yzbl* (HD 31; vgl. Parayre, *supra*, S. 44, Fig. 19) (Falke?), auf den aramäischen Siegeln des *yʿdrʾl* (VSA 19), des *mṅtḥr* (B 12), des *ʾlbrḱ* (CAI 7 = H 26) und des *ʾbgd*˙ (CAI 54a = H 2) sowie auf den Siegeln des *ʿmsʾl* (CAI 72 = H 126), des *šṅʾb* (CAI 35 = H 145), des *ʿbdʾyṁ* (B 16 = H 118), des *yznʾl bn ʾlḥnn* (CAI 8 = H 79), des *tmkʾl bn ḥgt* (CAI 14 = H 151) und auf dem Siegel des *ʾbgd* (CAI 60 = H 3, Falke?).

1.4. Vierflügliger Skarabäus

Das Motiv des vierflügligen Skarabäus, der die Sonnenscheibe vor sich herrollt und stets von zwei 'Standarten' (s.u. 7.A) flankiert wird, ist auf fünf ammonitischen Siegeln bezeugt, nämlich auf den Siegeln des ...]*ʾlḥnn* (H 30), des *ʾlḥnn bn ʾẇrʾl* (H 28), des *mnḥm ḃn ynḥm* (**Abb. 19**), des *šwḥr hnss* (**Abb. 23**) und auf dem Siegel(abdruck) des *mlkm ʾwr ʿbd bʿlyšʿ* (**Abb. 16**).

Von diesen Siegeln, die aus dem (späten) 7. Jh. v. Chr. stammen, sind zwei Beamtensiegel mit den Titeln *ʿbd* bzw. *h-nss*. Möglicherweise ist das Motiv des vierflügligen Skarabäus – über Phönizien (?) – aus dem Nordreich Israel (Tushingham 1970; 1971; VSE 137; Younker 1989) und/oder dem Südreich Juda übernommen worden; dort war es z.B. auf einem nicht unerheblichen Teil der Königs- (z.B. Welten 1969: 10ff) und gelegentlich auch auf Beamten-Siegeln (HD 47; Lachish III: 348, Pl. 45:167) verbreitet.

Anhand des Siegel(abdruck)s des *mlkmʾwr ʿbd bʿlyšʿ* (**Baʿalyiṯaʿ*), eines hohen Beamten des letzten literarisch (vgl. auch Jer. 40,14; Fl. Josephus, Ant. 10,9,2f [§ 160.164]) und epigraphisch erwähnten ammonitischen Herrschers, hat R.W. Younker (1985; 1989) zeigen wollen, daß das Motiv des vierflügligen Skarabäus, der von zwei 'Standarten' flankiert wird, das offizielle ammonitische Staatssymbol gewesen sei. Auch wenn es durchaus möglich ist, daß das Motiv aus dem Nordreich Israel – nach (?) dessen Untergang – übernommen worden ist, war es deshalb nicht das Symbol des ammonitischen Staates, noch war Milkom eine Astralgottheit oder eine Variante des phönizischen Gottes Baʿal Ḥammon (Younker 1989).
Als ammonitisches Staatssymbol ist es aus mehreren Gründen unwahrscheinlich: Erstens weist nur ein weiteres ammonitisches Beamtensiegel das gleiche ikonographische Motiv auf, nämlich das Siegel des *šwḥr h-nss* (**Abb. 23**); zweitens sind andere ammonitische Beamtensiegel anikonisch wie z.B. die Siegel des *ʾdnnr ʿbd ʿmndb* (**Abb. 2**), des *bṯš nʿr brkʾl* (**Abb. 12**) oder des *ʿbdʾ nʿr ʾlrm* (H 116); drittens weisen zwei ammonitische Beamtensiegel ganz andere Bildmotive auf (geflügelter Dämon; Harpokrates und schreitender Stier), nämlich das Siegel des *ʾdnplṭ ʿbd ʿmndb* (**Abb. 3**) oder das Siegel des *bydʾl ʿbd pdʾl* (**Abb. 13**); und viertens ist der Zusammenhang zwischen dem theophoren Element *mlkm* des Personennamens des Siegelbesitzers (*mlkmʾwr*) und den ikonographischen Elementen weder zwingend noch beweisbar; weder das Siegel des *mlkmgd* (**Abb. 17**) noch das Siegel des *zkʾ br mlkmʿz* (H 72) oder das Siegel des *tmkʾl br mlkm* (**Abb. 26**) noch das Siegel des **Mannu-ki-Inurta* (vgl. **Abb. 18**) weisen einen vierflügligen Skarabäus oder eine 'Standarte' auf.
Überhaupt gibt es m.E. bei ammonitischen – und anderen nordwestsemitischen – Siegeln nur selten einen erkennbaren Zusammenhang zwischen den ikonographischen Elementen einerseits und den verwendeten Titeln oder theophoren Elementen der Personennamen andererseits (zum ammonitischen Onomastikon vgl. Jackson 1983b): (1) Mehrfach verteilen sich gleiche ikonographische Motive auf mehrere verschiedene Siegelbesitzer, deren Personennamen verschiedene theophore Elemente (oder aber als Hypokoristika auch keine) aufweisen. (2) Gleiche Personennamen können verschiedene ikonographische Motive zugeordnet sein. (3) Die Siegel **Abb. 16-18, 26** mit dem theophoren Element *mlkm* weisen völlig verschiedene ikonographische Motive auf (vor allem vierflüglige Skarabäen, Adoranten, Sphingen und Quadrupeden). (4) Auch nach der sozialen Schichtung der Siegel sind keine ikonographischen Unterschiede erkennbar: Auf den Privatsiegeln sind die gleichen 'Ikonen' möglich wie auf den Beamtensiegeln.

Das Motiv des vierflügligen Skarabäus ist auf nordwestsemitischen Siegeln häufig nachgewiesen, auf phönizischen (z.B. BAALIM VI: 490f, Fig. 8, flankiert von zwei *ʿnḫ*-Zeichen; Siegel des *mq̇n*, Lemaire 1986: Nr. 2 = H 104; VSF 21; vgl. Gubel, *supra*, S. 117, figs. 33-35, und S. 122), israelitischen (s.o.; Samaria, vgl. Sass, *infra*, S. 216-217, Motiv B2.3), judäischen und aramäischen (z.B. VSA 3, 24) Siegeln, vgl. auch das Siegel des *ʾlntn* (CAI 32 = H 42).

1.5. Skorpion

Der Skorpion ist schon auf einem proto-ammonitischen Stempelsiegel aus Saḥāb (Ibrahim 1983: 48, Abb. 5a, Taf. 3A)[5] und dann wieder auf einem aus Ḫirbet Ḫulde stammenden anepigraphischen perserzeitlichen Stempelsiegel lokaler (?) Produktion bezeugt (**Abb. 34**). Er dürfte das Attribut-Tier einer oder mehrerer vorderasiatischer Liebes- und Fruchtbarkeitsgöttinnen, vor allem wohl ʿAstartes bzw. Ištars, gewesen sein (in Mesopotamien der Göttin Išḫara: Lambert & Frantz-Szabó 1980: 176-178; Seidl 1989: 156f; in Ägypten der Göttin Selqet: von Känel 1984; Behrens 1984). Das Motiv ist auf Stempelsiegeln verschiedener Zeiten in Palästina mehrfach belegt, z.B. in Dibon, Umm el-Biyāra (?), Tell el-Fārʿa Nord und Süd, Taʿanach, Tell en-Naṣbe, Sichem, Bet-Schemesch, Geser, Lachisch und Megiddo (z.B. Keel 1980: 89.114ff; Keel & Schroer 1985: 26ff; Bennett 1966: 396, Pl. 24a).

2. Menschen

Adoranten sind auf dem Siegel des *ʾlʿz bn mnḥm* (**Abb. 9**) und dem Siegel des *ʾlšmʿ* (H 51) belegt. Auf dem Siegel des **Mannu-ki-Inurta* ist auf der kreisrunden Basis des Konoïds eine weitverbreitete mythologische Kampfszene in Drillbohrertechnik eingraviert: Ein Heros (Heimpel & Boehmer 1975; Seidl 1989: 206f; Braun-Holzinger 1990: 101) packt mit der einen Hand ein vogelköpfiges, geflügeltes Mischwesen am Schopf und holt mit der anderen mit einem Krummschwert zum tödlichen Schlag aus (vgl. Ornan, *supra*, S. 55, Fig. 1). Auf der Langseite des Konoïds gegenüber der Inschrift ist ein Adorant in assyrisierendem westsemitischem Stil (schreitend, mit erhobenen Händen und mit einem Schurzrock bekleidet) eingraviert (**Abb. 18**, vgl. Ornan, *supra*, S. 68f mit Fig. 71), der seine Parallelen in den eben genannten ammonitischen Siegeln hat. Der Konoïd dürfte einschließlich der mythologischen Aktionsszene auf der Basis aus Mesopotamien nach Ammon importiert worden sein und dort dann der Konusmantel von einem lokalen Siegelschneider auf einer Seite mit der Inschrift, auf der anderen mit einem Adoranten versehen worden sein.

---

5. Vgl. z.B. Tell Kēsān (Keel et al. 1990: 210-217), Bet-Schemesch (ebd. 386, Abb. 94), Geser (Dever et al. 1986: 127, Pl. 62:17, 120:B), Bet-Zur (Sellers 1968: 82, Pl. 41c).

Auf dem Siegel des *ʾlʾmṣ bn ʾlšʿ* (**Abb. 5**; vgl. Ornan, *supra*, S. 70, Fig. 77) ist der Adorant in einem langen Gewand in einer assyrisierenden Form wiedergegeben. Adoranten in langem Gewand kommen z.B. auch auf dem Siegel des *ʾlrm bn tmʾ* (CAI 15 = H 49), dem aramäischen Siegel des *ʾbgd*: (CAI 54a = H 2) und dem Siegel *ʾbgdh* (CAI 24 = H 4) vor.

Auf einem importierten anepigraphischen Stempelsiegel aus dem Grab des *ʾdnnr* in Rabbat-Ammon (Harding 1953: 53f, Nr. 6; Hübner 1992a: Kap. 2. 10.2; 6) ist auf der Basis des facettierten Konoïds ein Adorant abgebildet, der vor dem Mondgott auf der Mondsichel steht. Parallelen dieser Adoranten-Form liefern auch die Importsiegel mit den Symbolen des Marduk und Nabû (s.u. 3.4.B).

Das Motiv des Adoranten (Verehrers) ist auf zahlreichen nordwestsemitischen Siegeln nachweisbar, z.B. auch auf moabitischen (Timm 1989a: Nr. 8, 11, 15, 27), phönizischen (z.B. Siegel des *yznʾl bn ʾlḥnn*, CAI 8 = H 79; des *mq̇n*, Lemaire 1986: Nr. 2 = H 104; des *šr*:, CAI 128 = H 148; des *krzy*, VSA 57) und aramäischen Siegeln (z.B. des *ʾbgd*, CAI 82 = H 1; vgl. Ornan, *supra*, S. 63-71 mit diesen und weiteren Parallelen).

3. Gottheiten

3.1. "Herr der Tiere"

Auf einem anepigraphischen Rollsiegel aus Meqābelēn (Harding 1950: 46, Nr. 34, Pl. 15:10) ist das Motiv des "Herrn der Tiere" belegt: Ein Heros hält in den beiden ausgestreckten Händen je eine Capride an den Hinterbeinen. Das Motiv (Lux 1962: 54ff; Wozak 1966; Calmeyer 1975) ist auf nordwestsemitischen beschrifteten und zahlreichen anderen Siegeln aus Palästina und Syrien nachweisbar (z.B. Keel u.a. 1989: 121f; B 131, 138; vgl. Ornan, *supra*, S. 54f).

3.2. Nackte Göttin

Das Motiv der nackten Frau *en face*, die ihre Hände unter ihre Brüste hält (und mit zwei scheibenförmigen Ohrringen geschmückt ist), ist auf dem ammonitischen Siegel des *bdʾl bn ndbʾl* belegt (**Abb. 11**). Wahrscheinlich handelt es sich bei der dargestellten *dea nutrix* um die weibliche Paredros des ammonitischen National- und Staatsgottes Milkom, wie sie auch in zahlreichen ammonitischen Terrakotten (ʿAmr 1980: Nr. 23ff; Hübner 1992a: Kap. 6.3) und weiblichen Doppelköpfen aus ʿAmmān (Abou Assaf 1980: Nr. 21-24) verkörpert ist.[6]

---

6. Römische Münzen aus Philadelphia (Spijkerman 1978: 242ff) zeigen Darstellungen der Göttin Asteria, die mit Zeus/Jupiter den tyrischen Herakles zeugte, der wiederum nichts anderes ist als die *interpretatio graeca* des tyrischen Melqart (Bonnet 1988), der über eine tyrische Kolonie in Rabbat-Ammon mit Milkom identifiziert worden sein dürfte (Hüb-

Das Motiv der nackten Göttin ist auf nordwestsemitischen Stempelsiegeln der Eisen-II-Zeit relativ selten nachweisbar, z.B. auf dem Siegel des *mnḥm bn smk ʿbd mlk* (CAI 102 = H 98), das wegen der gepunkteten Rahmenlinie (vgl. dazu VSE 38, 67, 424-425; B 45; A [25b,] 52, 69, 83, auch VSE 24; Sass, *infra*, S. 206) als judäisch oder israelitisch interpretiert werden kann – sofern es sich bei der ungrammatischen Titulatur *ʿbd mlk* statt *ʿbd h-mlk* nicht um einen Schreibfehler eines antiken Siegelschneiders, sondern um den eines modernen Fälschers handelt. Umso häufiger ist das Motiv der nackten Göttin dagegen – dreidimensional – in zahllosen Terrakottafigurinen innerhalb sämtlicher palästinischer Kulturen der Eisenzeit belegt (Hübner 1989c).

3.3. Harpokrates

Das ägyptisierende Motiv des Harpokrates ist auf drei ammonitischen Siegeln belegt, auf dem Siegel des *ʾlšmʿ bn b.. ʾl* (H 54), auf dem des *bydʾl ʿbd pdʾl* (**Abb. 13**) und auf dem des *mtʾ bn šʿl* (H 108; vgl. zudem jüngst Aufrecht 1992: Nr. 2; Hübner 1992c: *lẓnr bn ʾlʿzr*). Der jugendliche Sonnengott – mit dem Gestus 'Finger am Mund' oder 'Riechen am Lotus' oder einfach essend (?) – sitzt bzw. hockt auf einer Lotusblüte, d.h. über dem Urozean, und ist so ein Sinnbild für das Entstehen allen Lebens (Morenz & Schubert 1954: 14ff). Auf mindestens zwei der drei ammonitischen Darstellungen geht die Ikonographie offenbar nicht allein auf reine Harpokrates-Vorlagen, sondern zugleich auch auf Darstellungen hockender, fressender Affen zurück (vgl. die Affen-Terrakotta vom Tell Ṣāfūṭ: Königsweg: Nr. 125); insofern dürfte es sich um eine provinziell mißverstandene Mischung aus Affen- und Harpokrates-Darstellungen handeln.

Das ägyptisierend-phönizisierende Motiv (Meeks 1977) des Harpokrates hat zahlreiche Parallelen auf nordwestsemitischen Stempelsiegeln, z.B. auf dem Siegel der *ʾlšgb bt ʾlšmʿ* (CAI 9 = H 50), auf dem israelitischen Siegel des *ʿšyw bn ywqm* (VSE 38) und dem des *ʾbyw ʿbd ʿzyw* (VSE 65; vgl. Sass, *infra*, S. 228f, Motiv F3, dazu auch die Samaria-Elfenbeine).

3.4. Mesopotamische Gottheiten

Auch mesopotamische Gottheiten sind auf in die Ammonitis importierten Siegeln belegt:

A Auf dem schon genannten anepigraphischen Stempelsiegel aus dem Grab des *ʾdnnr* in Rabbat-Ammon ist auf einer Seite des facettierten Konoïds die Heilgöttin Gula eingraviert (**Abb. 31**). Sie sitzt auf einem Thron, an dessen Rücklehne mehrere Punkte bzw. Sterne angebracht sind. In ihrer linken

---

ner 1992a: Kap. 6). Zu erinnern ist in diesem Zusammenhang auch an einen der wechselnden Namen Rabbat-Ammons: Laut Stephanus von Byzanz hieß die Stadt in römischer Zeit ʾΑσταρτη.

Hand hält sie einen Ring, von dem eine Leine zu ihrem Postament-Tier, dem Hund, führt (vgl. Frankena & Seidl 1971: 695-697; Heimpel & Seidl 1975: 494-497; Seidl 1989: 140f). Aller Wahrscheinlichkeit nach handelt es sich bei dem Siegel um einen Import aus Mesopotamien; gleichwohl zeigen solche Funde, wie vertraut Ammoniter der Oberschicht mit diesen nichtammonitischen Bildern waren. Parallelen des Motivs sind auch auf weiteren nach Palästina importierten Siegeln der Eisenzeit und auf einem aramäischen Siegel (Ornan, *supra*, S. 62, Fig. 34) bezeugt.

B Die Götter Marduk und Nabû sind über ihre Attribute Hacke (*marru*) und Griffel (*qan ṭuppi*) identifizierbar (Pomponio 1978: 213-215; Seidl 1989: 117-125.197-193; Sommerfeld et al. 1990), die auf einem Podest aufgestellt sind, vor dem ein Adorant steht. Sie sind auf anepigraphischen Stempelsiegeln vom Tell Ṣāfūṭ (**Abb. 29**), aus Meqābelēn (Harding 1950: 46, Pl. 13:2; 15:9), ʿAmmān (**Abb. 30**; Dajani 1962: 124f, Pl. 4:8) und aus Ḫirbet Ḫulde (Yassine 1988: 21, Fig. 8:3) mehrfach nachgewiesen. Parallelen des Motivs sind auf importierten und imitierten Stempelsiegeln der Eisenzeit in Juda (z.B. Geser, En-Gedi, Tell eṣ-Ṣāfī), in Phönizien (z.B. ʿAtlīt, Tell Kēsān) und in Israel (z.B. Bet-El, Samaria) häufig bezeugt; vgl. auch das Siegel des *mnḥm* (CAI 29 = H 92) und andere aramäische Siegel (Ornan, *supra*, S. 65, Fig. 36-46).

4. Mischwesen bzw. Fabeltiere[7] und Dämonen

A Das Motiv des schreitenden, geflügelten Sphingen ist auf vier ammonitischen Siegeln überliefert, nämlich auf dem Siegel des *tmkʾl* (H 150), dem des *ndbʾl bn tmkʾ* (H 113), dem des *ʾlybr bn mnḥm* (**Abb. 6**) und dem des *bqš bn ʿzʾ* (**Abb. 14**).

Das Motiv findet sich häufig auf nordwestsemitischen Siegeln, z.B. auf dem Siegel des *pdʾl* (CAI 33 = H 129), dem des *ʿbdʾdd bn ʾddʾl* (CAI 131 = H 116), dem judäischen Siegel des/der *ḥnh* (VSE 351; vgl. Sass, *infra*, S. 227, Fig. 123), auf dem moabitischen Siegel des *ʾḥyšʿ* (Timm, *infra*, S. 192, Abb. 7) und dem edomitischen Siegel des **qwsg[br] mlk ʾ[dm* (Bartlett 1989: Nr. 5; vgl. Lemaire, *supra*, S. 23, Fig. 6). Vgl. auch dazu die Samaria-Elfenbeine.

B Das Kompositionsmotiv zweier antithetisch angeordneter, geflügelter Sphingen, die vor einem mit einer Lotus-Blüte kombinierten *ʿnḫ*-Zeichen sitzen, ist auf dem Siegel des *mlkmgd* (**Abb. 17**) bezeugt.

---

7. Sphingen, Drachen, Greifen (zum Motiv z.B. Bisi 1965: 80ff; Braun-Holzinger 1990: 97-102; Börker-Klähn 1971; Dessenne 1957; Gubel 1985; Seidl 1989: 171ff u.ö.; Unger 1938b; Welten 1977b).

Parallelen sind verschiedentlich auf nordwestsemitischen und anderen Siegeln nachweisbar, z.B. auf dem moabitischen Stempelsiegel des *kmšdn* (Timm, *infra*, S. 166f mit Abb. 4), dem aramäischen Zylindersiegel des *mtrš br š*ʿ*y* (B 128), einem Zylindersiegel aus Aseka (Bliss & Macalister 1902: 153, Pl. 83:2z) und auf bronzezeitlichen und spät-neoassyrisch-neobabylonischen Zylindersiegeln (z.B. Keel 1984: Abb. 49, 97; Porada 1948: Nr. 739; Hazor III-IV: Pl. 319:2).

C Das Motiv des schreitenden, geflügelten und mit einem Löwenkopf (?) versehenen Fabeltieres (Braun-Holzinger 1990) ist auf dem Siegel des *ʾlndb* (H 39) und einem anepigraphischen Stempelsiegel aus dem Grab des *ʾdnnr* in ʿAmmān (Harding 1953: 53, Pl. 6:5) überliefert. Parallelen sind verschiedentlich auf nordwestsemitischen Siegeln nachgewiesen (vgl. Ornan, *supra*, S. 55f mit Fig. 6).

D Auf dem Siegel des *ʾdnplṭ* ʿ*bd* ʿ*mndb* (**Abb. 3**) ist unterhalb einer Mondsichel und einer Scheibe ein geflügelter Dämon (*ugallu* (?), AHw 1402) mit einem Löwen- oder Caniden(?)-Kopf zu sehen (vgl. B 117), der einen Dolch (Seidl 1989: 132f) in der Hand hält (vgl. Unger 1938a; Ellis 1977; Green 1984: 85-87; 1986; Wiggermann 1992: 170-172; doch vgl. Ornan, *supra*, S. 56, die von einem Vogelkopf spricht). Ein ähnliches Motiv (Green 1986: 165.231f, Pl. 40:152) stammt von dem facettierten Konoïd aus dem Grab des *ʾdnnr*, der unter anderen Motiven auch die Heilgöttin Gula darstellt (s.o.).

Ikonographie und Stil des assyrischen Motivs auf dem Siegel deuten darauf, daß es kaum von einem Ammoniter gestaltet worden sein dürfte. Wahrscheinlich handelt es sich um einen Import, der erst in Ammon von einem ammonitischen Siegelproduzenten für seinen ammonitischen Auftraggeber beschriftet wurde. Zu Parallelen vgl. z.B. Unger 1938a; Green 1986; zur Identifikation der Mischwesen allgemein nun Wiggermann 1992.

E Auf dem doppelseitig gravierten Siegel (ovale, leicht bikonvex bombierte Platte) des *šbʾl* (H 136; vgl. Ornan, *supra*, S. 57 Fig. 8, S. 59 Fig. 17) aus dem Grab des *ʾdnnr* in ʿAmmān ist auf der einen Seite eine fragmentarisch erhaltene, vierflüglige menschliche Figur in einem langen assyrischen Gewand zu sehen, auf der anderen Seite ein geflügelter Stiermensch (*kusarikku* (?), AHw I 514; Wiggermann 1992: 174-179), darunter die Inschrift. Die Ikonographie ist neoassyrisch (stark beeinflußt), die Inschrift ammonitisch.

Parallelen zu dem Motiv des vierflügligen ‘Genius’ sind auf nordwestsemitischen Siegeln häufig bezeugt (z.B. Keel 1977: 194ff; moabitisch Timm, *infra*, S. 165f mit Abb. 3, vgl. S. 175ff mit Abb. 11-13; phönizisch CAI 107 = H 86; VSF 89; B 19f; aramäisch VSA 33, 68; HD 131; vgl. Gubel, *supra*, S. 123ff mit Fig. 64-70), zum Stiermenschen mehrfach (z.B. Keel 1977: 207ff; HD 136; B 117; vgl. Ornan, *supra*, S. 56f und Fig. 9).

[**F** Ob das Motiv des vierflügligen Uräus (Keel 1977: 70ff) in der ammonitischen Glyptik vorkam, ist ungewiß. Es ist auf einem anepigraphischen Stempelsiegel belegt, das in ʿAmmān gekauft wurde (**Abb. 28**) und möglicherweise ammonitisch ist – falls es sich nicht doch um ein Importstück aus Juda oder Israel handelt. Parallelen sind auf nordwestsemitischen Siegeln häufig nachweisbar, so z.B. auch auf dem (israelitischen?) Siegel des *ʾlšmʿ [b(n)] pll* (CAI 95 = H 56) oder den judäischen Siegeln des *yḥmlyhw mʿś-yhw* (VSE 51) und des *ʾlšmʿ bn h-mlk* bezeugt (VSE 72, vgl. VSE 89; A 201; dazu Sass, *infra*, S. 213f, Motiv B1.3).]

5. Pflanzliche Motive

A Das Lotus-Motiv ist auf dem Siegel des *tmkʾl bṙ mlkm* (**Abb. 26**), dem des *bydʾl ʿbd pdʾl* (**Abb. 13**), dem des *ʾlʾmṣ bn tmkʾl* (H 155) (?) und dem des *ʾlšmʿ bn b..ʾl* (H 54) (?) bezeugt. Auf dem Siegel des *mlkmgd* (**Abb. 17**) ist ein mit einer Lotus-Blüte kombiniertes *ʿnḫ*-Zeichen eingraviert, das von zwei Sphingen flankiert wird. Die Statue des *yrḥʿzr* aus ʿAmmān hat ebenfalls eine Lotus-Blüte in der Hand.

Die Lotus-Blüte ist ein heilvolles, lebensdienliches Symbol, das Liebeshauch, erfrischtes Leben und neue Kraft (Keel 1984: 63ff; 1986a: 79ff u.ö.; van Loon 1986; Bleibtreu 1990) andeutet. Das Motiv hat zahlreiche Parallelen auf nordwestsemitischen Siegeln, z.B. auf dem Siegel *ʾbgdh* (CAI 24 = H 4; vgl. auch Sass, *infra*, S. 209f, Motiv A3.1, sowie die Samaria-Elfenbeine).

B Daneben sind auch der Lebensbaum auf einem anepigraphischen perserzeitlichen Zylindersiegel vom Tell el-ʿUmēri (**Abb. 35**) und stilisierte Zweige auf dem Siegel des *ʾlndb* (H 39) belegt.

C Granatäpfel (zum Motiv vgl. z.B. Börker-Klähn & Röllig 1971; Keel 1986a: 134-136), Motiv des Lebens und Attribut der Aphrodite/ʿAstarte/Ištar, flankieren auf einem anepigraphischen Siegel (**Abb. 28**) einen vierflügligen Uräus. Die Herkunft des Siegels ist ungewiß; es kann sich um einen judäischen Export in die Ammonitis handeln (s.o. 4.F). Vgl. auch die Granatapfel-'Standarten' auf dem Siegel des *šʿl bn ʾlyšʿ* (**Abb. 24**).

6. Astralsymbole

A Der (acht-strahlige bzw. -zackige) Einzel-Stern ist auf dem Siegel des *tmkʾl bṙ mlkm* (**Abb. 26**) belegt. Er ist Symbol einer weiblichen, kriegerischen Gottheit, meist Ištars (Seidl, Hrouda & Krecher 1971: 485; Wilcke & Seidl 1980: 74-89; Seidl 1989: 100f). Einzelne Sterne sind auf nordwestsemitischen Siegeln häufig bezeugt, etwa moabitischen (z.B. Timm 1989a: Nr. 6, 15, 18, 21-24; *infra*, S. 192f, Abb. 2, 5, 15-20), phönizischen (z.B. B 4, 23) und aramäischen (z.B. B 85, 94f, 97f, 101, 103 u.ö.).

B Die Mondsichel ist auf ammonitischen Siegeln mehrfach belegt, vor allem auf den Siegeln des *ʾdnplṭ ʿbd ʿmndb* (**Abb. 3**), des *ḥnʾ bn bydʾl* (H 77), des *plṭ* (H 130), des *plṭy* (**Abb. 21**) und des *tmkʾl bṙ mlkm* (**Abb. 26**). Sie ist Symbol des Mondgottes (Sîn von Ḫarrān, Seidl 1989: 97f), der auf einem anepigraphischen Import-Siegel aus dem Grab des *ʾdnnr* auch *in personam* (?) auf der Sichel vor einem Adoranten abgebildet ist (s.o.; vgl. Ornan, *supra*, S. 61f, Fig. 23-26.30-33) und im ammonitischen Personennamen *yrḥʿzr* (Sockelinschrift der Statue aus ʿAmmān, Hübner 1992a: Kap. 2.1, Nr. 3) bezeugt ist.

Die Mondsichel ist innerhalb der nordwestsemitischen Glyptik häufig nachgewiesen, etwa auf moabitischen (z.B. Timm 1989a: Nr. 2, 6, 9, 15, 17f, 21-24, 27; *infra*, S. 192f, Abb. 2, 5f, 16-20), edomitischen (Bartlett 1989: Nr. 1, 7) und aramäischen Siegeln (z.B. B 85, 96f, 101, 103 u.ö.).

C Das Motiv der (Sonnen- oder Mond-)Scheibe ist innerhalb der ammonitischen Glyptik ebenfalls häufig belegt, nämlich auf den Siegeln des *ʾdnplṭ ʿbd ʿmndb* (**Abb. 3**), des *ʾyʾ bn tmkʾl* (**Abb. 4**), des *ʾlḥnn bn mnḥ* (H 29), des *ʾlndb* (H 39), des *btʾl* (H 70), des *plṭ* (H 130), des *plṭy* (**Abb. 21**) und auf dem ammonitischen (?) anepigraphischen Stempelsiegel von **Abb. 28**. Die Scheibe dürfte in der Regel das Symbol des Sonnengottes (Šamaš, Seidl 1989: 98-100) oder auch des Mondgottes Sîn sein. Sie hat zahlreiche Parallelen auf nordwestsemitischen Stempelsiegeln.

D Die Flügelsonne ist auf dem Siegel des *ʾln bn ʾmrʾl* (**Abb. 8**) und dem des *ʾlšmʿ bn bʿrʾ* (H 55) bezeugt. Sie ist das Symbol der geordneten Welt, des Sonnengottes Šamaš oder kann auch Königssymbol sein und ist u.a. auf judäischen, israelitischen, moabitischen, phönizischen und aramäischen Siegeln häufig nachweisbar (Parayre 1990a; vgl. *supra*, S. 27ff).

7. 'Standarten' und ʿnḫ-Zeichen

A Das Motiv der 'Standarten' (Szepter, stilisierte Pflanze?)[8], die innerhalb der ammonitischen Glyptik stets paarweise erscheinen und den vierflügligen Skarabäus flankieren (s.o. 1.4.), ist auf den Siegeln des ...]*ʾlḥnn* (H 30), des *mnḥm ḃn ynḥm* (**Abb. 19**), des *šwḥr h-nss* (**Abb. 23**) und auf dem Siegel(abdruck) des *mlkmʾwr ʿbd bʿlyšʿ* (**Abb. 16**) belegt.

Parallelen sind auf nordwestsemitischen Siegel mehrfach, freilich jeweils einzeln, belegt, etwa auf phönizischen Siegeln (vgl. Gubel, *supra*, S. 118ff mit Abb. 42-53, jeweils Szepter).

---

8. Sie werden von R.W. Younker (1985; 1989) als *caduceus* (*κηρικειον*) bezeichnet, also als Symbol der Heroldswürde des Hermes bzw. Mercur verstanden (Samter 1897; Ariel 1990: 13ff, S 104-110, S 152, S 190f, S 327), eine kultur-, form- und sachfremde Bezeichnung für dieses ikonographische Element nordwestsemitischer Glyptik.

B Das ursprünglich aus Ägypten stammende *ʿnḫ*-Zeichen (Collon 1983: 240f) ist auf dem Siegel des *mlkmgd* (**Abb. 17**) bezeugt. Es hat zahlreiche Parallelen auf nordwestsemitischen Siegeln (moabitisch z.B. Timm 1989a: Nr. 9f, 13, 26, phönizisch z.B. BAALIM VI: 490f, Fig. 8). Vgl. auch die Samaria-Elfenbeine.

8. *Mehrfach belegte Motiv-Kombinationen bzw. -Kompositionen*

A Die Astralsymbole Mondsichel und Scheibe sind häufig unmittelbar über- bzw. ineinander dargestellt auf dem Siegel des *plṭ* (H 130), dem des *plṭy* (**Abb. 21**) und auf einem anepigraphischen Stempelsiegel aus dem Grab des *ʾdnnr* in ʿAmmān (**Abb. 32**). Parallelen sind auf nordwestsemitischen Stempelsiegeln häufig bezeugt.

B Das Motiv des "Tierkopfes *en face*", der von zwei Vögeln flankiert wird, ist innerhalb der ammonitischen Glyptik mehrfach nachweisbar (s.o. 1.1.A, 1.3., vgl. unten S. 150).

C Der vierflüglige Skarabäus, der von zwei 'Standarten' flankiert wird, ist innerhalb der ammonitischen Glyptik ebenfalls mehrfach nachweisbar (s.o. 1.4.).

D Auch der Quadruped, der von zwei 'Standarten' o.ä. flankiert wird, ist innerhalb der ammonitischen Glyptik mehrfach belegt (s.o. 1.1.).

V. GRUNDZÜGE DER IKONOGRAPHIE DER AMMONITISCHEN SIEGEL

Was ist – ikonographisch gesehen – typisch ammonitisch an den ammonitischen Siegeln? Die Frage nach dem Proprium der Ikonographie der ammonitischen Siegel hat nicht nur den gleichen Schwierigkeitsgrad, sondern auch die gleiche Problematik wie die so beliebte Frage nach dem Proprium der vorexilischen Religion Israels. Deshalb ist die Frage nur sehr relativ zu beantworten. Zunächst ist festzuhalten, daß die gemeinsamen kulturellen, religiösen, sprachlichen, sozialen und ökonomischen Grundlagen, die die eisenzeitlichen Ammoniter mit den ihnen benachbarten Völkern und Staaten verbanden, weitaus größer waren als das sie Trennende. Die wenigen und oft nur mühsam erkennbaren Unterschiede lagen nicht im Grundsätzlichen, sondern in den Details.

Dem entspricht, daß es innerhalb der ammonitischen Glyptik so gut wie kein Motiv gibt, das nicht auch außerhalb Ammons belegt wäre: Fast alle Bildelemente, Motive und Ornamente sind in (mehr oder weniger) verwandter

Form auch in den zeitgenössischen Nachbarstaaten Ammons gut bezeugt (zu Kompositionen s.o. IV.8; zum liegenden Widder s.o. IV.1.1.D).

Darüber hinaus ist kein Motiv innerhalb der ammonitischen Siegel so häufig belegt und dabei gleichzeitig innerhalb der nordwestsemitischen Siegel so stark auf Ammon beschränkt, daß man es für typisch ammonitisch halten könnte. Daher sind Zweifel zumindest nicht unberechtigt, ob Siegel aufgrund ihrer Ikonographie Ammon überhaupt zugewiesen werden können (vgl. Timm 1989a: 160f mit entsprechenden Zweifeln bezüglich Moabs). Zwar fehlen bislang vielfach genaue Studien zu einzelnen Bildelementen oder Bildkompositionen und ihrer Verbreitung innerhalb der nordwestsemitischen Siegel, aber selbst Untersuchungen wie die von D. Parayre (1990a) über die Flügelsonne haben für die auf ammonitischen Siegel belegten Formen der Flügelsonne nur – und m.E. zu Recht – nachweisen können, daß diese Form ("types orientaux sans volutes, empennages doubles asymétriques") typisch für den südsyrisch-aramäischen, ammonitischen und moabitischen Bereich ist; man hat danach also aufgrund der Ikonographie immer noch eine drei- bzw. vierfache Möglichkeit der Zuweisung, nämlich in den aramäischen, den ammonitischen, den gileaditischen oder den moabitischen Bereich. (Methodisch ist dabei anzumerken, daß D. Parayre die Zuweisungen der Paläographen weitgehend übernommen hat und ihre ikonographischen Untersuchungen darauf aufbauend durchgeführt hat, was letztlich ein Zirkelschluß ist, sofern es um die Frage der Zuweisung aufgrund der Ikonographie geht.)

Auffälliger ist vielleicht schon das *Fehlen* mancher Motive in der ammonitischen Glyptik: So fehlt z.B. Löwe (sofern CAI 52 = H 120 eine Fälschung ist [Hübner 1989b: 224ff] und die Siegel CAI 7, 21, 72, 6 = H 26, 106, 126, 128 nicht bzw. nicht wahrscheinlich ammonitischer Herkunft sind; zur eisenzeitlichen (?!) Löwenplastik aus ʿAmmān vgl. Zayadine 1977-78: 34, Pl. 16). Ebenso fehlen etwa Bogenschütze, Leier, Palmette, Pleiaden, Jagdszenen, zweiflügliger Skarabäus, Bes, *w3ś*-Szepter, *nb*- und *nfr*-Zeichen und wohl auch das Motiv des vierflügligen Uräus (s.o. IV.4.F). Allerdings ist das – vermeintliche oder tatsächliche (?) – Fehlen der genannten Motive auch ein Problem des Überlieferungszufalls und zudem abhängig von der Frage, welche Siegel man für ammonitisch hält und welche nicht. Dennoch scheint mir der bisher bekannt gewordene Überlieferungszustand der ammonitischen Glyptik nicht ganz zufällig zu sein. In ihm spiegelt sich ein Repertoire wieder, das für den am Ostrand Palästinas gelegenen Zwergstaat typisch zu sein scheint: ein in den Motiven her begrenztes, etwas provinzielles Repertoire. Das zweifache kulturelle Gefälle, das einerseits vom West- zum Ostjordanland hin zunahm und sich andererseits in Transjordanien von Nord nach Süd (von Phönizien aus) über die südlichen Aramäerstaaten, Gilead, Ammon, Moab und Edom verstärkte, machte sich auch in der ammonitischen (Miniatur-)Kunst bemerkbar (zum assyrischen Einfluß s.u. VI.).

Selbstverständlich kann man davon ausgehen, daß es ammonitische Siegelwerkstätten bzw. einzelne individuelle ammonitische Siegelschneider gab; der Nachweis ihrer Existenz ist allerdings schwierig. D. Parayre (1990a: 283, Nr. 120f) glaubt, daß die beiden Siegel des *ʾln bn ʾmrʾl* (**Abb. 8**) und des *ʾlšmʿ bn bʿrʾ* (CAI 88 = H 55) auf einen Siegelschneider bzw. eine Werkstatt zurückgingen. Diese Hypothese ist einleuchtend, wird allerdings dadurch etwas eingeschränkt, daß nur mit dem gleichartigen Aufsatz auf der Sonnenscheibe argumentiert wird, aber die sonstigen Unterschiede ikonographischer (und paläographischer) Art nicht beim Namen genannt und erklärt werden; mit ihrer Hilfe könnte man auch zum gegenteiligen Schluß gelangen.

Eher könnte man schon bei den eng miteinander verwandten Widder- bzw. Stierköpfen, die von Vögeln flankiert werden, auf eine Werkstatt in der Ammonitis schließen (**Abb. 1**, **7**, das Siegel des *plṭ* H 130, vgl. das Siegel des *ṁtnʾl bn ʾẇrʾ* aus dem gileaditischen Tell Dēr ʿAllā, CAI 106 = H 109; s.o. IV.1.3) und darin insofern eine typisch – aber nicht ausschließlich – ammonitische Motiv-Komposition erkennen. Ähnlich könnte es – dem Stil nach – bei dem Motiv des angreifenden Stieres (IV.1.1.B) bzw. springenden Capriden (IV.1.1.C) sein: Auch hier könnte es sich jeweils um Produkte ein und derselben Werkstatt handeln (vgl. besonders **Abb. 4**, **22**, **24**, **25**), doch sind die Motive deshalb nicht zwingend exklusiv ammonitische. Darüber hinaus muß man vielleicht in beiden Gruppen näher zwischen dem Siegelschneider, der die Bilder, und dem oder denen, die die Inschriften gravierten, unterscheiden. Außerdem ist mitzubedenken, daß die Siegel mit dem Motiv eines springenden Quadrupeden ebenso ungesicherter Herkunft sind wie die mit dem Motiv des 'Tierkopfes *en face*' (von dem Siegel des *ṁtnʾl bn ʾẇrʾ* vom Tell Dēr ʿAllā abgesehen). Möglicherweise sind die Motive in der Tendenz *transjordanisch* (vgl. die spezielle Form der Flügelsonne laut Parayre 1990a), also südaramäisch, gileaditisch, ammonitisch und/oder moabitisch.

Gleichzeitig fällt das relativ häufige Vorkommen von Stempelsiegeln auf, deren Siegelfläche in drei horizontale Register eingeteilt ist, in deren oberem und unterem Register (fast) immer die (zwei- oder dreizeilige) Inschrift eingraviert ist und in deren mittlerem Register eine zentrale 'Ikone' von Vögeln, Pflanzen, 'Standarten' und/oder zwei Buchstaben der Filiation flankiert wird; die 'Ikone' kann häufig ein Quadruped (**Abb. 4**, **15**, **22**, **24f** [, **26**]; H 71, 77) oder ein Tierkopf (**Abb. 1** und H 33, 130) sein, aber auch ein vierflügliger Skarabäus (**Abb. 16**, **19**, **23** und H 30), ein geflügeltes Mischwesen (**Abb. 14** und H 113) oder eine Flügelsonne (**Abb. 8**). Daneben fällt die relativ häufige Verwendung des Stieres bzw. Stierkopfes und des Widders bzw. Widderkopfes unter den verwendeten Einzelmotiven auf.

VI. Die Entwicklung des ikonographischen Repertoires

Sieht man von den proto-ammonitischen, also den unbeschrifteten Siegeln der Eisen-I-Zeit aus der Ammonitis ab, dann liegen die Anfänge der ammonitischen Siegelproduktion in der Eisen-II-Zeit (s.o. I.). Mit der Konsolidierung der Politie Ammon als Territorialstaat setzt – wie anderswo auch (vgl. Jamieson-Drake 1991; Moortgat-Correns 1971) – verstärkt der Gebrauch von Papyrus und Tinte als Schreibmaterial ein und damit der Gebrauch von Siegeln, mit deren Hilfe man Bullen u.a. stempeln konnte. Dieser (Neu-)Beginn der ammonitischen Glyptik verlief ganz im Rahmen der entsprechenden Entwicklungen in den vergleichbaren Nachbarstaaten: Es war ein Prozeß, der insofern autochthon bzw. lokal geprägt war, als hier Vorgegebenes aufgenommen wurde; zugleich war es ein Prozeß, in dessen Verlauf aus der Menge der theoretisch zur Verfügung stehenden Möglichkeiten ein lokaltypisch eingegrenztes Repertoire ausgewählt wurde.

Die Blüte der ammonitischen Glyptik lag – quantitativ wie qualitativ – in der Zeit der neoassyrischen Vorherrschaft (Hübner 1992a: Kap. 4.3). Aus dieser Zeit stammt der weitaus größte Teil der ammonitischen Namenssiegel, allesamt Siegel der ammonitischen Oberschicht. Tiglat-Pileser III. hatte Ammon in der 1. Hälfte des 8. Jhs. v. Chr. zum assyrischen Tributär und Vasallen gemacht. Seitdem befand sich der transjordanische Kleinstaat im Windschatten der *pax assyriaca*. Er bot Ammon – jenseits der Verpflichtungen eines Vasallen – den Schutz der Hegemonialmacht, außenpolitische und ökonomische Stabilität und ein gewisses Maß an innerer Autonomie. Die Oberschicht des Zwergstaates kollaborierte mit den Vertretern der mesopotamischen Großmacht und profitierte von der wirtschaftlichen Prosperität, wie die Grabinventare in Rabbat-Ammon/ʿAmmān und anderswo in der Ammonitis zur Genüge belegen (Hübner 1992a: Kap. 5-6). Der assyrische Einfluß (Bennett 1978; 1982; Weippert 1987; Hübner 1992a: Kap. 4.3) zeigt sich nicht nur in der Ikonographie (Mischwesen, Heros, Dämon, Stiermensch, s.o. IV.4.) und im Onomastikon (**Mannu-ki-Inurta*, H 90) der ammonitischen Siegel, sondern z.B. auch in der ammonitischen Keramik (z.B. Oakeshott 1978: 133ff) und Kleinplastik (Reiter-Terrakotten aus Meqābelēn, La Voie royale: Nr. 137f). Parallel zu den außenpolitischen Entwicklungen verlief die freiwillig-unfreiwillige Aufnahme und Adaptation neoassyrischer und dann auch neobabylonischer Einflüsse bzw. assyrisierender und babylonisierender Bildelemente: Sie sind Ausdruck der politischen Hegemonie und der Pressionen der mesopotamischen Großmächte gegenüber dem transjordanischen Kleinstaat.

Gleichzeitig begann etwa um 700 v. Chr. eine gewisse Aramaïsierung der ammonitischen Kultur, die sich in der achämenidischen Zeit verstärkte. Aramäische Einflüsse sind nicht nur in der Schrift, sondern auch in der Sprache der Inschriften zu beobachten, sofern man z.B. die Filiation *br* (anstatt *bn*) als hinreichendes Indiz dafür ansieht, daß eine von Ammonitern geschriebene Inschrift in aramäischer Sprache verfaßt sein soll, vgl. die Siegel des *zkʾ br mlkmʿz* (H 72) und des *tmkʾl br mlkm* (**Abb. 26**). Auch die Zunahme der Astralsymbole könnte eine Folge dieser Aramaïsierung sein. Auf israelitischen Einfluß dagegen könnte das Motiv des vierflügligen Skarabäus zurückgehen.

Phönizische Einflüsse (Homès-Fredericq 1987; Hübner 1992a: passim) und Importe sind in der ammonitischen Kultur relativ häufig nachweisbar, z.B. bei den Tridacna-Muscheln (Stucky 1984; Brandl 1984; Hübner 1992a: Kap. 5), beim Import von Glas, Schmuck und Keramik (Hübner 1992a: Kap. 5), bei der Verwendung tyrischer Münzen seit dem 4. Jh. v. Chr. (Ḫirbet el-Ḥağğār, Thompson 1987; Ǧebel el-Aḫḍar, 2. Jh. v. Chr., Zayadine 1985a: 152), sowie in der Identifizierung Milkoms mit Melqart. Dabei wurden die Waren in den Häfen von Tell Abū Huwām und Akko angelandet und dann auf dem Landweg über Bet-Schean und Pella nach Transjordanien importiert; im Gegengeschäft wurden z.B. Sklaven (Vitelli 1917: Nr. 406, 3. Jh. v. Chr.) und Erzeugnisse der Weihrauchstraße aus der Ammonitis exportiert.

Anepigraphische phönizische Import-Siegel sind in Transjordanien z.B. aus es-Salṭ (Zazoff 1975: Nr. 16; Gubel 1990b: Nr. 151) und Gadara (?) (Henig & Whiting 1987: Nr. 4) bekannt.

Die phönizisierenden Elemente der ammonitischen Siegel sind im Grunde nichts anderes als die ägyptischen Einflüsse bzw. ägyptisierenden Elemente, die Ammon *via* Phönizien übernommen hatte (Hölbl 1989: 318-325). Zu diesen ägyptischen Einflüssen bzw. ägyptisierenden Elementen sind das nur gelegentlich vorkommende *ʿnḫ*-Zeichen und die wenigen Harpokrates-Darstellungen zu zählen. Diese Elemente gehen nicht auf direkten ägyptischen Einfluß zurück, sondern sind vor allem über den Handel mit der phönizischen Mittelmeerküste vermittelt worden; sie sind somit Ausdruck der wirtschaftlichen Bedeutung der phönizischen Hafenstädte für den transjordanischen Binnenstaat.

Nebukadnezzar II. beendete 582/581 v. Chr. die staatliche Existenz Ammons und inkorporierte es als babylonische Provinz in sein Imperium (Fl. Joseph., Ant. 10,9,7 [§§ 181f]; Contra Ap. I 19f [§§ 132.143]; Hübner 1992a: Kap. 4.3). Die Symbole Marduks[9] und Nabûs, Hacke und Griffel, das Symbol der Heilgöttin Gula, der Hund, und andere Gottheiten (Inurta) auf aus der Ammonitis stammenden Siegeln belegen den assyrischen bzw. babylonischen Einfluß auf die ammonitische Kultur und Religion. Auch die

---

9. Marduk und Ṣarpanītu waren schon in der spätbronzezeitlichen Ammonitis bekannt, wie ein Zylinder-Siegel aus Mārkā zeigt (Tournay 1967).

Wiederaufnahme des Zylinders als Siegelform (Meqābelēn, Tell el-ʿUmēri) geht auf mesopotamischen Einfluß zurück.

Der Anfang vom Ende der ammonitischen Siegelproduktion kam mit der Zerschlagung des ammonitischen Staates durch Nebukadnezzar II. und vollzog sich innerhalb weniger Jahrzehnte während der Zeit der spätbabylonischen und frühachämenidischen Vorherrschaft (Hübner 1992a: Kap. 4.4). Die einheimische Bevölkerung hatte durch Tote, Flüchtlinge und Deportationen (?) sowie durch Abwanderungen abgenommen, die Oberschicht, insbesondere die Beamtenschaft am ammonitischen Königshof ihre Bedeutung, z.T. wohl auch ihr Leben verloren.

In der Mitte des 5. Jhs. v. Chr. ist Ammon als persische Subprovinz innerhalb der 'Satrapie' *eber nāri* /*ʿbr nhr*ʾ belegt (Hübner 1992a: Kap. 4.4). Der Rückgang der urbanen und überhaupt der seßhaften Bevölkerung hörte nach und nach auf, halbnomadische Bevölkerungsteile nahmen weiter zu. Die Wirtschaft fing aber langsam an, sich zu stabilisieren; neue Importe waren aufgenommen worden, insbesondere die der attischen Keramik (Ḫirbet el-Ḥaǧǧār, Ḫirbet Ḫulde, Ruǧm el-Malfūf Süd, Tell el-ʿUmēri, Umm Uḏaina). Die Aramaïsierung von Schrift und Sprache schritt weiter voran. Achämenidische Einflüsse auf die Ikonographie ammonitischer Siegel sind vor allem stilistischer Art, wie man an den anepigraphischen Stempelsiegeln aus Ḫirbet Ḫulde (Yassine 1988: 21f, Fig. 8:3-5, vgl. **Abb. 33-34**) und den beiden anepigraphischen Zylindersiegeln vom Tell el-ʿUmēri (**Abb. 35-36**) sehen kann.

Doch letztlich versiegte die Siegelproduktion in Ammon; daran konnte auch die leichte Zunahme anepigraphischer Stempel- und Zylindersiegel in der spätbabylonischen und frühachämenidischen Ammonitis nichts mehr ändern. Sie war in hohem Maß an die staatliche Existenz Ammons gebunden. Ohne sie verloren die Siegelproduzenten den gesellschaftlichen Hintergrund, den Absatzmarkt und jenes Maß an ammonitischer Identität, die allesamt notwendig gewesen wären, um weiter ammonitische Siegel herstellen und verkaufen zu können.

Insofern sollte man die Amulett-Funktion der ammonitischen Namenssiegel nicht überbewerten; die zentrale Funktion dieser Siegel war juridischer und administrativer Natur. Die einzelnen ikonographischen Elemente und Szenen haben – wie anderswo auch – stets gleichzeitig dekorativ-ästhetische, apotropäisch-religiöse und propagandistisch-politische Funktionen, ebenso die Inschriften der Siegel; letztere unterstreichen die administrativen und juridischen Funktionen (vgl. zu dieser Frage auch Uehlinger, *infra*, S. 273-274).

VII. Schluss

Will man den Charakter des ikonographischen Repertoires der ammonitischen Siegel beschreiben, dann paßt er nahtlos in das Gesamtbild der ammonitischen Kultur: In der Tendenz ist es peripher wie die Sprache (vgl. *bʿlyšʿ* < **baʿalyiṯaʿ*; Knauf & Maʿani 1987; insgesamt Jackson 1983a); es weist provinzielle Züge auf, wie sie Zwergstaaten eigen sein können. Im Prinzip ist es so viel oder so wenig eigenständig wie das ikonographische Repertoire seiner Nachbarn; die gegenseitige kulturelle Durchdringung der palästinischen Kleinstaaten der Eisen-II-Zeit war enorm. Insofern ist es legitim, von einem innerpalästinischen Kulturinternationalismus zu sprechen, der die Kulturen und ikonographischen Repertoires der palästinischen Territorialstaaten trotz ihres politischen Separatismus massiv prägte.

In der Ikonographie der ammonitischen Siegel spiegeln sich der begrenzte Polytheismus der ammonitischen Religion (Hübner 1992a: Kap. 6) ebenso wie der begrenzte Kosmopolitismus bzw. die begrenzte Internationalität der ammonitischen Kultur wieder, die sich die ammonitische Gesellschaft aufgrund ihrer zentralen Randlage im mittleren Transjordanien leisten wollte, konnte und mußte.

Auswahlkonkordanz zu den beschrifteten ammonitischen Siegeln

Hübner 1992a	Abb. hier	CAI	Vattioni	CIS / RÉS	G	Andere
6	1	114				
14	2	40	VSE 164			
15	3	17	VSE 98		99	
17		49	VSE 194			
20	4	132				B 72
23	5	18	VSE 115	RÉS 1888	128	AOB^2 579
25		134				B 82
28		122				
29						Avigad 1989a: Nr. 11
30		141				Avigad 1989a: Nr. 13
31	6	39	VSE 133			
33		38	VSE 117			
34	7	79	VSE 317			B 81
37						Avigad 1989a: Nr. 15
38	8	118				
39		108	VSE 442			

Hübner 1992a	Abb. hier	CAI	Vattioni	CIS / RÉS	G	Andere
45	9	96	VSE 353			
48		135				B 83
51	10	105				B 77
54		111	VSE 448			
55		88	VSE 386			
59		67	VSE 259			
61	11	103	VSE 400			
62	12	54	VSE 221			
65	13	13	VSE 403 = VSA 9	CIS II,1 76		B 69
68	14	140				
70						Avigad 1989a: Nr. 12
71		116				
72		136				B 84
77		99	VSE 449			
80	15					Wolfe & Sternberg 1990: Nr. 443
87		101	VSE 445			
88	16	129				
89	17	127				
90	18	55	VSE 225			B 76
96	19	42	VSE 166			
102	20	92	VSE 390			
108		110	VSE 447			
110		70	VSE 263			
113		85	VSE 383			
116		53	VSE 217			
127		44	VSE 116			
130		87	VSE 385			
131	21					Wolfe & Sternberg 1989: Nr. 22
135	22	5	VSF 17			B 74
136		41	VSE 165			
138	23	68	VSE 261			
142						Geraty 1988: 250, Pl. 27
144		75	VSE 298			B 70
146	24	30	VSE 41		28	
149	25	3	VSE 318		27	B 73
150		84	VSE 382			
153	26	1	VSA 16	CIS II,1 94		
155						Younker 1990: 25, Pl. 25

LISTE DER ABBILDUNGEN

Die jeweils letzte Angabe in Klammern bezeichnet die Quelle der verwendeten Abbildung.

1. Alphabet-Siegel (H 6).
2. Siegel des *ʾdnnr ʿbd ʿmndb* (H 14; Herr 1978: Fig. 38:1).
3. Siegel des *ʾdnplṭ ʿbd ʿmndb* (H 15; G 99).
4. Siegel des *ʾyʾ bn tmkʾl* (H 20).
5. Siegel des *ʾlʾmṣ bn ʾlšʿ* (H 23; G 128).
6. Siegel des *ʾlybr (bn mnḥm)* (H 31; Sukenik 1945: Nr. 3).
7. Siegel des *ʾlyšʿ bn grġr* (H 34; Zeichnung Hildi Keel-Leu nach B 81).
8. Siegel des *ʾln bn ʾmrʾl* (H 38).
9. Siegel des *ʾlʿz bn mnḥm* (H 45; Zeichnung Hildi Keel-Leu nach Puech 1976: Pl. 2).
10. Siegel des *ʾlšmʿ* (H 51; Zeichnung Noga Z'evi, vgl. Ornan, *supra*, S. 69, Fig. 72).
11. Siegel des *bdʾl bn ndbʾl* (H 61; Zeichnung H. Keel-Leu nach Avigad 1977a: fig. 1b).
12. Siegel des *bṭš nʿr brkʾl* (H 62; Herr 1978: Fig. 40:31).
13. Siegel des *bydʾl ʿbd pdʾl* (H 65).
14. Siegel des *bqš bnʿzʾ* (H 68).
15. Siegel des *ynḥm* (H 80; Zeichnung H. Keel-Leu nach Wolfe & Sternberg 1990: Nr. 443).
16. Siegelabdruck des *mlkmʾwr ʿbd bʿlyšʿ* (H 88; Herr 1985: 169).
17. Siegel des *mlkmgd* (H 89; Zeichnung Ines Haselbach nach Avigad 1985: Pl. 1C).
18. Siegel des *mngʾnrt (*Mannu-ki-Inurta)* (H 90; Zeichnung Noga Z'evi nach B 76, vgl. Ornan, *supra*, S. 69, Fig. 71).
19. Siegel des *mnḥm bṅ ynḥm* (H 96; Gubel 1991a: Fig. 3,h)
20. Siegel des *mnr* (H 102).
21. Siegel des *plṭy* (H 131).
22. Siegel des *ṣnr bn ʾlʾmṣ* (H 135; Levy 1869: Taf. 2:4).
23. Siegel des *šwḥr h-nss* (H 138; Zeichnung Ines Haselbach nach Museumsphoto, IMJ 68.35.187).
24. Siegel des *šʿl bn ʾlyšʿ* (H 146; G 28).
25. Siegel des *tmkʾ bn mqnmlk* (H 149; Moscati 1966: 485, Abb. XXV, korrigiert nach B 73).
26. Siegel des *tmkʾl bṙ mlkm* (H 153; Photo Trustees of the British Museum).
27. Anepigraphisches Stempelsiegel aus ʿAmmān, Grab des *ʾdnnr* (Zeichnung Hildi Keel-Leu nach Harding 1953: 54, Nr. 7).
28. Anepigraphisches Stempelsiegel angeblich aus ʿAmmān (Ward 1968: 135, Fig. 1:1; Keel 1977: Abb. 94).
29. Anepigraphisches Stempelsiegel vom Tell Ṣāfūṭ (Wimmer 1987: 281, Fig. 3).
30. Anepigraphisches Stempelsiegel aus ʿAmmān, Grab des *ʾdnnr* (Zeichnung Hildi Keel-Leu nach Harding 1953: 53, Nr. 4).
31. Anepigraphisches Stempelsiegel aus ʿAmmān, Grab des *ʾdnnr* (Zeichnung Ines Haselbach nach Harding 1953: 53f, Nr. 6).
32. Anepigraphisches Stempelsiegel aus ʿAmmān, Grab des *ʾdnnr* (Zeichnung Ines Haselbach nach Harding 1953: 53, Nr. 5).
33. Anepigraphisches Stempelsiegel aus Ḫirbet Ḫulde (Zeichnung Ines Haselbach nach Yassine 1988: 22, Fig. 8:5).
34. Anepigraphisches Stempelsiegel aus Ḫirbet Ḫulde (Zeichnung Ines Haselbach nach Yassine 1988: 21f, Fig. 8:4).
35. Anepigraphisches Zylindersiegel vom Tell el-ʿUmēri (Porada 1989: 381ff, Fig. 23:1).
36. Anepigraphisches Zylindersiegel vom Tell el-ʿUmēri (Porada 1989: 381ff, Fig. 23:2).

1

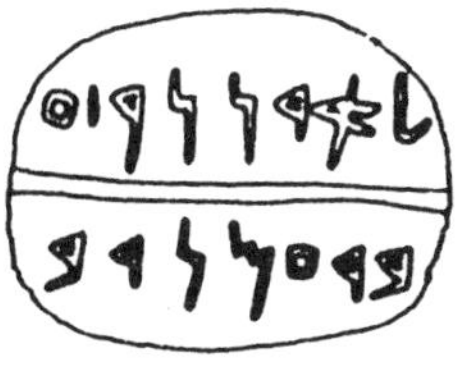

2

3

4

5

6

7

8

9

10

11

12

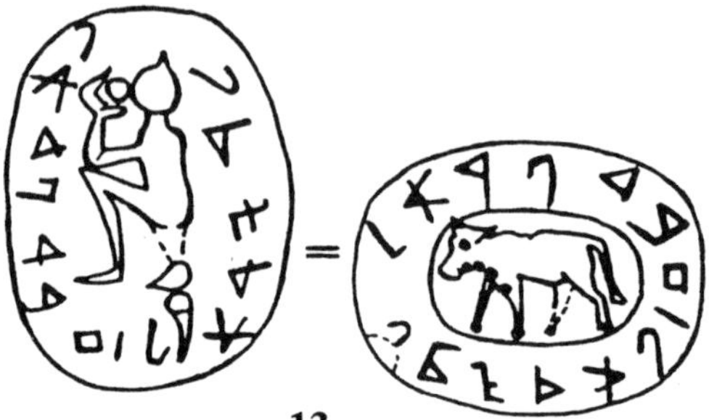

13

14

15

16

17

18

19

20

21

22

23

24

25

26

27

28

29

30

31

32

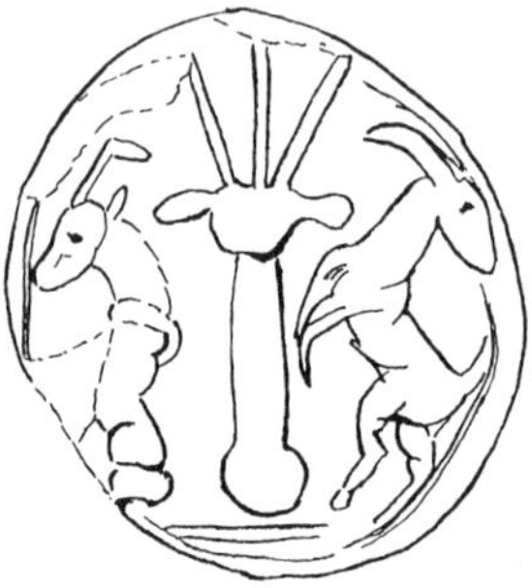
33

34

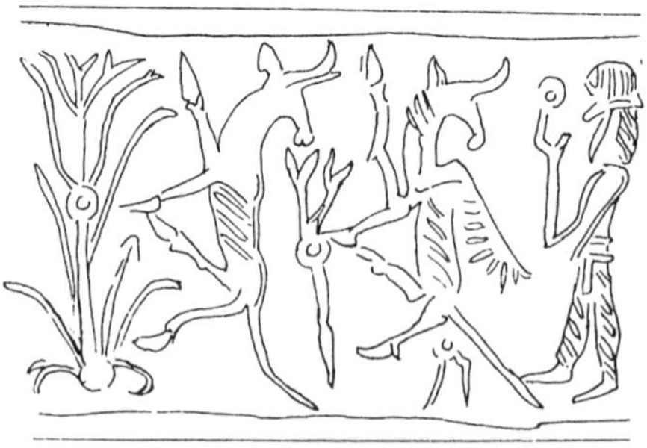
35

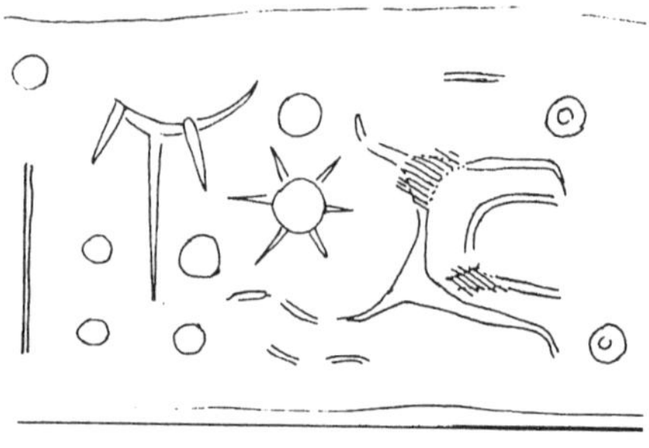
36

DAS IKONOGRAPHISCHE REPERTOIRE DER MOABITISCHEN SIEGEL UND SEINE ENTWICKLUNG: VOM MAXIMALISMUS ZUM MINIMALISMUS*

Stefan TIMM
Universität Kiel

I. Die Ausgangslage

Daß sich bis in die Gegenwart hinein überhaupt moabitische Siegel erhalten haben, ist noch vor einigen Dezennien generell bezweifelt worden. In Nachfolge W.F. Albrights (1947: 14-15, vgl. auch Thomsen 1951: 150) hat seinerzeit z.B. A.H. van Zyl bezweifelt, ob die ihm bekannten zwei "moabitischen" Siegel aus der Kollektion A. Reifenberg (das anikonische Siegel des *kmšʿm kmšʾl hspr* [Timm 1989a: 168ff Nr. 3] und das Siegel des *mšʿʾ* bzw. *mšʿ* [ebd. 254f Nr. 42]) überhaupt authentische antike Siegel seien und nicht vielmehr moderne Fälschungen (van Zyl 1960: 31). In den nun mehr als dreißig Jahren seit van Zyls Studie hat sich die Anzahl derjenigen Siegel, die als moabitisch angesprochen werden, enorm vermehrt. F. Israel hat in einer kenntnisreichen Abhandlung 35 Siegel als moabitisch klassifiziert (1987b; beachte das Postscriptum a.a.O. 122 mit einem Hinweis auf Heltzer 1985: 25-29). Der Autor dieser Studie hat 1989 47 Siegel diskutiert, die mit mehr oder weniger starken Argumenten für moabitisch angesehen werden (Timm

* Für die Hilfe bei der redaktionellen Gestaltung des Manuskripts ist Herrn Dr. Ch. Uehlinger herzlich zu danken.

1989a: 159-264). Seitdem haben neue Funde, neue Publikationen, aber auch neue Klassifizierungen schon länger bekannter Stücke weitere Siegel den Moabitern zugewiesen, und es ist damit zu rechnen, daß künftig noch weitere Siegel auftauchen, die als moabitisch deklariert werden (vgl. jüngst etwa Wolfe & Sternberg 1989: Nr. 24; NAAG 1991: Nr. 23 [s. Anm. 2]; Avigad 1992a). Wie schon zu W.F. Albrights Zeiten wird aber auch künftig vielfach strittig bleiben, ob ein Siegel, das sich in irgendeiner öffentlichen oder privaten Sammlung befindet, überhaupt authentisch und zu Recht als moabitisch zu klassifizieren ist. Auch die nachfolgende Darstellung wird durchgängig von dieser Grundsatzfrage bestimmt sein: Mit welchen Gründen können überhaupt palästinische Siegel der Eisenzeit als moabitisch klassifiziert werden? Für mehr denn zwanzig als "moabitisch" klassifizierte Siegel hat der Autor dieser Studie die Authentizität der Siegel oder deren Zuweisung nach Moab in Frage gestellt (Timm 1989a: 225-263 Nr. 27-47). Da ihm bislang keine durchschlagenden gegenteiligen Argumente bekannt geworden sind, bleiben diese Stücke – unter denen teilweise sehr bekannte oder berühmte sind! – denn auch im folgenden unberücksichtigt.

Ob alle bislang bekannten "moabitischen" Siegel authentisch sind, ist generell noch nicht zu sagen. Nur zwei der nachfolgend zu besprechenden Siegel stammen aus wissenschaftlich kontrollierten Ausgrabungen, keines davon aus Moab (**Abb. 18** aus Umm Uḏaina bei ʿAmmān, das anikonische Siegel des *kmšntn* aus Ur, vgl. zu letzterem Timm 1989a: 182ff Nr. 7). Keines der anderen "moabitischen" Siegel ist bislang mit modernen technischen Hilfsmitteln jemals auf seine Authentizität hin untersucht worden. Ihre Herstellung in der Antike wird also – ungeprüft! – überall vorausgesetzt. Ob diese ungeprüfte Voraussetzung auch weiterhin gültig bleibt, wird die Zukunft erweisen.[1] Daß die Authentizität der Siegel eine ungeprüfte Prämisse ist, sei hiermit nachdrücklich unterstrichen.

II. Siegel mit *KMŠ*-Namen

Bislang sind sieben[2] Siegel bekannt, die mindestens einen vollständigen Personennamen in ihrer Beschriftung enthalten, der mit dem Namen des moa-

1. Zu modernen Fälschungen von Rollsiegeln, die durch subtile vergleichende ikonographische Studien als Fälschungen erkannt sind, vgl. Teissier 1984: Nr. 692ff; Collon 1987: 94ff. Ein modernes technisches Hilfmittel zur Erkennung von Fälschungen durchbohrter Siegel stellen Gorelick & Gwinnet 1978 vor.

2. Zwar spricht Bordreuil (1986a: 61 Anm. 29) unter Hinweis auf Lemaire (1983: 26) von neun Siegeln mit *kmš*-Namen, doch ist dies ein aufklärbarer Rechenfehler: Lemaire hatte a.a.O. neun *kmš*-Namen zusammengestellt, die aber auf sieben Siegeln belegt sind. Auf einem Siegel aus Samaria liest Lemaire zwar auch *kṁ*[*š*], doch ist dort nur das Kaf wirk-

bitischen Gottes Kamosch (*kmš*; zur Aussprache vgl. Israel 1987c) gebildet ist.[3] Davon sind zwei anikonisch: das Siegel *lkmšʿm kmšʾl hspr*, angeblich in ʿAlēy im Libanon gefunden (Israel 1987b: Nr. III; Timm 1989a: 168ff Nr. 3), und das im É - n u n - m a ḫ-Tempel in Ur oberhalb eines Muschelflurs der persischen Zeit gefundene Siegel des *kmšntn* (Israel 1987b: Nr. IX; Timm 1989a: 182f Nr. 7). Die verbleibenden fünf Siegel mit *kmš*-Namen und ikonischem Dekor sind im folgenden kurz vorzustellen.

Das Siegel des *kmšyḥy* (**Abb. 1**)

Die Siegelfläche ist dreigeteilt. Im obersten Drittel befindet sich die extrem stilisierte Darstellung einer geflügelten Sonne mit je einem Punkt (= stilisiertem Stern?) zur Rechten und Linken. Davon ist durch eine doppelte Trennlinie die erste Zeile Beschriftung abgesetzt; darunter steht, durch eine einfache Trennlinie abgehoben, die zweite Zeile Beschriftung (zum Namen vgl. Timm 1989a: 164f).

Die geflügelte Sonnenscheibe ist ein uraltes ägyptisches Motiv, das schon im 2. Jt. über ganz Vorderasien Verbreitung fand. Die vergleichbaren Darstellungen der geflügelten Sonne auf syro-palästinischen Siegeln des 1. Jts. (vgl. schon Galling 1941: 148f; Welten 1969: 19-30; Wildung 1977; Keel 1982: 463-466; Mayer-Opificius 1984; ausführlich Parayre 1990a, vgl. *supra*, S. 27ff) sind aber bei weitem nicht so stark stilisiert, daß das Motiv kaum noch zu erkennen ist.[4] Es ist – mit den zwei 'Punkten' zur Rechten und Linken (= stilisierten Sternen?) – das einzige dekorative Element der Siegelfläche. Die Datierung dieses Siegels ist – wie die aller Siegel – schwierig. Die starke Abstraktion der geflügelten Sonne steht in gewisser Spannung zu den Buch-

---

lich lesbar (vgl. Ornan, *supra*, S. 67, Fig. 56; Sass, *infra*, S. 232 mit Anm. 88). Eine Lesung *kṁ[hm/n]* ist ohne weiteres möglich; vgl. zu anderen Vorschlägen schon Israel 1987b: Nr. XXII. Zum Siegel HD 117 mit der Zeile, die Lemaire einst *l<k>mšpṭ* las, vgl. Timm 1989a: 252f Nr. 41; vgl. nun aber Lemaire, *supra*, S. 16 mit Fig. 24.
Ein achtes Siegel mit einem *kmš*-Namen (*kmšḥsd*) und dem Titel *hspr* zeigte P. Bordreuil freundlicherweise dem Autor dieser Zeilen während der Tage in Fribourg. Dafür sei ihm herzlich gedankt. Das anikonische Siegel (vgl. die vorläufige Publikation in NAAG 1991: Nr. 23) muß in den nachfolgenden Ausführungen ebenso unberücksichtigt bleiben wie der neunte Beleg, eine jüngst von N. Avigad (1992a) publizierte Bulle *kmšʿz hspr*.

3. Für die Literatur zu den nachfolgenden Siegeln wird jeweils nur die Erstpublikation und ausgewählte Corpora angegeben. Für weitere Literaturangaben sei verwiesen auf die Zusammenstellungen bei Israel 1987b und Timm 1989a: 159-264.

4. Die beiden Darstellungen der geflügelten Sonnenscheibe, die D. Parayre in ihrem Katalog der hiesigen stilisierten Form zur Seite gestellt hat (1990a: 283f Nr. 115-117; *supra*, S. 43, Fig. 14-15): B 64 (s.u. **Abb. 19**) und B 63 (vgl. Israel 1987b: Nr. XXVIII; Timm 1989a: 205f Nr. 17) sind deutlich verschieden von der hier vorliegenden Form.

stabenformen, die in den Anfang des 7. Jhs. datiert werden (Bordreuil 1986a: 61).[5]

Das Siegel des *kmšmʾš* (**Abb. 2**)

Im oberen Drittel seiner Siegelfläche liegt ein Halbmond über einem ‘Strich’. Links von ihm befindet sich ein vielzackiger Stern (oder eine Strahlensonne?).[6] Symmetrisch dazu war ehedem auch rechts neben der Mondsichel etwas abgebildet, was heute durch die Erosion der Siegeloberfläche nicht mehr erkennbar ist. Der rechte Gegenstand muß jedoch nicht auch ein Stern gewesen sein (vgl. das Siegel des *yrʾ* bei Avigad 1954b: Nr. 7 = Israel 1987b: Nr. XI). Die zwei Zeilen seiner Beschriftung[7] sind von der bildlichen Darstellung durch je zwei Trennstriche abgeteilt.

---

5. Die Lesung der Buchstaben bereitet keine Schwierigkeiten. Die Form des Ḥet ( ) gilt als moabitische Sonderform (Bordreuil 1986a: 61; Timm 1989a: 164 Anm. 5, 282f). Der Standardform auf der Meschaʿ-Inschrift ( ) entspricht das Ḥet auf dem Siegel des (= *l*)*ʿbdḥwrn* (B 2), das L.G. Herr (1978: 17f Nr. 16) als aramäisch, F. Israel (1986: 71f) und P. Bordreuil (a.a.O.) als phönizisch klassifiziert haben, wogegen A. Lemaire es für moabitisch hält (*supra*, S. 14f mit Fig. 20). Die ikonographische Darstellung des Opfergabentisches auf diesem Siegel ist im syro-palästinischen Raum bislang ohne Parallele. Vergleichbare “Lotosszepter” gibt es u.a. auf neohethitisch-nordsyrischen Darstellungen (vgl. Orthmann 1971: 366-393). Einen Anschluß an phönizische Darstellungen für dieses Stück versucht E. Gubel (1987b: 247-249). Eine sichere Zuordnung des Siegels in den phönizischen, aramäischen (?) oder moabitischen Raum ist noch nicht möglich.
   Inzwischen ist aus Ḏībān eine beschriftete Scherbe bekannt geworden, die neben einem ʾAleph ein Ḥet und ein (um 90° verdrehtes) Šin (oder ein um 90° verdrehtes und rechts beschädigtes Mem) aufweist (Morton 1989: 318, Fig. 12). Das Ḥet auf dieser Scherbe hat die Form . Die Folge ist, daß für den moabitischen Schriftraum nunmehr mit *drei* verschiedenen Ḥet-Formen zu rechnen ist.
6. Auch wenn eine endgültige Klärung noch aussteht, ob es sich bei dem “Stern” wirklich jeweils um einen Stern handelt – es könnte an manchen Stellen auch eine Darstellung der Sonne gemeint sein (vgl. schon Bordreuil & Lemaire 1976: 52 zum Siegel des *rpʾ*, unten **Abb. 20**) –, sei das Motiv hier weiterhin als Stern bezeichnet.
7. Auf der mittleren Partie stehen die Buchstaben *lkmšm*, auf der untersten zwei anscheinend ein ʾAleph und ein Šin. Die beiden Mem auf diesem Siegel sind untereinander etwas verschieden. Das zweite hat unter seinem mittleren horizontalen Balken noch einen zusätzlichen kleinen Strich. Da sich dieses kleine, aber auffällige Detail bei anderen moabitischen Mem wiederholt, hat diese Buchstabenform als typisch moabitisch zu gelten (vgl. Timm 1989a: 290-293; Lemaire, *supra*, S. 4, 6).
   Die Lesung des ʾAleph ist nicht ganz sicher; doch ergibt sich nur bei der Lesung mit ʾAleph ein Personenname, der im nordwestsemitischen Onomastikon eine Parallele hat. Aufgrund dieses Namens sind auch andere Siegel mit dem Namen *mʾš* als moabitisch klassifiziert worden. Der Name *mʾš*, von der Wurzel *ʾ(W)Š* gebildet, ist jedoch auch außerhalb des moabitischen Sprachraums bezeugt (vgl. B 51 *lmʾš bn mnḥ hspr*, dazu auch Timm 1989a: 169 Anm. 17), und somit kein hinreichendes Argument für die Klassifikation irgendeines Siegels als moabitisch (vgl. noch die hebräischen Namensbildun-

Die Datierung des Siegels ist unsicher (vgl. Timm 1989a: 166 Anm. 10). Man wird eher für eine jüngere Entstehung (letzte Hälfte des 7. Jhs.) plädieren. Die Darstellung einer Mondsichel wird sich auf weiteren moabitischen Siegeln wiederholen (vgl. **Abb. 5-6, 17-19**).

Das Siegel des *kmšṣdq* (**Abb. 3**)

Die Siegelfläche ist dreiteilig, wobei zwei Drittel der oberen Siegelfläche von der bildlichen Darstellung einer vierflügligen, anthropomorphen Gestalt eingenommen werden. Durch einen Doppelstrich abgetrennt steht darunter in einer Zeile *lkmšṣdq*. Darunter befindet sich, nochmals durch einen einfachen Trennstrich abgeteilt, eine stilisierte geflügelte Sonne. Sie bildet hier nur ein untergeordnetes Bildelement, ist aber mit diesem Siegel ein weiteres Mal für Moab bezeugt, dazu in viel weniger abstrahierter Form als auf dem Siegel des *kmšyḥy* (**Abb. 1**). Als Entstehungszeit des Siegels ist das 8./7. Jh. anzunehmen (vgl. Timm 1989a: 171 Anm. 20).[8]

Neben einer Deutung der dargestellten vierflügligen Figur als weiblich (so Galling 1941: 152f, 186), als weibliche Göttin (Keel 1977: 196), als männliche solare Gottheit (Barnett 1969: 420), als vierflügliger Seraph (Culican 1977: 3) bzw. als göttliches Wesen (Israel 1987b: 109f) ist auch die als Genius vorgeschlagen (Giveon 1961: 38-42 = 1978: 110-116). Die Argumente für oder gegen die genannten Deutungen sollen hier auf sich beruhen (vgl. noch unten), versuchen derartige Deutungen doch generell, die jeweils vorliegende vierflüglige Figur im Kontext weiterer vergleichbarer, zeitlich und örtlich aber erheblich differenter Darstellungen zu deuten. Es kann jedoch nicht erwiesen werden, daß eine generelle Deutung auch für das ostjordanische Moab Geltung haben muß.[9] Unstrittig sollte in jedem Fall sein, daß der Kopfschmuck der abgebildeten Figur – ein Nachklang der ägyptischen Roten oder gar der Doppelkrone – in der ägyptisierenden Tradition der syro-palästinischen Siegelkunst steht. Die vier Flügel der Figur aber stammen aus der Bildtradition, die im 15./14. Jh. v. Chr. in Assyrien und Nordsyrien auftretend (vgl. Ward 1968: 139; Giveon 1961: 40, mitannische Herkunft vermutend; Keel 1977: 194), in den ersten Jahrhunderten des 1. Jts. in den neohethisch-aramäischen Staaten Nordsyriens ihren Ausdruck auch in Großplastiken gefunden hat

---

gen von der Wurzel *ʾ(W)Š* bei A 30 u.ö. sowie Zadok 1988: 25 mit Anm. 91 u.ö., andere nordwestsemitische bei Maraqten 1988: 125 s.v. *ʾYŠ*).

8. Während noch für M. Lidzbarski die bemerkenswerte Darstellung im obersten Teil der Siegelfläche ein Argument war, die Authentizität des Siegels zu bestreiten (ESE I: 136-142), hat K. Galling etliche Parallelen dazu beitragen können (1941: 152f, 186), wonach das Siegel heute als authentisch gilt (vgl. Israel 1987b: Nr. II; Timm 1989a: 171ff Nr. 4).

9. Vgl. auch Boardman & Moorey 1986: 43 zu einem unbeschrifteten Siegel in Paris, Cabinet des Médailles, mit einer vierflügligen Figur (a.a.O. 36 Nr. 2): "there is no reason to think it is one and the same genius or deity who is always represented".

(Genge 1979: Abb. 73f, 91f, 100 u.ö.; Orthmann 1971: 316-319; Börker-Klähn 1982: Nr. 294). Wahrscheinlich ist das Zusammenkommen dieser beiden Traditionslinien in einem moabitischen Siegel die Ursache dafür, daß die zwei Objekte (Pflanzen bzw. Tiere?), die die dargestellte Figur in ihren Händen hat, bislang nicht eindeutig identifiziert werden konnten. Will man den Versuch wagen, die abgebildete vierflüglige Figur in Bezug zu setzen mit den Gestalten des immer noch unzureichend bekannten moabitischen Pantheons (vgl. dazu Mattingly 1989: 211-238), so muß gleichzeitig angenommen werden, daß im 8./7. Jh. in Moab ägyptisierende Bild- und Religionsvorstellungen mit solchen aus dem nordsyrischen Raum bei diesem Genius(?) eine neue, unlösbare Verbindung eingegangen sind.

Das Siegel des *kmšdn* (**Abb. 4**)

Die Siegelfläche ist fast kreisrund, aber stark erodiert. Etwas mehr als die Hälfte nimmt eine bildliche Darstellung ein, darunter, durch einen einfachen Trennstrich abgeteilt, eine Zeile Beschriftung (zum Namen vgl. Timm 1989a: 179 Anm. 39). Darunter ist rudimentär noch die Andeutung eines eigenartigen Symbols zu erkennen.

Die stark erodierte bildliche Darstellung ist nur noch zur Hälfte erkennbar. Anscheinend standen sich ehedem spiegelbildlich zwei Sphinx- bzw. Greifendarstellungen gegenüber. Die Kopfpartie des allein erhaltenen rechten Greifen bzw. des rechten Sphinx ist auf dem publizierten Foto nicht klar erkennbar. Eine erneute Überprüfung während des Fribourger Symposions ergab, daß oberhalb der Kopfpartie definitiv keine Andeutung einer Krone oder eines Federbusches mehr geboten ist.[10] Als ein geographisch nahestehendes Beispiel für spiegelbildliche Darstellungen von Sphingen sei vor allem auf das ammonitische Siegel des *mlkmgd* verwiesen (Avigad 1985: Nr. III; vgl. Hübner, *supra*, S. 161, Abb. 17).[11]

Aufgrund der Buchstabenformen, besonders des Mem und Nun, hatte A. Lemaire als Ersteditor eine Datierung des *kmšdn*-Siegels ins 7. Jh. vorgeschlagen (1983: 26). Bislang gibt es keine moabitische Inschrift, die sicher ins 7. Jh. datiert werden kann. Die spiegelbildliche Greifen- bzw. Sphinxdarstellung hat erst in späterer Zeit Parallelen. So muß dessen Entstehung wohl um ein Jahrhundert herabdatiert werden (6. Jh.). Die Form des Nun entspricht einem solchen Ansatz (vgl. dazu Timm 1989a: 294).

10. Für die Hilfe bei der Klärung des Sachverhalts sei A. Lemaire an dieser Stelle herzlich gedankt.

11. Avigad verwies für die spiegelbildliche Sphinx-Darstellung auf jenem Stück auf zwei mesopotamische Rollsiegel, von denen eines aus neubabylonischer, eines aus achämenidischer Zeit stammt (Wiseman 1958: Pl. 71 und 106). Weitere Beispiele auf Siegeln bieten etwa Frankfort 1939: Pl. 42n, 44n; Porada 1948: Nr. 76, 980, 985; Dessenne 1957: Nr. 76, 79, 92f, 119, 121, 129, 171, 176.

Bildlich und sachlich umstritten ist das Motiv im untersten Register. A. Lemaire hatte die weitgehend abgegriffene Darstellung – fragend – als ein zweiflügliges Insekt gedeutet (1983: 26) und dafür auf ein Siegel mit umstrittener Lesung *lmš* verwiesen, das sich heute im Israel Museum Jerusalem befindet (HD 117; vgl. Timm 1989a: 252f Nr. 41; Lemaire, *supra*, S. 16 mit Fig. 24). F. Israel (1987b: 117) hat als weiteres Beispiel das Siegel des *mšʾ* bzw. *mšʿ* benannt (HD 115, vgl. dazu Timm 1989a: 254f Nr. 42). Die besten Beispiele bieten aber ein Siegel mit der Beschriftung *lšmʿl*, das in eṭ-Ṭafīle erworben wurde, vielleicht aber aus Buṣēra stammt (Harding 1937: 253-255, Pl. X:10), sowie ein Siegel im Hecht-Museum Haifa, von dem nur die ersten beiden Buchstaben als *yʿ*[.] sicher lesbar sind (Lemaire 1986: Nr. 9; Avigad 1989a: Nr. 23). Das Zeichen im untersten Register des *yʿ*[.]-Siegels deutete Lemaire als eine Art doppelter Halbkugeln, die zwei ägyptische *nb*-Zeichen repräsentieren könnten, worüber eine Art Dreizack eingraviert sei. Das *kmšdn*-, das *šmʿl*- und das *yʿ*[.]-Siegel legen allerdings nahe, daß jeweils das gleiche Motiv in abgewandelter Form vorliegt. E. Gubel hat während des Fribourger Symposions auf vergleichbare Darstellungen auf ägyptischen Skarabäen des Mittleren Reiches, der 12. Dynastie und früher, hingewiesen und damit den Ursprung des Motivs wahrscheinlich geklärt (vgl. Ward 1978: 68ff; Tufnell 1984: 270f, class 3A2; ebd. 300f, class 4A2; vgl. auch Gubel 1991b: Nr. 72). Folglich hat sich mit dieser Darstellung im Ostjordanland (*kmšdn*, *šmʿl* – die Herkunft des *yʿ*[.]-Siegels ist ungeklärt) ein Bildmotiv aus der Zeit der 12. ägyptischen Dynastie (und früher) bis in die Eisen-II-Zeit durchgehalten, auch wenn die Zwischenglieder dafür bislang noch fehlen.[12]

Das Siegel des *kmš* (**Abb. 5**)

Die Siegelfläche ist kreisrund und dreigeteilt. Im oberen Teil ist die stark erodierte Darstellung einer Mondsichel zu erkennen, daneben rechts ein kleiner Stern; davon durch einen Strich getrennt eine Zeile Beschriftung. Darunter, wiederum durch einen Strich getrennt, war einst ein Gegenstand abgebildet, der heute nicht mehr identifizierbar ist. Als Entstehungszeit des Stückes wird das 7. Jh. angenommen.

12. Freilich zeigen bereits manche Belege bei Ward (1978: 70, Fig. 15:6, 36, 54, 68, 79, 80), daß das Motiv leicht in Richtung der geflügelten Sonnenscheibe modifiziert und wohl auch als solche verstanden werden konnte, wie B. Sass während des Symposiums zu Recht bemerkt hat.

III. Die einzelnen Bildmotive

Die erörterten fünf Siegel mit *kmš*-Namen sind – zusammen mit den oben auf S. 161f genannten anikonischen Siegeln des *kmšʿm* und des *kmšntn* – die Grundlage und der Ausgangspunkt, um weitere beschriftete eisenzeitliche Siegel den Moabitern zuzuweisen. Ob derartige Zuweisungen berechtigt sind, muß sich aus den Kriterien ergeben, die anhand dieser sieben Siegel zu gewinnen sind. Was ist das typisch Moabitische dieser Siegel? Die Antwort ist einfach und klar: ihre *kmš*-Namen. Doch ist noch einmal festzustellen: keines der mit *kmš*-Namen beschrifteten Siegel ist durch Ausgrabungen in Moab aufgefunden. Angesichts der unklaren Herkunftsverhältnisse könnte man in fast allen Fällen – ausgenommen das bei Ausgrabungen in Ur gefundene anikonische des *kmšntn* – an der Authentizität der Siegel zweifeln.

Die Form ist bei den *kmš*-Siegeln ebenfalls different: drei Siegel sind Skaraboide (**Abb. 1-3** sowie die beiden genannten anikonischen Stücke), zwei sind Konoide (**Abb. 4-5**). Das Material, aus dem die Siegel hergestellt wurden, ist in allen Fällen verschieden.[13] Geht man einmal davon aus, daß die genannten Siegel authentisch sind, so haben die moabitischen Siegelschneider für deren Herstellung kein bestimmtes Material bevorzugt.

Dank der ausgeschriebenen Personennamen ist auch der Schriftcharakter einzelner Buchstaben ein Entscheidungskriterium für die Klassifizierung weiterer Siegel als moabitisch geworden. Man hat jedoch einzugestehen, daß dies ein sehr unsicheres Kriterium bleibt. Von den Buchstabenformen des Lamed her, das auf den sieben *kmš*-Siegeln insgesamt fünfmal bezeugt ist, wird niemand weitere Lamed auf anderen Siegeln als "moabitisch" klassifizieren können. Gleiches gilt für den Buchstaben Šin u.a. Der Buchstabe Ḥet, der bislang als Kriterium für eine moabitische Zuschreibung beigezogen wurde, ist neuerdings in anderer Form durch einen Ausgrabungsfund aus D̠ībān belegt (s.o. Anm. 5). Er hatte auch früher schon vergleichbare Parallelen im hebräischen Schriftraum. Auch Charakteristika bei anderen Buchstaben, die bislang als typisch moabitisch angesehen wurden, könnten sich bei anwachsender Beleglage als viel weniger typisch erweisen. Immerhin ist bei den Buchstaben Kaf und Mem ein kleiner Strich unter dem mittleren horizontalen Balken aufgefallen (Timm 1989a: 287-293, s.o. Anm. 7). Denselben kleinen Strich gibt es beim Nun auf dem Pariser Siegel des *bʿlntn* (**Abb. 11**), das aus anderen Gründen als moabitisch klassifiziert worden ist.

Sofern beschriftete eisenzeitliche Siegel keine *kmš*-Namen enthalten, kann ihre Zuweisung nach Moab nur durch eine kumulative Argumentation erfolgen. Kumulative Argumente dafür sind (vgl. im allgemeinen Lemaire, *supra*, S. 1ff):

---

13. *lkmšyḥy* Sardonyx, *lkmšmʾš* Achat, *lkmšʿm* … gelblicher Kalkstein (Geyserit), *lkmšṣdq* Porphyrit, *kmšdn* roter Kalkstein, *kmš* Alabaster, *kmšntn* Lapislazuli.

(a) Der Fundort des Siegels sollte nach Möglichkeit im antiken Moab liegen oder wenigstens in geographischer Relation dazu stehen (vgl. *kmšdn*, **Abb. 4**, aus Kerak, anders aber *kmšntn* aus Ur!).
(b) Die Buchstabenformen müssen in Übereinstimmung stehen mit den auf den monumentalen moabitischen Denkmälern und den *kmš*-Siegeln belegten Formen.
(c) Die auf den beschrifteten Siegeln erhaltenen Personennamen sollten sich dem bislang bekannten moabitischen Onomastikon einfügen.
(d) Dekorative oder ikonographische Darstellungen müssen sich an diejenigen Bildelemente anschließen, die auf den *kmš*-Siegeln nachgewiesen sind. Letzteres ist ein besonders heikles Kriterium. Von den sieben *kmš*-Siegeln bieten nur fünf ikonographische Elemente. Von diesen ausgehend eine Entwicklung der moabitischen Ikonographie aufzeigen zu wollen, ist kein aussichtsreiches Unterfangen. Der Belegumfang ist für generelle Aussagen zu gering und noch mit der zusätzlichen Schwierigkeit belastet, daß die Datierung der Siegel alles andere, nur nicht gesichert ist.

Solche Kautelen vorausgeschickt, dürfen das Siegel des *kmšmʾš* (**Abb. 2**) und das des *kmšṣdq* (**Abb. 3**) als die beiden ältesten moabitischen Siegel gelten (8.-7. Jh.).

1. Zu Mondsichel und Stern

Im *kmšmʾš*-Siegel (**Abb. 2**) wird eine Darstellung der Mondsichel geboten, im obersten Register der Siegelfläche stehend, links neben sich ein Stern, rechts ein heute undefinierbarer Gegenstand. Den Strich unter der Mondsichel könnte man für einen sekundären Einschnitt halten, wenn sich nicht auf der Siegelfläche des *mnšh bn hmlk*-Siegels, das aus anderen Gründen als moabitisch anzusehen ist (**Abb. 17**), ein vergleichbarer Strich fände. Auf dem Hintergrund der vielen syro-palästinischen Siegel, die eine Mondsichel mit einer Standarte auf einem Podest abbilden (vgl. Spycket 1973; 1974; Keel 1977: 284-296; Weippert 1978; GGG: §§ 174ff), wird man den Strich unter der Mondsichel als rudimentäre Andeutung eines Podestes deuten dürfen. Damit ist zugleich auch gesagt, daß hier weder der assyrische Typ eines solchen Podestes, noch der palästinische Typ vorliegt (dazu Keel 1977: 284ff). Es ist vielmehr eine eigenständige Entwicklung aufweisbar, die nur noch einen entfernten Anklang an die Vorlage(n) hat.

Der Sichelmond steht auf moabitischen Siegeln fast immer an prominenter Stelle im obersten Bildregister, so z.B. im Siegel des *kmš* (**Abb. 5**), das ins 7. Jh. datiert wird, wo er von einem (weitgehend erodierten) Stern begleitet ist. Auch auf anderen Siegeln, die als moabitisch klassifiziert wurden, steht der Sichelmond fast immer im obersten Bildregister (anders **Abb. 7, 19**).[14] Ein Beleg für einen Sichelmond (mit einbeschriebener kleiner Neumondscheibe oder Sonnenscheibe) findet sich auch auf einem wenig bekannten Stück, dessen Siegelfläche ansonsten von einem springenden Vierfüßler (Capriden?) dominiert wird (**Abb. 6**).[15] Eine ganze Reihe von palästinischen Beispielen mit vergleichbarem Motiv gehören mehrheitlich ins 8./7. Jh. (vgl. Shuval 1990: 105 Anm. 4, 111 Tabelle 4), ein vergleichbarer Diskoid (Shuval 1990: Nr. 0101) ans Ende des 7. Jhs. So wird auch dieses anepigraphische Siegel eher ins 7. Jh. gehören (vgl. GGG: § 188).

Damit legt sich die Annahme nahe, daß für die moabitischen Siegelschneider (und ihre Kunden) die Darstellung des Sichelmondes mit einer konkreten theologischen Vorstellung verbunden war. Von den *kmš*-Siegeln her ist auch klar, daß die Mondsichel eine viel wichtigere Rolle spielte als die geflügelte Sonnenscheibe. Thetisch formuliert: In Moab ist eher mit einem Mondkult als mit einem Sonnenkult zu rechnen.[16]

2. *Zur geflügelten Sonnenscheibe*

Auf einem der beiden ältesten moabitischen Siegel kommt auch das uralte Motiv der geflügelten Sonne vor. Auch wenn die geflügelte Sonne auf dem Siegel des *kmšṣdq* (**Abb. 3**) nur ein ganz untergeordnetes Bildmotiv ist, sie ist immerhin da. Welche Abstraktion für dieses Motiv möglich ist, zeigt das Siegel des *kmšyḥy* (**Abb. 1**). Sofern dessen Datierung ins 8./7. Jh. richtig ist, könnte man meinen, daß sich dieselbe Abstraktion auf noch späteren moabitischen Siegeln wiederholt. Das ist nicht der Fall. Man wird die hier vorliegende, völlig abstrahierte, Form der geflügelten Sonne vorerst für einen Sonderfall anzusehen haben. Es ist allerdings auffällig, daß auch beim *kmš*-

---

14. Daß sich die Monsichelstandarte auf ostjordanischen Siegeln nicht überall zu einer strichförmigen Andeutung verringert hat, belegt u.a. ein Siegel aus dem edomitischen Ṭawīlān mit einem überaus betonten Podest (Bennett 1967-1968: 53-56; 1969: 389, pl. VIb; vgl. Keel 1977: 288, Abb. 209; GGG: 343, Abb. 298a).

15. Die Verbindungen, die Kenna (1973) bei diesem Stück aufgrund der Diskoidform und einzelner Motivausführungen zum kretischen und helladischen Raum ausgezogen hat, und die ihn zu einer Datierung ins 14. Jh. v. Chr. führten, sind so wenig zu halten wie das frühe Datum.

16. Auch wenn zwischen den eisenzeitlichen Siegeln aus Moab mit Mondsicheldarstellungen und der arabisch beeinflußten, aber aramäisch geschriebenen Inschrift aus Kerak, die J.T. Milik (1959) bekannt gemacht hat (vgl. Lipiński 1975: 261f), ein großer zeitlicher und kultureller Abstand besteht, so ist es doch gewiß kein Zufall, daß der Dedikator jenes Textes, der sich ausdrücklich als *ʿbdkmš* bezeichnet, den schönen Namen "Neumond(sichel)" Sohn des ʿAmmaʾ trug (*hll br ʿmʾ*). Schon Milik (a.a.O. 339) hatte zu Recht diese Etymologie für den Namen des Dedikanten jener Inschrift vorgeschlagen – ohne allerdings auf die Neumondsichel auf moabitischen Siegeln zu verweisen.

ṣdq-Siegel (**Abb. 3**) dieses Motiv ganz nebensächlich, an fast versteckter Stelle, im untersten Bildregister geboten wird. Daraus ergibt sich, daß auf moabitischen Siegeln mit dem Bildmotiv der Flügelsonne anscheinend keine klare emblematische Vorstellung mehr verbunden war.[17] Wie das Bildmotiv in Moab im einzelnen gedeutet wurde, ist unbekannt.

3. Zur vierflügligen Gestalt

Die Siegelfläche des *kmšṣdq*-Siegels (**Abb. 3**) wird von einer vierflügligen Gestalt dominiert. Über die Bedeutung der vierflügligen Gestalt besteht kein Konsens (s.o.). Wenn es denn aber so ist, daß in assyrischer Bildtradition bei vergleichbaren vierflügligen Figuren nur *ein* Bein der Figur von der Kleidung bedeckt ist bzw. die Bekleidung hinter dem einen Bein noch durchscheint (Giveon 1961: 40f; Keel 1977: 200), so steht die hier vorliegende Figur eindeutig *nicht* in solcher Tradition. Für den Kopfschmuck der vorliegenden Figur gilt, daß er zwar nicht wirklich eine ägyptische Krone oder Doppelkrone ist, aber doch nur verstanden werden kann, wenn man ägyptische Kronendarstellungen als Vorlage annimmt. So steht die vierflüglige Figur auf diesem moabitischen Siegel des 8./7. Jhs. in der ägyptisierenden Bildtradition der syro-palästinischen Siegelkunst, aber (noch) nicht unter direktem Einfluß der assyrischen Glyptik.

4. Zwischenbilanz

Insgesamt sind auf den sieben *kmš*-Siegeln nur wenige bildliche Motive bezeugt. Die auffälligste und auch umstrittenste Darstellung ist die vierflüglige Gestalt auf dem Siegel des *kmšṣdq* (**Abb. 3**). Weiterhin gibt es Darstellungen der Mondsichel (**Abb. 2, 5**) und der geflügelten Sonne (**Abb. 1, 3**), dazu noch eine spiegelbildliche Greifen- oder Sphinxdarstellung (**Abb. 4**) und – auf demselben Siegel – vielleicht ein Bildrelikt aus dem Mittleren Reich. Das ist wahrlich keine Fülle an verschiedenen Bildmotiven, sondern ein beklagenswerter Mangel, der generalisierende Aussagen nicht erlaubt. Vermehrt werden die erörterten Bildmotive nun aber durch Siegel, die zwar keine *kmš*-Namen aufweisen, aber aus anderen Gründen als moabitisch klassifiziert wurden.

---

17. Bezeichnenderweise hat C. Bonnet in ihrer Studie zum Sonnengott im kanaanäisch-phönizischen Raum (1989) die geflügelte Sonnenscheibe nicht als Repräsentation des Sonnengottes aufgenommen.

IV. Siegel mit Namen ohne *KMŠ*-Element

Auch im folgenden bleiben anikonische Siegel unberücksichtigt, die allein von der Form ihrer Buchstaben her als moabitisch klassifiziert wurden.[18] Die nachfolgende Erörterung faßt einige Siegel nach der jeweils dominierenden ikonographischen Darstellung auf ihrer Siegelfläche zu 'Gruppen' zusammen. Wenn dabei nicht allein die ikonographische Darstellung diskutiert wird, sondern immer wieder gefragt werden muß, ob das Siegel zu Recht als moabitisch deklariert ist, unterstreicht das erneut die schwierigen Unterscheidungskriterien zwischen phönizischen, hebräischen und moabitischen Siegeln.

1. Greif oder Sphinx

Das Siegel des *ʾḥyšʿ* (**Abb. 7**)

Die Siegelfläche ist dreiteilig. Im obersten Teil, mehr als die Hälfte der Siegelfläche einnehmend, findet sich die Darstellung eines stilisierten geflügelten Löwen mit einem großen Schurz zwischen seinen Vorderpranken. Das Mischwesen schreitet auf dem Siegel nach rechts. Sein Kopf ist so erodiert, daß nicht sicher erkennbar ist, ob es sich um einen menschenartigen (= Sphinx; so zuletzt Lemaire 1990b: 99 Anm. 10) oder um einen vogelartigen Kopf (= Greif) handelt. Vor dem Kopf des Tieres steht ein hohes *ʿnḫ*-Zeichen (oder Thymiaterion?), hinter ihm ein kleineres. Von der Darstellung ist die Beschriftung durch einen Doppelstrich getrennt. Unten, wiederum durch einen Doppelstrich getrennt, erscheint die Darstellung einer Mondsichel, rechts davon ein mehrzackiger Stern.

Ist eine phönizische Klassifikation (so HD 119) ausgeschlossen[19], so läßt sich auch eine Zuweisung nach Moab paläographisch nicht zwingend beweisen.[20] Die Greifen- bzw. Sphinxdarstellung, die hier im unteren Register

---

18. Etwa das Siegel eines *nḥm bn ḥmn* (Timm 1989a: 211f Nr. 19) und das eines *klkl mnḥm* (Timm 1989a: 203f Nr. 16; zum Namen *klkl* vgl. noch Silverman 1970: 481; Zadok 1988: 31 s.v. *klkl* und *klklyhw*). Besonders letzteres wäre schriftgeschichtlich wichtig, weil auf ihm die Form des Mem mit einem kleinen Strich unter dem mittleren horizontalen Balken zu finden ist, die bislang nur auf moabitischen Siegeln nachgewiesen wurde. Würde das Siegel – wie vom Ersteditor des Siegels vorgeschlagen (Avigad 1979: Nr. 9) – weiterhin als hebräisch klassifiziert, so liefe das darauf hinaus, daß die Form des Mem generell kein Klassifikationsmerkmal für moabitische oder hebräische Siegel mehr sein könnte. Vgl. noch unten die Diskussion zum Mem auf dem Siegel des *mypʿh* (**Abb. 13**).

19. Der Name des Siegelinhabers ist – entgegen der Erstpublikation – aus dem Nominalelement *ʾḥ* und der Verbalwurzel *YŠʿ* zusammengesetzt. Letztere ist im Phönizisch-Punischen nicht nachgewiesen.

20. A. Lemaire (1980: 496) hat für die Ḥet-Form auf moabitische Parallelen verwiesen und damit eine moabitische Klassifikation begründet (vgl. 1990b: 100 Anm. 6). In den

begleitet ist von der Darstellung eines Sichelmondes und eines Sterns, ist also für die Klassifikation maßgeblich. Sie hat eine Analogie in der (spiegelbildlich verdoppelten) Darstellung auf dem Siegel des *kmšdn* (**Abb. 4**). Sofern das *ʾḫyšʿ*-Siegel weiterhin als moabitisch anzusehen ist, wäre für Moab eine frühe Darstellung eines einzelnen Greifen bzw. eines einzelnen Sphinx bezeugt.

Das Siegel des *ʾmrʾl* (**Abb. 8**)

Die ellipsoide Siegelfläche wird zu mehr als der Hälfte eingenommen von einem Greifen, der nach links schreitet.[21] Dessen Kopfputz besteht aus vier Strahlen. Zwischen seinen Vorderläufen befindet sich ein Schurz. Vor dem Greifen steht ein hohes *ʿnḫ*-Zeichen (oder Thymiaterion?). Unter der Greifendarstellung, davon durch eine einfache Trennlinie abgeteilt, steht *ʾmrʾ*. Darunter befindet sich eine letzte Trennlinie. Parallel zur letzten Trennlinie ist ein verdrehtes Lamed eingraviert, für das der Raum hinter dem letzten ʾAleph offensichtlich falsch berechnet war.[22]

Die moabitische Klassifikation dieses Siegels, das um 750 v. Chr. datiert wird, ist von seiner Beschriftung her ebensowenig zu sichern wie von seiner Ikonographie. Greifen- bzw. damit eng verwandte Sphinxdarstellungen gibt es ja außerhalb der moabitischen Glyptik häufig (vgl. Gubel 1985; Lemaire 1990b).

Das Siegel des *ydlʾ* (**Abb. 9**)

Die Siegelfläche wird von etwas mehr als zur Hälfte von einem stilisierten geflügelten Löwen (?) eingenommen, dessen Kopf in einen Federbusch von vier Strahlen ausläuft. Zwischen seinen Vorderläufen befindet sich wieder ein Schurz. Vor dem Löwen (?), der auf dem Siegel nach links schreitet, steht ein 'Pfahl', der sich oben zu drei 'Ästen' verzweigt. Mittels einer Doppellinie wird die Beschriftung *ydlʾ* davon abgeteilt. Dabei folgt auf das ʾAleph noch ein vertikaler Strich. Darunter steht nochmals ein Doppelstrich.

---

moabitischen Monumentalinschriften oder den *kmš*-Siegeln ist ein vergleichbares Ḥet freilich nicht nachgewiesen. Eine vergleichbare Form gibt es auf dem Siegel des *ḥšk ʾmhẏ*, das ebenfalls als moabitisch deklariert worden ist (B 68; Israel 1987b: Nr. XVII), bei dem aber für eine solche Klassifikation und überhaupt an der Authentizität ernste Zweifel anzubringen sind (Timm 1989a: 232f Nr. 31). Das Šin auf dem Siegel des *ʾḫyšʿ* ist nicht sicher erkennbar. Die übrigen Buchstaben ermöglichen zwar eine Datierung ins 8. oder 8./7. Jh., jedoch keine sichere Zuweisung nach Moab.

21. Es handelt sich – anders als auf **Abb. 7** – eindeutig um die Darstellung eines Greifen, nicht eines Sphinx.

22. Auch die obere, zweite Trennlinie zwischen der Greifendarstellung und der Beschriftung kann so gedeutet werden, daß unter dem eigentlichen, einfachen Trennstrich noch ein weiteres verdrehtes Lamed liegt, dessen Abstrich mit dem ersten ʾAleph der Inschrift eine Ligatur eingegangen ist. So ergäbe sich als Beschriftung *l!//ʾmrʾ///l* (anders noch B 62; Israel 1987b: 108; Timm 1989a: 189f Nr. 10).

Unter Hinweis auf die Greifen- bzw. Sphinxdarstellungen der "moabitischen" Siegel, speziell des *ʾmrʾl*-Siegels (**Abb. 8**), hat A. Lemaire kürzlich vorgeschlagen (1990b: 100 Anm. 16), die Buchstabenformen dieses Siegels paläographisch dem moabitischen Schriftraum zuzuweisen.[23] Ausschlaggebend für diese Klassifikation ist gewiß mehr die ikonographische Darstellung auf dem Siegel als die Formen von Yod, Dalet, Lamed und ʾAleph (vgl. Lemaire, *supra*, S. 15 mit Fig. 21). Für alle vier Buchstaben lassen sich aber auch im hebräischen Schriftraum Parallelen finden, so daß die neue Klassifikation noch nicht das letzte Wort für die künstlerische Heimat des Siegels ist.[24]

Das Siegel des *mʾš* (**Abb. 10**)

Die Siegelfläche wird mehr als zur Hälfte von einem Greif ausgefüllt, der nach links schreitet. Sein Kopf ist verziert mit einem dreistrahligen Federbusch. Zwischen seinen Vorderläufen befindet sich wieder ein Schurz. Darunter eine doppelte Trennlinie, darunter die Beschriftung.

P. Bordreuil (1986f) hat dieses Stück aufgrund der Buchstabenformen, der Darstellung und des Namens[25] als moabitisch klassifiziert und darauf hingewiesen, daß Abbé Starcky ehedem noch weitere Siegel aus Transjordanien in seiner Sammlung hatte. Eine (ehedem spiegelbildlich verdoppelte) Darstellung eines Sphinx oder eines Greifen ist auf dem Siegel des *kmšdn* (**Abb. 4**) bezeugt. Insofern könnte auf einem zeitlich früheren moabitischen Siegel sehr wohl auch eine einzelne Greifen- oder Sphinxdarstellung auftreten. Die Buchstabenformen erlauben allerdings nur eine Datierung in die Mitte des 7. Jhs., aber keine eindeutige Zuweisung nach Moab.[26]

Auffallend ist bei den vier hier erörterten Siegeln mit einer Sphinx- oder Greifendarstellung, daß die Kopfpartie des Greifen bzw. des Sphinx zwar bisweilen mit einer Art Federbusch versehen ist, keine der Darstellungen aber

---

23. P. Bordreuil hatte das Siegel um 750 v. Chr. datiert und als phönizisch klassifiziert; die Verbalwurzel (*DLH*) des Personennamens sei für das Phönizische freilich neu. Das nachfolgende ʾAleph repräsentiere einen Gottesnamen (B 3). Letzterem ist angesichts vieler Hypokoristika mit der Endung ʾAleph nicht zuzustimmen.

24. Eine moabitische Parallele zu Personennamen der Wurzel *DLH* fehlt. Zu hebräischen vgl. Zadok 1988: 25, 30, 31, 39, 96; Avigad 1989a: Nr. 10 (Siegel des/der *dlh* oder *dly* samt zwei weiteren Belegen auf Siegeln).

25. Daß der Name *mʾš* in Moab gebräuchlich war, bezeugt seine Langform *kmšmʾš*. Allerdings hat es diesen Namen z.B. auch im hebräischen Sprachraum gegeben, wie z.B. das Siegel des *mʾš bn mnḥ hspr* (B 51) erweist.

26. Ein typisch moabitisches Mem mit zusätzlichem Strich unter dem horizontalen Mittelbalken gibt es auf dem Siegel des *mʾš* jedenfalls nicht. Sein ʾAleph und Šin sind für die Datierung relevant, reichen jedoch nicht, um eine moabitische Klassifikation über jeden Zweifel erhaben sein zu lassen.

eine eindeutig ägyptische Krone zeigt, wie sie doch für einen ägyptischen Sphinx erwartet werden dürfte und auch oft genug auf anderen Siegeln belegt ist (vgl. schon G 1-7, andeutungsweise auch G 10-11; Gubel 1985; Lemaire 1990b). Angesichts dessen, daß ein moabitischer Siegelschneider die vierflüglige Figur auf dem Siegel des *kmšṣdq* (**Abb. 3**) mit einer Krone von der Art der ägyptischen Königskrone versehen hat, sollte man annehmen dürfen, daß auch ein so typisch ägyptisches Wesen wie ein Sphinx (oder der damit ikonographisch eng verwandte Greif) mit einer ägyptischen Krone hätte versehen werden können. Doch ist dies hier nicht der Fall. Vielleicht handelt es sich um eine Besonderheit gerade moabitischer Sphinx- bzw. Greifdarstellungen.[27] Da die (ehedem spiegelbildliche) Sphinx- oder Greifendarstellung auf dem moabitischen Siegel des *kmšdn* (**Abb. 4**) oberhalb der heute allein erhaltenen rechten Figur keinen Federbusch aufweist, unterscheiden sich die vier zuletzt erörterten Siegel davon freilich in einem wichtigen Detail. War ihre Klassifizierung als moabitisch schon durch ihre Buchstabenformen nicht sicher zu erweisen, so kann auch die Zuordnung ihrer Greifen- bzw. Sphinxdarstellungen zum Repertoire der moabitischen Glyptik nicht als endgültig gesichert gelten. Wenn aber auch nur eines der vier Siegel im Land der Moabiter hergestellt wurde – was vorerst nicht sicher erweisbar ist –, so würde sich damit eine ikonographische Kontinuität zur Darstellung auf dem Siegel des *kmšdn* ergeben, und das dort vorliegende Motiv wäre dann für Moab nicht mehr singulär.

Was emblematisch mit dem Motiv des Sphinx oder des Greifen in Moab ausgesagt werden sollte, entzieht sich noch unserer Kenntnis. Man wird es am ehesten mit dem Königtum verbinden.

2. Vierflüglige Gestalt

Die Siegelfläche des *kmšṣdq*-Siegels (**Abb. 3**) wird von der Darstellung einer vierflügligen Gestalt dominiert. Vergleichbare Gestalten finden sich u.a. auf vier weiteren, ebenfalls als moabitisch klassifizierten Siegeln.

Das Siegel des *bʿlntn* (**Abb. 11**)

Das Siegel ist im letzten Jahrhundert von E. de Sarzec in Tello in Mesopotamien gefunden worden. Mehr als die Hälfte seiner Siegelfläche ist von einer nach links schreitenden vierflügligen Gestalt ausgefüllt, die etwas Schlangenähnliches in ihren Händen hat. Es ist nicht auszuschließen, daß die

---

27. Dann wäre allerdings auch das Siegel des *šmʿ*, mit einer deutlich erkennbaren Krone auf dem Haupt des Sphingen (G 3), von den hier erörterten Darstellungen abzusetzen, als nicht-moabitisch anzusehen (anders noch Timm 1989a: 224 Nr. 26) und im westjordanischen Raum Syrien-Palästinas zu belassen (so schon Gubel 1985: 106f).

Figur eine Maske vor dem Gesicht trägt.[28] Auf dem Haupt der Figur befindet sich eine stilisierte ägyptische Krone, wobei vor und hinter dem Haupt sonderbare 'Bänder' von oben herabreichen, die auch als Lamed gedeutet werden könnten. Bekleidet ist die Figur mit einem kurzen Gewand, das noch nicht einmal bis zu den Knien reicht. Unterhalb der Figur, vor und hinter ihr, findet sich je ein liegendes spitzes Dreieck (dazu Timm 1989a: 194 Anm. 29). Unterhalb der Darstellung, durch einen Doppelstrich getrennt, steht die Beschriftung.

Die Buchstabenformen dieses Siegels sind anfänglich als phönizisch oder hebräisch deklariert worden, dann als phönizisch (Delaporte 1920: 26, Pl. 242), aber auch als aramäisch (VSA 20). Zuletzt hat sie L.G. Herr (1978: 158 Nr. 8) als moabitisch klassifiziert, worin ihm nunmehr gefolgt wird (vgl. B 61; Israel 1987b: Nr. XVI; Timm 1989a: 194f Nr. 12).[29]

Der Name *bʿlntn* ist noch mehrfach auf Siegeln belegt. Neben dem in Rede stehenden Siegel hatte schon P. Schroeder (1880: Abb. 8) ein zweites mit der Inschrift *bʿlntn* publiziert, das sich damals in der Slg. Dr. J. Mordtmann, Konstantinopel, befand. Es zeigt zwei sich gegenüberstehende, die senkrechte Namensinschrift flankierende Falken über einer Flügelsonne, darunter zwei Uräen, die ein *ʿnḫ*-Zeichen flankieren. Jenes Stück soll aus Chalzedon bestanden haben. Ein Skaraboid aus Achat mit gleicher Darstellung und gleichem Namen *bʿlntn* findet sich heute im Bible Lands Museum in Jerusalem und ist von M. Heltzer als hebräisches Siegel angesprochen worden (1981: 311f Nr. 270); der Skaraboid ist mit dem Stück aus der Slg. Mordtmann wohl identisch. Ein Siegel im Israel Museum (HD 120) zeigt auf seiner Siegelfläche einen geflügelten Sphinx mit ägyptischer Krone und Schurz zwischen den Vorderläufen, der nach links auf einen stilisierten Lebensbaum zuschreitet. Hinter ihm steht ein *ʿnḫ*-Zeichen, unter der Darstellung, getrennt durch einen einfachen Trennstrich, die Inschrift. Ein sehr einfaches, anikonisches Siegel im Hecht Museum, Haifa, mit dem Namen *bʿlntn* hat kürzlich N. Avigad bekannt gemacht (1989a: Nr. 21).

Da im Phönizisch-Punischen die semitische Wurzel *NTN* im Grundstamm Perfekt regelmäßig als *YTN* erscheint (vgl. Friedrich & Röllig 1979: §§ 158-160), sind Verbalformen mit Nun am Anfang im Phönizisch-Punischen als Textfehler oder als irreguläre Assimilitionsformen anzusehen (vgl. noch den Namen *bʿntn* (sic!) auf

28. Vgl. zu solchen Masken, vorwiegend – aber nicht ausschließlich! – aus Gräbern, Ciasca 1988. Eine Zusammenstellung der syro-palästinischen Funde solcher Masken samt dem Versuch, ihre Funktion(en) zu bestimmen, bedarf einer Einzelstudie.

29. Die auffälligsten Buchstabenform dieses Siegels sind seine zwei Nun, die voneinander differieren. Das erste hat deutlich einen Querstrich unter seinem horizontalen Balken, das zweite nicht. Derartige zusätzliche Striche unter dem horizontalen Querbalken sind zuvor schon nachgewiesen bei den Buchstaben Kaf und Mem. Sie sind keine Gravurfehler des Siegelschneiders, sondern Eigenarten der moabitischen Schriftentwicklung (Timm 1989a: 290-293). So kann dieses Siegel trotz des weit entfernten Fundortes als moabitisch gelten.

einem Krug aus Tell ʿArqa, Bordreuil 1983: 751ff). Will man nicht mit einem ständig wiederholten Schreibfehler rechnen, so sind Siegel mit dem Personennamen *bʿlntn* als nicht-phönizisch zu klassifizieren (anders Avigad 1989a: 18). Hilfsweise könnte vermutet werden, daß man die ikonographischen Darstellungen auf den *bʿlntn*-Siegeln zwar in phönizischen Werkstätten angefertigt, die Beschriftung jedoch in einem Bereich vorgenommen hat, wo man das Verb "geben" mit Nun in der ersten Silbe sprach. Doch deutet auf den *bʿlntn*-Siegeln nichts darauf hin, daß ihre Beschriftung anderswo als in der Werkstatt der ikonographischen Abbildung vorgenommen wurde.

Wohin gehören also die *bʿlntn*-Siegel? Sie stammen gewiß nicht alle aus der gleichen Zeit und auch nicht alle aus der gleichen Werkstatt. Das älteste von ihnen dürfte das Pariser Siegel mit der vierflügligen Gestalt sein (**Abb. 11**; B 61: Mitte 8. Jh.), das jüngste, mit ganz offener ʿAyin-Form, das Stück in Haifa (Avigad 1989a: 17f: 7.-6. Jh.). Obgleich das Motiv der vierflügligen Gestalt viel älter ist, hatte es im 9.-8. Jh. im nordsyrischen Raum eine neue Blütezeit. Die ägyptisierenden Kronen derartiger Figuren – wie auf **Abb. 11** – verwies K. Galling in eine phönizische Werkstatt des 8. Jhs. (Galling 1941: 151ff; vgl. zur ganzen Gruppe auch Gubel, *supra*, S. 123-125). Die Frage ist aber, ob der Ausdruck "phönizische Werkstatt" allein geographisch auf das phönizische Mutterland bezogen werden muß. Galling hatte es wohl so gemeint. Inzwischen verdichten sich jedoch die Gründe dafür, daß mit Siegelwerkstätten in phönizischer Handwerkstraditon Mitte des 8. Jhs. auf dem Boden des Nordreiches Israel zu rechnen ist (Garbini 1982; Lemaire 1990b: 100f; GGG: Kap. VII). Die Annahme, daß "phönizische" Werkstätten nicht nur im phönizischen Mutterland selbst, sondern auch auf west- und ostjordanischem Boden gearbeitet haben, ist z. Zt. die beste Erklärung dafür, daß Siegel mit dem von der nordsyrischen Glyptik und Reliefkunst her beeinflußten Motiv der vierflügligen Gestalt, verbunden mit dem phönizischen Motiv der ägyptischen Krone(n), eine Beschriftung erhalten haben, die im phönizischen Sprachraum nicht möglich war.

Bleibt es bei der moabitischen Klassifikation des Pariser *bʿlntn*-Siegels, so ist damit zu rechnen, daß das Stück in einer Werkstatt auf dem Boden (West- oder Ost-)Palästinas angefertigt wurde, die eine nordsyrisch-phönizische Bildtradition pflegte. Im übrigen ist dann mit dem Namen *bʿlntn* der Gottesname Baal erstmals auch für Moab bezeugt.

Daß ein moabitischer Eigentümer eines Siegels mit der Darstellung einer vierflügligen Gestalt darin die Wiedergabe seines Gottes Kamosch erblicken konnte (vgl. den Namen *kmšṣdq* auf **Abb. 3**), ist möglich. Angesichts des Siegels von **Abb. 11** war aber offenbar das gleiche Motiv auf den Gott Baʿal (vgl. den Namen *bʿlntn*) übertragbar. Eine solche Interpretation der beiden Siegel würde freilich voraussetzen, daß zwischen dem Namen des Siegeleigentümers und der ikonographischen Darstellung auf seinem Siegel eine enge inhaltliche Relation besteht. Dafür gibt es zwar einige Beispiele auf syro-palästinischen Siegeln, doch ist eine solche Relation keineswegs immer gegeben.[30]

Das Siegel des *ʿzʾ* (**Abb. 12**)

Das Siegel stammt aus dem Umkreis des Kibbutz Dan bei Tell el-Qāḍi in Israel. Es hat in seiner Beschriftung mit den Buchstaben des Pariser *bʿlntn*-Siegels nur das Lamed und ʿAyin gemeinsam. Leider gehören Lamed und ʿAyin zu denjenigen Buchstaben, bei denen voneinander abweichende Formen im phönizischen, hebräischen, moabitischen und aramäischen Schriftraum kaum nachzuweisen sind. Ein Zayin wie auf dem *ʿzʾ*-Siegel ist auf moabitischen Denkmälern nur auf der Meschaʿ-Inschrift bezeugt, allerdings entspricht jene klassische Form der hier vorliegenden nicht genau. Eine typisch phönizische Form des Buchstabens liegt jedoch auch nicht vor. Eine aramäische Klassifikation des Siegels und eine Datierung ins 9.-8. Jh. (so Herr 1978: 47f Nr. 99) ist auch noch nicht das letzte Wort (vgl. Timm 1989a: 213f Nr. 20). Eine moabitische Klassifikation des Siegels wird erst gesichert sein, wenn eines Tages zum Buchstaben Zayin auf dem Siegel des *ʿzʾ* vergleichbare Formen auf unbestreitbar moabitischen Inschriften auftauchen.

Die Darstellung steht in Parallele zu etlichen weiteren Beispielen. K. Galling hatte seinerzeit – wie oben erwähnt – die vergleichbaren Darstellungen auf dem Pariser Siegel des *bʿlntn* (**Abb. 11**), auf dem Siegel des *kmšṣdq* (**Abb. 3**) und auf dem Siegel des/der *mmh* (dazu Timm 1989a: 243f Nr. 37) einer phönizischen Werkstatt des 8. Jhs. zugeordnet (Galling 1941: 151ff). Das letztgenannte Siegel muß aber aufgrund seiner Buchstabenformen, die eine moabitische Klassifikation jedenfalls ausschließen, von den übrigen abgesetzt werden (vgl. Timm, a.a.O.).

Das Siegel des *mypʿh* (**Abb. 13**)

Fast drei Viertel der Siegelfläche werden eingenommen von einer vierflügligen Gestalt, die nach rechts schreitet. Auf ihrem Kopf trägt sie eine ägypti-

30. Damit, daß der Gottesname Kamosch und der Gottesname Baʿal auf je einem moabitischen Siegel mit je einer vierflügligen Gestalt bezeugt sind, ergäbe sich ein weites Feld für Erwägungen und Spekulationen, z.B. ob man aus den beiden Siegeln schließen darf, daß der Gott Kamosch bei den Moabitern von Baʿal unterschieden war, oder ob Baʿal dort auch nur eines unter mehreren Epitheta des Kamosch bildete. Daß der Gott Kamosch von den Moabitern als Baʿal tituliert wurde, ist jedenfalls nicht selbstverständlich (vgl. Koch 1979: 466). Gesetzt den Fall, der Gott Kamosch war bei den Moabitern vom Gott Baʿal unterschieden, hatten sich dann die religiösen Vorstellungen über Kamosch den religiösen Vorstellungen über Baʿal einander so stark angenähert, daß ein Verehrer des Kamosch auf seinem Siegel eine ganz ähnliche Darstellung benutzen konnte wie ein Verehrer des Baʿal? Mangels weiterer Quellen – und der generellen Unsicherheit bei der Korrelation von Siegeldekor und theophorem Element im Namen des Siegelsbesitzers – sind derartige Erwägungen hier abzubrechen.

sche Doppelkrone, deren Vorderteil sich fast kugelartig über das Haupt erhebt. Die Darstellung der ägyptischen Doppelkrone hat ihre nächste Parallele auf dem *kmšṣdq*-Siegel (**Abb. 3**). Vor dem Gesicht der Gestalt scheint sich ziemlich deutlich eine Gesichtsmaske zu befinden (s.o. zum Pariser Siegel des *bʿlntn*). In beiden Händen hält die Gestalt je einen Gegenstand, den Avigad (1990: 43) als Lotosblume deutet. Die 'Rippen' der vier Flügel sind bis auf den Leib der Figur durchgestaltet. Das Kleid bedeckt auch beim Ausschreiten der Figur deren oberste Beinpartien nicht, so daß es wie ein Hosenanzug wirkt. Assyrische Siegelschneider hatten bessere Fertigkeiten entwickelt, eine schreitende Person bis an die Knie noch von einem Kleid bedeckt sein zu lassen.

Die einzeilige Inschrift ist von der bildlichen Darstellung durch eine Doppellinie abgetrennt. Von ihrem Duktus her hat Avigad das Siegel ins 7. Jh. datiert. Die Buchstabenfolge *mypʿh* war bislang nur als Name der moabitischen Ortschaft Mefaa(t) bekannt.[31] Avigad hat für die Deutung des Siegeleignernamens darauf hingewiesen, daß im Hebräischen öfter Ortsnamen als Personennamen in Gebrauch waren, vgl. Anatot, Betuel, Efron, Eschtemoa, Gilead, Hebron, Jafia, Sichem, Sif und Socho (1990: 42). So liege mit diesem Stück kein Siegel der moabitischen Stadt Mefaa(t) vor, sondern das eines Moabiters, der seinen Personennamen nach der Stadt Mefaa(t) hatte. Daß das Siegel einem Moabiter gehörte, ist also aus dem Namen des Siegeleigners gefolgert, nicht aus den Formen der Buchstaben.[32] Das Gewicht des moabitischen Ortsnamens Mefaa(t) wird den epigraphischen Befund zwar auch künftig verdrängen. Aber so sehr der (Orts-)Name Mefaa(t) und die vierflüglige Gestalt ins Repertoire moabitischer Siegel passen mögen: nach dem epigraphischen Befund ist hinter die moabitische Klassifikation des Siegels ein unübersehbares Fragezeichen zu setzen.

---

31. Im Alten Testament מפעת und מיפעת geschrieben (Jos 13,18; 21,37; Jer 48,21 Ketib; 1 Chr 6,64). Die Meschaʿ-Inschrift (KAI Nr. 181) bietet die Endung *-h* bei den Ortsnamen *qrḥh* (Z. 3, 21, 25) und *nbh* (Z. 14). So kann die hier auf dem Siegel vorliegende Graphie mit He am Ende statt wie im Hebräischen mit Taw als korrekte moabitische Schreibung des Ortsnamens gelten.

32. Besonders beim Mem ist schon Avigad aufgefallen (1990: 43), daß es nicht die zu erwartende moabitische Form aufweist. Der Leerraum auf dem Siegel hätte in jedem Fall gereicht, ein Mem mit einer gerundeten Unterlänge einzugravieren (zu den moabitischen Mem vgl. Timm 1989a: 290-293). Unter den fünf Buchstaben des Siegels müßte das Mem als *das* Kriterium gelten, epigraphisch zwischen moabitischer oder hebräischer Herkunft zu unterscheiden. Das vorliegende Mem hat aber keine typisch moabitische Form. Vergleichbares läßt sich auch vom He sagen, auch wenn für dessen Entwicklung im moabitischen Schriftraum viel weniger Belege zur Verfügung stehen. Ein moabitisches He sollte im 7. Jh. eine horizontale Oberlänge über dem rechten vertikalen Balken hinaus haben (vgl. Timm 1989a: 281f). Nach den sonstigen Schriftdenk-

Die Siegel des *kmšṣdq* (**Abb. 3**) und des *bʿlntn* (**Abb. 11**) zeigen wie die beiden Siegel des *ʿzʾ* (**Abb. 12**) und des *mypʿh* (**Abb. 13**), deren moabitische Klassifikation allerdings problematisch ist (s.u.), jeweils sehr ähnliche Darstellungen. Wenn in deren Bildtradition ein Motiv aus dem nordsyrischen Raum vermehrt wurde um die ägyptisierende Krone aus dem phönizischen Kulturkreis, muß man für die Deutung der dargestellten vierflügligen Gestalt in Moab mit sehr komplexen Einwirkungen von außen rechnen. Wenn sich bestätigt, daß die vierflüglige Gestalt auf **Abb. 11** eine Gesichtsmaske trägt und auch die auf **Abb. 13** mit einer solchen Gesichtsmaske versehen ist, wird die Interpretation der Gestalt als einer (männlichen oder weiblichen) Gottheit ganz fraglich. Man wird sie dann eher als eine Mittlerfigur deuten müssen, die angesichts der/einer Gottheit/des Numinosen ihr Antlitz zu verbergen hat (vgl. auch – anders? – Ex 34,29ff; dazu – nicht völlig überzeugend – Jaroš 1976). Darüber hinaus gehört die vierflüglige Gestalt – anders als etwa die geflügelte Sonne – nicht zu den ältesten Motiven der eisenzeitlichen Siegel aus Palästina. So ist diese Darstellung ein Beleg dafür, daß die Siegelschneider der Moabiter im 8. und 7. Jh. neuen ikonographischen und religiösen Einflüssen durchaus offen gegenüberstanden.

3. Adorationsszene

Das erste Siegel mit einer Szene, in der sich zwei Personen an einem altarähnlichen Gegenstand ehrfurchtsvoll gegenüberstehen, das als moabitisch klassifiziert worden ist, war das Siegel des *ʾmṣ hspr* (**Abb. 14**). Über dieses berühmte Siegel des "Schreibers Amoṣ" hinaus sind inzwischen noch zahlreiche weitere Siegel mit vergleichbaren Darstellungen[33] als "moabitisch" klassifiziert worden.[34]

Man kann zuweilen geradezu den Eindruck haben, jedes syro-palästinische Siegel, das eine vergleichbare Adorationsdarstellung aufweist, müsse neuerdings als "moabitisch" klassifiziert werden. Überprüft man indes die verschiedenen Buchstabenformen dieser Siegel mit Adorationsdarstellungen, so fallen erhebliche Unterschiede zu den bislang auf den *kmš*-Siegeln belegten Buchstabenformen auf. Legt man ganz strenge Maßstäbe an für einen derartigen epigraphischen Vergleich, so wird sogar die Zuweisung des berühm-

---

mälern aus Moab können die auf diesem Siegel vorliegenden Buchstaben jedenfalls nicht als moabitisch gelten.

33. Auch wenn andere Benennungen für diese Darstellung vorgeschlagen wurden (B 67: "cérémonie d'alliance"; Bordreuil 1987a: 284 "scène d'alliance"), seien derartige Darstellungen hier weiterhin als Adorationsszene benannt (vgl. Keel 1990c: 17 Anm. 8).

34. Vgl. Timm 1989a: Nr. 8, 13 (= **Abb. 15**), 15, 21, 27, 35; B 102; Avigad 1989a: Nr. 18 (= **Abb. 16**), 22; Lemaire 1990b: Nr. 3 (aus es-Salṭ im Ostjordanland). Zur ganzen Gruppe vgl. Ornan, *supra*, S. 66f, figs. 48-50, 56-65.

ten *ʾmṣ hspr*-Siegels an einen Moabiter wieder fraglich.[35] Ein minuziöser "buchstäblicher" Vergleich der Schriftformen zwischen den als moabitisch klassifizierten Siegeln mit Adorationsdarstellungen mit den Buchstabenformen auf den moabitischen Inschriften oder den *kmš*-Siegeln kann hier nicht vorgenommen werden. An zwei beschrifteten Siegeln mit einer Adorationsszene sei die Problematik aber verdeutlicht.

Das Siegel des *ḥkm*! (**Abb. 15**)

Zwei Drittel der Siegelfläche bilden eine sehr schön ausgeführte Adorationsszene, in der sich zwei Personen einander gegenüberstehen. Über ihnen schwebt ein vielzackiger Stern. Zwischen den beiden Personen befindet sich ein Ständer, dessen oberer Teil als liegender Halbmond geformt ist. Links neben dem Ständer ist noch ein undeutbarer Kreis zu sehen. Hinter den beiden Personen steht jeweils ein stilisiertes *ʿnḫ*-Zeichen. Für die sehr schön ausgeführte Adorationsszene hat O. Keel eine Reihe nordsyrischer, aramäischer Beispiele beigebracht (1990c: 15f); die Darstellung steht – unabhängig von der paläographischen Klassifikation des Siegels als moabitisch oder aramäisch – unter starkem aramäischen Einfluß aus Nordsyrien (Ḥarrān). Als Datierung des Siegels wird die letzte Hälfte des 8. Jhs., aber auch die erste Hälfte des 7. Jhs. vorgeschlagen (vgl. Timm 1989a: 197 Anm. 32).

Unter der Szene, durch einen Doppeltrennstrich abgeteilt, ist die Inschrift *lḥkṁ* eingraviert. Sie ist in sehr ungelenken Formen ausgeführt.[36] Die Zuordnung des Siegels zum moabitischen Schriftraum hatte erstmals N. Avigad (1978a) mit der Lesung *lḥkš* vorgeschlagen, wobei die Form des Buchstabens Ḥet wahrscheinlich das (unausgesprochene) Argument bildete, da sie auf dem Siegel des *kmšyḥy* (**Abb. 1**) ein genaues Pendant hat. L.G. Herr (1978: 51) hatte das Stück bei der Lesung *lḥkm* als "Possible Aramaic Seal" bezeichnet.[37] Der epigraphische Befund kann die Klassifikation des Siegels als moabitisch nicht begründen.[38]

---

35. Das gilt dann auch für das Siegel des *ʾḥyḥy* (vgl. Timm 1989a: 185f Nr. 8) und das Siegel des *km*[...] aus Samaria (vgl. dazu oben Anm. 2). Ersteres wird hauptsächlich deswegen als moabitisch angesehen, weil das Siegel des Schreibers Amoṣ so klassifiziert ist, letzteres nur aufgrund einer weitgehend ergänzten Lesung.

36. Herr (1978: 51) hatte wegen der vorzüglichen Darstellung und der gleichzeitig völlig unbeholfenen Buchstabenformen (vgl. Kaf und Mem) eine moderne Fälschung nicht ausschließen wollen.

37. Die Ḥet-Form sei "all right in Aramaic", die Form des Kaf allerdings für den aramäischen Schriftraum "unique". Das letzte Zeichen las Herr als (eindeutiges) Mem, das – wenngleich verdreht – "a good...Aramaic form" sei.

38. In der (Neu-)Publikation des Siegels durch P. Bordreuil wird das Stück – wiederum mit der Lesung *lḥkš* – in die Gruppe der moabitischen Siegel eingereiht, wobei die Form des Buchstabens Ḥet das epigraphische Argument bildet, die vergleichbare Darstellung auf dem Siegel des Schreibers Amoṣ (**Abb. 14**) das ikonographische (B 67). Der Le-

Das Siegel des *mʾš* (**Abb. 16**)

Die Siegelfläche wird zu mehr als der Hälfte eingenommen von einer Adorationsdarstellung. In dieser Darstellung steht aber nur eine Person rechts vor einem altarähnlichen Ständer. Über diesem leuchtet links ein neunstrahliger Stern. Links des Ständers steht der Sichelmond. Im Rücken der Figur ein Ständer – ähnlich dem Altar – mit zwei kreuzweisen Querbalken.

Unter der Darstellung, durch eine doppelte Trennlinie abgeteilt, findet sich die Beschriftung. Avigad (1989a: 16) datiert das Siegel nach den Buchstabenformen ins 8./7. Jh. Die Abbildung des Siegels zeigt beim steifen Mem den typischen Querstrich, der auch auf anderen moabitischen Mem aufgefallen war. Der Name *mʾš* ist mit seiner Langform *kmšmʾš* (**Abb. 2**) für Moab sicher nachgewiesen, er ist aber auch außerhalb des moabitischen Sprachraums bezeugt und kann nicht als ein sicheres Kriterium für eine moabitische Klassifikation gelten.

Hinter gelegentlich geäußerten Vorbehalten, Adorationsszenen wie auf dem Siegel des Schreibers Amoṣ, des *ḥkm* oder des *mʾš* u.a. dem Corpus der hebräischen Namenssiegel zuzuordnen, steht oft – wenn auch vielfach unausgesprochen – die Annahme, daß derartige Szenen einem Israeliten oder Judäer nicht zuzumuten seien, zumal die Darstellungen durch emblematische Symbole wie den Sichelmond oder Sterne auf pagane Gottheiten verweisen. Bislang ist in der Tat kein Siegel mit einer Adorationsdarstellung und einem jahwehaltigen Namen bekannt geworden, so daß die Annahme, derartige Darstellungen seien grundsätzlich als nicht-hebräisch zu klassifizieren, noch nicht

---

sung *lḥkš* und der Klassifikation als moabitisch schlossen sich Israel (1987b: Nr. XV) und der Verfasser (Timm 1989a: 197f Nr. 13) an. Der Name des Siegeleigentümers blieb bei dieser Lesung jedoch rätselhaft und war auch mit einem Hinweis auf eine palmyrenische Namensform *ḥkyšw* (Stark 1971: 88) im Grund nicht erklärt.

Wie schon Herr gesehen hatte, ist der letzte Buchstabe aber als verdrehtes Mem zu deuten, worauf auch A. Lemaire während des Fribourger Symposions insistierte (cf. *supra*, S. 16f mit Fig. 25). Damit ergibt sich für dieses Siegel zweierlei: (1) Erfreulich: ein von der Wortwurzel *ḤKM* "weise sein" her deutbarer Name (vgl. zu Namen dieser Wurzel Zadok 1988: 98 mit Anm. 67), der allerdings in der hier vorliegenden Form anderweitig bislang nicht bezeugt ist. (2) Fatal: ein neuer Beleg des Buchstabens Mem für den moabitischen Schriftraum (s.o. Anm. 18), der in dieser Form singulär ist.

Schließt man sich aufgrund des Ḥet einer moabitischen Klassifikation des Siegels an, wofür die parallele Form auf dem Siegel des *kmšyḥy* (**Abb. 1**) spräche, während für eine solche Form eindeutige aramäische Beispiele fehlen (anders Herr 1978: 51, vgl. aber ebd. Fig. 27), so ist gleichzeitig zu sagen, daß die Form des Mem den reichlich belegten moabitischen Formen definitiv entgegengesetzt ist. Man mag das für eine individuelle Sonderform auf diesem Siegel halten, wie es ja auch anderswo auf Siegeln ungewöhnliche Buchstabenformen gibt. Gleichzeitig muß aber konzediert werden, daß es zur Form des Ḥet auch im hebräischen Schriftraum eindeutige Parallelen gibt (vgl. Timm 1989a: 284 Anm. 20).

eindeutig entkräftet werden konnte. Der epigraphische Befund läßt jedoch in manchen Fällen deren bisherige, gerade auch die “moabitische” Zuordnung fraglich und eine hebräische Zuordnung möglich erscheinen. Warum darf eigentlich das Siegel des *kṁ*[...] (Ornan, *supra*, S. 67, Fig. 56), obwohl es in Samaria ausgegraben wurde, nicht als hebräisch klassifiziert werden (vgl. Sass, *infra*, S. 232 mit Anm. 88)?

Wenn freilich auch nur ein oder zwei Siegel mit Adorationsdarstellungen weiterhin als moabitisch gelten können, so ist das von besonderem Belang. Denn sie bieten dann eine ikonographische Darstellung, die auf *kmš*-Siegeln bislang nicht bezeugt ist, und sind weiterhin ein Zeichen dafür, daß im 8./7. Jh. v. Chr. auch in Moab unter aramäischem Religionseinfluß eine Entwicklung stattfand, die von einer emblematischen Gestaltung der Siegel weg zu typischen Darstellungen geführt hat. Es ist ein erheblicher Unterschied, ob man auf Siegeln nur – oder in erster Linie – emblematische Elemente wie die geflügelte Sonne oder die Mondsichel mit ihrem Verweischarakter auf die damit gemeinte Gottheit abbildet, oder ob man eine Anbetungsszene darstellt, in der sich der Siegeleigner selbst wiederfinden konnte (zum Hervortreten von Verehrerdarstellungen in der nordwestsemitischen Glyptik der Eisenzeit II C vgl. Ornan, *supra*; Uehlinger, *infra*, S. 262-265; GGG: §§ 183-186).

4. Mondsichel und Stern

Zwei *kmš*-Siegel, das des *kmšmʾš* (**Abb. 2**) und das des *kmš* (**Abb. 5**) enthalten neben ihrer Beschriftung noch jeweils im obersten Bildregister die stilisierte Darstellung eines liegenden Halbmondes und eines strahlenden Sterns. So simpel diese beiden ikonographischen Elemente auch sind, sie können auf den Siegeln in einer erstaunlichen Variabilität auftreten.

Die Mondsichel- und Stern-Darstellung ist geradezu ein Klassifikationsmerkmal für “moabitische” Siegel geworden (vgl. Israel 1987b: 112). Hält man diesem Klassifikationsmerkmal jedoch wieder die epigraphische Form der Buchstaben auf diesen Siegeln entgegen, so wird eine moabitische Zuweisung bei vielen Stücken erneut problematisch. Vier Siegel seien hier noch diskutiert.

Das Siegel des *mnšh bn hmlk* (**Abb. 17**)

Die Siegelfläche ist dreigeteilt. Im obersten Register steht der Sichelmond mit einem untergesetzten kleinen Strich (Andeutung eines Podestes?). Links daneben befindet sich ein sechsstrahliger Stern. Darunter, abgeteilt durch je zwei Doppelstriche als Trennungslinien, die Beschriftung.

Das Siegel wurde vom Ersteditor – und ihm folgend vielen anderen – als hebräisch angesehen. Manche identifizierten den hier bezeugten *bn hmlk* gar mit dem Prinzen Manasseh, der später König in Juda wurde (vgl. Herr 1980b: 69f). J. Naveh hat das Siegel aber aufgrund der Buchstabenformen dem moabitischen Schriftraum zugewiesen (1966: 29 Anm. 24), worin ihm vielfach gefolgt wird (vgl. Israel 1987b: Nr. VII; Timm 1989a: 207ff Nr. 18). Damit wäre auch in Moab der Titel *bn hmlk* bezeugt.[39]

Das Siegel des *plṭy bn mʾš hmzkr* (**Abb. 18**)[40]

Die Siegelfläche hat vier Register. Das oberste weist zwei kleine Striche auf, gefolgt von der Mondsichel-Stern-Darstellung. Die übrigen Register sind ausgefüllt durch die Beschriftung, auf die am Ende noch ein kleiner Strich (als Raumfüller?) folgt. Die einzelnen Register sind jeweils durch einen Doppelstrich abgeteilt. Aufgrund der Buchstabenform wird das Siegel ins 8./7. Jh. datiert.

Die Mondsichel-Stern-Darstellung hat die verwandte Darstellung auf dem Siegel des *kmš* (**Abb. 5**) zur Seite. Dort steht der Stern rechts neben dem Mond, hier links. Außerdem finden sich hier auf dem Siegel zwei kleine Striche vor der Darstellung, die es an dieser Stelle anderswo nicht gibt. Die nächste Parallele zur Mondsichel-Stern-Darstellung von **Abb. 18** bietet das eben erörterte Siegel des *mnšh bn hmlk* (**Abb. 17**). Dort steht aber noch ein kleiner Strich (rudimentäres Podest?) unter der Mondsichel. Bei aller Ähnlichkeit in den beiden Darstellungen haben die Siegelschneider also doch zwei verschiedene Darstellungen geboten.

Das Siegel des *rʿṣ* (**Abb. 19**)

Seine Siegelfläche ist dreigeteilt. Im obersten Register findet sich eine Mondsichel-Stern-Darstellung, wobei der Stern rechts der Mondsichel steht.

---

39. N. Avigad hat neuerdings ein weiteres Siegel mit der Aufschrift *mnšh bn hmlk* veröffentlicht (1987a: Nr. 7; vgl. Sass, *infra*, S. 214 mit Fig. 85). Ein Vergleich zwischen diesem und dem bislang bekannten von **Abb. 17** zeigt etliche Unterschiede: (1) geflügelter Skarabäus und drei Punkte vs. Mondsichel-Stern-Darstellung; (2) andere Zeilentrennung: *lmnšh b//n hmlk* vs. *lmnšh bn//hmlk*; (3) erheblich verschiedene Buchstabenformen. Man wird die beiden Siegel nicht nur verschiedenen Eignern, sondern auch verschiedenen Schrifträumen und verschiedenen Zeiten zuordnen müssen. Insofern unterstützt die Darstellung der Mondsichel und eines Sternes auf dem schon länger bekannten Siegel von **Abb. 17** auch dessen Zuordnung nach Moab. Die Diskussion der beiden Siegel könnte künftig wichtige Kriterien für die Unterscheidung moabitischer von hebräischen Buchstabenformen bieten.

40. Vom Fundort des Siegels her ist anfänglich eine ammonitische (Hadidi 1987: 101), vom Schrifttyp der Buchstaben her eine hebräische (Younker 1985: 179 Anm. 2) Klassifikation vorgeschlagen worden. Doch haben dann zugleich F. Zayadine (1985b) und M. Abu Taleb (1985) das Siegel als moabitisch bestimmt, worin ihnen nunmehr gefolgt wird (vgl. Israel 1987b: Nr. XXV; Timm 1989a: 217ff Nr. 22; vgl. Lemaire, *supra*, S. 2-3). Für die moabitische Klassifikation des Siegels sind in erster Linie seine Buchstabenformen maßgeblich gewesen, dann auch die Darstellung der Mondsichel mit dem Stern. In der Tat haben die meisten der 15 Buchstaben dieses Siegels

Links neben der Mondsichel stehen zwei kleine Striche. Darunter kommt eine Zeile Beschriftung, wiederum darunter die stark stilisierte Darstellung der geflügelten Sonne, kopfstehend (vgl. Parayre 1990a: 301, Pl. X:116; *supra*, S. 43, Fig. 6). Die einzelnen Register sind voneinander durch eine Doppellinie abgeteilt. Aufgrund der Buchstabenformen und der ikonographischen Elemente hat P. Bordreuil (B 64) das Siegel ins 8. Jh. datiert und als moabitisch klassifiziert.

Die Buchstabenformen haben auf der Meschaʿ-Inschrift, aber auch im hebräischen Schriftraum ihre Parallelen (vgl. Herr 1978: Fig. 50-52). So ist das entscheidende Argument für eine moabitische Klassifikation des Siegels die Darstellung der Mondsichel und eines Sternes im obersten Register sowie die Darstellung einer geflügelten Sonne, kopfstehend, im untersten. Daß mit dem Motiv im untersten Register wirklich eine geflügelte Sonne gemeint ist, zeigt das Siegel des *rpʾ*.

Das Siegel des *rpʾ* (**Abb. 20**)

Seine Siegelfläche ist durch zwei Doppelstriche dreigeteilt. Im obersten Register steht eine geflügelte Sonne, im mittleren die Schriftzeile, im untersten die Mondsichel, die einen achtzackigen Stern rechts neben sich hat. Aufgrund der Buchstabenformen[41] und der ikonographischen Darstellung hat F.

---

ihre engsten Parallelen im moabitischen Schriftraum. Doch gilt einschränkend auch, daß weder bei dem hier vorliegenden Kaf, noch bei dem hier vorliegenden Mem der horizontale Strich unter dem mittleren Querbalken auftritt, der sonst als typisch moabitisch anzusehen ist (s.o. Anm. 7). Auch die hier belegte Form des Buchstabens Yod ist so, mit kleinem Abstrich, noch nicht auf *kmš*-Siegeln nachgewiesen. Auch das *mypʿh*-Siegel (**Abb. 13**) zeigt ein anderes Yod. Die Beispiele auf dem Siegel des *yḥṣ* (Israel 1987b: Nr. XXVII; Timm 1989a: 234f Nr. 32; vgl. Ornan, *supra*, S. 66, Fig. 55) und dem Siegel des *ylʾ* (Israel 1987b: Nr. XXXI; Ornan, *supra*, S. 67, Fig. 63) sind wahrscheinlich *beide* nicht moabitisch (anders noch Timm 1989a: 201f Nr. 15 zum Siegel des *ylʾ*). Ganz eigenwillig ist schließlich die Form des Ṭet. Sie wird gern für aramäisch beeinflußt angesehen (Abu Taleb 1985: 24; van der Kooij 1987: 113 Anm. 32: "imitations from Aramaic or Ammonite traditions"). Doch gibt es bislang auf Siegeln kein klar bezeugtes moabitisches Ṭet, so daß die Annahme aramäischen Einflusses unbeweisbar ist (zur Form des Ṭet auf der Meschaʿ-Stele vgl. Timm 1989a: 284-285). So sind besonders für die Formen des Yod und Ṭet auf diesem Siegel bislang noch keine moabitischen Beispiele beizubringen.
Der Name *kmšplṭ* ist in einem aramäischen Papyrus aus der Zeit 472/471 v. Chr. aus Ägypten als moabitisch bezeugt (Timm 1989a: 218f). Seine Kurzform *plṭy* könnte gut moabitisch sein, hat aber auch etliche hebräische Belege zur Seite (Timm 1989b: 195ff).

41. Die Buchstaben sind freilich – bis auf das Reš – ziemlich standardisiert und bieten keine Charakteristika, die sie eindeutig als hebräisch oder moabitisch ausweisen würden. Der Name *rpʾ* ist auf Siegeln allein und in Verbindung mit jahwistischen Namen mehrfach belegt (vgl. Timm 1989a: 221 Anm. 82; Zadok 1988: 30 mit Anm. 64, S. 64, 91, 96 mit Anm. 16, S. 130).

Israel es als moabitisch rubriziert (Israel 1987b: Nr. XXX; vgl. Timm 1989a: 221 Nr. 24).

Die Darstellung der geflügelten Sonne im obersten Bildregister erklärt die Darstellung der stilisierten Flügelsonne im zuvor erörterten Siegel des *rʿṣ*. Die hiesige Flügelsonne hat aber einen vogelartigen dreieckigen Schwanz. Sie steht damit in assyrischer oder assyrisierender Bildtradition (vgl. Mayer-Opificius 1984; Parayre 1990a: 301 Nr. 114), was einer Datierung des Siegels ins 8./7. Jh. entsprechen mag.

Von den vielen Mondsichel- und Stern-Darstellungen auf "moabitischen" Siegeln sind hier nur wenige behandelt worden. Für die Typik dieses Motivs am eindrücklichsten ist die Darstellung auf dem Siegel des *mnšh* (**Abb. 17**). Die vielen sonstigen Darstellungen des Motivs auf anderen Siegeln, die als "moabitisch" deklariert worden sind, halten bei einer minutiösen paläographischen Überprüfung einer solchen Klassifikation wahrscheinlich nicht stand. Daß das Motiv bei den moabitischen Siegelschneidern insgesamt aber recht beliebt war, zeigen die zwei Siegel mit *kmš*-Namen (**Abb. 2**, **5**).

Während es sonst eine Fülle palästinischer Siegel gibt, auf denen die Mondsichel auf einer Standarte und einem Podest abgebildet wird – bislang allerdings noch nie auf westsemitischen, beschrifteten Stempelsiegeln! –, ist diese Darstellung für Moab nicht belegt.[42] Die moabitischen Mondsichel-Stern-Darstellungen zeichnen sich gerade dadurch aus, daß sie unter die Mondsichel nur einen einfachen 'Strich' setzen. Man wird deshalb künftig darauf zu achten haben, ob nicht noch weitere Mondsichel-Stern-Darstellungen mit einem 'Strich' unter dem Sichelmond als moabitisch gelten können.

Insgesamt bleibt das Mondsichel-Stern-Motiv auf moabitischen Siegeln stets prominent und wird nicht – wie etwa die geflügelte Sonne – zu völlig neuen Formen abstrahiert.

---

42. Aus dem eisenzeitlichen Grab Nr. 20 bei der Stadt Nebo/Ḫirbet el-Muḫayyeṭ stammt ein anepigraphisches Rollsiegel (des späten 8./7. Jhs.), das wahrscheinlich schon wegen seiner mesopotamischen Rollsiegelform nicht als einheimisches Produkt anzusehen ist und auch von seinem Fundort her nur unter vielen Vorbehalten als moabitisch gelten könnte. Es zeigt zwei musizierende Verehrer vor einer Sichelmondstandarte mit ausgeprägten 'Troddeln' auf einem hohen Podest (Saller 1965-1966: 187-192, Fig. 7; vgl. Weippert 1978: 55 Nr. 16; zuletzt GGG: § 176 und Abb. 300, nunmehr mit richtiger Szenentrennung der Siegelabrollung). Die Szene hat zwar typologische Parallelen in den Adorationsdarstellungen auf den als moabitisch deklarierten Siegeln des *ʿzrʾ* und des *ylʾ* (vgl. Israel 1987b: Nr. XII, XXXI; Timm 1989a: 215f Nr. 21, 201f Nr. 15; beide Siegel bei Ornan, *supra*, S. 67, Fig. 59, 63), doch sind im einzelnen die Stellung der Figuren, deren Kleidung und die sonstigen Attribute zur Szene in allen drei Stücken so verschieden, daß eine Zusammengruppierung als willkürlich gelten muß. Selbst die beiden zuletzt genannten Siegel können im übrigen aufgrund paläographischer Kriterien nicht sicher als moabitisch klassifiziert werden (anders noch Timm 1989a: Nr. 15 bzw. Nr. 21, aber s.o. Anm. 41).

V. Zusammenfassung und Schluss

Das Schwierigste bei den moabitischen Siegeln ist, hinreichende Merkmale für ihre Authentizität und ihre Klassifikation als moabitisch beizubringen. Nur ein einziges *kmš*-Siegel ist bislang bei archäologischen Ausgrabungen gefunden (*kmšntn* aus Ur, s.o. S. 162). Dieses stammt aus dem 6. Jh. (oder später) und ist – zufällig? – anikonisch. Bei keinem der sonstigen "moabitischen" Siegel in öffentlichen oder privaten Sammlungen ist bislang eine Prüfung der Authentizität mit modernen Hilfsmitteln vorgenommen worden.

Sieben Siegel (vgl. aber Anm. 1) sind heute bekannt, die wegen ihrer *kmš*-haltigen Personennamen in den moabitischen Kulturraum gehören. Damit ist das bislang einzig überzeugende Merkmal eines als moabitisch zu klassifizierenden Siegels gegeben: der *kmš*-Name des Siegeleigners. Davon abgeleitet dienen dann auch die Buchstabenformen als zweites Klassifikationskriterium. Die dekorativen oder ikonographischen Bildelemente bieten dagegen bislang für die moabitischen Siegel (noch) keine ähnlich zuverlässigen Kriterien. Nimmt man methodisch – wie hier geschehen – für die Darstellung der moabitischen Glyptik den Ausgangspunkt bei den fünf *kmš*-Siegeln mit Bildelementen, so ist deren ikonographisches Repertoire äußerst bescheiden:

1. die vierflüglige Gestalt
2. die geflügelte Sonne, gelegentlich äußerst abstrahiert
3. der Sichelmond mit oder ohne untergesetztem Strich, begleitet von einem oder zwei anderen Bildelementen, vermutlich Sternen
4. die (spiegelbildlich verdoppelte) Darstellung eines Sphinx oder eines Greifen
5. die Darstellung eines Bildelementes aus der Tradition der ägyptischen 12. Dyn. oder früher im unteren Bildregister auf dem Siegel des *kmšdn* (vgl. **Abb. 4**).

Wahrscheinlich war auf dem Siegel des *kmš* (**Abb. 5**) im untersten Register noch ein weiteres Bildelement geboten, das heute jedoch zerstört ist.

Weitet man die Dokumentation auf Siegel aus, die nicht wegen eines *kmš*-Namens, sondern aus epigraphischen Gründen als moabitisch zu klassifizieren sind, läßt sich

6. die Adorationsszene

hinzufügen. Dazu kommt schließlich

7. das Motiv des säugenden Muttertieres auf dem anepigraphischen Siegel von **Abb. 6**, das aus Rabbat Moab stammen soll.

Das älteste Motiv aus diesem bescheidenen Bildrepertoire[43] ist die geflügelte Sonnenscheibe. Auf **Abb. 3** steht sie an ganz versteckter Stelle, so

43. Anmerkungshalber sei darauf hingewiesen, daß keines der hier diskutierten moabitischen Siegel ikonographisch an Darstellungen anschließt, wie sie auf zwei anepigra-

auch auf **Abb. 19** und auf dem Siegel des *mlkyʿzr* (B 63), dessen Klassifikation als moabitisch wohl nicht zu halten ist (anders noch Timm 1989a: 205f Nr. 17). Auf **Abb. 1** erscheint sie dann in völlig abstrahierter Form im oberen Bildregister (vgl. noch die assyrisch beeinflußte Wiedergabe auf **Abb. 20**, dort ebenfalls im obersten Bildregister). Das ursprünglich ägyptische Motiv der Flügelsonne hat also in der moabitischen Siegelkunst mancherlei Wandlungen durchlaufen. Einen eindeutigen emblematischen Charakter konnte es nicht bewahren, wie seine fast völlige Abstraktion oder seine randständige Darbietung belegen.

Das ist anders bei der Mondsichel-und-Stern-Darstellung, die auf den *kmš*-Siegeln als einziges Bildmotiv neben der Flügelsonne zweimal erscheint, mehrfach auf weiteren Siegeln ohne *kmš*-Namen belegt ist und fast immer an prominenter Stelle im obersten Bildregister steht (anders nur auf **Abb. 7, 20**). Auch wenn bei weitem nicht alle Siegel mit Mondsichel-und-Stern-Darstellung, die bislang als "moabitisch" klassifiziert wurden, wirklich aus Moab stammen, so hat doch die Mondsichel-und-Stern-Darstellung stets einen prominenten Platz in der moabitischen Bildkunst behalten. Diese Beobachtung kann durch den Hinweis unterstützt werden, daß auf fast allen moabitischen Adorationsszenen immer auch der Sichelmond erscheint. Von der Ikonographie der Siegel her ist in Moab also eher mit einem Mondkult als mit einem Sonnenkult zu rechnen.

Mangels einschlägiger literarischer Quellen ist noch nicht sicher zu sagen, welche Vorstellungen man in Moab mit der Darstellung der vierflügligen Gestalt verband. Ikonographisch haben sich hier das nordsyrische Motiv der geflügelten Gestalt und die ägyptische Doppelkrone dank Vermittlung phönizischer Tradition zu einem neuen Ganzen verschmolzen. Dabei sind einige Einzelheiten der jetzigen Darstellungen noch nicht sicher deutbar: z.B. was die Gestalt auf **Abb. 3** in den Händen hält oder ob die Figuren auf **Abb. 11** und **13** eine Gesichtsmaske tragen. Der ikonographische – und damit verbunden gewiß auch religiöse – Einfluß aus dem phönizischen Raum ist jedoch unübersehbar. Am einfachsten ist er erklärbar, wenn für dieses Motiv mit "phönizischen" Werkstätten auf dem Boden Palästinas gerechnet wird.

Der Mangel an literarischen Quellen erlaubt es auch noch nicht anzugeben, was für Assoziationen oder Vorstellungen mit der Darstellung eines Sphinx oder eines Greifen in Moab verbunden waren. Man kann nur vermuten, daß damit auf das Königtum hingewiesen wird. Das Motiv ist auf **Abb. 4** in spiegelbildlich verdoppelter Form belegt. Sieht man andere Siegel ohne *kmš*-

---

phischen Siegelabdrücken der SB-Zeit bei archäologischen Ausgrabungen in D̲ībān zutage gekommen sind (Morton 1989: 244ff, 315f Fig. 9-10, 323f; Mussell 1989). Zu einem vergleichbaren Hiatus in Ammon vgl. Hübner, *supra*, S. 134-135. Ebensowenig ist ein Anschluß an die ins 7./6. Jh. zu datierende, ägyptische(?) Bulle von el-Balūʿ möglich (Worschech 1990: 87-90 mit Abb. 26a und Taf. X:1).

Namen wie **Abb. 7-10** weiterhin für moabitisch an, dann ist es noch öfter in Einzeldarstellung bezeugt.

Deutlich hebt sich von solcherart Darstellungen die Adorationsszene ab. Sie ist bislang noch nicht auf *kmš*-Siegeln bezeugt, sondern nur auf beschrifteten Siegeln, die aufgrund ihrer Buchstabenformen oder ihrer Personennamen als moabitisch gelten. Derartige Adorationsdarstellungen bilden wohl nicht den Siegeleigner persönlich bei seinem Kultvollzug ab, sondern wollen wahrscheinlich eine Szene zeigen, in der sich der Siegeleigner wiederfinden konnte. Fast alle moabitischen Siegel mit Adorationsszenen weisen im übrigen auch immer den Sichelmond mit auf. Das kann nur als Reflex eines starken Einflusses des Mondkultes von Ḥarrān gedeutet werden, der während der assyrischen Expansion nach Syrien-Palästina im 9. und 8. Jh. durch die aramäische oder aramaisierte Administration vermittelt wurde.

Das letzte ikonographische Motiv ist das sonderbare Element auf **Abb. 4** ganz unten, das wohl aus Ägypten aus der Zeit des Mittleren Reiches abzuleiten ist. Das Motiv hat zwar Parallelen auf anderen Siegeln, von denen auffälligerweise eines auch aus dem Ostjordanland stammt (s.o. S. 166). Was das Bildmotiv im Ostjordanland in der Eisen-II-Zeit besagen soll, ist bislang nicht bestimmbar.

Fazit: Eine typisch moabitische Ikonographie der Siegel läßt sich nach dem jetzigen Kenntnisstand noch nicht bieten. Ebensowenig ist es möglich, anepigraphische Siegel eindeutig als moabitisch zu klassifizieren, wenn nicht der Fundort eine solche Zuordnung wahrscheinlich macht. Die bislang bekannten Bildmotive sind nur ein kleiner Ausschnitt aus dem ikonographischen Repertoire, wie es auf ost- und westpalästinischen Siegeln der gleichen Zeit geboten wird. Dabei fehlen viele Bildmotive, die sonst auf west- oder ostjordanischen Siegeln gut bezeugt sind. Doch sollte man aus dem Fehlen vieler Motive bei dem noch so geringen Corpus der moabitischen Siegel keine vorschnellen Schlüsse ziehen. Bislang kann doch auch positiv gesagt werden, daß keines der moabitischen Siegel die einfache Kopie eines westjordanischen Siegels ist. Insofern haben die moabitischen Siegelschneider sehr wohl ihre eigenen Bildaussagen zu formulieren gewußt. Was sie im einzelnen damit haben ausdrücken wollen, können hoffentlich eines Tages neue literarische Nachrichten, die durch archäologische Arbeit aus dem Boden Moabs noch zutage gebracht werden müssen, näher erläutern.

LISTE DER ABGEBILDETEN SIEGEL

Die jeweils letztgenannte Angabe in Klammern bezeichnet die Quelle der verwendeten Abbildung.

1. Siegel des *kmšyḥy*, Skaraboid aus dunkelbraunem Sardonyx mit dunklen Adern aus Chalzedon, 2,53 x 1,95 x 0,91 cm. Das Siegel soll in Damaskus gekauft worden sein; heute in Paris, BN, Coll. de Clercq Nr. 2515 (vgl. B 66; Israel 1987b: Nr. I; Timm 1989a: 162ff Nr. 1).
2. Siegel des *kmšm'š*, Skaraboid aus braunem Achat, 1,7 x 1,5 x 1,0 cm. Das Siegel wurde in Jerusalem gekauft, heute in Tel Aviv, Slg. S. Harari (Avigad 1970a: Nr. 7; vgl. Israel 1987b: Nr. IX; Timm 1989a: 166f Nr. 2).
3. Siegel des *kmšṣdq*, Skaraboid aus Porphyrit, 2,5 x 1,8 x 0,8 cm; Herkunft unbekannt; heute im Vorderasiatischen Museum Berlin, Inv. Nr. VA 2826 (Sachau 1896: 1064 mit Abb.; vgl. Keel 1977: 199, Abb. 143; Israel 1987b: Nr. II; Timm 1989a: 171ff Nr. 4).
4. Siegel des *kmšdn*, konisches Siegel aus ziegelrotem Kalkstein; angeblich aus Kerak; heute in der Slg. V. Barakat (Lemaire 1983: Nr. 11, Tf. III:11; vgl. Israel 1987b: Nr. XIX; Timm 1989a: 178f Nr. 5).
5. Siegel des *kmš*, Konoid von 1,4 x 1,2 x 2,3 cm aus Alabaster, Durchbohrung im oberen Ende des Konus. Herkunft unbekannt; heute in Jerusalem, IMJ 73.19.22 (HD 114; vgl. Israel 1987b: Nr. XIV; Timm 1989a: 180f Nr. 6).
6. Anepigraphisches Siegel, Diskoid, wahrscheinlich aus Marmor; von V.E.G. Kenna 1969 in Rabbat-Moab erworben (Kenna 1973; Keel 1980: 113, Abb. 86).
7. Siegel des *'ḥyš'*, Skaraboid aus hartem, grauem Stein, 1,6 x 2,0 x 0,8 cm; Herkunft unbekannt; heute in Jerusalem, IMJ 75.47.145 (HD 119; vgl. Israel 1987b: Nr. XVIII; Timm 1989a: 187f Nr. 9; Zeichnung Hildi Keel-Leu nach Museumsphoto).
8. Siegel des *'mr'l*, Skaraboid aus braunem und graugelbem Achat, 2,3 x 1,56 x 1,17 cm; Herkunft unbekannt, heute in Paris, BN, Inv. Nr. 1972.1317.126 (B 62; vgl. Israel 1987b: Nr. XXXII; Timm 1989a: 189f Nr. 10).
9. Siegel des *ydl'*, Skaraboid aus rotem Jaspis, 1,75 x 1,38 x 0,76 cm; heute in Paris, BN, Inv. Nr. 1972.1317.130 (B 3; Zeichnung Hildi Keel-Leu nach Photo Jean Dufour).
10. Siegel des *m'š*, Skaraboid aus achatem Jaspis, 1,5 x 1,1 x 0,75 cm; Herkunft unbekannt; heute in Palma de Mallorca, Museo Biblico del Seminario diocesano, Inv. Nr. 230.108 (Baqués-Estapé 1976: Nr. 27; vgl. Bordreuil 1986f; Israel 1987b: Nr. XXIV; Timm 1989a: 243 Nr. 36).
11. Siegel des *b'lntn*, Skaraboid aus rotbuntem Achat, 2,2 x 1,55 x 1,14 cm; Herkunft unbekannt; heute in Paris, Louvre, Inv. Nr. MNB 1500 (B 61; vgl. Israel 1987b: Nr. XVI; Timm 1989a: 194f Nr. 12; Zeichnung Eric Gubel nach B 61 = *supra*, S. 125, Fig. 65).
12. Siegel des *'z'*, Skaraboid aus Karneol, 2,0 x 1,5 x ? cm; IAA 69-5530, ausgestellt im Bet Ussishkin, Kibbutz Dan (Giveon 1961: 38-41 = 1978: 110-116; vgl. Timm 1989a: 213f Nr. 20; GGG: 221, Abb. 211c).
13. Siegel des *myp'h*, Skaraboid aus Karneol, 1,8 x 1,4 x 0,9 mm; Herkunft unbekannt; heute in Jerusalem, Bible Lands Museum (Avigad 1990; Zeichnung Eric Gubel = *supra*, S. 125, Fig. 64).
14. Siegel des *'mṣ hspr*, Herkunft unbekannt; heute in Jerusalem, IMJ 71.65.177 (HD 1; vgl. Naveh 1982: 103, Fig. 89a; Israel 1987b: Nr. V; Timm 1989a: 191ff Nr. 11).

15. Siegel des *ḥkm*, Skaraboid aus Jaspis, 2,4 x 1,85 x 1,25 cm; Herkunft unbekannt; heute in Paris, BN, Inv. Chabouillet, Nr. 1052/2 = K 1830 (B 67; vgl. Israel 1987b: Nr. XV; Timm 1989a: 197f Nr. 13; Photo Jean Dufour).
16. Siegel des *m'š*, Skaraboid aus gelbgrauem Kalkstein, 1,8 x 1,6 x 1,15 cm; Herkunft unbekannt; heute in Haifa, Hecht Museum, Inv. Nr. H-920 (Avigad 1989a: Nr. 18; Zeichnung Noga Z'evi = Ornan, *supra*, S. 66, Fig. 49).
17. Siegel des *mnšh bn hmlk*, Skaraboid aus braunem Achat mit einem weißen Band, 1,3 x 1,2 x 0,6 cm; Herkunft und Verbleib unbekannt (Avigad 1963; vgl. Naveh 1982: 103, Fig. 89b; Israel 1987b: Nr. VII; Timm 1989a: 207ff Nr. 18).
18. Siegel des *plṭy bn m'š hmẓkr*, Skaraboid aus Achat, 2,2 x 1,7 x 0,8 cm; aus einem eisen-II-zeitlichen Grab in Umm Uḏaina im westlichen ʿAmmān, zum Fundkontext gehören noch etliche Objekte des 8.-4. Jhs. v. Chr.; heute im Archäologischen Museum ʿAmmān, Inv. Nr. J 14.653 (Abu Taleb 1985; Zayadine 1985b: 157; vgl. Israel 1987b: Nr. XXV; Timm 1989a: 217ff Nr. 22).
19. Siegel des *rʿṣ*, Skaraboid aus Achat; 1,64 x 1,52 x 1,05 cm; Herkunft unbekannt; heute in Paris, Musée Biblique de Bible et Terre Sainte, Inv. Nr. 5128 (B 64; vgl. Israel 1987b: Nr. XXXIV; Timm 1989a: 220 Nr. 23; Zeichnung Hildi Keel-Leu nach Photo Jean Dufour).
20. Siegel des *rp'*, Skaraboid aus rotgeädertem Jaspis; 1,49 x 1,29 x 0,85 cm; Herkunft unbekannt, heute in einer Privatsammlung (Bordreuil & Lemaire 1976: Nr. 19, damals als hebräisch klassifiziert und ins 8./7. Jh. datiert; vgl. Israel 1987b: Nr. XXX; Timm 1989a: 221 Nr. 24 [korrigiere die falsche Angabe des Aufbewahrungsortes!]).

1

2

3

4

5

6

7

8

9

10

11

12

13

14

15

16

17

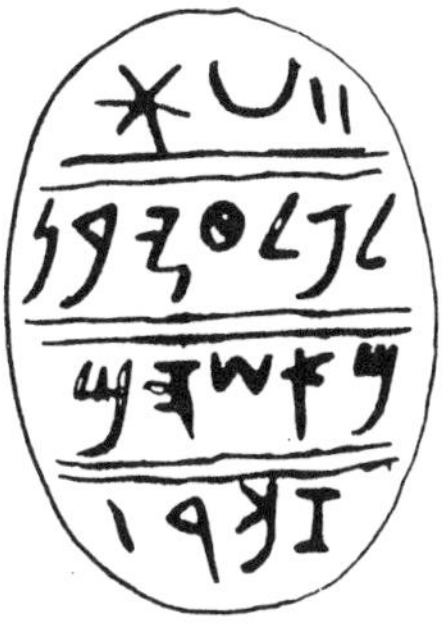

18

19

20

THE PRE-EXILIC HEBREW SEALS: ICONISM VS. ANICONISM

Benjamin SASS
University of Haifa and Israel Antiquities Authority

PRELIMINARY REMARKS

Kurt Galling's work on the iconography of West Semitic seals was published more than fifty years ago (Galling 1941), and a new treatment of the subject has been a desideratum for some time now. When Othmar Keel approached me in 1989 with the proposal of a joint research project of the above title, he already had in mind our symposium of some two years later and this volume. The present paper is to be viewed in this light, as a forerunner of my part of our planned book. It is intended mainly to present in abridged form the results of the first stage of the study – the documentation and classification of the iconographic material.[1] And when it will have appeared, our book will complement and possibly supersede the present study in scope and in its treatment of the material. The drawings usually illustrate only one example of each phenomenon;[2] where possible, I employed excavated pieces, and in their absence – bullae or stamped handles.

Obviously, the iconography of Hebrew glyptic cannot be studied in isolation, and indeed, in the preparatory stages of the book I collected all the West and South Semitic inscribed seals, as well as excavated anepigraphic parallels. While the non-Hebrew material finds little expression in this article, it was always influential in the background.

Most West Semitic personal seals are of unknown provenance, a handicap that will forever mar the study of this class. I have referred to the issue of authenticity time and again in the discussion of the iconography, particularly when the examples at our disposal of a certain motif occur only on unprovenanced seals. Where possible, I resorted to excavated anepigraphic parallels, but such efforts alleviate the situation only in part. This unsolvable problem is taken up at some length in the conclusions.

I. INTRODUCTION

1. *Classification*

The names, epigraphy, iconography, material, technique, shape and provenance are taken, to differing degrees, into consideration when the origin of a West Semitic seal is to be established.

– *The name* is the primary criterion for classification if theophorous or otherwise characteristic (like Hebrew *ṣpn*).

---

1. I acknowledge with thanks the advice and help that Othmar Keel, André Lemaire, Tallay Ornan and Christoph Uehlinger extended to me during the preparation of this paper.

2. The drawings are not to scale. Each may appear several times.

– *Epigraphy* matches the personal names in many clear-cut cases. If a name is equivocal, epigraphy gains in importance, and may serve as the main criterion for classification. It has its well-known limits, however, especially when the script is 'lapidary' (cf. Lemaire, *supra*, p. 5). Liable to constitute a circular argument, to which I shall return, the 'lapidary' script is usually thought to be an eighth-century feature.

– *Iconography* is inapplicable anyway in the case of most Hebrew seals, and of some of the others that are aniconic. As to the iconic seals, they may show Egypto-Phoenician, Syro-Mesopotamian or 'local' traits. If some motifs are considered to belong rather exclusively to a certain group, like the four-winged uraeus on Judaean seals, this observation was founded in the first place on the onomasticon or epigraphy. Theoretically, this could lead in turn to identification based on iconography, while in practice it has been demonstrated to be impossible in some cases, casting doubt on the potential others: if it contradicts the classification of the name or script, iconography is often eclipsed by onomastic and epigraphical considerations. The eighth-century seal of Milkiram (**fig. 81**; Avigad 1969: 7; Lemaire 1976: 88) can serve as an example: in spite of the four-winged uraeus in the central register (see pp. 213-214) it was considered Phoenician because of its name and script (alternatively, the script could be Aramaic, perhaps even Hebrew, though not characteristically so). It was the motif (see B1.3) that led Avigad not to rule out the Hebrew alternative.

Iconography is apt to be adopted and shared (cf. *supra*, the contributions by Parayre and Ornan), a case in point being the two worshippers facing each other, an altar or another object between them. This scene is considered by some to be characteristically Transjordanian, while epigraphy is equivocal enough to permit an Aramaic and perhaps Hebrew attribution (see GGG: §§ 177, 185; below, subject F5).[3] This means that in classifying anepigraphic seals too, iconography has weighty limits.

– *Material, technique and shape* may be of classificatory value, e.g. the use of chalcedony or the faceted conoidal shape that can help differentiate local seals from Mesopotamian or Mesopotamian-inspired ones. The techniques, Porada's four 'styles' and a few others, are closely related to the materials, and may assist in establishing the origin of a seal. Two rare sealing surface shapes, the square (**fig. 1**) and the doubly-truncated elongated oval (**fig. 2**), are encountered mainly, but not exclusively, among Hebrew seals. Two other

---

3. Intuitively this scene may look un-Hebrew indeed: "So far, not a single seal was found, that can be securely identified as Hebrew and which carries a pagan cult scene of this sort, and it is unlikely that such a seal will ever be found in the future" (Avigad 1977b: 108, about the seal of Ezra, cf. Ornan, *supra*, p. 67, fig. 59). But in view of the humans and divine and semi-divine figures represented, albeit rarely, on Hebrew seals, this scene too is not impossible.

shapes are the circle (**fig. 3**) and the very elongated oval (**fig. 4**). A few more shapes exist (e.g. **fig. 5**) in addition to the usual oval.[4]

– *Provenance* should be regarded as an auxiliary criterion at most, as more than one excavation produced a seal of demonstrably 'foreign' script (cf. Lemaire, *supra*, pp. 2-3, and below, note 74). This holds also true for aniconic seals, of course. Applied to a coherent group of seals exhibiting distinctive common features, the criterion may gain in importance when excavated examples point to a restricted geographical distribution.

All told, the name and script remain the touchstones for the classification of most inscribed seals. Where both are indecisive iconography may play a certain role; but if they exist at all, cases where the iconographical argument is not a circular one must be rare. I concur with Lemaire (*supra*, p. 6) that such seals be rather classified as, say, Phoenician-Aramaic or even Phoenician-Aramaic-North Israelite. In the relatively few instances the name and epigraphy are decisive but contradictory, some of the seals in question having probably belonged to internationals (but cf. Uehlinger, *infra*, pp. 257ff).[5]

2. *Quantities – iconic vs. aniconic seals*

Within my documentation of about 1150 late Iron Age inscribed West Semitic stamp seals the number of Hebrew seals and sealings is approaching 700. In this total are the seals represented by stamped handles and bullae,[6] and a few dozen unpublished pieces.[7,8] The two hoards of Judahite bullae, that from the City of David (Shiloh 1986) and that published by Avigad (1986a) represent together over 200 seals; none of these bullae was made by a known seal.[9] Statistically, this fact is instructive – it suggests that the seals known today are but a fraction of the original production.

Returning to the less than 700 Hebrew seals, close to 500 are aniconic or nearly aniconic. About three quarters of the latter, towards 370, bear merely the familiar two lines of script separated by a double or single line or by nothing at all. This biregistral layout was also current, though much less

4. 'Ad hoc' seals, like those of *ṭbšlm*, IR 136, or *dršyhw bn* ʿz..., HD 86, are a class for itself.

5. Such as the seal of *šʿnp* (*šʿnf*) *bn nby* (HD 85), an Arab with a Judean seal, or *bqšt bt ʿbdyrḥ*, an Ammonite(?) with a Hebrew seal (Lemaire, *supra*, pp. 12, 20 and note 22).

6. The *lmlk* handles being counted as two seals, but see Lemaire 1981.

7. These figures may be distorted by undetected forgeries, for which see pp. 245-246.

8. Avigad in 1987 (a: 195) counted just over 600, including a few exilic and post-exilic pieces not considered here.

9. Avigad suggested that a bulla published by Bordreuil & Lemaire (1976: no. 21) was made with a seal he himself published (1989b: no. 6). If this is so, this would be the first such match.

widespread, in other scripts, like in the Ammonite seal of Adoninur (CAI 40; cf. Hübner, *supra*, p. 157, fig. 2). The rest of the seals considered aniconic, about 130, should better be labelled not entirely epigraphic, as they contain a floral register divider (or, rarely, a border design), mostly stylized. This leaves us with under 200 iconic seals, less than 30% of the total, some with merely a branch or bird as space filler.

One would assume human or anthropomorphic figures to be the least common motifs on Hebrew seals, and indeed they adorn only some 30 pieces (another four portray human-headed fantastic animals). But even rarer are celestial bodies, only about a dozen.

It is this aniconic trend that must have motivated the more talented seal cutters to pay great attention to calligraphy and elaborate the register divider of the bipartite inscribed seal, the most common layout, into something approaching iconism.

As Avigad had shown (1986a: 118; already 1958a: 76, 81), the Hebrew artists in the eighth century produced more iconic seals than their seventh-century successors. This may be gleaned from the 4:1 majority of iconic seals of royal functionaries in the eighth century, and is manifest in the small proportion of iconic seals among the bullae from the city of David and from Avigad's hoard, dated about 600.

3. Chronology

Quite a few seals can be dated only broadly to the eighth to seventh centuries (Avigad 1986a: 113), the short seal-legends often lacking chronologically-significant letters. Palaeography serves in many cases as a *terminus post* at best, as the script of the seals may have been archaistic, honorific so to speak, or stiff because of the hard stone, lending the script a false senior air. (The script of many other seals is cursive of course, even in hardstone, imitating the ink inscriptions of their time.) It is to be asked whether seals with 'lapidary' script, that are usually ascribed to the eighth century, are correctly dated. Although Lemaire addressed this issue in our symposium (see his remarks on pp. 5-6), the subject was not specifically on the agenda, and is not treated in any length here.

The starting point for the chronology of Hebrew seals is the pieces mentioning the names of sovereigns or other personalities known from the biblical text. (Epigraphically, their value is not to be over-estimated, as they have to be considered with other contemporary inscribed media.) Royal seals have not survived, but five functionaries mentioned the names of their sovereigns on their seals. These are Shemaᶜ, Abiyaw and Shubnayaw, Eshnaᵓ and Yehozaraḥ son of Ḥilqiyahu who mention Jeroboam II of Israel (787-747) and Uzziah (ca. 773-735), Ahaz (742-726) and Hezekiah (725-697) of Judah respectively (**figs. 22-23, 29, 109, 148**). We have no royal names for the seventh century, but the hoard of bullae published by Avigad (1986a) is dated c. 600 by the sealings of Baruch son of Neriah the scribe (**fig. 14**) and Jerahmeel son of the king (Avigad 1978c). Less certain identifications are discussed by Avigad (1986a: note 164) and Schneider (1988; 1991).

We speak of a series originating in the second half of the ninth century (cf. Hübner, *supra*, pp. 131-132, 150-151). Cross (1962: note 12) dated the seal, of unknown provenance, of *šmʿyhw bn ʿzryhw* (**fig. 118**) to the ninth century on palaeographical grounds, mainly the shape of *mem*. Interestingly, the iconography of this seal is unique in Hebrew glyptic, but whether or not it is characteristically archaic remains to be seen. I dated to this time the seal of *ʾbʾ*, not necessarily a Hebrew one, found near Ekron in Philistia (Sass 1983). Several others are considered early, but the bulk of the series is thought to belong to the eighth to seventh centuries.

Keel & Uehlinger (GGG: chapters 7-8) would attribute to the ninth and eighth centuries (termed Iron Age II B) local seals and other products with Egypto-Phoenician iconography, and to the later eighth to seventh (Iron Age II C) those with Assyrian and/or Syrian iconography. This is most probably correct, not excluding, however, the possibility of continued Phoenician inspiration on the local imagery of the late eighth, seventh and sixth centuries (cf. next paragraph and GGG: § 203).

4. *Israel and Judah*

Even though the term 'Hebrew' for Judahite or Israelite seals might be considered inadequate, I need to wait a little longer before feeling confident enough to forsake it in other than the clearest cases. As to the differences between Israelite, or North Israelite and Judahite glyptic,[10] there are the seals with royal names and the theophorous components *-yw* and *-yhw* to guide us, but the latter are not always consistent (e.g., the name of king Uzziah of Judah, **figs. 23**, **148**, ends in *-yw*; cf. Avigad 1986a: 116; 1987a: 197). Phoenician influence is considered to be at the same time more 'Israelite' and more eighth-century, while some motifs seem more Judahite, perhaps also more seventh-century. But this is still a moot point: what about Phoenician elements in Judaean glyptic of the late ninth to eighth centuries, and the seventh? The four seals of eighth-century royal Judaean functionaries are instructive (cf. Uehlinger, *infra*, p. 285). In two, the cachets of Abiyaw, official of Uzziah (**fig. 148**) and Eshnaʾ, official of king Ahaz (**fig. 147**), the iconography is Phoenician, while on the seal of the other official of Uzziah, Shubnayaw (**figs. 132**, **151**), it is mixed, Phoenician and Assyrianizing. The fourth and latest (**fig. 22**) is aniconic. Phoenician cultural inspiration could have certainly been exerted at times when Judah was under Northern

10. Lemaire (e.g. 1990a), among others, has taken up the subject of Israelite iconography.

political influence, such as the reigns of Athaliah (845-840, 2 Kings 11) or Joash of Israel (802-787, 2 Kings 14:15-16), but not necessarily only then.

II. MOTIFS, SCENES, LAYOUTS

1. Additional criteria of classification

Before proceeding to the iconic subject-matter of the Hebrew seals, I wish to enumerate five criteria not mentioned above.[11]

1. Layout of sealing surface
   a. undivided (**figs. 5-7**)
   b. bipartite (**figs. 8-13, 32-46**)[12]
   c. tripartite (**figs. 14-21**)
   d. quadriregistral (**figs. 22-23**)[13]
2. Layout of text
   a. no special space – dispersed (**fig. 24**)[14]
   b. no special space – curving along edge (**fig. 25**)[15]
   c. register/column – (**figs. 26, 27**)[16]
   d. = a + c – exceeding bounds of exergue (**fig. 28**)[17]

---

11. Yet further criteria include: 1. the number of sealing surfaces, up to five, but in Hebrew seals not more than two (e.g. **figs. 132 + 151**); 2. axis of the picture and/or legend in relation to the sealing surface, latitudinal (**fig. 21**), longitudinal (**fig. 20**) or equal (**fig. 3**); 3. view of motif – in profile (most), *en face* (**figs. 138, 142, 144**), from above (cf. **pl. I:5**).
12. Bi- and tripartite seals can have registers or columns; all known quadripartite seals are registral. Register dividers may or may not be present (compare **figs. 9, 13, 20** with most others); columns are usually undivided. The relative widths, or heights of the registers/columns are to be accounted for – e.g. exergual is a biregistral seal of certain proportions.
13. A few more layouts exist, mostly not in Hebrew seals.
14. A subgroup being *bn* flanking the motif in the central, pictorial register of the text-picture-text arrangement (**figs. 42, 45**). This feature is particularly popular in Ammonite seals, e.g. B 73, 74 (= Hübner, *supra*, p. 159, fig. 22). The position of *bn* in **fig. 15** is unique.
15. Layouts a and b occur in undivided sealing surfaces and in pictorial registers. In some non-Hebrew seals the legend, no special space allocated, runs in an uninterrupted straight line (or lines) in the field (e.g. G 115)
16. Text being the only component of the register or column, otherwise we are dealing with layout a or b. The figures illustrate convex and concave texts only. Two convex text columns may give the impression of running around the whole edge, but true, coin-like circumscriptions are in fact known only from a few Ammonite seals, e.g. Hübner, *supra*, p. 158, fig. 13.

1

2

3

4

5

6

7

8

9

10

11

12

13

14

15

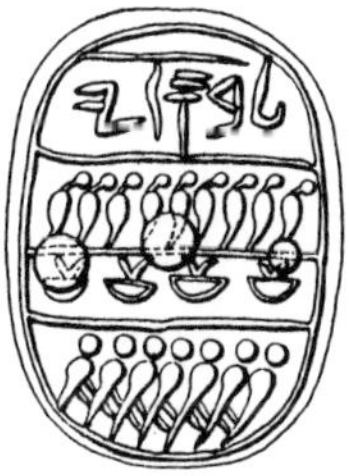
16

17

18

19

20

21

22

23

24

25

26

27

28

29

30

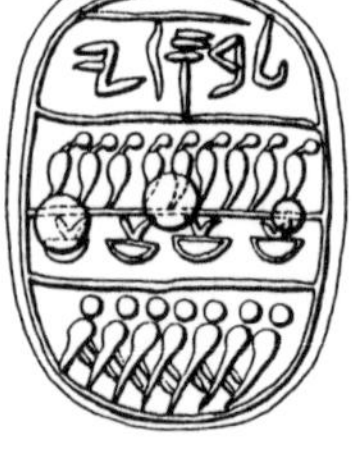

31

32

33

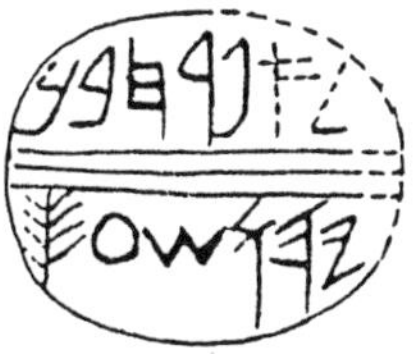
34

35

36

37

38

39

40

41

42

43

44

45

46

3. Text-picture relationships in registral/columnar layout[18]
   a. text-picture, picture-text, text-text (**figs. 8-11, 13, 32-46**)
   b. text-text-text and the tripartite combinations of text and picture, six in all (**figs. 14-21**)[19]
   c. text-text-text-text, picture-text-text-picture (**figs. 22-23**), picture-text-picture-picture (if **fig. 81** is Hebrew)
4. Status of subject[20]
   a. scene
   b. sub-scene, e.g. enthroned deity in **fig. 155**
   c. agglomerate of motifs, interrelationship unknown (**fig. 138**)
   d. sole or dominant motif or virtual scene (*šmʿ ʿbd yrbʿm* lion)
   e. motif in a, b, c; secondary motif in d
   f. motif as space filler (**figs. 60, 108**)
   g. motif as border design
   h. motif as register divider
5. Specific arrangements[21]
   a. antithetic/doubled motif (**fig. 29**)
   b. *tête-bêche* and reversed arrangements (**fig. 30**)[22]
   c. frieze (**fig. 31**)

2. Register dividers and border designs

Because of the importance of the owner's name most seals are registral or columnar (delimited or not), allocating a well-defined space to the inscription. Seals containing no decoration other than a register divider or border were classified as aniconic. This is obvious when the delimitation consists of a single or double line. But it becomes an arbitrary grouping with no few elaborate dividers and borders, geometric or vegetal; some of these evolved into motifs in their own right, almost virtual scenes (e.g. **fig. 54**; see also the

---

17. On some non-Hebrew seals the name exceeds in a straight line the bounds of the exergue; see G 130, 135.
18. In seals where each register or column (to be listed from top or from right) contains either text or a picture but not both. The direction of writing varies in columnar seals.
19. The seventh arrangement, picture-picture-text, is unknown, with the exception of the seal of *yḥn*, mentioned in note 85. The picture-picture-picture arrangement is to be found in non-Hebrew seals with dispersed legend, e.g. B 12 (= Gubel, *supra*, p. 117, fig. 38), and on the anepigraphic face of bifacial seals like **fig. 138**.
20. 'Subject' is used here as a term embracing 'scene' and 'motif'.
21. A and b are rare in inscribed Hebrew seals, but were common in local anepigraphic glyptic of the tenth and ninth centuries. The antithetic arrangement is characteristic of Phoenician glyptic, and most of its occurrences in Hebrew seals are on pieces of Phoenician make or influence.
22. See also the discussion of **fig. 61** (motif A3.1).

discussion of **fig. 58**). Certain seals are borderline cases in an additional sense – are they to be classified as bi- or as triregistral?[23,24]

Nearly three fourths of the Hebrew seals are oval, latitudinal, with a single border line and biregistral layout (see p. 197) and a majority has a bilinear register divider. This delimitation is also popular in longitudinal seals, exergual and triregistral. Other seals are undivided (**fig. 32**). Mono- and trilinear dividers exist too (**figs. 33-34** and cf. Weippert 1979: 174), the former mostly, the latter exclusively in Hebrew seals, all latitudinal and biregistral save one (Wolfe & Sternberg 1989: no. 11). As noted, the Hebrew seal cutter compensated with calligraphy, elaborate border designs, and especially with register dividers, for the aniconism preferred by most customers. A few examples follow:

Figs. 4, **35-37** display a design which looks like a double-ended *ʿankh* or stand. If cut in half, both variants, the one with loop ends and the one with fan-shaped ends, resemble depictions of this device on local seals (Uehlinger 1990). That our design could not have had a real existence lends support to Uehlinger's proposal that in certain combinations, even though 'one-ended', a symbol rather than an actual cult object was intended. **Fig. 36** appears to combine the motif under discussion with the thunderbolt, and if this is indeed so, we are faced with a 'first' in Judahite iconography, smuggling in by the back door, so to speak, the symbol of the storm god. The dividers in **figs. 38-39**[25] may also be variations on the '*ʿankh*/stand' theme. Conversely, although it looks like two joined candelabra supports, a floral motif is probably to be preferred for **fig. 38**, in line with **figs. 43-45**.

Fig. 40 shows a divider in the shape of two lotus buds growing from a central element, fairly popular in pre-exilic Hebrew seals (nearly thirty examples) and occurring sporadically elsewhere (e.g. Jakob-Rost 1975: no. 186 *lqwsgbr* [*mlk ʾd*]*m*). A crisply-cut unprovenanced piece (**fig. 41**) shows open lotus flowers instead of the buds (see also motif A3.1).[26]

Two back-to-back curves, with pomegranates, papyrus flowers etc. at their ends (**fig. 42**) constitute another group. Other types of biconcave dividers have fleurs de lys, pomegranates etc. growing between their ends (**figs.**

---

23. This uncertainty pertains to geometric and vegetal dividers/central registers, not to animal and human or anthropomorphic motifs of course (compare **fig. 8** with **fig. 96**).

24. Or tricolumnar: should the central motif in **fig. 54** be viewed horizontally or vertically? The seals with a human figure flanked by two lines of script are obviously tricolumnar, i.e. longitudinal with a vertical axis, the seal having to be turned sideways in order to be read. Note the different directions of the legends in **figs. 133** and **148**.

25. Provenanced examples are not known.

26. Positive about the genuineness of the seal, Avigad (1981: 303), related this motif to the lotus-bud divider.

43-45[27]). A unique, inexplicable biconcave divider can be seen in **fig. 46**, an unprovenanced seal.[28]

We have seen that most register dividers are biconcave (only the lotus-bud divider is somewhat convex), hence the phenomenon, unmatched in non-Hebrew seals, of the text lines curving inwards (**fig. 27**; cf. 2.1.2). Curving outwards, parallel to the edge, they are found on Hebrew and non-Hebrew seals of various layouts (**figs. 26, 62**; Avigad 1977a: fig. 1).

The border of very many West Semitic seals consists of a frame-line (others have no border at all), and more than fifty seals with a double line (**figs. 47-48**) are known, all Hebrew (in the Hecht Museum, Haifa, is an unpublished Hebrew seal with a triple-line border). The dot border (**figs. 49-50**) was less popular, with fewer than twenty examples, and all, save a single Ammonite seal (CAI 102),[29] are Hebrew. The dot border is usually delimited with a single line on the inside, and in a few unprovenanced cases by a double line or by none at all. Several Hebrew and other West Semitic seals have a rope, or ladder border (**fig. 51**), and this device is not uncommon in anepigraphic Phoenician seals, mainly of the Persian Period. Two Hebrew seals of unknown provenance (**fig. 52**) sport a pomegranate border (see also Lemaire, *supra*, p. 18, note 20).

3. Motifs and scenes[30]

This section is arranged by motif, and only seals with scenes containing human or anthropomorphic figures (section F) are grouped by scene. In dealing with the other few scenes it seemed more practical to list them according to their various motifs. These scenes are:

1. Uraeus or bird on flower
2. Animal or fantastic being facing a plant, stand etc.
3. Ibex suckling young
4. Animal contest (lion chasing ibex)

27. In crispness the latter recalls **fig. 41**; see section H.

28. It may help clarify the original shape of a damaged divider on a broken bulla, A 140.

29. It is the dot border that led Hübner (*supra*, p. 143) to question the Ammonite attribution of the seal. That it cannot be Hebrew is borne out by the script.

30. See section II.1.4. Omitted from this discussion were Egyptian hieroglyphs, *ʿankh* and stand-shaped motifs (many examples), and dots as decorative devices and space fillers.

47

48

49

50

51

52

53

54

55

56

57

58

59

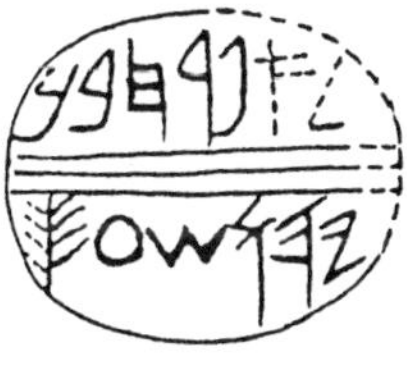
60

61

A Plants

A1 Palm tree and palmette

A1.1 Palm tree

The only more or less realistic palm tree, flanked by two persons (see F5), is to be found on the reverse of the seal of *ḥlqyhw bn pdy* (**fig. 53**), and there exists a good comparison to the scene and its style in an anepigraphic seal from Tell en-Naṣbeh (Naṣbeh I: pl. 55:63; cf. Schroer 1987b: 212-213). These seals share features with the Lyre Player group (Boardman 1990 with previous bibliography). A 205 is a broken anepigraphic bulla showing what appears to be a palm tree with bunches of dates. If correctly understood, the motif may be compared to Neo-Imperial renderings like Collon 1987: no. 773. Naturalistic palm trees are also rare in other inscribed West Semitic seals.

A1.2 Stylized, 'Proto-Aeolic' tree

The hoard of bullae published by Avigad contained two or three such pieces (A 116 = **fig. 54**, A 137, probably A 206) but they are broken and their restoration is not final. Should these impressions be viewed horizontally? That the text runs horizontally is not in itself reason to turn the picture the same way, cf. note 24. But could not an elaborate, double-ended register divider have been intended, somewhat like **fig. 37**? There are no non-Hebrew examples.

A1.3 Palmette with trunk

So common on metal bowls, ivories etc., this motif is seldom found in Hebrew (**fig. 55**) and other inscribed West Semitic seals. It also appears on B 58 (**fig. 124**), unique in several aspects.

A1.4 Trunkless palmette

It is common in Hebrew seals (**fig. 56**) and rare in all others.[31] Befitting tree-tops, nearly all the palmettes figure in the upper registers of triregistral seals. Palmettes in the bottom register (e.g. A 75) are exceptions, and to them should probably be added a motif in the same place, but reversed, in **fig. 67**, in a seemingly *tête-bêche* arrangement.

A1.5 Proto-Aeolic capital

Proto-Aeolic capitals appear on three Hebrew seals of unknown provenance, one in nearly mint condition (**fig. 57, pl. I:2**; cf. section H) and two worn

---

31. In fact only a few nondescript devices in a couple of non-Hebrew seals, if not malformed winged disks, *may* have been intended as palmettes (like in the bottom register of the seal of *kmšṣdq*, Timm, *supra*, p. 192, fig. 3; cf. also the seal of *mlkrm*, **fig. 81**).

specimens. Even though unfamiliar,[32] the separate depiction of a capital is in itself insufficient as an argument against the authenticity of these seals: if the trunkless palmette is so popular, why not a column- or pilaster-less capital?

A2 Branch

Did this motif symbolize a goddess for all seal owners who used it (cf. Hestrin 1987; 1991; Schroer 1987b; 1989: 96-113), or did some of them select it simply for its 'aniconism' (cf. also Uehlinger, *infra*, p. 275)?[33]

– *As sole motif* it appears on two seals (**fig. 58**). The illustrated seal serves as a good example for the importance the register divider gained in Hebrew glyptic: it overshadows the motif. In this status – as sole motif – the branch does not occur on non-Hebrew seals.

– *As a component* in the scene 'quadruped or composite being facing branch' (or stand etc.) it is very common on Near Eastern stamp seals, but its only occurrence in Hebrew glyptic is on the seal of *ṣpn nryhw* (**fig. 59**), faced by an ibex (section D2).

– *As space filler* (**fig. 60**) the branch is found on bipartite, otherwise aniconic Hebrew seals, in a similar role as the bird (motif C6).

A3 Flower

A3.1 Lotus flower

– *As sole or main motif* (**fig. 61**) it can be seen on three Hebrew examples; as all are unprovenanced there is no firm basis for discussion. This motif is not unexpected, however, and the lotus *bud* is very popular in Hebrew register dividers (**fig. 40**).[34] The seal in **fig. 61** is unusual in almost everything – in the occurrence of the lotus flower and rosette, doubling of the latter, reversed palmette (*tête-bêche* with the flower?) and in the undivided tri-registral layout.[35]

---

32. Architectural motifs are extremely rare in West Semitic seals. An obelisk adorns one (CAI 12), but unlike the capital the obelisk is an independent element, well known in Egyptian glyptic. A two-dimensional ivory capital was discovered at Samaria (Samaria-Sebaste 2: 42, pl. 22:1), and the excavators assumed it was part of a composition.

33. An anepigraphic seal from Lachish (Lachish III: 365; cf. note 86) has a branch-like tree in an adoration scene, whose focus is a female deity. See the most recent discussion of Keel & Uehlinger in GGG: § 193 with fig. 323. The goddess is not to be found on inscribed Hebrew seals and she is not very common on other inscribed West Semitic seals.

34. Regrettably, the only seal with lotus *flowers* in the same role, **fig. 41**, comes from the antiquities market as well.

35. Another seal with this motif (**pl. II:9**) belongs to what may be called the tasteful group, see section H. The flower in this seal has a close parallel on a cosmetic palette, Barag 1985: fig. 12, pl. 45:5, also from the antiquities market.

– *As a component* in the scene 'child on flower' (**fig. 62**) the flower, assumed to be a lotus, cannot always be identified as such. There are three Hebrew examples, all of unknown provenance, and in the one illustrated here the human figure is flanked by two falcon-headed deities also squatting on flowers (see subjects F3 and F7.2). It could have been the child that gave the Phoenician artist the idea to place various beings on flowers.[36, 37] Four-winged uraei on flowers (**fig. 64**) are depicted on two Hebrew seals.

A flower resembling the Babylonian 'cactus' (Porada 1947: 151; Collon 1987: 83) appears twice on Hebrew seals (**figs. 63, 65**), though a lotus flower may have been intended.[38] Rendered in such a general manner, it cannot be regarded as a distinct Babylonian-inspired element. On one of the seals (**fig. 63**, Reifenberg 1950: no. 12) the figure holds the 'cactus' in its hand, while in **fig. 65** this motif, doubled, embellishes the register divider, the seal being perhaps the only Hebrew specimen thus decorated (see the discussion of **fig. 46**).

A3.2 Rosette

So common in the Judaean seventh-century stamp (**fig. 66**; see GGG: § 204), it is otherwise surprisingly rare in Hebrew glyptic. In non-Hebrew seals the rosette, if this is what the ancients intended to depict, is usually composed of six or eight dots encircling a central one, like in **fig. 67**. A similar rosette adorns the sound-box of the lyre in the seal of *mʿdnh* (**pl. II:13**).[39]

A4 Pomegranate

Much less common in Hebrew glyptic than one might expect from a popular vegetal motif (and almost absent from the other West Semitic seals), the pomegranate appears mainly in register dividers and border designs (**figs. 68-70**).

---

36. Once (B 5 = Gubel, *supra*, p. 117, fig. 40) even a lion is squatting on a flower in a most uncomfortable position. In a similar way the four-winged scarab appears on two Phoenician(?) seals (B 10; Buchanan & Moorey 1988: no. 294), where the flower evolved into a kind of pole. Perhaps related is the bird on a pole or standard with floral finial, particularly common behind the human figure on seals showing a 'king' with staff (e.g. G 135 = Gubel, *supra*, pp. 119-120, figs. 50-52; cf. F4.1). While none of these is Hebrew, the bird is similarly positioned behind the main figure on a Hebrew seal, considered Moabite by some (**fig. 63**; cf. E3), with different subject-matter.

37. Outside this scene the Egypto-Phoenician lotus flower is rare on non-Hebrew seals.

38. This motif is not too widespread on other West Semitic seals (cf. Hübner, *supra*, p. 146). It appears once on a stamp seal with South Semitic inscription (Sass 1991: 50), this time in an unquestionably Babylonian scene.

39. See section H for this seal. An unpublished Hebrew seal in the Hecht Museum, a remarkably tasteful piece, has the rosette as its sole motif.

62

63

64

65

66

67

68

69

70

71

72

73

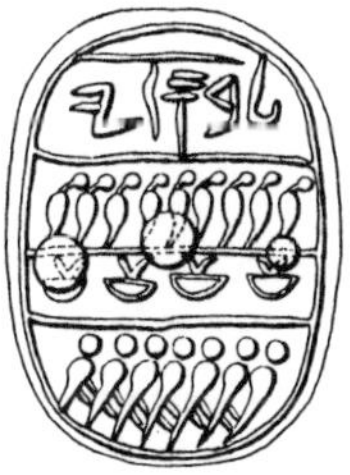
74

75

76

B Invertebrates, reptiles, fish[40]

B1 Uraeus

The Egyptian uraeus entered the Near Eastern imagery in the second millennium, and its popularity did not abate in the first, when it figured mainly in Phoenician or Phoenician-inspired art. Many of its representations are winged, and it were the Hebrews who adopted the winged version most vigorously. The four-winged uraeus was particularly popular, and, with very few exceptions, this variety is in fact exclusively Hebrew.[41]

B1.1 Unwinged uraeus

It is found quite often in Phoenician seals, and is less popular in Hebrew glyptic. Alone or duplicated, it may hover about or hang from the image it was meant to protect (**figs. 71-73**).[42]

– A uraeus *frieze*[43] appears on the seal of *bsy* (**fig. 74**), perhaps on that of *špṭ* (**fig. 12**); its location on the latter, in a kind of top exergue, is most unusual. The uraeus frieze is uncommon in the other groups of inscribed seals too.

B1.2 Two-winged uraeus

With wings spread forward, it is known on only one Hebrew seal, from Lachish (**fig. 75**).[44]

The uraeus with outstretched, sometimes asymmetric wings (**fig. 76**) appears on three Hebrew seals, two of which may be by the same hand (Avigad 1954b: 148).[45] These Hebrew uraei appear in the bottom register of triregistral seals. Perhaps this is dictated by the plano-convex outline of the being with its upturned wings.

---

40. Including winged uraei and beetles.

41. In the next section, B2, the uraeus is compared to the beetle, a motif of similar prominence in Hebrew glyptic.

42. In several cases, none of them Hebrew, it hangs from the kilt of a griffin or from the garment of a walking person (one example, the seal of Pataisi, HD 41, was found in Samaria).

43. Compare the bird frieze, C6.

44. The same motif, doubled and executed in a different technique, is depicted on the seal of *ʾlʾmr* from Megiddo (Megiddo I: pl. 67:34), which is more likely to be Phoenician than Hebrew, and on very few others.

45. Asymmetric are also the wings of a mysterious headless being with a bird's tail like a winged sun's on the seal HD 117 (cf. Parayre, *supra*, p. 48, fig. 47), possibly a Moabite seal. A pair of two-winged uraei(?) in *tête-bêche* arrangement, with sun disks on their heads, are depicted on the seal of *ʾlhʿm* (CAI 10; cf. Lemaire, *supra*, p. 23, fig. 7), considered Ammonite by some. But neither the Ammonite attribution nor the identification of the beings in question is final.

B1.3 Four-winged uraeus

It is usually the sole motif (for an exception see **fig. 78** and motif G1.1). More often than not the four-winged uraeus figures in triregistral seals, as noted; there it normally occupies the top register (**figs. 77-78**), never the bottom register. It looks as if it had been considered inappropriate to have one's name written *above* this symbol; the being was meant to hover over the name, providing divine protection. Why this did not apply to the two-winged uraeus remains to be explained; form seems to have played a more important role with the latter whereas substance dictated the position of the former.

In some triregistral seals with four-winged uraeus the top register is higher, occupying up to half the space; on other occasions the artist preferred the more spacious exergual layout (**fig. 79, pl. I:3**),[46] but then the exergue could not accommodate the owner's name, and part of it had to be scattered in empty spaces in the upper field. This, we see, was acceptable.

Like the sun child, the scarab and other motifs, the four-winged uraeus is positioned twice on a flower or palmette (**fig. 80**). The layout of the unillustrated seal (HD 37) is unique, though the name appears below the motif in accordance with what I assume to be the rule. The overall layout of **fig. 80**, as well of that of another bulla from the same lot (A 200), is not clear.

In the British Museum is an anepigraphic triregistral seal with a four-winged uraeus as its central motif (BM 102609). The winged cobra, with horns and coiled tail, occupies the central register, 'permissible' even if the seal were Hebrew, for there is no owner's name. Although there is statistical probability that we are dealing with a 'Hebrew' seal, I think this is not so.

The seal of Milkiram (**fig. 81, pl. I:4**) is not of straightforward Hebrew attribution (see section I.1).[47] Interestingly, the name of Milkiram is written above the uraeus. Several long-forgotten identical bulla impressions from Nineveh (Layard 1853: 155, bottom center [upside down] and left) display a four-winged uraeus wearing what seems a double Egyptian crown, with an illegible legend below. That these impressions were made with a non-Hebrew (Phoenician or Aramaic) seal is hinted by a second impression on each of these bullae (BM 84540-7, 84575) of the seal of ʿAtarʿezer (Barnett 1967a: 5*, pl. 7:4). Unlike the S- or Z-shaped bodies on certainly-Hebrew seals, the uraei on the Nineveh and Milkiram examples, as well as the uraeus on BM 102609, have a coiled tail. This could perhaps differentiate between the Hebrew and non-Hebrew renderings.

46. A yet unpublished handle, stamped with the same seal, comes from Y. Shiloh's excavations in the City of David, Jerusalem.

47. Like one four-winged beetle (**fig. 87**) the uraeus is flanked by *ʿankh* signs.

B2 Beetle

The beetle, mainly the winged variety, is among the most popular motifs in Hebrew glyptic, on par with the winged uraeus. Although these two share more than one layout, there are some marked differences. In contrast to the four-winged uraeus the beetle, also the four-winged variety, was a favourite motif of Israel's neighbours too, with the Ammonites more than with anyone else.

B2.1 Wingless beetle

The only example occurs on the seal of *ʿzʾ bn ḥts* (**fig. 82**), which is unique among the Hebrew seals in many aspects of its iconography (see F7.1). The wingless beetle is also rare in non-Hebrew glyptic.[48]

B2.2 Two-winged beetle

On a few Hebrew seals with a latitudinal axis (**fig. 83**) the two-winged beetle appears in the upper of two registers.[49] It should be noted that two-winged (or, for that matter, four-winged) uraei do not figure in inscribed latitudinal seals.

In longitudinal seals, most of which are exergual or triregistral, the two-winged beetle nearly always occupies the exergue or bottom register. This could have been due to practical considerations: the proportions of the insect and the – seemingly obligatory – up-curving wings. Only one of these seals is possibly Hebrew, the seal of *ʿšnʾl* (**fig. 84**).[50] The unprovenanced seal of Manasseh, the King's Son (**fig. 85**), has a straight-winged beetle in the top register, either suspect or an iconographic 'first'.[51]

B2.3 Four-winged beetle

Several anepigraphic examples with a latitudinal main axis are known, such as the bullae from Samaria, impressed with the same seal (**fig. 86**), and a very similar, unprovenanced seal published by Tushingham (1970). On how an inscription, dwarfed by the motif (or virtual scene), would have been fitted

---

48. It appears on the seal of *bnʾk* (?) (G 102), a Phoenician seal, and perhaps on one or two others.

49. In a few non-Hebrew latitudinal seals, exergual or with an undivided field, like B 89, it may hover freely.

50. Cf. Lemaire, *supra*, p. 17 with fig. 26; Millard (1991: pl. 156) takes the eighth-century script of this seal to be Ammonite or Hebrew. For this motif in non-Hebrew seals see B 5 (= Gubel, *supra*, p. 117, fig. 40) and HD 98.

51. In the same location, but not rendering, the insect is to be found on a few Phoenician seals, e.g. G 103. It occurs also in the top and bottom registers in *tête-bêche* arrangement, as on the anepigraphic seals, Buchanan & Moorey 1988: no. 276 and Museé Biblique de Bible et Terre Sainte in Paris, no. 5123 (unpublished). In such an arrangement the upper motif relates to the frame of the seal in the same way as the lower.

77

78

79

80

81

82

83

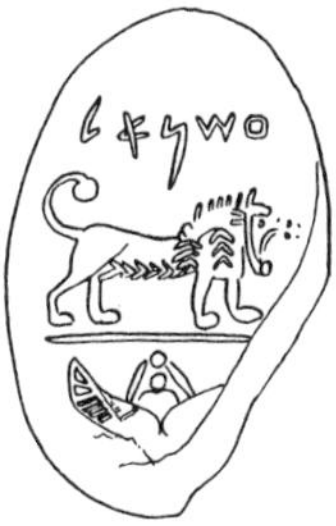

84

85

86

87

88

in one may learn from the Aramaic or Ammonite seal, with a round face, of *ʾlntn* (CAI 32). There are no inscribed latitudinal seals with four-winged uraei, as noted.

On longitudinal seals, as befits its volume, the four-winged beetle usually occupies most of the field, in the center or at the top. Of the five such Hebrew seals (several others are known), two (**figs. 87, 88**)[52] are exergual. Two are triregistral, one of them (**fig. 89**; cf. Lemaire 1981: esp. 57*) without dividers, the other (**fig. 90**) divided and the beetle is flanked by two birds.[53] In layout it is comparable to seals with a four-winged uraeus, cf. **fig. 77**. The layout of the fifth (HD 47) is not clear and the symbol seems to stand on a pedestal.

These seals reflect different solutions to the task of fitting the voluminous symbol and two words into a limited space. In the first example the name of the owner is written in the exergue, while the letters of his father's name are scattered between the upper wings of the beetle, in a fashion similar to the exergual seals with four-winged uraeus (see **fig. 79**).

In contrast to the seals portraying a tetrapterous uraeus, the similarly-winged beetle could be depicted *underneath* the legend (**fig. 89** and HD 47). There are, however, no Hebrew triregistral seals *with* dividers[54] that show a four-winged beetle in the central register, a common occurrence in Ammonite glyptic (see note 53).

Christoph Uehlinger (personal communication) offered the following view about the significance of the human-headed beetle (**fig. 88**) in an Israelite context: "As long as the local glyptic, anepigraphic seals included, does not provide us with comparanda (contrast Phoenician ivories), the seal of *blth* should best be regarded as a Phoenician import that received a Hebrew inscription. This could imply that the owner found the motif appealing, and it may well have had a religious meaning for him. The addition of a human head gives the beetle, symbol of the rising sun, a more personal (feminine?) aspect. This would certainly fit the general tendency of eighth-century Israelite art towards solar symbolism. However, as long as it remains isolated in its

---

52. A copy, presumed genuine, of the latter was donated to the Israel Museum a few years ago (IMJ 89.115.76; Israel Museum News 2/89 [August–December 1989], 8). The artist – he was one indeed – did not fully understand the ancient motif and text he was copying.

53. See motif C6 on the birds. This is the only such composition in Hebrew seals (in **fig. 87** the beetle is flanked by two *ʿankhs*). In Ammonite glyptic the four-winged beetle is usually accompanied by standards (Hübner, *supra*, p. 147 with figs. 16, 19, 23), and it is an animal head that the birds are escorting (see *ibid.*, pp. 139, 148 and 150 with figs. 1, 7).

54. And none whatsoever except **fig. 89**.

local context, it cannot be properly understood within the Israelite religious environment" (cf. Uehlinger, *infra*, pp. 276-277).

Asked about the relationship between scarab and uraeus, Uehlinger, in a letter of 9 November 1991, commented: "The beetle is clearly a metaphor for the movement and constant regeneration (*ḫpr*) of the sun. Its representation on seals does not mean the real, flying insect. In contrast, the winged uraei, even though similarly belonging to the realm of solar symbolism, were perceived as actual beings, or attribute beings, in Yahweh's heavenly environment, as the seraphim in Isaiah 6 show. This may explain why these creatures, indicating the presence of Yahweh, were unlikely to have been depicted underneath one's name" (on the role of the uraeus, or seraph, in Hebrew iconography see Keel 1977: chapter II; GGG: §§ 151, 161-162).

B3 Tortoise

Encountered sporadically in first-millennium Mesopotamian art (Seidl 1989: 153), and sometimes associated with Ea, this motif is not particularly popular in the contemporary Near East.[55] The tortoise appears on a single Hebrew seal (**fig. 91**). Could it have served as a family, or personal emblem (see next motif), or was it chosen for its symbolic or apotropaic value?

B4 Locust

Of five West Semitic seals that sport this motif two are Aramaic.[56] The other three are Hebrew, possibly North Israelite, the seal of *ḥmn* (**fig. 92**) on account of its Megiddonian provenance and Phoenician iconography, the seals of *ʿzryw hgbh* (**fig. 93**) and *ʿlyw* by virtue of the spelling with *-yw* (though this is not certain, see p. 199). In the first example the locust occupies the exergue, in the same manner as on the seal of *nnz*. The undivided latitudinal bi- and triregistral layout in text-picture, and text-text-picture arrangement of the latter two is rather rare on Hebrew seals and in West Semitic glyptic in general.[57]

---

55. It also adorns the coins of sixth-century Aegina.

56. They are the seals of *ʾḥṣr* (HD 130 = Ornan, *supra*, p. 57, fig. 11) and *nnz* (B 122). Interestingly, they share the type of voluted winged sun, attributed by Parayre (*supra*, p. 37 with figs. 37, 42) to Samʾal of the second half of the eighth century.

57. But in itself it is not enough to cast doubt (Garbini 1982: 170-171) on the authenticity of these unprovenanced seals. For undivided biregistral seals, two of the picture-text, and one of the text-picture type, two of them of known provenance, see **fig. 83**, Avigad 1969: no. 15 and Wright 1965: fig. 91; for undivided triregistral seals see IR 31 and **figs. 89, 96, 118**, one of the text-text-text and three of the text-picture-text composition, three of them of solid authenticity. Indeed, none matches the latitudinal text-text-picture format of the seal of *ʿzryw hgbh*, and in their arrangement they, too, are a minority among the Hebrew seals of these layouts. We are dealing, as it is, with a rare, but not unexpected design.

The role of the locust as a family emblem is obvious on the seal of ʿAzaryaw the 'Locust', probably implying the same function for the insect on the seal of ʿAlayaw (see also previous motif).

B5 Fish

With one uncertain exception, all West Semitic seals that depict fish are Hebrew, mostly Judahite if the provenanced ones are representative. Of these twelve examples ten show the fish in the upper register. The majority have the fish as their sole motif, and of these eight are triregistral (**fig. 94**), and one (Bordreuil & Lemaire 1982: no. 13) is biregistral. Another triregistral seal, of different workmanship, depicts the fish with additional motifs (**fig. 95**). Of the two remaining seals one is undivided triregistral of the text-picture-text type (**fig. 96**; see note 57). The other (**fig. 97**) is one of the most unusual Hebrew seals (see motif F7.1). Unlike all its counterparts the fish in this seal swims upwards.

Most seals seem to depict the same kind of fish, with rather plump, criss-cross body, fins and short tail. Was a specific family meant (Avigad 1976b: note 7) or do we simply see the form easiest to draw? All these seals are made of soft stone and are of simple design. The fish in **fig. 96** is somewhat different, with its elongated body and longer tail, while the fish in **fig. 97**, a hardstone seal with Phoenician iconography, is unlike all the others.

Obviously, fish stand for plenty and fertility, and may signify the life-giving quality of water (e.g. Keel 1978: 135-142). It remains to be found out whether this or a more specific symbolism was intended here.

C Birds

C1 Falcon

Of Phoenician, ultimately of Egyptian origin, the falcon appears on several Hebrew seals. As main motif, fit for a royal bird, it can be seen in **fig. 98**, with an exact parallel in the Phoenician seal of *yḥzbʿl* (HD 118 = Gubel, *supra*, p. 120, fig. 60). With protectively spread wings, like one of the stances of the two-winged uraeus, it is depicted on a seal (**fig. 99**)[58] and a bulla (Avigad 1989a: no. 10), and in **fig. 100** two hieracocephalous deities flank the child on the flower. For other possible falcons see C6 below.

C2 Dove

A bird with a round head, looking like a dove, occurs once in West Semitic glyptic, on the Hebrew jar-handle impression of *ʿrb nby* (**fig. 101**). If identified correctly, it would not seem to allude to the owner's name, for why show a dove on the seal of a man named 'Crow'? As expected from a dove, it 'nests' in the uppermost of the three registers.

---

58. Its back is shown in **pl. I:5**.

89

90

91

92

93

94

95

96

97

98

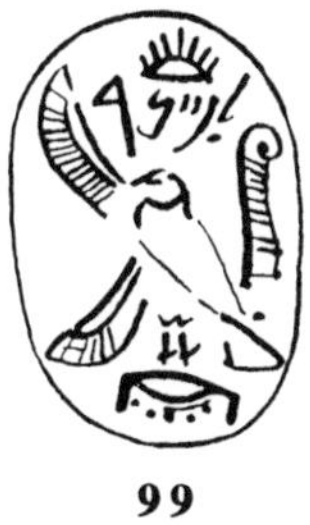
99

100

101

102

103

Pottery vessels stamped with seals that contain both text and picture (**figs. 50, 79**) were rare in ancient Israel outside the *lmlk* stamps.

C3 Rooster
Fighting cocks are shown on two Hebrew seals, one of them from the Tell en-Naṣbeh excavations (**fig. 102**). It could be due to either their flightless character or the curve of their bodies that they occupy the lowermost of three registers.[59]

C4 Duck
Duck heads seem to adorn the prow and stern of the boat on the seal of *ʾlšmʿ bn gdlyhw* (**fig. 103**), the only inscribed seal showing this motif. Several anepigraphic seals with the same or similar scene (for which see F6 below) are of Palestinian origin (GGG: §§ 178-179).

C5 'Emblematic' bird (eagle?)
A schematic, linearly-rendered bird with spread wings appears on a single, possibly Judahite seal (**fig. 104**). Depicted in the lowermost of three registers because of the curve of its wings, it does not manifest the consideration evident in the positioning of several other motifs.[60]

C6 Indeterminate bird
Fig. 105 shows a bird on a flower or pole (see A3.1) as a secondary subject. In **fig. 106**, a seal whose proper publication is still awaited, two identical birds flank the central motif. The antithetic arrangement is very widespread in West Semitic glyptic, but can be seen only sporadically on Hebrew seals.[61]

– In a *frieze* the bird, possibly a falcon, is rare outside Hebrew glyptic. To the examples in the seals of ʿEzer (Avigad 1979: no. 7) and *bsy* (**fig. 107**)[62] I suggest to add the seal of *šlm* (HD 81), the clear (though sloppily-executed) birds in the first degenerating to a stick-figure like rendering in the second, to

59. A different rooster appears, incised after firing, on pottery vessels from Gibeon (Pritchard 1961: 20, fig. 47).

60. Together with another whose iconography is relevant (**fig. 128**) our seal probably sets a date prior to the emergence of inscribed seals for the floruit of a distinct group of anepigraphic, mostly bone seals from Judea and the coastal plain (Keel-Leu 1991: 75-78; GGG: §§ 157-159; Sass forthcoming): the seemingly minimal overlap of that group with our inscribed seals may indicate that one was on the decline when the other made its debut (see GGG: § 204). The script of our seal is not particularly early.

61. This observation may be no longer valid if Lemaire (1985b: 40) is right in regarding as North Israelite seals like G 52-54 (cf. Gubel, *supra*, p. 117, figs. 37, 39), hitherto considered Phoenician.

62. The latter was classified as Aramaic by Herr (1978: Ar 51).

a series of oblique lines in the third.[63] Bird and uraeus friezes may appear together on the same seal, like in **fig. 107**.

– As *space filler* in otherwise aniconic seals (**fig. 108**) the bird is an exclusively-Hebrew device, with the exception of the seal of *yʿdrʾl* (Bordreuil, *supra*, p. 89, fig. 20). The flail in our figure identifies it as a falcon, and could indicate that the other birds belong to the same kind. As with the branch in that role (motif A2, **fig. 60**), one may ask if the bird retains its symbolic significance or serves a decorative purpose only.

D Mammals

D1 Lion

Striding and roaring, the lion (**fig. 109**) is a popular motif on inscribed seals. He is often the virtual scene and appears alone, or accompanied by secondary motifs, almost tertiary to judge from the disproportion – bucephalus, two-winged beetle, falcon – whose relationship with him is seldom self evident. Sometimes he can be accompanied by a larger figure too. All these seals are latitudinal, exergual or with undivided field. The lion is depicted in this position on anepigraphic seals too, including one from the excavations of Tell en-Naṣbeh (Naṣbeh I: pl. 55:74; IAA I.5954). In longitudinal seals, the lion assumes a slightly less important role. Only two of these are epigraphic, the seal of *ʿšnʾl* (**fig. 110**), classified by Lemaire (see note 50) as probably Hebrew and a South Semitic one (Sass 1991: fig. 38).

Lemaire (1990a, with previous bibliography) considered most these seals Aramaic or probably Aramaic, and a few Hebrew or probably Hebrew. The seal of *tnʾl* (*ibid.*: no. 10), enumerated among the latter, and another one classified as 'probably Aramaic' have a bucephalus in profile in the field. This may hint, considering the near-total avoidance of bovine motifs in Hebrew glyptic (see D4 below), that the seal of *tnʾl* is not Hebrew.

Our lion seals figure prominently among the 'lapidary' seals attributed to the eighth century that do not lend themselves easily to epigraphical classification (see section I.1). That the Hebrew ones among them are expected to be North Israelite (Lemaire 1990a), is borne out by the identification of the majority of this class as Aramaic or probably Aramaic, from the popularity of the roaring lion in North Syrian monumental art and from the provenance – Megiddo – of the seal of *šmʿ ʿbd yrbʿm*, the most majestic of all Hebrew seals. But this may be a circular argument, probably arising from inadequate acquaintance with eighth-century Judahite iconography: if North Syrian influence penetrated as far south as Tell en-Naṣbeh (see above), could it not have reached Jerusalem, only 13 km to the south? And why should not some of the roaring-lion seals be Phoenician? Several of the legends are equivocal enough

63. The bird frieze is to be found on contemporary anepigraphic seals from excavations at Megiddo (Megiddo I: pl. 72:12) and Jerusalem (Couroyer 1970: pl. 10h, j).

to merit that possibility, and the roaring lion does appear on anepigraphic Phoenician seals (like Buchanan & Moorey 1988: no. 276); in different positions, the king of beasts figures on yet other epigraphic Phoenician pieces.

A lion is carved in relief on the back of a Phoenician-inspired Hebrew seal, the only West Semitic inscribed seal to be thus decorated (**pl. I:4**; its sealing surface is in **fig. 99**).[64]

What did the lion stand for in the eyes of Shemaʿ, the official of king Jeroboam II, and of other Israelite seal owners? And did it have a different meaning to contemporary non-Israelites? It is not at all clear whether these solitary lions represent just their own natural, or apotropaic might as guardian lions, or whether they stand for the king, or a deity (cf. Ornan, *supra*, p. 63; GGG: § 118).

A lion chasing an ibex can be seen on some inscribed registral seals of Phoenician inspiration, though not necessarily workmanship, none of them Hebrew (cf. Lemaire 1986: 307-309). This ancient theme (Tufnell 1984: pl. 36; GGG: § 12) figures in the bottom register of an anepigraphic seal from Megiddo, this time of what looks like Phoenician workmanship (Mutesellim II: fig. 63; Culican 1974: pl. 36a).[65] From the Ramat Raḥel excavations comes a handle of a *lmlk* jar, impressed with a seal that had the same contest scene as its sole decoration (**fig. 111**). Even though anepigraphic, the type of jar indicates this was an official Judahite seal of the late eighth century (Barkay 1992: 128; see also motif D5).[66] If in Egypt this scene can be understood as expressing pharaoh's triumph over his non-Egyptian foes, a comparable Near Eastern significance is not obvious. Depicted separately, each of these two animals played a positive role. Symbolic significance, however, depends on the context among other factors, and the same animal may be positive in one context and negative in another (Christoph Uehlinger's observation).

---

64. A comparable lion, portrayed from above in intaglio, exists on a Phoenician seal (Avigad 1985: pl. 1A). The depiction of a motif from that point of view is unparalleled in inscribed seals.

65. On inscribed seals (cf. Gubel, *supra*, p. 117, figs. 34-36) this scene appears in the lowermost pictorial register, the legend occupying the bottom register.

66. There are no Hebrew seals showing a human or anthropoid figure vanquishing a lion, and also among other late Iron Age inscribed stamp seals the leontomachy is extremely rare; for a possible explanation see Ornan, *supra*, p. 54. Only one Hebrew seal depicts an anthropomorphic figure in combat, against a griffin; see **fig. 129**.

104

105

106

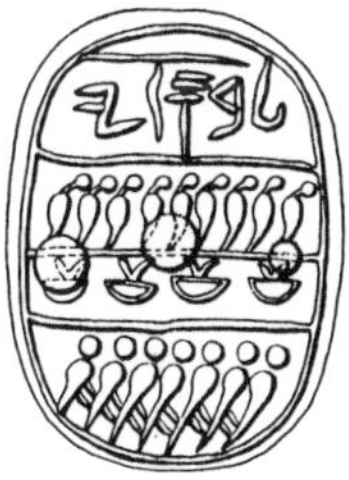

107

108

109

110

111

112

113

114

115

116

117

D2 Ibex

In addition to the hopeless contest with the lion (**fig. 111**), the ibex figures in only two or three Hebrew seals. Galloping, it serves as virtual scene on one (**fig. 112**). The reverse of the seal of *ṣpn nryhw* (**fig. 113**) shows an ibex facing a branch, with a star and a rhomb (cf. section G) in the field. Rather than considering it an abbreviation of the two antithetic creatures facing a plant, so common on contemporary Mesopotamian cylinder seals, this scene could descend from local traditions current since the Middle Bronze Age (Tufnell 1984: pl. 36; GGG: §§ 11, 93, 188).[67, 68]

Fig. 113 has good parallels in Aramaic and Ammonite glyptic, while the lone, galloping ibex (**fig. 112**) is otherwise unknown on inscribed seals. Keel & Uehlinger (GGG: §§ 11, 116) take the ibex, when sole or main motif, to have originally denoted vitality and the ability to survive in a hostile environment.

D3 Deer

Among inscribed West Semitic seals the grazing she-deer is exclusively Hebrew. It is usually depicted in the top register of bi- and tripartite seals (**fig. 114**), fitting the plano-convex outline of the animal in grazing position. A tripartite bulla (**fig. 115**) with the deer in the middle register is exceptional not only in the location of the grazing animal, but in its being the sole triregistral Hebrew seal in the text-picture-text arrangement (see above, p. 204).[69]

Considering Avigad's bullae as Judahite, we may have three such provenanced examples – A 169, probably A 125 and an unpublished bulla from the city of David.[70] This might indicate that Hebrew seals depicting a grazing she-deer are exclusively Judahite (cf. GGG: § 117, and *infra*, p. 275).

A walking cervine(?) is depicted on the seal of *mḥsyhw nby* (**fig. 116**), and two seals with unusual shape and layout, probably by the same hand (**fig. 117** and G 37), show galloping deer. Exceptional in Hebrew glyptic,

---

67. A worshipper facing a plant appears on a few West Semitic examples (Ornan, *supra*, figs. 73, 74), but none is Hebrew (cf. F4.3).

68. An outwardly-male ibex suckling its young (cf. Keel 1980: note 150a and p. 117; GGG: §§ 91-92) is depicted on a seal on which some read *šnyw* (Reifenberg 1938: no. 8; cf. VSE 132; Herr 1978: undistinguishable 3), but regarding the signs as pseudo-script would probably be closer to reality. This scene is not represented, then, in the Hebrew repertoire; but compare GGG: § 188 for anepigraphic seals of the seventh century.

69. The same motif, doubled, appears in the bottom register of an anepigraphic, seemingly Phoenician-style seal of unknown provenance in Berlin (G 174; Jakob-Rost 1975: no. 168). Examples are known from other media, e.g. a painted male on a Spanish-Phoenician ostrich egg (Moscati 1968: 240).

70. Kindly brought to my attention by Baruch Brandl.

but widespread on Ammonite, Moabite and South Semitic seals, is the *tête-bêche* arrangement seen in **fig. 117**.

D4 Bull

While seals depicting bovines are fairly common in the West Semitic realm, especially in Ammonite glyptic (Hübner, *supra*, pp. 136-138 with figs. 13, 15, 21 etc.), there is only one such Hebrew seal, the seal of Shemaᶜyahu son of ᶜAzaryahu (**fig. 118**; see p. 198 on its possible ninth-century dating).[71] The near-absence of bovines, associated with the storm god, from inscribed Hebrew seals, and their abundance on Ammonite seals, is certainly not accidental (cf. Hübner, p. 137; GGG: § 119).[72]

D5 Horse

The horse as main or secondary motif is virtually missing from inscribed West Semitic stamp seals.[73] But it figures prominently and beautifully on handles, all stamped with the same anepigraphic seal, of *lmlk* jars from En Gedi, Jerusalem etc. (**fig. 119**; Barkay 1992a). Unlike the linear, or flat character of most Hebrew glyptic art, our *lmlk* horse, that must date to the late eighth century, is cut in the best modelled style. Was the seal imported (from where?) or made by a gifted local seal cutter? Was the horse chosen as a family or office emblem, or as an allusion to the owner's name (Barkay 1992a: 128)? That the seal served an official function is almost certain from its use on *lmlk* jars (*ibid.*; see also motif D1 – lion chasing ibex). An association of this rare motif with the "horses of the sun-god" (2 Kings 23:11; cf. Schroer 1987a: 282-300, esp. 298-300, with bibliography) would be rather difficult to prove, in contrast to the clear solar connotations of the two *lmlk* beings (see GGG: § 199 for a recent assessment of 2 Kings 23:11 and archaeological correlates).

---

71. See motif D1 on the combination of a bull's head with the striding lion.

72. As attribute animal of the national deity, the four-winged uraeus in Hebrew seals (motif B1.3) could have played a role comparable to the bull's in Ammonite seals.

73. But see a rather unusual South Semitic seal, Sass 1991: 62-63. Unharnessed horses may be seen on Phoenician bronze bowls, e.g. Moscati 1968: fig. 20, and in other two-dimensional representations. The horse is an obvious component of chariot scenes, so popular on cylinder seals (on such scenes in South Semitic stamp seals see Sass 1991: 59-61). Anepigraphic Iron Age stamp seals with a chariot scene come from the excavations at Gezer (Gezer II: 328 no. 391, III pl. 209:12), Hazor (an impression, Hazor III-IV: pls. 196:27, 360:9) and Dan (Biran 1977: pl. 37C), but the provenance is in itself no proof of their being Israelite.

E Fantastic animals

E1 Griffin

Many Israelites had seals decorated with Phoenician griffins as virtual scenes (**figs. 120-121**), and, probably deterred by the human head, only few opted for winged sphinxes (next motif, **fig. 123**). The creature is either alone, or facing an *ʿankh*-shaped symbol, once enclosed in a cartouche. The relatively large number of griffin seals of Israelite provenance[74] or *-yw* names led Lemaire (1990b: 97-101) to propose an Israelite, possibly Samarian workshop. Indeed most of these seals share a longitudinal, exergual or similar arrangement, and the creature, the dominant motif, is normally shown walking; **fig. 121** (**pl. I:6**) has a recumbent griffin (cf. Gubel 1985).

Unique in West Semitic glyptic is the seal of *yqmyhw* (**fig. 122**), that depicts a man slaying a griffin (see motif F2 and note 66; Gubel, *supra*, pp. 107-108).

E2 Winged sphinx

The winged sphinx is less popular than the griffin, as noted, and this pertains also to non-Hebrew seals, but not to the same extent. Most winged sphinxes on West Semitic stamp seals, including our Hebrew example (**fig. 123**) show Phoenician inspiration. There is one Palestinian exemplar, the seal of Elʾamar from Megiddo (Megiddo I: pl. 67:34), with non-Hebrew script. A few human-headed winged quadrupeds go back to northeastern prototypes. Among them stands out a Hebrew seal depicting an *aladlammû*-like being (**fig. 124**) (cf. Ornan, *supra*, p. 60 with note 11, and F8.3 below).

E3 Miscellaneous

Otherwise unknown in West Semitic glyptic, a human-headed winged being with a scorpion's tail (**fig. 125**) appears as main motif on the seal of *ḥmlk* which could be Hebrew or Moabite.[75] It combines Phoenician features with those of the Mesopotamian scorpion-man (for the latter see Ornan, *supra*, p. 56 with fig. 7).

The human headed four-winged beetle is quite common in Phoenician glyptic of the Persian Period, while earlier examples do not abound. It is all the more surprising that the only inscribed piece among the latter should be Hebrew (**fig. 126**; see motif B2.3 and Boardman 1971: 196).

---

74. One of them, the seal of Pataisi from Samaria (HD 41), is non-Hebrew (see p. 197 on provenance).

75. Herr (1978: He 146) is for a Hebrew, Timm (1989a: 199-200) for a Moabite attribution, while to me the script looks decidedly indecisive: it is true that the distinct, two-bar *ḥet* is more at home in Moabite, but this and each of the other three letters has its parallels in Yahwistic seals; the name is hopelessly equivocal too. Cf. Lemaire, *supra*, p. 6, note 1.

118

119

120

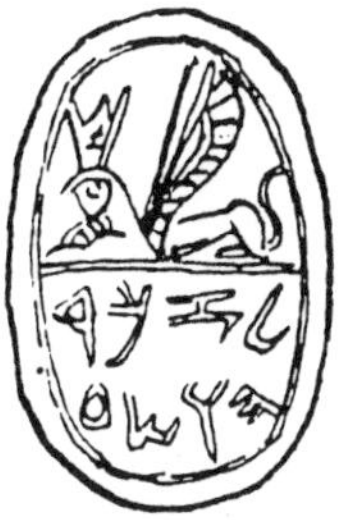

121

122

123

124

125

126

127

128

As to the unusual subject-matter of these two seals, we have already seen that the most 'heretical' motifs do occur occasionally on Hebrew seals. The latter motif, like its conventionally-headed version, must have been a solar symbol, whereas the former remains to be explained.

F Human and anthropomorphic figures[76]

F1 Stick and outline figure

Stick figures (**fig. 127**) appear on the reverse of oval plaques, predominantly of bronze, giving the impression of distinct workshops. In addition to the seals mentioned here, there are several unpublished examples, including one with four figures that is on exhibit in the Hecht Museum. None of these seals is provenanced, and they seem to have appeared on the market in recent years only. In itself, this fact does not discredit them, but a degree of doubt must remain. I suggest to wait for reliable evidence before 'admitting' the stick figure into the iconographical repertoire of the inscribed Hebrew seals.

A seal with an outlined and hatched human figure (**fig. 128**) evokes an earlier style (see discussion in motif C5).[77]

F2 Contest scene

Fig. 129 shows a man slaying a griffin,[78] strictly speaking not a contest scene, for the griffin does not offer even token resistance. Unique in West Semitic glyptic, this scene is comparable, however, to depictions on Phoenician bronze bowls and ivories (cf. Gubel, *supra*, pp. 107-108 with figs. 12-15).[79]

F3 Child on flower

Common in Phoenician art, the boy is supposed to squat like the infant Horus, but in two of the three Hebrew examples (**figs. 130, 148** vs. **pl. I:1**) he is in a position recalling *Knielauf*, well-known in Mesopotamian iconography (cf. Ornan, *supra*, p. 57, figs. 11-12).[80] In **pl. I:1** he is bareheaded, while in **figs. 130** and **148** he wears what appears to be a debased

---

76. See E2 and E3 for fantastic, human-headed beings.

77. The seal with what appears to be a pseudo-legend, read *šnyw* by some, has a 'shrugging', *en face* near-stick figure turned 90° to the main scene. This seal has several unique features (see note 68). A similar figure is to be seen on several seals (G 22, 53, possibly G 16; see motif C6).

78. Cf. motifs D1 and D2 for lion chasing ibex.

79. The seal of *ʾny*, G 6, shows a griffin trampling a human (or protecting him, as Gubel, *supra*, p. 108, prefers), another 'first' on seals, and again with parallels on Phoenician metal bowls and ivories. This could be a variation on the Egyptian theme of the victorious pharaoh in lion or in sphinx form.

80. A close parallel, without flower, is to be found on an impression from Hazor Stratum VI (eighth century; Hazor II: pls. 67:13, 162:7).

Egyptian double crown or a horned disk. Instead of holding one hand to his mouth, as in the Egyptian prototype, he is raising both in a gesture of prayer or blessing.[81, 82]

F4 Man alone

Always shown in profile, a man walking or standing, alone or as main motif is popular on West Semitic stamp seals (cf. Ornan, *supra*, pp. 68-71). There are three main variants:

1. Man holding staff in one hand, the other hand hanging beside his body **(fig. 131)**.
2. Man holding staff in one hand and gesturing with the other **(fig. 132)**.
3. Man gesturing with both hands **(fig. 133)**.

We may dub them 1. dignitary/king; 2. worshipping/blessing dignitary/king; 3. worshipper. The first two variants exist in both Phoenician and Mesopotamian-inspired versions, while the third always belongs to the latter. The persons vary in hairdo and headdress, garment, and in the secondary motifs surrounding them.

The staff and occasional Egyptian double crown may designate authoritative the first two figures. It was Bordreuil who suggested (1985), followed by Gubel (1990a; 1991a; cf. *supra*, pp. 118-121 with figs. 42-57), that seals showing a man with staff belonged, according to the presence or absence of the crown, to kings or royal functionaries. High office, Bordreuil argued, could be expressed in personal seals by means of characteristic iconography alone, uniform throughout the late Iron Age Levant; taken a step further I understand this to imply that every human figure in a central position on a seal depicts the owner: a 'common' worshipper, a dignitary, a king. This is most probably right in some cases, perhaps more so in the worshipper variety (see F4.3). But, like the pharaoh or his cartouche in Egyptian glyptic, could not the image of a dignitary or king fulfil a purpose approaching that of a deity, namely to invoke his power or denote the owner's association with him? In that case one may be justified to ask whether the gesture of his hands is meant to show the person praying or blessing (see GGG: § 186).

The point raised by Bordreuil touches upon another issue, the omission of the title from officials' seals, iconic and aniconic. In his proposal Bordreuil

81. In Ammonite glyptic the squatting child tended to merge with or turn into a squatting monkey; see Hübner, *supra*, p. 158, fig. 13a. This metamorphosis is also evident in an unpublished conical limestone seal from Tel Batash, Israel, found on the surface before the excavations, IAA 77-57. Identical in style and layout to its Ammonite counterparts, the seal seems to be anepigraphic, but its edges are so badly damaged, that one cannot be sure. A monkey is depicted on an anepigraphic seal from Lachish, cf. notes 33, 86.

82. For a uraeus and other beings on flowers see A3.1.

attempted to show that the near-absence of royal West Semitic seals is an optical illusion. Is he right? In fact we have here his approach juxtaposed with another:

– 1. Any seal showing a man with staff may belong to a dignitary, and if he is crowned he is likely to be a king; looking up the name in biblical or extra-biblical records suffices in many cases to identify the owner of such a seal.

– 2. In order to securely identify the owner of a seal his name, patronymic and title, or at least two of these should match the ancient records (Avigad 1987a; Schneider 1991; cf. Lemaire, *supra*, pp. 13-14).

Regarding Bordreuil's addition of the iconographical criterion I prefer a midway position: 'royal' or 'official' iconography of a seal could imply royal or official ownership, but this cannot be proved if the office or at least the patronymic were not indicated; a person may have chosen to depict his sovereign on his seal, perhaps even his superior, as a manifestation of his loyalty or esteem.

Two phenomena are clear and consistent: 1. none of the empty-handed figures wears an Egyptian-inspired crown;[83] 2. the crowned figure always holds a staff (but not vice versa). In comparing the present group with that of persons in front of deities, symbols or cult objects another phenomenon becomes apparent: it is chiefly the empty-handed man that one sees in the latter contexts; the sovereign or dignitary appear in most cases in their own right (among the few exceptions are G 130 and B 2). Though impossible to prove, it stands to reason, then, that the dignitary or king is normally not praying for his own salvation on his own seal, but is blessing the owner of another, his subordinate or subject.

F4.1 Man with staff

The first variant, the figure that does not gesture (**fig. 131**), an uncommon one in West Semitic seals, is represented in two clumsily carved seals that are regarded as Hebrew.[84] A similar figure might appear on another seal, of uncertain attribution, known only from a drawing (G 135). The same stance is also found on two non-Hebrew seals, HD 124, with a bare-headed person in Mesopotamian-inspired style and B 23 (= Gubel, *supra*, p. 119, fig. 44), with a Phoenician-style figure wearing the Egyptian double crown.

83. The question of possible Mesopotamian or Syrian royal headdress requires further study.

84. Their Hebrew attribution, and alternatively their genuineness, are not beyond doubt.

F4.2 Man with staff, gesturing
Cut mainly in Phoenician style, this is the most widespread variant of the three. Only one Hebrew seal belongs here (**fig. 132**), one of the few inspired by Mesopotamian glyptic (cf. Ornan, *supra*, p. 69, fig. 68).

F4.3 Man gesturing with both hands
There are many West Semitic seals of a man, presumably the seal owner (a priest praying on his behalf is less likely), depicted as an adorer gesturing with both hands. There are even more specimens of the worshipper before a plant, offering stand, altar, divine symbol or attribute or deity (Ornan, *supra*, figs. 36-49, 53, 69, 80). We have only one Hebrew example of the former (**fig. 133**), and none of the others.[85, 86]

The seal of Peqaḥ (**fig. 134**), although portraying a person in profile, does not fit within the first two of the above-mentioned subgroups, probably also not within this one, the third.[87] Both hands of the man are extended forwards and upwards, either holding an object or gesturing (there is a break at this point). The object before him is perhaps a 'vegetal' standard, reminiscent of that in Ornan, *supra*, p. 69, fig. 74, an Aramaic seal.

F5 Two men
Two worshippers before a plant, offering stand, altar, divine symbol(s) or attribute(s) or a deity were very common in the West Semitic realm, but, as with depictions of a single worshipper in such a context, they are extremely rare in Hebrew glyptic.

Only one such seal, in an unusual style, is certainly Hebrew (**fig. 135**). It is an oval bifacial plaque that may have belonged to Ḥilqiyahu, son of Padi (the legend is much damaged). On the reverse two men (the owner, doubled?) are kneeling, or dancing, under a palm tree (see motif A1.1).

Two worshippers flanking a stand(?) and crescent appear on a seal from Samaria (Ornan, *supra*, p. 67, fig. 56). Only the first letter of the owner's

85. Unless the seals of *stmk* (Avigad 1989a: no. 22; Ornan, *supra*, p. 66, fig. 48) and *kpr* (NAAG 1991: no. 25; Ornan, p. 69, fig. 69), considered Moabite, turn out to be Hebrew. The seal of *yḥn* (Aufrecht 1992: no. 1) is most probably Moabite, not Hebrew.

86. In Lachish was found a late Iron Age anepigraphic seal (Lachish III: 365) depicting, in Mesopotamian-influenced Levantine style, a worshipper facing a *'dea nutrix'* (cf. note 33). Another, the seal of *šlm*, G 100, shows an Egyptianizing scene of a human(?) figure before a mummiform deity. *Šlm* is a very common Hebrew name, but the script of this seal, known only from a drawing, cannot be checked: the *mem*, curved in Galling's drawing, is straight-legged in Levy's (1869: no. II,1). The whereabouts of the seal are unknown to me.

87. Upon examination of the original carnelian plaque in Berlin and the excellent photograph in Bordreuil 1986c it becomes evident that the spidery figure is a disgrace to the seal cutters' profession, eighth century BC or 19th century AD. But even if genuine, why need the seal of Peqaḥ be Hebrew?

name, a *kap*, is well preserved,[88] and the letter could be Hebrew as well as Moabite. The seal belongs to a distinct subgroup (Ornan, *supra*, p. 68 with figs. 56-65) that was probably Aramaean-inspired and may have enjoyed a distribution wider than originally thought (GGG: § 185; Keel 1990c; see also p. 196 above, and note 3; Timm, *supra*, pp. 180-183).[89]

F6 Enthroned anthropomorphic deity

Two inscribed Hebrew seals show an enthroned figure.[90] Quite common in the Syrian-inspired 'deity in boat' scene and its boatless relatives between 'cypresses', altars etc., mostly on anepigraphic seals,[91] the figure is taken to be the moon god, or an El-type deity with lunar aspects (GGG: §§ 178-179; for an earlier view, see Keel 1977: 306-311). Of Egyptian origin, an enthroned solar deity or pharaoh, in a boat or boatless, is found in the glyptic of the earlier centuries of Iron Age Palestine (Keel 1982: esp. 460-461; GGG: § 83; cf. Sass 1983: 174). Standing in a boat, a lunar deity appears in a cult scene on a late-second-millenium Assyrian cylinder seal from Samsat (cf. Matthews 1990: no. 534).

On the reverse of one of the two Hebrew seals mentioned (**fig. 136**), the enthroned deity travels in a boat. The other seal (**fig. 137, pl. I:7**; GGG: fig. 305c),[92] bifacial as well, shows on the reverse an enthroned gesturing man, his head consisting of a mere drilling with a hint of a beard at 8 o'clock. He is seated in front of an *ʿankh*-shaped stand, above which appears to be an

88. Possibly *km̊*[...; *klm*... was restored in Samaria-Sebaste 3: 87, pl. 15:21, but examination of the original reveals that the legend is almost totally destroyed beyond the first letter.

89. An anepigraphic seal showing two human(?) worshippers flanking a Bes(?) figure was found in Hazor Stratum VI (Hazor III-IV: pls. 187:22, 360:4, 5; cf. the corrected drawing in GGG: fig. 228).

90. The seal, with a related scene, of *ʿšnyhw ʿbd hmlk* from Tel Qasile (VSE 125) is a forgery.

91. From Shechem in the Israelite (or ex-Israelite) heartland comes an anepigraphic seal showing a similar figure between two 'cypresses' (Wright 1965: fig. 52:7; Keel 1977: 286, note 47, 307-308, fig. 238c; GGG: fig. 304).

92. This seal (IAA I.8915), of unknown provenance, seems to have escaped scholarly attention although it was acquired in Jerusalem by the Palestine Department of Antiquities as early as 1930. It is a biconvex of reddish limestone, 14 x 12 x 10 mm, drilled from both ends but the drillings do not meet. The legend on the obverse is not well preserved, and the reading *lʾšyhw mšmš* is not absolutely certain. If correctly read, both names are attested in Hebrew, the owner's better than his father's (e.g. A 33, A 70; our seal is mentioned in Avigad's discussion of A 70).

129

130

131

132

133

134

135

136

137

138

139

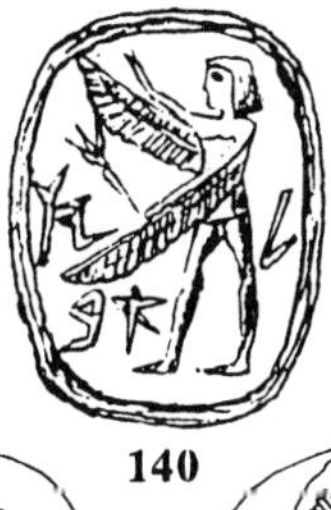
140

141

142

143

144

oblique crescent,[93] both malformed. A fairly similar scene, with additional elements, is to be found on the seal of *šlmʾl* (Avigad 1989a: no. 19; GGG: fig. 305a; cf. Lemaire, *supra*, pp. 17-18; Uehlinger, *infra*, p. 264, fig. 6), which is Aramaic or Ammonite.

Devoid of divine attributes, it may be argued that the figure in the latter two seals is a worshipper of rank, a king perhaps, but **fig. 136** and its parallels indicate that a god, always basically the same one, is represented. That the two Yahwistic seals may portray Yahweh in his lunar aspect is an intriguing possibility. Such a concept is at any rate a plausible one in Judah in the seventh century, a time when Sin of Haran enjoyed unprecedented prominence (GGG: §§ 173-179, 181-182; Uehlinger, *infra*, pp. 263-265).

It was the general tendency in the Neo-Imperial West to prefer the depiction of mortals (cf. Ornan, *supra*), and the near-absence of Mesopotamian-inspired anthropomorphic deities from inscribed Ammonite and Moabite seals underlines this. The presence, if a rare one, of a hominiform god in inscribed seventh-century Judaean seals is unusual, then, in more than one respect.

F7 Animal-headed deity

F7.1 *En face* head of Sekhmet(?)

The exceptional seal of *ʿzʾ bn ḥts* (**fig. 138**) has this image, unique in West Semitic glyptic, as its central motif.[94] Of Phoenician workmanship or strong influence, this bifacial scaraboid stands out in its choice of motifs, while their layout is less unusual. The blend of different motifs with no apparent relationship is sometimes to be found (e.g. Rahmani 1964: pl. 41F), and the tri-registral layout *without* dividers has Phoenician anepigraphic parallels (Culican 1974: pl. 36d; our seal face, too, is uninscribed).

---

93. Described in the IAA inventory card as a bird(?) which the seated figure is supposed to be holding. While I see no reason to doubt that a crescent is represented, its role as the divine attribute is not self-evident: the crescent presides over many contemporary scenes, including scenes with different deities or with none at all (Ornan & Sass 1992: 63).

94. Analogous aegis-shaped amulets, the head and a broad collar, are known in the early first millennium (e.g. Gubel 1991b: no. 218, a 22nd-Dynasty piece). With various heads, the same device appears on seals too (e.g. G 103; probably Gubel, *supra*, p. 117, fig. 34), occasionally growing wings (B 24, HD 98). But when the rendering is sketchy, and often headless, it may be undistinguishable from a pomegranate. Couroyer (1970: 251-252), discussing an uninscribed seal from Kenyon's excavations in Jerusalem, maintained that all are pomegranates. That aegises, really broad collars, were meant in some of the cases becomes evident from examples like B 17 or Megiddo I: pl. 67:44 (IAA 36.946), on which the details rule out the fruit. In the only Hebrew seal with this device (**fig. 107**) the flat-topped rendition is again more suitable for a collar.

F7.2 Falcon-headed anthropomorphic deity
Squatting on flowers, wearing Egyptian double crowns and holding staffs, two such figures (a somewhat corrupt variant of Gardiner's sign C2; cf. motif C1 above) flank the child on the flower (**fig. 139**). This is their only appearance among the inscribed West Semitic seals. The doubling of the design is common on Phoenician seals, but rather unusual in Hebrew glyptic (cf. motif C6).[95]

F8 Winged anthropomorphic figure
Under this heading were listed several different beings. Of the two-winged humans shown in profile on West Semitic seals (there is none in frontal view), some are actually to be regarded as four-winged, only one pair being visible. Others, like the two Hebrew examples listed below (F8.1), are truly two-winged. There are only few bipterous examples in West Semitic glyptic, all different, some showing Phoenician and others Mesopotamian traits. But most winged humans, also those whose head and body are depicted in profile, have four visible wings. These fall into two main groups:[96]

1. Male figure in profile with (mostly debased) Egyptian double crown, holding an object, usually a papyrus stalk, in each hand (none is Hebrew).
2. Frontally-rendered woman (see F8.2) of Mesopotamian inspiration, holding a staff in each hand.

F8.1 Two-winged male
Two Hebrew seals depict, as their virtual scenes, Egyptianizing male figures with two wings spread forward. These have no exact counterparts on West Semitic seals, but the ivories abound in parallels. The first seal (**fig. 140**), probably an Israelite eighth-century piece, was found in a late tomb in Carthage; only a drawing was published. The figure is blessing with the right hand and holds a flower(?) in the left. The other seal (**fig. 141**)[97] is of unknown provenance; strictly speaking, the falcon-headed figure should have been listed under F7.2, but I preferred to pair it with the previous seal. The figure is brandishing a mace in its right hand and holds a bent, *ʿankh*-shaped object in its left.[98] The two-winged figure of B 58 is discussed in F8.3 below.

---

95. Another falcon-headed deity is listed under F8.1.

96. There are exceptions and borderline cases like G 90, a seal of which only a drawing was published, where the figure does not wear the Egyptian crown, and the four-winged deity(?) in **fig. 143** (see F8.3). All but the last one function as virtual scenes.

97. Classified as Aramaic by Herr (1978: Ar 52).

98. The deity on the seal of *ṣdyrk* (Ornan, *supra*, p. 62, fig. 35) holds a comparable object.

F8.2 *En face* four-winged woman

Frontality is a way of exhibiting female nudity and indeed, of the *en face* women on inscribed West Semitic stamp seals only one, B 92, is dressed. A mere two examples depict the four-winged, frontally-rendered nude woman holding a staff in each hand, our Hebrew example (**fig. 142**) and the seal of *ykl*ʾ (cf. Ornan, *supra*, p. 59, figs. 20-21). The naked woman recalls the unwinged so-called *'dea nutrix'* known from two Ammonite seals (Avigad 1977a).[99] In these seals the woman is holding her breasts, but in the already-mentioned Ammonite or Aramaic seal B 92 (cf. Bordreuil, *supra*, p. 90 with fig. 24) she is clothed and holds, or rather waves, two floral staffs in a gesture similar to that of the naked, four-winged goddess on **fig. 142**. On the significance of our naked woman see GGG: §§ 196-197; *infra*, p. 276.

F8.3 Winged figures on B 58

In quality, design and subject-matter this scaraboid seal (**fig. 143**) stands out among the inscribed West Semitic stamp seals. In fact the complexity of the composition is more suitable for a cylinder seal.

In the lower half a kind of *aladlammû* ("*lamassu*") with divine headdress (horned mitre with sun disk above), is standing, face to the front, before a tree of Phoenician inspiration; above them a two-winged male deity (actually four-winged, see above and Bordreuil's description) with horned headdress faces a four-winged, beardless anthropomorphic figure, divine or semi-divine and apparently female (cf. GGG: 389; Uehlinger, *infra*, p. 276). I could not find a comparison to the composition as a whole, but some elements have parallels, mainly in Urartian and North Syrian art.[100]

Should the whole be regarded as a single scene? Theoretically the seal could be horizontally divided into two,[101] but from a compositional point of view a single scene seems more likely.

---

99. Cf. Hübner, *supra*, pp. 142-143, who accepts only one as Ammonite, but see our note 29. The female deity on an anepigraphic seal from Lachish is partly clad (see notes 33, 86).

100. Nearly unheard of in Assyria, North Syrian and Urartian representations of the first millennium show a winged deity on a quadruped (Carchemish III: pl. B33b) and on a fantastic quadrupedal being (Merhav 1991: 314-315). Winged, human-headed quadrupeds looking to the front are known outside Assyria in Urartian art (Merhav 1991: 110-111, nos. 75-77) and elsewhere, e.g. on Phoenician ivories from Nimrud and Khorsabad, but the headdress with disk, ultimately of Hittite origin, is usually reserved for deities (Carchemish III: pl. B36b; Merhav 1991: 85, fig. 39; 113, no. 80). Comparisons for a winged deity with one foot on a stylized palm tree and the other on the fantastic being just mentioned are not readily available, but cf. Merhav 1991: 85, no. 39; 90, no. 48 for a winged deity on an animal on a tree.

101. If biregistral, the composition in the bottom register poses no problems (see E1); the pair of winged figures in the top register would remain to be explained.

The layout of the legend is another first; even though several empty spaces were left in the field of this originally uninscribed seal, the owner's name was written in one of them only, seemingly in three lines, each containing three(?) letters.

No wonder that this cluster of enigmas led me at one stage to doubt the authenticity of this seal. A good look at the worn original in the Bibliothèque Nationale took away much of my skepticism, however, but it should be borne in mind that our comparisons pertain only to single elements in the scene (cf. GGG: § 197, esp. p. 389 with fig. 331b).

F9 Mummiform female(?) deity *en face*

Fig. 144 is another seal with unique iconography among West Semitic inscribed stamp seals, the Egyptianizing figure indicating possible Phoenician influence. Unique are also the layout and empty spaces.

F10 Soldier leading captive

Even though the first of its kind was published by Sukenik (1928) over sixty years ago,[102] awareness of the distinct type came late (Lemaire 1986: 313-314). As indicated by their plain backs, all examples that could be examined are well-fired dockets, not bullae.[103] The script of Sukenik's Samarian piece (**fig. 145**), inscribed *lšr*, is indistinct, and Hebrew is only one possibility.[104] The *lmlk* Lemaire made out on the docket he published (1986) is not more instructive. The same word (and probably another one) may be written on an unstratified docket from Ashdod (Ashdod IV: 46, IAA 69-2026; Dothan suggested to read *lmn...* or *lmt...*). Though the Philistine provenance of this piece has to be borne in mind, the remnants of the letters are not unlike Hebrew.

One docket inscribed *lšr* and two possibly reading *lmlk*, all with the same scene and at least two of them perhaps Hebrew, are an interesting phenomenon. Suffice it to say that these could well be official dockets. Did they serve to mark booty, about to enter the exchequer? The scene, a local interpretation of an Assyrian subject (it has no exact Assyrian parallels),[105] is certainly suitable.

F11 'Investiture'

The two *šrhʿr* bullae picture an official in front of the king in an Assyrianizing style (**fig. 146**; cf. Ornan, *supra*, p. 71 with fig. 66), and since the

---

102. He bought the stamped clay lump from children in Samaria.

103. An Aramaic docket is mentioned by Lemaire, *loc. cit.*, and a seemingly anepigraphic impression was found at Sheikh Zuweyid (Anthedon: 11, pl. 30:8).

104. The present whereabouts of the original are unknown. In 1991 it could not be located in the Institute of Archaeology of the Hebrew University.

105. Christoph Uehlinger's observation; cf. GGG: § 156.

legend names the Governor of the City, probably of Jerusalem, the scene may well have been intended to illustrate the delegation of authority to the official in question and to emphasize his loyalty to the crown (GGG: 409 with reference to G. Barkay's interpretation).

G Celestial bodies

Celestial bodies are even more scarce on Hebrew seals than human figures, and contrary to the latter they appear only rarely on the anepigraphic face of bifacial seals (the small sample may be misleading in this respect, however). The emergence and prominence of astral symbols, and of the moon in particular, in late-eighth- and seventh-century Judah (GGG: §§ 172-188) may find another corroboration: The star and the crescent, dated in Judah to the seventh century (see below), are never in our small sample of inscribed Hebrew seals accompanied by the winged sun,[106] an association known from Aramaic and Moabite seals (e.g. B 63, 64, 98). In the late ninth and eighth centuries this combination was not expected in Israel, probably also Judah, because of the supremacy of the sun, mostly rendered in Egypto-Phoenician style (GGG: §§ 148-153, 160-162). But it should be asked if seals with archaizing 'lapidary' script were not still being cut in seventh-century Judah, and if Phoenician iconographic inspiration and solar symbolism did not perpetuate side by side with the new fashion.

G1 Sun

G1.1 Sun disk

In Hebrew seals with Phoenician iconography the Egyptian sun disk was not avoided outright, but its rarity speaks for itself. Elaborately crowned (compare Perrot & Chipiez 1885: fig. 188), it serves as a virtual scene in the seal of *ʾšnʾ ʿbd ʾḥz* (**fig. 147**). What looks like cow's horns and a disk, but may be a Phoenician misrepresentation of the Egyptian double crown, can be seen on the head of the 'sun child' in another courtier's seal (**fig. 148**).

G1.2 Winged sun

With the notable exception of the *lmlk* stamps (**fig. 149**),[107] the winged sun is rare on Hebrew seals, and very common elsewhere. It could be argued that this motif was reserved for royalty and government, but the four-winged *lmlk* scarab, another solar motif (**fig. 89**), quite frequent on Hebrew personal seals, contradicts this. If the winged sun was an unwelcome motif in Hebrew glyptic, as were other celestial bodies, why was it chosen to grace an official stamp? An important difference between the *lmlk* stamps and most other

106. The crescent or star are paired with the rhomb, though not with one another, in a few Hebrew seals; see below.

107. Cf. Lemaire 1981: esp. 57*; Parayre 1990a: nos. 103-105, pl. 13, and *supra* p. 43, fig. 10.

inscribed seals is in the impersonality of the former, but whether this quality could make the association with a heavenly body more permissible is far from clear.

When not a central motif, the most obvious place for the winged sun is in the upper part of the field (**fig. 150**).[108] Two Hebrew seals (**figs. 151, 152**) have a winged sun in the bottom register, however (the former has another, different one, in the top register).[109, 110] Two seals (**fig. 152** and VSE 168),[111] have the winged sun associated with a winged uraeus, a being from Yahweh's sphere (see motif B1). Even if, as stands to reason, this pairing is not incidental, it conveys an exception.

Parayre (1990a: 288-289, 291-292; cf. *supra*, pp. 30-32) classified as Egyptianizing, or Phoenician, all the above winged disks except the *lmlk* examples; the latter, with a doubly curved upper line and up-curving tips, is attributed to Anatolian prototypes (see note 107).[112] If accurate, and if Phoenician inspiration indeed equals North Israelite origin and eighth-century date (see above, section I.4), Parayre's observation would fit well the chronology of the seals, most, if not all of which seem to date by epigraphy to that century.

G2 Moon

Like the depiction of the deity with lunar connotations (subject F6), the new moon is exceedingly rare in Hebrew seals, in contrast to its prominence on uninscribed and inscribed non-Hebrew examples (Keel 1977: 284-296; Uehlinger 1990; GGG: §§ 185-188). It is almost as if only the boldest dared to have a crescent displayed next to their name. Nearly giving the impression of being disguised it appears, together with a rhomb, on two Hebrew seals (**fig. 153** and HD 70), and possibly frames the legend of another (**fig. 154**).[113,114] Rendered as a boat it can be seen in **fig. 155**, and the crescent

---

108. Another seal with this motif, the seal of *nʿmʾl pʾrt*, was considered Hebrew by Lemaire (1985b: 38-41; cf. *supra*, p. 18 with note 20).

109. While the man on the reverse is rendered in an Assyrianizing style, the top, and perhaps the bottom sun on this seal, the seal of *šbnyw ʿbd ʿzyw*, is Egyptianizing. This mixture is not unexpected from the second third of the eighth century onwards.

110. This arrangement can be seen in non-Hebrew seals too (e.g. B 93), though it is not very common outside *tête bêche* and similar designs.

111. And B 16, if Lemaire (1985b: 40) is right in attributing it to Israel.

112. See also Parayre's discussion of her fig. 46, a jar-handle impression from En Gedi.

113. The seal's border, together with the stalks of the two flowers supporting the falcon-headed deities form a crescentic space, into which the owner's name was inserted.

114. The Aramaic seal of *šmšʿzr ʿbdšhr*, with crescent and star, has a legend displaying a "surprisingly great similarity to the formal cursive hand of the Hebrew seals" (Avigad 1986b: 53; see Bordreuil, *supra*, pp. 98 with fig. 37).

hovers near the head of the enthroned deity in **fig. 156** (see F6 for the latter two).[115]

The crescent on a pole or stand is not represented in Hebrew seals (it is also very rare in seals with other scripts[116]), but an anepigraphic City of David bulla (Barkay 1991: 38; GGG: fig. 297a) has it as virtual scene.

Save one, our seals are straightforward late First Temple period Judaean pieces. As to **fig. 154**, it was dated by Avigad and by Hestrin & Dayagi-Mendels (cf. HD 39) to the eighth century, and by Herr (1978: He 85) to the late eighth. Admittedly, there is no proof that the artist who made this seal intended to produce a crescentic shape, and even if he did, his inspiration belongs to a different world: The crescent, perhaps doubling as a boat, could have been carrying the child on the flower, in a way comparable to its depiction on Phoenician metal bowls (Moscati 1968: fig. 23).

G3 Star

The winged female figure in **fig. 157** holds staffs, or sceptres, crowned with stars, similar to the standards that flank the scene in Ornan, *supra*, p. 67, fig. 59. In **fig. 158** the star is paired with a rhomb on the anepigraphic reverse. Together with the central figure, an ibex (see subject D2), this is the only Hebrew scene of its kind among many inscribed 'Syro-Transjordanian' and anepigraphic occurrences.

G4 Rhomb

Of an uncertain meaning (Uehlinger 1990: 328; Black & Green 1992: 153; Bordreuil, *supra*, p. 96 note 28), the rhomb is listed in this section for its association with heavenly bodies, evident in many seals. In Hebrew glyptic it is known on three seals (**figs. 153, 158** and HD 70), always paired with a crescent or star.[117]

---

115. The crescent adorns the upper part of the field on several seals depicting worshippers, with script akin to Hebrew, that are generally regarded as Moabite (Ornan, *supra*, pp. 66-67, figs. 48, 56 [for which see above, subject F5 with note 88], 69).

116. One could assume this rarity to be an 'optical illusion', inscribed seals in hardstone showing the anthropomorphic god within his crescent instead (cf. Keel 1990c). But Ornan (*supra*, figs. 23-26, 30-33) claimed convincingly that these hardstone seals belonged to the Aramaean population of Mesopotamia or to Mesopotamians in the West. The near-absence of the crescent on a pole from name seals of the western Near East is yet to be explained.

117. Perhaps it appears also on the seal of *gdyhw*... (Avigad 1989a: no. 2).

145

146

147

148

149

150

151

152

153

154

155

156

157

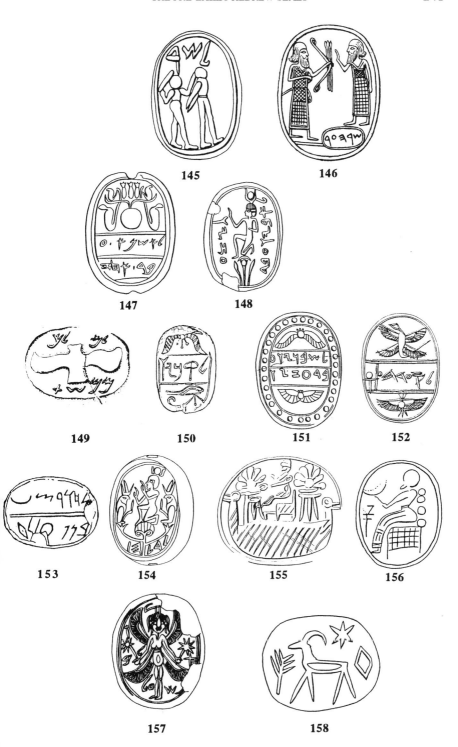

158

H Tasteful recent acquisitions

Certain recently acquired,[118] epigraphically and onomastically correct seals share several technical and iconographical traits. Crisply cut, often in attractive stones, they are executed in a well-balanced and -spaced, restrained, primarily linear style. Inscribed in an elegant, mostly seventh-century Judahite hand, a relatively large proportion of these masterpieces belongs to daughters, sons and stewards of kings, so far unnamed. If genuine, the mint condition of these pieces is surprising, and if not, why did the artist not 'age' them?

Not all these seals are iconic, but many of those which are have the longitudinal triregistral layout in common, usually of the picture-text-text type (**pl. II:8-10**). Because of the prominence of the motif, the top register may occupy up to half the field, sometimes more. The number of register dividers varies, as do the motifs, and most of the latter are uncomplicated, not unanticipated, and beautiful.

Two motifs, the boat and the lyre (**pl. II:12, 13**), are more complex and less expected, in fact unparalleled.[119] Both seals seem to have appeared on the market in the seventies, and it could be that while simpler pieces continue to reach collections, such complex seals ceased to turn up.

Two seals (**pl. II:10, 11**) are the only West Semitic examples in which the bilinear border is partly augmented with an additional line, gracefully curving inwards and terminating in dots.[120]

Several of the aniconic seals of this group, mostly latitudinal and biregistral, stand out in their minute size, calligraphy (almost micrography) or innovatively-aesthetic, though generally not unexpected register dividers (e.g. **figs. 41, 45**). Some contain several small dots in the field, possibly overdoing (in good taste) a device, usually of larger size, occurring in moderation on unquestionably authentic pieces.

Another group, a successor to or competitor of the 'tasteful group' if my doubts about its authenticity turn out to be founded, may be labelled the 'nouveaux riches' group. Characterized by an inferior taste, it tends to employ fancy stones and abounds with pomegranates. Several of the specimens sport a beaded, coin-like border, a possible misinterpretation of the dotted border (cf. p. 206). Some of its space-fillers and register dividers are strikingly remi-

---

118. Starting in the seventies?

119. "Except for its conventional shape, every aspect of this seal [the seal of Maʿadanah] is unfamiliar: its decoration, the name of its female owner, and her title. Neither do I remember having met with the exact colour of the stone among the seals known to me. ...the lyre of our seal is the only one which stands by itself as a separate motif or emblem. In all the other instances cited above it is held by a musician" (Avigad 1978d: 146, 150). Sharing the faith of several scholars in the authenticity of the seal, the Bank of Israel chose this very lyre to adorn the half-shekel coin.

120. Trilinear register dividers are well-known, however, see **fig. 34**.

niscent of those found in Avigad's bullae, not always, it seems, correctly understood. This group shares with the tasteful group the penchant for names with titles.

Without a reliable authenticity test (see below, pp. 245-246) a conclusion that the seals of these two groups are fakes would be a mistake. I think it is impossible to pronounce them authentic either. It is my wish to emphasize here the doubt shrouding many of these pieces.

III. CONCLUSIONS

1. Epigraphy and chronology

Although not concerned with epigraphy, this study is dependent on its chronological consequences. In voicing skepticism about the epigraphical dating of seals I am aware that, in a certain context, this could be an easy and unfair way of dealing with the learning and labour invested by so many scholars. Yet, the clear cases notwithstanding, should not more seals be dated in a general way to the eighth to seventh centuries than was hitherto the practice? It is well-known that seal legends are brief, and that the chronologically-diagnostic letters are limited in number (see above, pp. 198-199).

2. Aniconic vs. iconic seals; the selection of motifs

The shrinking production of iconic seals in the last pre-exilic century is evident in Avigad's and the City of David bullae, and relating this to *Weltanschauung* seems obvious. True, the archaeological finds attest to increasing literacy since the eighth century, and the predominance of aniconic seals could be ascribed to this development (e.g. Naveh 1982: 71): in such a cultural climate seal pictures became less necessary from the practical point of view. They remained appreciated for other reasons, however. The avoidance of figurative seals, with certain motifs shunned more than others, seems to be of ideological origin, then. How was the situation before, say, 850 BC? Obviously people had nothing against the written personal name, and yet they had only anepigraphic, or iconic seals in Israel and elsewhere in Iron I and the early part of Iron II. This is one of the testimonies to the limited spread of writing, that was confined to a scribal élite at that time. There was almost certainly an inscribed royal seal in Israel and its neighbours, though none had been found. Other people could not have had blank seals!

Most jar-handle impressions, mainly on *lmlk*-type jars, are aniconic (Garfinkel 1984), and only a handful combine picture with text (**figs. 50, 79, 89, 149, pl. I:3**).

As to the iconographic differences between Israel and Judah, these have to be compared for the eighth century, when the two kingdoms existed side by side. Let me just review the four seals of Judaean royal stewards (**figs. 28 + 223, 34, 88, 37**; cf. Uehlinger, *infra*, p. 285): one is of mixed Syro-Mesopotamian and Phoenician iconography and two of straightforward Phoenician influence; the fourth and latest is aniconic. This indicates that eighth-century Judah did share Israel's taste for things Phoenician.

Motifs occurring chiefly in Hebrew glyptic include the four-winged uraeus, fish, rooster and grazing she-deer. Most vegetal register dividers, and the use of the branch and bird as space fillers are also characteristically Hebrew. The trunkless palmette is to be found almost exclusively on Hebrew seals. Many of these motifs and features seem, at least intuitively, to be Judaean, although this observation may be linked with the belief that most Phoenician-inspired Hebrew seals are North Israelite.

Phoenician inspiration on Hebrew glyptic is often considered an eighth-century Israelite phenomenon. But that seals with Phoenician palmettes (motif A1.4) were widespread in Judah in the last pre-exilic decades is clear from Avigad's bullae, though it could be argued that this motif became universal by then. Seals like **figs. 62** and **88** could date to, say, the early seventh century by their epigraphy. And does not the Egypto-Phoenician falcon in **fig. 98** (motif C1) come from the hoard of bullae dated c. 600 BC? Should all these be considered heirlooms or originally-anepigraphic seals inscribed later?

Even though it seems not to have eliminated Phoenician influence and its solar emphasis (cf. GGG: §§ 203-204 for Judah, and Hübner, *supra*, pp. 139-141 for Ammon), a new and powerful astral symbolism, of Aramaean origin, entered Judah when the rest of the country came under Assyria's domination (GGG: chapter VIII). In glyptic this symbolism finds its main expression in anepigraphic seals. Had we at our disposal the inscribed Judean seals alone, this symbolism would have been virtually invisible, whereas on Aramaic and Transjordanian inscribed seals the astral trend is eye-catching.

The 'unwelcome' motifs – human figures, astral symbols and certain animals – were less shunned in Hebrew glyptic when on their own, that is on the anepigraphic face of bifacial seals (**figs. 155, 156, 158**), and on uninscribed seals), as if they were considered permissible if not in direct juxtaposition with the name of the owner. This implies that even in the eighth century, at least the human image and celestial bodies were not widespread on inscribed seals. But in the seventh, in Judah, they must have been even less popular. Seals with human figures constitute about 4% of all Hebrew examples, while in Avigad's bullae, considered to date about 600 BC, there are only two out of about 200, c. 1%. And in the City of David hoard of some 50 bullae there is none. The same holds true for celestial bodies.

To visualize an abrupt drop in iconic seals during the reign of Josiah might prove as futile as Aharoni's dating, based on the biblical narrative, of the destruction of the shrine at Arad to that king's reign in contradiction to the stratigraphy of the site. The image ban could not, even not by royal decree, have penetrated instantly all strata of society (cf. GGG: §§ 207-208, 215; and see now Uehlinger, *infra*, pp. 278-288). The progress of the aniconic trend among the Hebrews may have reflected, with an indigenous, possibly more pronounced flavour in Judah, a general Near Eastern tendency (cf. Ornan, *supra*). This trend may be perceived as an ongoing process, that did not reach its peak until exilic times, and as a matter of fact was never total; it is in none than the seventh century that the image of a deity is found on Hebrew seals. But certain combinations, such as a worshipper before a deity, may have been totally out of bounds (cf. Uehlinger, *infra*, pp. 263-265).[121] By and large the 'puritan' Hebrew iconography is almost reminiscent of the Muslim image ban; vegetal motifs clearly predominate, especially so when we move towards the late seventh century (cf. GGG: § 208).

3. Legally and illicitly excavated seals; forgeries

The proportion of demonstrably genuine Hebrew seals rose dramatically to nearly half the total of c. 700 with the discovery of the City of David and Avigad bullae.[122] But the rest, and most other West Semitic personal seals, are of unknown provenance. With the astonishing supply of seals to an ever-demanding market, one cannot help wondering, Are they really all originals, clandestinely excavated, or do they include a proportion of cunningly crafted flawless fakes? One school of thought maintains: "If the material, shape, technique, iconography, epigraphy and names pass our test, the seal must be genuine." André Lemaire put it differently in our conference: "You may be able to prove a seal to be a fake; you cannot prove its genuineness", or if I am permitted a paraphrase, "Any seal is presumed genuine until proven false." The underlying feeling is indeed a grave one: If most inscribed stamp seals are in doubt, what is left for us to do? But can the doubt hanging over a great proportion of the unprovenanced seals be sublimated forever? Gifted craftsmen continue to be born, and the materials and tools at their disposal are no worse than those used by the ancients. Neither is the ability to study authentic pieces and to follow scholarly publications reserved for academics alone. Endless variations on the themes found, say, in Avigad's hoard of bullae are possible, and it may well be that the effects are felt in the collections and

121. But see on the seal of *šlm* in note 86.

122. There is no reason to doubt the genuineness of the latter in spite their illegal origin. Concerning their authenticity, jar-handle impressions belong to a similar category, though who can guarantee against recently carved pieces?

museums for some years. Surely forgers stumble, but is it realistic to expect that all forgers always do?

Now that several bullae of biblical personalities have been discovered (Avigad 1986a, 1987b; Schneider 1988, 1991), we may witness a trickle of similar seals to the market.

Fakes may be 'too good' too. The following is quoted from the chapter on the faking of classical gems in Rome in the 18th and early 19th centuries (Jones 1990: 147, by Judy Rudoe):

> "The engravers who worked for dealers like Jenkins were often very talented; both the English gem-engraver Nathaniel Marchant, and the Italian engraver Benedetto Pistrucci were known to have made convincing imitations of antique gems which were sold as ancient. Neoclassical work, however, tended to follow the conventions of the time in restrained, well-spaced and sometimes sentimental compositions. It also responded to the specific demands of collectors of the period. Discussions by authors like Maffei, ... of ancient signatures stimulated a strong demand for signed pieces, while Lippert's Daktiliothek (1767), a catalogue accompanied by plaster casts, made collection by subject fashionable. As a result, Neoclassical fake gems frequently feature subject-matter unknown to the classical repertoire and bear signatures otherwise known only from ancient literature."

If classical gems with their hard stones and intricate subject-matter could be so artfully reproduced, then West Semitic seals, mostly in soft stone and with simpler iconography must be, if I may be allowed an exaggeration, a *Kinderspiel* for a talented forger. Who can tell which of the unprovenanced seals, 'tasteful' or otherwise, are fakes and which are not? On the other hand, it is well known that controlled excavations yield from time to time unusual finds that, if acquired on the antiquities market, would raise suspicion.

It is not by accident that the question of forgeries is dealt with at length in the concluding section of this paper; willing or not, our work is hinging on this question. And until unprovenanced seals can be subjected to a reliable authenticity test (Hübner 1989b: 220-221; cf. *supra*, pp. 132-133, and Uehlinger, *infra*, pp. 270-271) a sizeable measure of doubt will remain. The results of many glyptic studies, the present one not excluded, must be judged in this light.

1

2

3

4

5

6

7

8

9

10

11

12

13

CHECKLIST OF SEALS MENTIONED

The inscribed seals in the Bibliothèque Nationale, Cabinet des Médailles, are listed according to their Bordreuil numbers.

SEAL	PROVENANCE	COLLECTION	REFERENCE	FIG./PL.
ʾbyw	?	ex Reifenberg, Jerusalem	HD 36	17
ʾbyw ʿbd ʿzyw	?	BN	B 40	148
ʾdnyhw šmʿ	?	Hecht H-2031	Avigad 1989b: 93	127
ʾḥyqm mtn	?	Hecht H-1744	Avigad 1979: 123	95
ʾḥmlk smk	Lachish	IAA 36.1829	HD 48	11, 28, 87
ʾlyhw yqmyhw	Gezer?	IAA 74-1888	Herr 1978: He 154	44
ʾlyšb bn ʾšyhw	Arad	IAA 67-663	HD 11	4
ʾlyšb bn šʿl	?	?	Bordreuil & Lemaire 1976: no. 17	37
ʾlqnh	?	?	Avigad 1987a: fig. 4	112
ʾlšmʿ bn gdlyhw	?	?	D 100	103, 136, 155
ʾlšmʿ bn smkyhw	Jerusalem	IAA 84-139	Shiloh & Tarler 1986: 203 top right	47
ʾlšmʿ bn hmlk	?	ex Clark, Jerusalem	G 65	77
ʾmryhw bn yhwʾb	?	IMJ 76.22.2313	A 31	42
ʾnyhw bn myrb	?	?	Avigad 1982	pl. II:12
ʾprh bn yhwšʿ	? (bulla)	Jerusalem, Sasson	A 20	34, 60
ʾryhw	?	Hecht H-1490	Herr 1978: He 79	108
ʾryhw ʿzryhw	En Gedi	IAA 67-1330	Herr 1978: He 27	1
ʾšyhw mšmš	?	IAA I.8915	-	137, 156, pl. I:7
ʾšnʾ	?	IMJ 73.19.27	HD 40	131
ʾšnʾ ʿbd ʾḥz	?	lost?	Bordreuil 1985: 23	29, 73, 147
blth	?	Péronne Municipality	Boardman 1971: no. 2	88, 126
bsy	?	IMJ 73.19.16	HD 38	16, 31, 74, 107
brkyhw bn nryhw hspr	? (bulla)	IMJ 76.22.2299	A 9	14
gʾl bn šʿl	?	BN	B 44	6, 48, 142, 157
gdyhw bn hmlk	?	IMJ 85.15.22	Bordreuil & Lemaire 1979: no. 1	45
dlh	?	IMJ 68.35.197	HD 39	62, 100, 130, 139, 154

SEAL	PROVENANCE	COLLECTION	REFERENCE	FIG./PL.
dlyhw bn gmlyhw	?	Hecht REH-027	Avigad 1979: 122	pl. II:10
dršyhw ḥml	?	Tel Aviv, Braun	VSE 338	38
hwdyhw mtnyhw	?	?	Bordreuil & Lemaire 1976: no. 9	27
hwšʿyhw ḥlṣyhw	?	IMJ 76.22.2315 etc.	A 47	56
hwšʿyhw bn šlmyhw	?	IMJ 71.46.88	HD 53	35
zkr hwšʿ	?	BM 48487	G 10	121, pl. I:6
zkr ʿzr	?	BN	B 42	114
zkryw khn dʾr	?	IMJ 85.15.20	Herr 1978: He 57	76
ḥwrṣ bn pqll	?	BN	B 46	153
ḥlqyhw bn pdy(?)	?	Private, France	Lemaire 1986: no. 4	53, 135
ḥmyʾhl bt mnḥm	Jerusalem	IAA 75-466	HD 34	96
ḥmlk	?	IAA J.895	Herr 1978: He 146	7, 63, 105, 125
ḥmn	Megiddo	IAA 34.1490	HD 42	92, 120
ḥnh	?	Oxford, Ashmolean, Gibson loan	Buchanan & Moorey 1988: no. 300	123
ḥnnyhw ʾmt	?	Harvard Semitic Museum	Albright Institute brochure	90, 106
ḥnnyhw bn ʿzryhw	?	Berlin, VA 32	G 78	52, 70
y…	?	BN	B 58	124, 143
yʾznyhw ʿbd hmlk	Naṣbeh	IAA 32.2525	HD 5	19, 102
yhwzrḥ bn ḥlqyhw	? (bulla)	IMJ 74.16.45	HD 4	22
ywʾbʾ/ʾbyw	Carthage	?	G 97	140
yqmyhw	?	IAA J.894	HD 44	122, 129
yqmyhw bn nḥm	? (bulla)	Jerusalem, Sasson	A 77	20, 133
yrm zmryhw	?	Oxford, Ashmolean, 1889.433	Buchanan & Moorey 1988: no. 297	71
yšʿyhw bn ḥml	? (bulla)	IMJ 76.22.2307	A 83	49
mḥsʾ	?	private, California	Zuckerman 1987: pl. 8	144
mḥsyhw nby	?	Hecht H-2030	Avigad 1989b: 91	116
mky yqmyh	?	IMJ 71.46.103	HD 84	33
lmlk... (winged sun)	Judaean, numerous			21, 149
lmlk... (beetle)	Judaean, numerous			89

SEAL	PROVENANCE	COLLECTION	REFERENCE	FIG./PL.
mlkyhw ḥlq	? (bulla)	IMJ 76.22.2324	A 98	94
mlkrm	?	Private, France	Herr 1978: Ph 8	61, pl. I:4
mnr	?	?	Bordreuil & Lemaire 1982: no. 15	99, pl. I:5
mnšh mlkyhw	?	?	Bordreuil & Lemaire 1982: no. 5	46, 65
mnšh bn hmlk	?	?	Avigad 1987a: fig. 7	85
mʿdnh bt hmlk	?	IMJ 80.16.57	Avigad 1978d	pl. II:13
mtn	?	?	Bordreuil & Lemaire 1976: no. 16	128
mtn bn plṭyhw	? (bulla)	Jerusalem, Sasson	A 116	54
nmšr bn šʿl	? (bulla)	Jerusalem, Sasson	A 123	36
nryhw mtn	?	?	Bordreuil & Lemaire 1982: no. 2	pl. II:8
nryhw bn hmlk	?	private, France	Avigad 1987a: fig. 8	57, pl. I:2
ntbyhw nʿr mtn	?	Hecht REH-015	Avigad 1981: no. 1	41
ntnyhw bn ʿbdyhw	?	BN	B 49	30, 117
sʿdh	?	?	Avigad 1989b: 91	78, 152
ʿzʾ bn ḥṣ	?	Jerusalem, HU, 4000	Herr 1978: He 125	72, 82, 97, 138
ʿzr	?	Hecht REH-044	Avigad 1979: 126	10
ʿzryw hgbh	?	London, Moussaieff?	Herr 1978: He 127	93
ʿzrqm bn prpr	? (bulla)	Jerusalem, Sasson	A 138	43
ʿmdyw	Dan	Jerusalem, HUC	Biran 1988	5
ʿrb nby	?	Jerusalem, Spaer	Avigad 1981: no. 3	50, 101
ʿšyhw bn ḥwyhw	?	?	Bordreuil & Lemaire 1976: no. 7	91
ʿšyw bn ywqm	?	BM 48494	Herr 1978: He 131	32, pl. I:1
ʿšnʾl	?	BM 48489	Millard 1991: 138	84, 110
pdh	?	London, Moussaieff	Herr 1978: Ar 52	141
pdyhw špl	?	?	Avigad 1989b: 94	pl. II:9
pdyhw bn hmlk	?	Hecht H-1984	Avigad 1992b	pl. II:11
plʾyhw mttyhw	?	IMJ 85.15.26	Avigad 1980b	68
plṭh	Jerusalem	IAA 80-1315	Barkay 1986: 34	8, 58
plṭyhw bn hwšʿyhw	? (bulla)	?	A 147	40

SEAL	PROVENANCE	COLLECTION	REFERENCE	FIG./PL.
pqḥ	?	Berlin, VA 35	G 137	134
pšḥr	?	?	Avigad 1989b: 95	61, 67
pšḥr bn mnḥm	? (bulla)	IMJ 76.22.2328	A 152	2
ṣpn nryhw	?	?	Bordreuil & Lemaire 1976: no. 2	59, 113, 158
qnyw	?	Berlin, VA 2830	Herr 1978: He 60	150
šbnyhw	?	ex Clark, Jerusalem	G 77	24, 55
šbnyw/šbnyw ʿbd ʿzyw	?	Paris, Louvre, AO 6216	B 41	13, 23, 132, 151
šbʿ yḥmlyhw	?	Jerusalem, Spaer	Avigad 1975b: no. 14	39
šḥr bn gdy	? (bulla)	IMJ 76.22.2339	A 25	3, 51
šḥr bn gdyhw	? (bulla)	IMJ 76.22.2317 etc.	A 24	69
šmʿ ʿbd yrbʿm	Megiddo	lost	HD 3	109
šmʿyhw…	? (bulla)	Jerusalem, Sasson	A 163	26
šmʿyhw bn ʿzryhw	?	ex de Vogüé, Paris	G 31	118
šmr…	Judeideh	?	G 56	9, 83
špṭ	?	IMJ 71.70.220	HD 37	12, 25
špṭyhw ʿšyhw	Lachish	IAA 38.123	HD 50	18, 75
šr	Samaria?	?	Sukenik 1928	145
šrhʿr	? (bulla)	Jerusalem, Sasson	A 10	146
…yhw bn ʿmlyhw	?	Hecht H-1741	Avigad 1979: 121	104
… bn gdyhw	? (bulla)	Jerusalem, Sasson	A 169	15, 115
… ṣpnyhw	Lachish	BM, no number	Lachish III: pl. 47	79, pl. I:3
…ḥm(?) ….bʿ	? (bulla)	Jerusalem, Sasson	A 202	98
Four-winged beetle	Samaria	IAA 33.3143, 8, 9	Samaria-Sebaste 3: pl. 15	86
Four-winged uraeus	? (bulla)	IMJ 76.22.2345	A 201	64, 80
Horse	Judaean, several		Barkay 1992a: 127, fig. 2A	119
Lion and ibex	Ramat Raḥel	IAA 64-1783	Ramat Raḥel II: pl. 40:7	111
Rosette	Judaean, numerous			66

LIST OF FIGURES

NO.	SEAL	SOURCE
47.	*ʾlšmʿ bn smkyhw*	Shiloh & Tarler 1986: 203
48.	*gʾl bn šʿl*	Ornan, *supra*, fig. 20
49.	*yšʿyhw bn ḥml*	A 83
50.	*ʿrb nby*	Avigad 1981: no. 3
51.	*šḥr bn gdy*	A 25
52.	*ḥnnyhw bn ʿzryhw*	D 24
53.	*ḥlqyhw bn pdy*(?)	Schroer 1987b: fig. 26
54.	*mtn bn pltyhw*	A 116
55.	*šbnyhw*	G 77
56.	*hwšʿyhw ḥlṣyhw*	A 47
57.	*nryhw bn hmlk*	drawing Noga Z'evi
58.	*plṭh*	Barkay 1986: 34
59.	*ṣpn nryhw*	GGG: fig. 317a
60.	*ʾprḥ bn yhwšʿ*	A 20
61.	*pšḥr*	drawing Noga Z'evi
62.	*dlh*	GGG: fig. 241c
63.	*ḥmlk*	Sukenik 1942a: fig. A2
64.	Four-winged uraeus	A 201
65.	*mnšh mlkyhw*	drawing Noga Z'evi
66.	Judaean rosette	Bliss & Macalister 1902: pl. 56:42
67.	*pšḥr*	drawing Noga Z'evi
68.	*plʾyhw mttyhw*	Avigad 1980
69.	*šḥr bn gdyhw*	A 24
70.	*ḥnnyhw bn ʿzryhw*	D 24
71.	*yrm zmryhw*	ESE I: 11
72.	*ʿzʾ bn ḥts*	drawing Noga Z'evi
73.	*ʾšnʾ ʿbd ʾḥz*	Sukenik 1941: 17
74.	*bsy*	drawing Noga Z'evi
75.	*špṭyhw ʿšyhw*	Keel 1977: fig. 85
76.	*zkryw khn dʾr*	Keel 1977: fig. 87
77.	*ʾlšmʿ bn hmlk*	drawing Noga Z'evi
78.	*sʿdh*	drawing Noga Z'evi
79.	... *ṣpnyhw*	drawing Hildi Keel-Leu
80.	Four-winged uraeus	A 201
81.	*mlkrm*	Keel 1977: fig. 95
82.	*ʿzʾ bn ḥts*	drawing Noga Z'evi
83.	*šmr...*	Bliss & Macalister 1902: fig. 45
84.	*ʿšnʾl*	drawing Hildi Keel-Leu
85.	*mnšh bn hmlk*	drawing Noga Z'evi
86.	Four-winged beetle	Samaria-Sebaste 3: pl. 15:29
87.	*ʾḥmlk smk*	Lachish III: pl. 45:167
88.	*blth*	G 63
89.	*lmlk* (beetle)	Naveh 1982: fig. 63
90.	*ḥnnyhw ʾmt*	Albright Institute brochure
91.	*ʿšyhw bn ḥwyhw*	drawing Noga Z'evi
92.	*ḥmn*	Sukenik 1942a: fig. A1
93.	*ʿzryw hgbh*	OLB 1: fig. 93
94.	*mlkyhw ḥlq*	A 98

NO.	SEAL	SOURCE
95.	*ʾḥyqm mtn*	drawing Noga Z'evi
96.	*ḥmyʾhl bt mnḥm*	drawing Noga Z'evi
97.	*ʿzʾ bn ḥts*	drawing Noga Z'evi
98.	*...ḥm*(?) *....bʿ*	drawing Noga Z'evi
99.	*mnr*	Bordreuil & Lemaire 1982: 15
100.	*dlh*	GGG: fig. 241c
101.	*ʿrb nby*	Avigad 1981: no. 3
102.	*yʾznyhw ʿbd hmlk*	D 69
103.	*ʾlšmʿ bn gdlyhw*	GGG: fig. 306a
104.	*...yhw bn ʿmlyhw*	drawing Noga Z'evi
105.	*ḥmlk*	Sukenik 1942a: fig. A2
106.	*ḥnnyhw ʾmt*	Albright Institute brochure
107.	*bsy*	drawing Noga Z'evi
108.	*ʾryhw*	drawing Noga Z'evi
109.	*šmʿ ʿbd yrbʿm*	ESE II: 140
110.	*ʿšnʾl*	drawing Hildi Keel-Leu
111.	Lion and ibex	drawing Noga Z'evi
112.	*ʾlqnh*	drawing Noga Z'evi
113.	*ṣpn nryhw*	GGG: fig. 317a
114.	*zkrʿzr*	G 36
115.	*... bn gdyhw*	A 169
116.	*mḥsyhw nby*	drawing Noga Z'evi
117.	*ntnyhw bn ʿbdyhw*	D 32
118.	*šmʿyhw bn ʿzryhw*	de Vogüé 1868: no. 34
119.	Horse	Bliss & Macalister 1902: pl. 56:33
120.	*ḥmn*	Sukenik 1942a: fig. A1
121.	*zkr hwšʿ*	Levy 1869: pl. 3:9
122.	*yqmyhw*	drawing Noga Z'evi
123.	*ḥnh*	GGG: fig. 249
124.	*y...*	Ornan, *supra*, fig. 22
125.	*ḥmlk*	Sukenik 1942a: fig. A2
126.	*blth*	G 63
127.	*ʾdnyhw šmʿ*	drawing Noga Z'evi
128.	*mtn*	drawing Noga Z'evi
129.	*yqmyhw*	drawing Noga Z'evi
130.	*dlh*	GGG: fig. 241c
131.	*ʾšnʾ*	drawing Noga Z'evi
132.	*šbnyw*	GGG: fig. 263a
133.	*yqmyhw bn nḥm*	A 77
134.	*pqḥ*	GGG: fig. 263c
135.	*ḥlqyhw bn pdy*(?)	Schroer 1987b: fig. 26
136.	*ʾlšmʿ bn gdlyhw*	GGG: fig. 306a
137.	*ʾšyhw mšmš*	GGG: fig. 305c
138.	*ʿzʾ bn ḥts*	drawing Noga Z'evi
139.	*dlh*	GGG: fig. 241c
140.	*ywʾb/ʾbyw*	Berger 1907
141.	*pdh*	drawing Noga Z'evi
142.	*gʾl bn šʿl*	Ornan, *supra*, fig. 20

NO.	SEAL	SOURCE
143.	*y...*	Ornan, *supra*, fig. 22
144.	*mḥsʾ*	drawing Noga Z'evi
145.	*šr*	drawing Noga Z'evi
146.	*šrhʿr*	A 10
147.	*ʾšnʾ ʿbd ʾḥz*	Sukenik 1941: 17
148.	*ʾbyw ʿbd ʿzyw*	GGG: fig. 241b
149.	*lmlk* (winged sun)	Naveh 1982: fig. 63
150.	*qnyw*	Welten 1977c: 301
151.	*šbnyw ʿbd ʿzyw*	GGG: fig. 263b
152.	*sʿdh*	drawing Noga Z'evi
153.	*ḥwrṣ bn pqll*	D 22
154.	*dlh*	GGG: fig. 241c
155.	*ʾlšmʿ bn gdlyhw*	GGG: fig. 306a
156.	*ʾšyhw mšmš*	GGG: fig. 305c
157.	*gʾl bn šʿl*	Ornan, *supra*, fig. 20
158.	*ṣpn nryhw*	drawing Noga Z'evi

LIST OF PHOTOGRAPHS IN PLS. I-II

NO.	SEAL	SOURCE
1.	*ʿšyw bn ywqm*	Trustees of the British Museum, photographs B. Sass
2.	*nryhw bn hmlk*	Private collection, France, photograph B. Sass
3.	*... ṣpnyhw*	Trustees of the British Museum
4.	*mlkrm*	Private collection, France, photograph B. Sass
5.	*mnr* (back)	A. Lemaire, photograph J. Dufour
6.	*zkr hwšʿ*	Trustees of the British Museum
7.	*ʾšyhw mšmš*	IAA, photographs S.J. Schweig and B. Sass
8.	*nryhw mtn*	A. Lemaire
9.	*pdyhw špl*	from Avigad 1989a: 94
10.	*dlyhw bn gmlyhw*	Hecht Museum
11.	*pdyhw bn hmlk*	Hecht Museum, photograph G. Larom
12.	*ʾnyhw bn myrb*	from Avigad 1982
13.	*mʿdnh bt hmlk*	Israel Museum

NORTHWEST SEMITIC INSCRIBED SEALS, ICONOGRAPHY AND SYRO-PALESTINIAN RELIGIONS OF IRON AGE II: SOME AFTERTHOUGHTS AND CONCLUSIONS*

Christoph UEHLINGER
Biblical Institute, Fribourg

In this concluding article, there is no need to summarize the papers presented at the Fribourg symposium. I should only emphasize, in a necessarily selective way, some of the issues raised by the authors, add a few methodological afterthoughts, and present an outlook on some perspectives for future research on iconography and the history of Iron Age religions in Syria and Palestine.

I. Description, classification and the "significant series"

The two contributions by *André Lemaire* and *Dominique Parayre* should be read in close conjunction, as they complement each other and both discuss

---

* Comments of Othmar Keel and Stewart Watson are gratefully acknowledged. Particular thanks are due to Benjamin Sass, who made significant contributions to improve style and argument of this contribution.

the crucial problem of classification in a general perspective. While Parayre focusses exclusively on iconography, Lemaire offers an overview of non-iconographical criteria for 'ethnic' classification, which include geographical and archaeological provenance,[1] seal type, material and dimensions,[2] palaeography and layout of the inscription, language and onomasticon. His discussion makes it very clear that the classification of an individual seal should rely, wherever possible, on the cumulative weight of a number of converging criteria.

Decorated and inscribed seals show a complex interplay between the material object, its figurative design, and its inscription. If one takes into consideration the different stages of a seal's production as distinguished by Lemaire (*supra*, p. 19), the examination, description and interpretation[3] of the seal should proceed accordingly, i.e. in similarly distinguished and temporarily independent stages:[4,5]

(1) material and formal criteria:
A. material, seal type and shape, dimensions;
B. layout of sealing surface (vertical or horizontal, registral or columnar division, dividers and border design, etc.), spatial relation of picture and text;[6]

---

1. From an archaeological point of view, one might be somewhat surprised that the provenance criterion should be accorded relatively limited weight, and suspect that low esteem for provenance is a typical feature of the antiquities market – where the vast majority of inscribed seals comes from. However, it is true that seals travelled easily in antiquity (cf. Collon 1987: 138), and many compelling examples of dislocation exist (Lemaire, *supra*, pp. 2-3; Gubel, *passim*; Timm, p. 162; Sass, p. 197). An inscribed seal bought in Amman, displaying the typically Judaean motif of a four-winged uraeus (Hübner, *supra*, p. 146 and fig. 28), might well belong to that category. As it happens, the provenance criterion gains in importance when a whole group of seals with common features (a "significant series") is concerned (cf. Parayre, *supra*, p. 29, and see below).

2. Regarding the latter criteria, Lemaire's discussion (*supra*, pp. 3-4) rightly implies that they are often more significant for workshop attribution than for 'ethnic' classification (but note Sass, pp. 196-197).

3. "Interpretation" is here understood in a largely descriptive sense, to be compared to semantic and syntactic analysis in the linguistic domain; the ideological component and religio-historical aspect, to which I shall turn below, should not interfere at this stage in the classification process.

4. Compare Parayre, *supra*, pp. 28-29; Sass, pp. 195-197.

5. Geographical and archaeological provenance do not appear as a separate classificatory stage, as they enter the discussion of each "significant series"' distribution on all three levels.

6. On the latter, see Parayre 1990a: 286-288; Sass, *supra*, pp. 200-206.

(2) iconographical criteria: choice, execution (technique, morphology, style) and relative position of specific motifs, motif constellations and scenes (i.e., figurative 'vocabulary' and 'syntax') – to be analyzed against the background of (A) inscribed seals, (B) anepigraphic seals and (C) other media of figurative art such as ivories, tridacna shells, metalwork, jewellery, monumental art, etc.;

(3) epigraphical criteria: palaeography, language and onomasticon.[7]

One would wish that future publications of new seals[8] as well as general discussions of 'ethnic' or 'national' glyptic corpora might conform to a common standard and address the classification issue in its real complexity.[9] As noted by Lemaire, the significance of one criterion taken in isolation is generally limited; only the cumulative weight of some or all criteria might put classification on a basis firmer than mere assumption. When all relevant aspects are considered, one has still to ask whether they are in agreement or simply in non-contradiction. Where it is not possible to reach a cumulative argument pointing to a single direction (see the examples given by Lemaire, *supra*, pp. 18-21, and other examples discussed below), one should consider the apparent contradictions rather than rely on one or another arbitrarily favoured criterion.[10] It is not the least merit of Lemaire's paper to insist on the fact that contradictions between various criteria do indeed exist, and that a commentator's predilection for clear-cut certitudes should not be allowed to blur that evidence.

Point (2) of our scheme underlines the potential use and relative importance of an adequate iconographical discussion. Much in the same way as any other craft, writing included, figurative art developed alongside lines of tradition. These embrace not only the figurative models, but also the technical means to realize them in various materials. They developed and were trans-

---

7. Material aspects may of course condition the technical execution of icon and inscription; contrariwise, the formal layout of the sealing surface may depend at least in part on the iconographical motifs selected. Wherever pertinent, the interdependence or relative autonomy of the three sets of criteria should therefore be discussed.

8. As a matter of fact, classification is too often based on limited discussions of arbitrarily isolated criteria, especially onomasticon or palaeography, and sometimes also iconography. See below, n. 10.

9. As it stands, the contributions to the present volume are not all based on identical criteria of classification, a problem that was repeatedly addressed at the symposium; see below, section III.

10. This would apply, for instance, to a seal in the Borowski collection (Aufrecht 1992: no. 1), recently published as Hebrew on tenuous palaeographical grounds, while layout and iconography – especially the juxtaposition of star, crescent and stroke (or another star?) in the upper register (compare Timm, *supra*, 192-193, figs. 2, 5, 17-19) – rather point to a Moabite origin (cf. Sass, *supra*, p. 231, n. 85).

mitted in specialized workshops, forming distinct 'schools', each producing objects conditioned by respective *canones*, tools, and competence.

Facing a multitude of individual objects, usually isolated from their original context, the modern iconographer tries, on the basis of typological comparison and classification, to identify "significant series" that concur in the analogous treatment of one or several iconographic features. Wherever possible, such a series may first be limited to inscribed seals only, but should then be gradually expanded to include uninscribed seals and non-glyptic material such as ivories,[11] tridacna shells,[12] metalwork,[13] jewellery,[14] or monumental art. The "significant series" method[15] may eventually result in locating workshops or at least general areas of production[16] and, vice versa, a workshop's products' distribution on the regional or international market.

Dominique Parayre has undertaken the painstaking documentation and typological analysis of one iconographical motif, the "winged disk", one of the most common and prominent features in the Northwest Semitic glyptic repertoire. She considers not only the morphology of the "winged disk", but also its placement within the overall layout (its 'syntactical' position) of a seal's decoration. The full extent and argument of her research will be presented in her forthcoming book, a revised version of a doctoral thesis. Together with her more elaborate 1990 studies (a, b), the condensed paper published in the present volume already demonstrates *ad oculos* how promising this kind of approach may be for future research on Northwest Semitic glyptic.

---

11. For the identification of styles and schools in ivory carving, of crucial importance for glyptic studies as well, cf. especially Barnett 1982; Herrmann 1986, 1989, 1992a, b; Winter 1976, 1981, 1982, 1983, 1989, 1992. See below, n. 37.

12. Cf. Stucky 1974; Geva 1980; Brandl 1984a, b; Reese 1988.

13. Cf. Markoe 1985; Curtis 1988.

14. Cf. e.g. Culican 1986; Barnett & Mendleson 1987; Lancel 1991.

15. Cf. Parayre 1990a: 269f, and her methodological remarks *supra*, pp. 28-29.

16. Note, in principle, Winter's neat remark on method: "When portable objects...found at a particular site in association with a series of fixed monuments, can be demonstrated to partake of virtually identical properties when compared to those monuments, and can be equally distinguished from fixed monuments of other sites within the same cultural 'region', then...it is a reasonable conclusion that the portable objects were made within the same locale as the larger works" (1983: 185). Cf. e.g. Parayre, *supra*, pp. 29, 36-37 on Zincirli. As is well known, however, this method based on the priority of monumental art cannot operate in a South Syrian and Palestinian context, where known remains of figurative art are almost exclusively limited to portable, minor objects (for Palestine, see the overview in Keel 1985: 11-20).

II. THE NEED FOR SEPARATE STUDY OF FORMAL CRITERIA, ICONOGRAPHY, AND EPIGRAPHY

1. General observations

An important and particularly difficult issue for our symposium, addressed time and again, was the problem of agreement or contradiction of epigraphical and iconographical criteria and/or classification. Let us consider briefly the more complicated instance of contradiction between epigraphical and iconographical criteria. Parayre is right in claiming (*supra*, p. 28) that the image and the inscription appearing on a single seal should not be artificially separated. As noted in the introduction (*supra*, pp. XIff), the long neglect of iconography in the study of Northwest Semitic inscribed seals is due precisely to such an artificial splitting of scholarly interest.

On the other hand, Lemaire has demonstrated (*supra*, pp. 18-21) that contradictions may occur between iconography and inscription, as the figurative design and the inscription need not necessarily be the product of a single workshop nor even come from the same geographical area. To cite but one clear-cut example in addition to Lemaire's: At the present stage of our knowledge on Judaean glyptic of the eighth and seventh centuries BC, it seems highly improbable that the seal *yḥ*[*y*ˀ]*hw* [*š*ˀ]*lm* (**fig. 11**; B 58, as tentatively reconstructed by Puech 1989: 590)[17] should have been produced in Israel or Judah in spite of its fragmentary Hebrew inscription. Its iconography undoubtedly points to a North Syrian origin at the time of Sargon or Sennacherib, with possible Urartian influence. While this example is admittedly extreme, we have to account for numerous cases where the contradiction would be somewhat more discreet or even invisible to us.

From a strictly methodological point of view, then, the possibility of contradiction should always be taken into account. Consequently, iconographical and palaeographical analysis should proceed independently from each other first (points [2] and [3] on pp. 258-259), each producing its own "significant series". If both series concur, the 'ethnic' classification of a seal would gain further probability. In the opposite case a more complex picture could emerge, as with the document B 58 just mentioned, an originally anepigraphic North Syrian seal that had an inscription added somewhat later in Judah. We should certainly prefer either result to the a priori suspicion of circular reasoning that is sometimes expressed against any attempt to 'ethnic' or 'national' classification on iconographical grounds.[18]

The same methodological principle is valid with regard to the material and formal aspects of a seal, which should be considered as an independent evid-

17. Cf. Ornan, *supra*, p. 60 with note 11 and fig. 22; Sass, pp. 236-237 with fig. 143.

18. See the remarks of Hübner, *supra*, p. 149, and Sass, p. 196.

ence, to be studied and classified on its own (point [1] above) before relating it to the other sets of criteria.

2. An example: the incompatibility of mortals and deities

The strict application of this methodological postulate yields significant results e.g. in *Tallay Ornan*'s paper on "The Mesopotamian influence on West Semitic seals". Ornan's introduction (*supra*, pp. 52-53) aptly distinguishes between (a) seals of Mesopotamian manufacture bearing a West Semitic inscription and (b) seals of Syro-Palestinian origin with such an inscription and originally-Mesopotamian[19] iconographic elements. The two categories should obviously not be addressed as products of one and the same "West Semitic seal-cutter" whose contribution to seals of the first, 'Mesopotamian' category was for sure very limited. Contrariwise, it would seem necessary to restrict the notion of "Mesopotamian influence" to those seals which were produced in the West but nevertheless show typically Mesopotamian iconographical features, i.e. part of the seals belonging to the second category.[20] Furthermore, we should clearly distinguish different levels or domains of "influence",[21] e.g. formal, iconographical, or conceptual.

A short conspectus of the seals illustrated in Ornan's paper gives a rather clear-cut picture:

(1) Whereas in the first category 'Mesopotamian' seal shapes, especially the faceted or rounded conoids, abound,[22] with only a few seals of more 'Western' shape,[23] the former are conspicuously absent from the second category.[24] The layout of the 'Western' group seems to reserve a pre-planned

19. But see n. 29.

20. As an example, one may cite the seal of *ʾḥyḥy* (*supra*, p. 67, fig. 62), unique among the seals of the 'two worshippers' group in its arched element usually considered to represent a sacred tree (but note Ornan's caution on p. 71, note 23).

21. The concept of "influence", together with related terms, and the various levels on which "influence" may operate would merit thorough discussion and definition, a task beyond the scope of the present article.

22. Note especially figs. 1+71, 3-4, 7+14, 8+17, 10, 12+13, 16, 23-27, 32-33, 34+44, 36-43, 45-47, 53-54, 81; fig. 9 is most likely a cut-down conoid (Buchanan & Moorey 1988: 59 on no. 371). To these could be added Mesopotamian, mostly Assyrian cylinder seals with Aramaic inscriptions that were beyond the subject of Ornan's study; see e.g. G 151-161; Bordreuil, *supra*, pp. 77ff, figs. 5-11, 13.

23. Besides Ornan's fig. 22 just mentioned, another ovoid (fig. 15, the seal of a high-ranking Ammonite official of the seventh century), and the round stamp with flat back of fig. 6 (G 12: Babylonian, sixth century).

24. Ornan's figs. 48-52, 55-65, 68-69, 72-77, 79-80, 82 are all scaraboids or ovoids, the only exceptions being figs. 70 and 78 (conoids with 'Ammonite' inscriptions; see Hübner, p. 157, figs. 5 and 9).

space for the inscription, while in the first group the legend's positioning appears sometimes rather secondary.

(2) Regarding iconography, the first, 'Mesopotamian' group shows such typical Assyrian semi-divine figures as the *girtablullû*, the *kusarikku*, the *ugallu* and the like,[25] but also the anthropomorphic moon god (Sîn) appearing in the crescent, or the worshipper standing in front of the cultic symbols of Marduk and Nabû.[26] On the other hand, the depiction of mortals as the main motif, be it in the 'two worshippers' constellation (**fig. 1**) or as a single 'worshipper' (**fig. 2**),[27] is almost entirely restricted to the second, 'Western' group.[28]

(3) Considering epigraphy, Ornan briefly notes that the first group displays almost exclusively Aramaic inscriptions (if not names, cf. pp. 52-53).

The three sets of characteristics considered together, Ornan's thesis that the "West Semitic seal-cutter" – at least in some rather appreciated workshops – showed a marked preference for the depicition of mortals would seem to be wholly justified. In light of the foregoing argument we may even add that such preference was apparently not due to Mesopotamian influence, as it is a conspicuous feature of the 'Western' group only. If one takes into consideration Ornan's premise (*supra*, p. 53) that the pictorial repertoire of the 'Western' stamp seals discussed represents a selection of motifs taken from larger and more complex scenes on cylinder seals,[29] the deliberate choice of some

25. See Ornan's discussion on pp. 54-60; and Hübner, pp. 144-145.

26. Ornan, *supra*, pp. 60-64.

27. *Ibid.*, pp. 68-71; for the 'two worshippers' group, cf. also Timm, pp. 180-183.

28. Ornan's figs. 71 and 81 (both conoids) are notable exceptions. Note Hübner's opinion on the former (*mngʾnrt*), thought to have been engraved on the base (divine combat, Ornan's fig. 1) in Mesopotamia with the worshipper and the inscription added by an Ammonite seal cutter (*supra*, pp. 141-142), a very plausible suggestion in view of the marked differences in style and technique between the two iconic designs. Regarding the worshipper on the seal of ***nrglslm*** (Ornan's fig. 81), Ornan & Sass (1992: 63-64) similarly argue for a Western origin.

29. I may be allowed, however, to remark that a minute comparison of 'Western' stamps and Mesopotamian cylinder seals will have to be performed before this premise can be taken for granted. Most 'two worshipper' representations have no immediate prototype on cylinder seals (the *ʾḥyḥy* example [p. 67, fig. 62] is not representative for the group), but the pictorial constellation of two identical human figures facing each other in a gesture of greeting or worship is known on Syro-Palestinian scarabs since the Middle Bronze age. This could indicate that we have to consider more closely the local, 'Canaanite' background of the constellation.
The 'one worshipper' group, on the other hand, does not look very homogeneous. While some examples may well show worshippers and ultimately derive from Mesopotamian prototypes (e.g. figs. 48-49, 69, 77-81), others (e.g. figs. 51, 67-68, 72-75, 82) compare more closely to Bordreuil's (1985, 1986b) and Gubel's (1990a; *supra*, pp. 118-121) 'royal or official' series (note esp. the attributes of authority on figs. 51, 68

1

2

3

4

5

6

7

8

Western workshops to represent men engaged in worship or blessing rather than deities or semi-divine intermediaries should obviously be of considerable interest for religio-historical research.

A similar tendency to underline acts of worship ('prayer' or music) rather than their addressee may be observed on some uninscribed stamp seals of Palestinian manufacture (**fig. 3** from Tell Keisan; GGG: 347, figs. 302a-d) dating to the seventh century BC. They belong to a larger group of uninscribed ovoids, apparently produced by the same workshops, that show one or two worshippers facing a standard positioned on a podium and crowned by a tasseled crescent (**fig. 4** from Shiqmona; GGG: § 176) – i.e. the cultic symbol of the moon god of Harran (Keel 1977: 284-296; 1990c). At the same time, however, another group of seals, again closely related in shape, material, style and technique and apparently also of central Palestinian or Gileadite origin, shows a male deity, in a gesture of blessing, enthroned in a boat. One recently published example of this group, inscribed *lšlmʾl* (**fig. 6**), is discussed by Lemaire (*supra*, pp. 17-18) and Sass (p. 234) who consider it to be Ammonite or Aramaic. To this and other examples already noted (Keel-Leu 1991: 114-115; GGG: § 178; cf. **fig. 5** from Shechem, **fig. 8** from Yoqneʿam),[30] we may now add a recently published limestone ovoid of unknown provenance, kept at the Australian Institute of Archaeology in Mel-

and 82, and cf. Sass, *supra*, pp. 229-231). This would imply that they represent no selection from the repertoire of cylinder seals at all, and that their identification as worshippers is open to doubt.

30. One famous example, inscribed in Hebrew *lʾlšmʿ bn gdlyhw*, is discussed by Sass, *supra*, pp. 232-234 with fig. 136 (and compare *ibid.*, fig. 137).

bourne (**fig. 7**). O. Keel and the present writer tentatively identify this god as a lunar, El-type deity (GGG: §§ 178-181).[31] Clearly, the 'cult standard & worshipper' and the 'enthroned deity' series are closely related in shape, material, style and iconography.[32] In light of this evidence it would seem that at least for some "Northwest Semitic seal-cutters", it was not so much the representation of a divine figure as such that should be avoided, but rather the simultaneous representation of an anthropomorphic god and a human worshipper in one single scene,[33] a rather common feature in contemporary Assyro-Aramaean glyptic.[34]

III. 'ETHNIC' OR 'NATIONAL' GLYPTIC REPERTOIRES

1. General observations: methodological disparities

Turning now to the five articles presenting the repertoire of specific 'ethnic' entities, we face a problem which is closely related to the issue of classification discussed above. As a matter of fact, the criteria that guided our contributors' choice of Aramaic, Phoenician, Ammonite, Moabite, or Hebrew inscribed seals for the review of their respective iconographic repertoires were not strictly identical. The different approaches are partly due to the paucity of preliminary studies, but there are other factors, and it should be noted that our authors have based their work on different methodological principles and presuppositions. This obviously precludes an immediate comparative evaluation of their results.

The five studies devoted to 'ethnic' or 'national' repertoires proceed along quite different avenues, which may be briefly outlined as follows:

– *Pierre Bordreuil*, from the very outset of his study, has, with one exception, chosen not to consider uninscribed material, not even for comparative purposes. His selection of 'Aramaean' cylinder and stamp seals is based on a threefold epigraphical criterion (Aramaic script, language, and onomasticon). However, no attempt has been made to present an exhaustive catalogue of seals which could be considered Aramaean on that ground. Instead, the article

31. This has been doubted by Helga Weippert, who would like to identify the deity as a sun god (private communication).

32. To my knowledge, no seal of the 'cult standard & worshipper' series is inscribed, as against the 'enthroned deity' series, where inscribed and anepigraphic exeamples occur side by side.

33. See GGG: §§ 183-188 for an explanation of this separation in the general religio-historical context of seventh-century Syria and Palestine.

34. E.g. GGG: 333, figs. 285-287, 288c; Ornan, *supra*, p. 61, figs. 23-29; Bordreuil, pp. 77, figs. 5-6, and 81, figs. 7-8.

offers detailed descriptions and comments of select items. Based on iconographical and/or stylistical criteria, he distinguishes four sub-categories, termed Assyrian,[35] Syrian, Egyptianizing,[36] and Persian.

Much more research is needed to connect the seals discussed by Bordreuil – and those he deliberately left aside – with stylistically and iconographically related parallels in order to establish "significant series" which could point to distinct workshops and traditions. Consequently, his classification of some seals in one or another sub-category will probably need revision.[37]

– From the point of view of method and classification, *Eric Gubel*'s presentation of Phoenician glyptic follows a very different line, which is more apt to produce a synthetical overview because it takes into account selected uninscribed seals and non-glyptic material such as metalwork and ivories. Gubel attempts to compute approximate statistics on the basis of a maximum of available data, and he clearly demonstrates the use of typological classification according to shape, material, layout of sealing surface, etc.

---

35. That Assyrian 'mythological' iconography predominates on cylinder seals with Aramaic inscriptions (*supra*, p. 77, figs. 5-6, p. 81, figs. 7-9, p. 85, figs. 10-11, 13, p. 93, figs. 33-34) comes as no surprise, for these cylinders are simply products of Assyrian workshops. These workshops were receptive to Egypto-Phoenician motifs at least since the time of Sargon II. Even the seal of *ʿbdkdʾh* (p. 85, fig. 13), for which D. Collon (1986b: 426; 1987: 83, 85), followed by Bordreuil, has suggested a Phoenician origin, might easily have been cut in late eighth-century Assyria. The extremely sophisticated technical execution of this seal points to a first-class, i.e. royal, workshop. Contrast the seal of *srgd* (p. 85, fig. 12), which is a fine example of a typically Phoenician cylinder seal with Aramaic inscription!

36. As Bordreuil does not give general definitions of his sub-categories, one has to identify distinctive traits on the basis of his descriptions alone. I confess that on this basis, the two sub-categories termed "iconographie syrienne" and "iconographie égyptisante" remain somewhat enigmatic to me: "Syrian" apparently cannot mean "not Egyptianizing", as the so-called "Syrian" cylinders of *srgd* and *ʿbdkdʾh* (on which see the preceding note) both contain obvious Egyptianizing motifs. Contrariwise, if "Syrian" should imply "not specifically Egyptianizing" (which would make sense for p. 85, fig. 14, and p. 89, figs. 15-16, 18-20), the two cylinders mentioned should be excluded. On the other hand, the seal of *mrʿly* (p. 89, fig. 24), briefly discussed within the "Egyptianizing" group, should surely be termed "Syrian" (or more precisely: "South Syrian" or "Ammonito-Aramaean"), as nothing except the scarab shape of the stone is "Egyptianizing".

37. See the preceding notes for a short review of this writer's suggestions. It is precisely at this point, that uninscribed seals and non-glyptic material should be considered in future studies. Note that research on ivory carvings has contributed considerably to our ability to distinguish between North Syrian, 'Intermediate', coastal Phoenician, and South Syrian styles, each having been produced by a number of distinct workshops or schools (cf. Barnett 1982: 43-55; Herrmann 1989, 1992b; Winter 1976, 1981, 1983, 1989, and now 1992: 135-140 on classification and terminology).

Not surprisingly, in view of the cosmopolitan character and distribution of Phoenician culture, Gubel's overview discusses a considerable number of seals which are also included in other authors' 'national' corpus. Consequently, one has to face a well-known *crux* of Syro-Palestinian archaeology: What is actually "Phoenician", and what is *specifically* "Phoenician" in Phoenician iconography?[38] Only when this question has been answered will research on the degree of penetration of "Phoenician" art and symbolism into the different areas of Syria and Palestine make any progress.

– With *Ulrich Hübner*'s contribution on Ammonite glyptic, still another methodological stance is taken.[39] Among the problems of a projected Ammonite "glyptography", Hübner explicitly addresses the issue of forgeries, an issue which he thinks is generally underrated. His selection of decorated seals and bullae that may be considered certainly or probably Ammonite on the basis of cumulative criteria – corresponding, in principle, to those discussed in Lemaire's article, plus an iconographical criterion – nevertheless amounts to some 40 items, plus 20 anepigraphic seals or impressions. Taken together, these allow a tentative compilation of an iconographic repertoire which Hübner, however, thinks not to be specifically Ammonite (see esp. on pp. 148-150).[40] This reservation notwithstanding, he feels confident enough to venture into an *argumentum e silentio* and list some motifs that seem to be absent from Ammonite glyptics.

– There is a certain degree of consensus on method between U. Hübner and *Stefan Timm*, although the latter's approach, in practice, is more restrained and takes a deliberately and explicitly "minimalist" stand that precludes any *argumentum e silentio*. One single criterion, the *kmš*-element in personal names, is taken to be decisive for the Moabite classification of a seal, and the primary 'corpus' (five items!) and related iconographic 'repertoire'[41] that emerge are of necessity very limited. The Moabite attribution of most

38. See the preceding note.

39. For the complete argument, one has to refer to Hübner's just published book (1992a); but see already Hübner 1989b on forgeries.

40. However, a close look at the parallels listed in Hübner's discussion of individual motifs is necessary, as these are sometimes of a very general nature (same or similar motif), i.e. not differenciated according to iconographic context, style, technique, material etc. Hübner appears to be more critical in the detection of forgeries (see his 1989b article) than in his use of parallels here. It would seem therefore that the "significant series" method has not yet been fully exploited and might still yield some more positive results.

41. It is somewhat difficult to use this term for a collection of motifs that are – except for the star, crescent and winged disk, the latter in two or three totally different renderings – attested only once each in Timm's primary selection.

other 14 other seals discussed remains open to doubt in Timm's eyes.[42] He restricts his judgement with regard to 'ethnic' attribution entirely to palaeographical considerations and prefers statements on the iconography of one or two seals with *kmš*-names to a more thorough and critical examination of the full potential of iconographical method.[43]

– *Benjamin Sass*, by contrast, handles a corpus much larger than that of any other group of inscribed seals and seal impressions: ca. 700, of which about 200 show some figurative decoration, while the remaining 500 items are entirely or nearly aniconic. The burden of a larger documentation is compensated by the real possibility to establish a "significant series" even within one 'ethnic' group.[44] Sass' study is admittedly preliminary and part of a larger project. It thus restricts itself to the discussion of methodological issues, i.e. criteria of classification,[45] and the presentation of a large repertoire[46] of iconographical motifs and scenes attested on Hebrew seals.[47] Some motifs appear to be characteristic, if not entirely restricted to Hebrew glyptic, others are part of an artistic *koinè*, while a few motifs may be considered 'unwelcome' or are missing altogether.[48] The latter issue, of course, is

---

42. Such doubt is not claimed, however, for the seal of *bʿlntn* (p. 193, fig. 11), which is certainly Moabite according to Timm's judgement, and that of *ʿzʾ* (*ibid.*, fig. 12), both showing a four-winged genius. This is surprising, as both seals have been found far outside the territory of Moab; their palaeography and onomasticon are not unequivocal, and their iconography, which differs in several respects from that of the *kmšṣdq* seal (p. 192, fig. 3), is considered typically Phoenician by many (cf. Gubel, *supra*, pp. 123-125).

43. As a matter of fact, Timm does not consider formal, iconographical, and epigraphical aspects on an equal level, nor independently from one another (see above, section II, on this methodological premise).

44. At the symposium, slides were shown that assembled the relevant items to series, whereas for practical reasons the paper restricts itself to one illustration per motif.

45. This discussion fully integrates formal, epigraphical, and iconographical aspects, with the formal criteria outlined in more detail than elsewhere.

46. Note that this repertoire is not considered complete, as it does not yet include inanimate objects (e.g. architecture, stands, altars, weapons, etc.) nor hieroglyphs and other signs.

47. Sass remains cautious with regard to a clear-cut distinction between Israelite and Judaean seals; see his comments *supra*, pp. 199-200.

48. In this author's opinion, the term 'unwelcome' should not necessarily be taken in a specific religious sense which would imply a somewhat anachronistic clear-cut distinction between 'orthodoxy' or 'heterodoxy' in Israelite and Judaean religion of the eighth and earlier seventh centuries, but simply point to the fact that the repertoire of Hebrew glyptic is the result of significant choices, guided by whatever motives and reasons (cf. Holladay's 1987 distinction between "established" and "non-conformist" worship, but see GGG: 400, n. 378).

thorny and has been the subject of much wishful thinking by prominent scholars. One understands that Sass remains equally cautious about clear-cut chronological conclusions or models that would too straightforwardly relate the rise of aniconic seals with e.g. a religious reform undertaken by king Josiah (on this issue, see below, pp. 281ff). At the end of his article, Sass takes up the problem of forgeries.

This short review may suffice to show that various aspects of method and procedure need further clarification. Future studies should share a minimum of common premises in order to be able to achieve comparable results.[49]

2. Need for methodological clarification, issues for further study

As there is a definite need for clarification and concert, I would point out the following aspects:

1. Our symposium already benefited from a general consensus on what non-iconographical criteria should be applied for the classification of a seal into a specific 'ethnic' or 'national' corpus; in practice, however, these criteria were not handled evenly by all our contributors. At the same time it had to be recognized that many examples exist where palaeographical and linguistic criteria do not allow a clear-cut 'ethnic' attribution.

Future studies will need to thoroughly discuss the potential and methodological status of iconographical criteria for classification. In particular, the "significant series" method as used e.g. in the work of D. Parayre, will have to be further implemented and tested by extension to additional iconographical subjects.

2. In many instances, the application of the "significant series" method could be seriously hampered by the relatively narrow basis of our documentation as long as one does restrict oneself to inscribed seals only. As a matter of fact, too many publications of inscribed seals treat them as unique gems with respect to iconography, without relating them to others, whereas these seals must have been produced by workshops which were in constant interaction and exchange with each other, and with non-glyptic crafts. Scholarly argument and hypothesis are difficult to prove or disprove as long as they are based on a *unicum*.

Future studies on the iconography of Northwest Semitic inscribed seals will have to devote more consideration to anepigraphic seals[50] and to non-

49. Detailed proposals for classification, which will be helpful for future research, are presented by Sass, *supra*, esp. pp. 194-206.

50. On the initiative of O. Keel, a research project of the Swiss National Fund for Scientific Research has documented all excavated – or, at least, clearly provenanced – Neolithic to Iron age stamp seals from Palestine/Israel (cf. Keel 1986; Keel & Uehlinger

glyptic sources.[51] The way opened by Galling fifty years ago has to be taken up more seriously, so to speak. Non-epigraphic material will enlarge our knowledge of materials, shapes, techniques, repertoires, styles, etc., essential for workshop studies. Furthermore, anepigraphic seals are more often provenanced than inscribed ones, and they may set the locating of workshops and of their products' distribution on a much firmer basis.

3. Our symposium was confronted time and again with the problem of authenticity.[52] A great majority of our documents are unprovenanced and have passed many hands until acquired on the antiquities market for some private or public collection. To retrace their way to their findspot is often impossible. The disparity in number between Hebrew and other Northwest Semitic inscribed seals may by itself raise suspicion.[53] It is thus understandable that a participant of the symposium advocated a strict limitation on a critically established minimum of seals. Others rightly insisted that the genuineness of an unprovenanced seal is impossible to prove. Every one agreed that the radical solution to restrict one's interest to excavated material alone would not be very helpful for this area of research.

While it is virtually impossible to escape the dilemma, scholars should at least find some basic agreement on how to cope with it in practice.[54] If

1990: 135-141). This documentation of ca. 10,000 items is based at the Biblical Institute of the University of Fribourg and may be consulted. The planned corpus will be published by O. Keel. A detailed introductory volume with full bibliography and another volume including ca. 1800 seals are in an advanced stage of preparation.

51. See notes 11 and 37 above.

52. Compare Hübner 1989b, and *supra*, pp. 132-133; Timm, p. 162; Sass, pp. 245-246.

53. Of about 1200 Northwest Semitic inscribed seals or seal impressions, about 700 are Hebrew. Even if one sets apart the recently published hoards of bullae (Avigad 1986; Shiloh 1986), more than 400 remain. For several reasons which may be easily guessed, the demand for Hebrew seals on the antiquities market is today much stronger than for any other group, and it is more profitable to produce a Hebrew seal than, say, an Ammonite one. It is surprising, then, that a recent exhibition on "Fakes and Forgeries from Collections in Israel" (Eretz Israel Museum, Tel Aviv, 1989) did include scarabs, cylinder seals, and coins, but not a single inscribed seal or bulla. (Forged bullae may of course be produced and I am told that they have made their appearance on the market.)
Note, on the other hand, that due to social and cultural context, the discovery of an authentic Hebrew seal and its subsequent appearance on the market is an event that has better statistical chance to happen than the discovery of an Edomite inscribed seal for instance. This should be kept in mind whenever statements are made on the extent of literacy among the Hebrews as compared to neighbouring peoples.

54. It appears clearly from the history of archaeological discovery and research that scholarly work affects the antiquities market (cf. Hübner 1989b: 217-220; Eretz Israel Museum 1989: 7*-26*) as it may influence to some extent the valuation of antiquities, entertain expectations of dealers and collectors alike, and consequently condition the

authenticity can hardly be proven, it cannot simply be taken for granted either. Publications of new material should, as a matter of principle, address the issue and argue in detail, on the basis of comparative material, on what grounds a new item may be presumed to be genuine. Furthermore, they should include a presentation of as much detail of an object's 'history' as is possible to reconstruct (from purported provenance to market).[55] This will never outweigh the necessity of developing reliable authenticity tests (Gorelick & Gwinnet 1978), and it does certainly not render superfluous research on forgeries (cf. Clermont-Ganneau 1885; Diringer 1934: 319-325; Herr 1978: 185-188; Hübner 1989b).

4. To sum up these observations, it would be beneficial to future studies if we would aim at some consensus on uniform handling of the "significant series" method. In our attempt to establish 'ethnic' or 'national' glyptic corpora, we should also reach some practical agreement on what may be termed a "concentric circles" approach. When dealing with 'ethnic' classification and authenticity, this method will make an explicit distinction of various levels of probability. It should be able to replace the overtly "minimalist" approach and re-admit into the discussion a considerable part of the available documentation. The sources on which our study has to rely are too scarce to allow us to disregard dozens of potentially significant items.

5. Last but not least, it goes without saying that while our symposium concentrated on 'ethnic' or 'national' corpora with the aim of identifying *specific* features, possibly even *diagnostic* choices of figurative motifs or scenes, the foregoing studies make it very clear that the 'national' repertoires contained a relatively large number of 'regionally' shared or even common 'international' motifs. This regional or international *koinè*, of which the winged disk is a prominent example, will be of prime importance for future studies as it offers by far the most promising field for workshop studies.

---

production of forgeries. In this respect, the choice of subjects of scholarly study is not devoid of significance.

55. It should be noted that earlier studies often contained more information on the place and date of the acquisition of an individual seal than most modern publications. This is regrettable, as the reconstruction of an object's 'history' on the antiquities market could in some cases help to evaluate the authenticity not only of the single piece, but of whole groups of objects.

IV. PERSPECTIVES FOR RELIGIO-HISTORICAL RESEARCH

1. General observations

The limits of comparison due to methodological disparities notwithstanding, some characteristic features of 'national' glyptic repertoires seem to emerge with sufficient clarity. Among these, one could mention the representation of bovines, rather prominent in Ammonite glyptic, rare in Hebrew[56] and Phoenician glyptic, and missing from the Moabite repertoire; the similar distribution of a squatting monkey replacing Harpocrates; the relative prominence of astral symbolism in the Moabite repertoire, rather 'unwelcome' on Hebrew seals according to Sass; the prominence, on the other hand, of various winged beings on eighth-century Israelite seals or the apparently characteristic and specific representation of four-winged uraei or she-deer on Judahite seals of the seventh century BC. Consequently, this brings us to the question whether the iconographical material studied in this volume has any definite relevance for the study of the Syro-Palestinian national religions in the Iron Age II.[57]

The issue has been addressed by all authors on various levels, but methodological problems abound and not much preliminary research is available in this somewhat neglected field.[58] These problems concern not only icono-

56. That the only bull on a Hebrew inscribed seal seems to have belonged to a Judaean (*šmʿyhw bn ʿzryhw*, cf. Sass, *supra*, p. 227, fig. 118) is noteworthy. Two crudely cut scaraboids from ninth- to eighth-century Samaria show an anthropomorphic deity standing on a bull (GGG: 217, figs. 207a-b), but Israelite inscribed seals, ivories etc. seem to have completely ignored the subject. This is surprising, as biblical texts insist on bull worship in Northern Israel (1 Kings 12:26ff; 2 Kings 10:29; 17:16; Hos. 8:5f; 10:5f; 13:2 etc.), and the latter is usually considered to be a distinct feature of Israelite national religion (be it Yahwism or El worship, as recently argued by Wyatt 1991). For an assessment of iconographical evidence for bull representations in Israel, cf. GGG: § 119. Clearly, the glyptic evidence of ninth- and eighth-century Israel shows that solar symbolism (cf. GGG: §§ 148-153), probably related to Yahweh as "Lord of Heaven" similar to the Phoenician Baʿalshamem, was then much more important than bull symbolism related to a Hadad-type weather-god.

57. As noted earlier, inscribed seals are often considered a source for religious history, but most commonly with restricted regard to the theophorous personal names (e.g. Tigay 1986; Fowler 1988; Avigad 1987a: 195-197; 1988: 8-9).

58. O. Keel's studies are fundamental in this respect, but they have rarely touched upon Northwest Semitic inscribed seals of the Iron Age II (cf. however Keel 1977; 1986a; 1990c). A synthetic discussion of the bearing of iconographical sources on the religious history of Israel and Judah has been presented by Tigay (1986: 91-96, see esp. his remarks on seals and ivories *ibid.*: 94-95).
Disappointingly, the new six-volume "Anchor Bible Dictionary" (ed. D.N. Freedman, 1992), designed to be a standard reference work for biblical studies including archaeology for years to come, does not contain an entry on seals in general. There is a brief

graphical method in general and its practical implementation.[59] The reluctance to use inscribed seals as a source for religious history also stems from our relative uncertainty regarding (a) the actual use and function of decorated inscribed seals in ancient society (are they to be considered simply seals or rather "seal-amulets"?), (b) the significance of a seal's decoration in terms of religion and belief, and (c) even when obviously religious in content, the status of a seal's decoration within the religious "symbol system" of its manufacturer, its owner and of their respective cultural environment(s).

2. Seals or seal-amulets?

Studies on the use and function of seals in ancient Northwest Semitic society usually stress administrative and legal, i.e. definitely instrumental aspects, such as the safeguarding of property or the authentication of commercial transactions and documents (for an overview, cf. Gibson & Biggs 1977). For obvious reasons, this approach is especially prominent in the case of the so-called "functional" (title without personal name, attested almost exclusively by impressions) and "official" seals (title + personal name), but there is clear evidence for the official use of so-called "private" seals too, as impressions of 'private' seals on jar handles and bullae are numerous, especially in Judah.[60] In light of this evidence, some scholars would minimize the seals' apotropaic significance and function as an amulet (cf. Hübner, *supra*, p. 153), and they are certainly right with regard to aniconic seals, iconic seals with purely ornamental designs, or more elaborately decorated seals which display clearly 'secular' subject matter such as the Judaean *šrhʿr* scene (cf. Ornan, *supra*, p. 67, fig. 66; Sass, p. 241, fig. 146).[61]

On the other hand, the material of the stone itself, especially semi-precious stone, may lend the seal the character of a jewel.[62] Jewellery always has a

article by B.S. Magness-Gardiner on Mesopotamian (!) seals, mostly cylinders (vol. 5, 1062-1064), and in an article on ancient Israelite jewellery by E.E. Platt, one may find a few comments devoted to seals as symbols of aristocratic office (vol. 3, 829-830). However, both articles completely ignore relevant literature on Palestinian glyptic, inscribed or not.

59. For a general overview of the history of research on iconography and religion cf. Keel 1992a: 369-372; for some case studies – not related, however, to Northwest Semitic inscribed glyptic – cf. Keel 1992b.

60. H. Weippert rightly remarks that the distinction between 'official' and 'private' seals is purely terminological and has no relevance to the seals' respective function (1988: 675).

61. Note, however, that to display one's loyalty to a 'secular' authority may well have a definitely apotropaic effect in certain social environments!

62. Not to mention that specific materials may have been thought to have distinct apotropaic qualities by themselves. Unfortunately, while Mesopotamian texts contain clear references to specific healing and protecting qualities of various seal materials in

practical function of adornment and embellishment, and a symbolic one related to power and prestige. For this reason alone, the significance of seals obviously transcends their administrative or legal use. Furthermore, one should recognize that while function, adornment and prestige may all condition the choice of a specific design as a decoration of one's personal seal, other, more symbolical or belief-related criteria did also operate in antiquity. Some "glyptic metaphors" in biblical and other Ancient Near Eastern literature imply that a seal could be considered to represent one's most personal feelings and beliefs and function as an apotropaic or beneficial amulet (cf. Hallo 1983). Most famous among them is the metaphor of Cant. 8:2, where the girl compares herself to a seal-amulet capable of protecting her beloved against death (cf. Keel 1984: 114-119; 1986a: 245-251). It seems to me that the term "seal-amulet", coined by Hornung & Staehelin (1976) with regard to Egyptian scarabs and scaraboids, does more justice to many of the objects discussed in this volume, especially if one does not consider decorated inscribed seals in isolation, but as a distinguished sub-category of glyptic art in general.

3. The religious significance of glyptic iconography

It is true that the properly religious significance of the iconographical repertoire attested on inscribed seals is not always self-evident. The large spectrum of motifs and scenes ranges from representations of anthropomorphic deities or their symbols, which have an unquestionable religious meaning, to mere icons of prosperity, vitality and strength. While representations of various winged beings and hybrid creatures have already been recognized by Galling and Reifenberg to have a definitely religious significance, be it as apotropaic protectors or mediators between the human and the divine, many representations are somewhat ambiguous. Are the running bulls on Ammonite seals or the more 'international' roaring lions to be understood as attribute animals of definite deities, or do they simply denote super-human strength and vigour?[63] This question was formulated fifty years ago by Galling (see *supra*, p. XV), and it has still not found a clear-cut solution.

There may be some religious significance implied even in cases where this is not immediately apparent, as two examples may suffice to illustrate: First, the grazing she-deer is exclusively attested on Hebrew seals (**fig. 9**; cf. Sass, *supra*, pp. 224-225) in contrast to other areas' preference for male deer. In his opening address to our symposium, O. Keel suggested that the

magic and ritual (cf. Goff 1939; Haussperger 1991: 265-290), nothing comparable about such valuations is known from the Northwest Semitic area.

63. Cf. Ornan, *supra*, p. 63; Sass, pp. 222, 225.

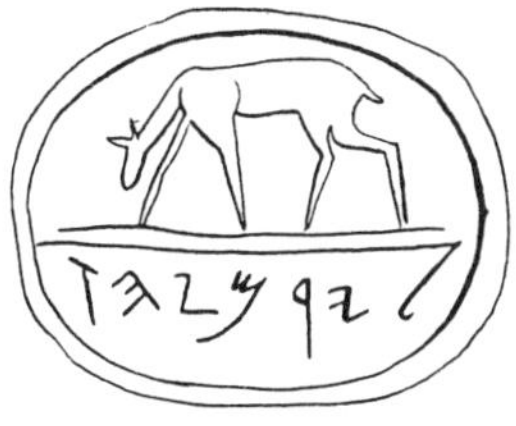

9

10

grazing she-deer may be understood as a symbolic representation of the seal-owner's own personality (his *nefeš*), seeking God "as a (she-)deer on flowing waters" (Ps. 42:2;[64] cf. GGG: § 117). Second, one may recognize among the rare late-seventh–sixth century Judaean seals and bullae that are not strictly aniconic a certain preference for either vegetal (twigs, pomegranate, lotus and other buds or flowers) or architectural symbolism (pillars, capitals; cf. **fig. 10**; but see Sass, *supra*, p. 208). These may be related to the Temple of Jerusalem, its cult and festivals, whose influence and status increased especially at that period, at least among the educated élite represented by the seals and bullae in question (GGG: § 208).

4. Workshop supply, individual choice and the cultural symbol system

How does a seal's iconography relate to the religious "symbol system" of its manufacturer and/or of its owner or of their respective culture? A. Lemaire maintains that the iconography of a seal is informative about the "personality" of its engraver rather than that of its owner, as the figurative decoration could be cut on a seal before it was sold, while the name could be added only as a result of the transaction (Lemaire 1988: 224; cf. *supra*, p. 21). This makes the use of the seals' iconography as a source for religious history somewhat more complicated, as the choice of a subject has to be evaluated in terms of both, the manufacturer and the client's, cultural and religious contexts. These could indeed be quite different as probably in the case of *yḥ*[*y*?]*hw* [*š*?]*lm* (**fig. 11**)[65] already mentioned (see above, p. 261). However, a customer's choice, even when facing a limited offer, is as much a choice as that of the manufacturer, and we may understand any owner of a name-seal to have adopted a certain motif, be it local or foreign, as his own, personal sealing subject.

64. Read *ʾayyelet* instead of *ʾayyāl* in v. 2a, as the following verb-form *taʿarog* needs a feminine subject. The latter also fits better the parallelism with feminine *nefeš* in v. 2b. The *taw* of *ʾayyelet* was probably lost by haplography.

65. Cf. Ornan, *supra*, p. 60 with note 11 and fig. 22; Sass, pp. 236-237 with fig. 143.

11

12

13

Lemaire has rightly remarked that the seals "nous mettent directement en relation avec des personnages du passé dont ils nous donnent une sorte de carte d'identité abrégée" (Lemaire 1988: 221). If the iconographical subject of a seal has religious significance, we may confidently regard it as an interesting aspect of the seal owner's religious identity, too.

Such choices and identities could be quite individual, as may be demonstrated once again by B 58. As a matter of fact, we possess numerous examples of seals that remain, for the time being, simply unique and unparalleled. One should not exaggerate ancient society's tendency to traditionalism and conformism when dealing with decorated inscribed seals.

True, historical interpretation has definite limits where it faces individual conscience rather than collectively shared concepts and processes. To remain with our example, B 58 shows a religious representation in which its Judaean owner *might* have recognized Yahwe and the "Queen of Heaven", possibly identified with Asherah (cf. GGG: § 197). But as the seal remains unique for the time being, we have no other documentary evidence to test such an hypothesis against other documentary evidence. And nothing compels us to deny that another Israelite or Judaean individual, *gʾl bn šʿl*, could have recognized the four-winged naked goddess holding astral staffs shown on *his* seal (**fig. 12**; B 44)[66] as a representation of the "Queen of Heaven" either. Fascinating as both documents may be, they remain unique, and their weight for religious history is thus limited in comparison to other seals which, being more conventional, may be related to a "significant series" (cf. GGG: §§ 196-197 for a discussion of both seals and the "Queen of Heaven" issue).

The seal of *blth* (**fig. 13**)[67] is another example, for which I would adopt Lemaire's opinion referred to above: The decorative design, a four-winged, apparently woman-headed scarab holding a sun-disk, is until now unparalleled in Israelite or Judaean figurative art but has several good parallels in

66. Cf. Ornan, *supra*, p. 59, fig. 20; Sass, p. 241, fig. 157.

67. Cf. Gubel, *supra*, p. 123, fig. 61; Sass, p. 215, fig. 88 = p. 227, fig. 126.

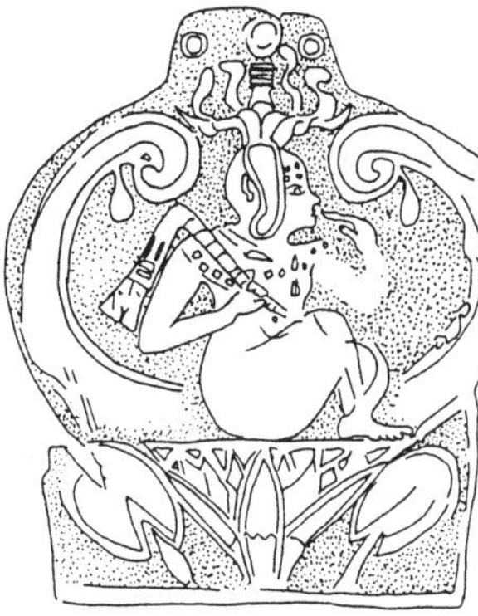

14

15

16

17

Phoenician metalwork, ivories, jewellery and somewhat later seals (cf. Gubel, *supra*, p. 122; Sass, p. 226). The seal is obviously a product of a Phoenician workshop and has been classified as "Hebrew" on palaeographical grounds only. While it might be easy to understand a woman-headed beetle in a Phoenician context as a representation of a female sun-goddess, i.e. either as a late survival of the goddess *Šapšu* already attested in Ugaritic texts, or as a female counterpart of solar Baᶜalshamem (cf. Bisi 1988), we cannot say much about its significance in an Israelite context (cf. Sass, *supra*, pp. 216-217).[68]

Religious history tries to reconstruct the religious "symbol system" of a certain area and period and asks for its coherence and plausibility. As has been said above, this can only be done on the basis of the "significant series" method, and the heuristic potential of unparalleled seals resulting from individual choices is thus somewhat limited: it attests to what may have been possible, while a "significant series" may document what was current or prominent. Consequently, the dozens of inscribed and uninscribed Israelite seals and several of the Samaria ivories which offer strong evidence for the prevalence of solar symbolism in Northern Israel during the eighth century BC (**figs. 14-17**; cf. GGG: §§ 148-153) are much more significant for the history of Israelite religion than the *blth* seal just mentioned, as they attest to the existence of a general religious 'ambiance' that clearly conditioned the religion and beliefs of many people among the Israelite elite.[69] Many of the seal

68. Hebr. *šemeš* is often feminine (cf. HAL IV 1469a).

69. The ivory carvings in question are typical luxury goods, and they have been found in the palace area of Samaria; they include Egyptian and Phoenician imports as well as local products. Most of the relevant provenanced seals come from Samaria and Megiddo. Neither ivories nor seals may be considered to belong to the domain of "popular religion ... where unsophisticated folk did not draw fine distinctions and so were always inclined to syncretism", as W.G. Dever (1990: 162) has maintained.

owners involved bear Yahwistic personal names, and it is simply unthinkable that the state religion of Northern Israel, i.e. 'official' Yahwism, should not have been affected by this 'ambiance' and emphasis on solar symbolism.

This example may demonstrate that whoever is interested in the reconstruction of the religious history of first-millennium Syria and Palestine should certainly not disregard the potential of iconographic sources in general, and of Northwest Semitic inscribed seals in particular.

V. ICONISM VS. ANICONISM AND THE BIBLICAL "IMAGE BAN"

1. General observations

As mentioned in the preface of this book (cf. *supra*, p. VII), the idea of a symposium devoted to the iconography of Northwest Semitic inscribed seals grew out of a larger research project, entitled "Origin and effect of the biblical image ban as reflected in inscribed Hebrew seals of the ninth to sixth centuries BC". While it is not possible to take up this issue at length within the limits of an article, some remarks on the subject might aptly conclude this volume.

How can inscribed Hebrew seals contribute to our understanding of the origin, implementation and effect of the biblical veto on images? The subject seems to be on the agenda of name-seal studies since the early days of the 19th century. Not surprisingly, some authors insist on the *presence* of pictorial representations on Hebrew seals which appeared to contradict the biblical image ban.[70] M.A. Levy was apparently the first to note that the *absence* of pictorial representations seems to be characteristic of Hebrew seals

70. According to de Vogüé, *šmʿyhw bn ʿzryhw*, whose seal shows a walking bull (see above, n. 56) was an Israelite exile in Babylonia "qui, tout en conservant les noms et l'écriture de la mère patrie, s'est laissé aller à enfreindre la loi mosaïque sur la représentation des animaux vivants" (1868: 131). A reference to the Bible is not cited, but de Vogüé probably thought of Dtn. 4:17 (16-19), the only place where a catalogue of prohibited representations including animals is given. De Vogüé knew of course from other Biblical texts that the Mosaic law had been transgressed by other, more prominent Israelites in their own country:"Salomon avait donné l'exemple du relâchement dans la décoration du temple et du trône royal: ses successeurs, moins orthodoxes encore, quelques-uns même tout à fait idolâtres, tels que Achaz et Manassé, les rois d'Israël, presque tous adonnés aux cultes phéniciens et syriens, habituèrent les yeux du peuple juif au spectacle des symboles figurés et des représentations animales. (...) Il n'est donc pas étonnant qu'un Juif, transporté en Assyrie de Samarie ou de Jérusalem, ou bien habitant la Palestine sous le règne d'un de ces rois prévaricateurs, ait fait graver sur son cachet la figure d'un taureau" (*ibid.*: 132). As a matter of fact, only the *šmʿyhw* seal is discussed in that way by de Vogüé, as the representation of a bull allowed a reference to the 'golden calf' of Bethel (1 Kings 12:28).

(1869: 33; cf. Sass, *supra*, pp. 197-198). He considered the cult of Yahweh to have been aniconic, but did not explicitly link the two phenomena. However, he considered many pictorial representations attested on Hebrew seals to be related to idolatry and noted that the latter had prevailed among the Hebrews until the return of the exiles.

Only progress in dating seals on the basis of palaeography or archaeological context and the recognition of the different spellings and orthography of the divine name in Israel and Judah, which allowed to differentiate Hebrew seals into Israelite and Judaean,[71] could lead to the conclusion that aniconic seals were especially numerous in Judaean glyptic since the seventh–sixth centuries BC. This was explicitly formulated by A. Reifenberg who was inclined to understand such seals as "symptoms of the growing consciousness of the Mosaic prescriptions that may be connected with the above-mentioned reformation [i.e., Josiah's reform] and the rigorous enforcement of the law after the return from exile" (1950: 17).

2. Israelite aniconism? A critique of some erroneous presumptions

Reifenberg's interpretation has been accepted, among other scholars, by N. Avigad, who found confirmation in the fact that among the 255 bullae published by him, only 13 display pictorial representations (Avigad 1986a: 118; cf. Sass, *supra*, p. 198).[72] In one of his latest statements on the subject, Avigad even maintained that "archaeological evidence proves that the Israelites did observe the prohibition of making images,[73] except for some minor attempts to form crude images in pottery. In the main, the Israelites remained an aniconic nation. However, it is evident that, notwithstanding the prohibition, they did not always abstain from using figurative art." Having reviewed figurative representations in the Temple of Solomon (e.g. the cherubim and the copper serpent), Avigad considered it "no wonder then that images of the kind sanctioned in the Temple became the standard pattern on individual seals", and he noted that "the iconography of the Hebrew seals contains, except for one or two uncertain instances, no pagan cultic scenes or emblems of the kind to be found on other seals, such as the worship of astral symbols or deities" (1988: 15).

Taken together, these observations clearly imply that the major motifs of the iconographic repertoire attested on Hebrew seals were considered not to

71. The variant spellings had been noted earlier (e.g. by Levy 1868: 41). Since the discovery of the Samaria ostraca (1910), where only the *-yw* orthography is attested, the latter is generally understood as a distinct Northern Israelite dialectal form (cf. Lemaire, *supra*, p. 11; but note Sass, p. 199).

72. I.e. 5%; the proportion does not alter significantly if one considers the three hoards of late Judaean bullae (City of David, Lachish, Avigad) together.

73. Avigad refers to the "second commandment of the Torah", i.e. Ex. 20:4 || Dtn. 5:8.

transgress the biblical prohibition because they related to the decoration of the Temple of Jerusalem, while heterodox symbolism or scenes of idolatrous worship were avoided by the Hebrew seal-cutters. In my opinion, Avigad's thesis, based upon the recognition of the Temple of Jerusalem as the single major sanctuary of Israel and Judah, sounds somewhat apologetic and is untenable for several reasons:

1. The iconographic repertoire attested on Hebrew seals is broader than what we know from descriptions of figurative art as displayed in Jerusalem's main sanctuary.[74] It includes, to cite but the more prominent features, winged sun-disks (**fig. 18**), a crowned sun-disk (**fig. 19**), two- and four-winged scarabs, various birds, she-deer (**fig. 9**) and ibexes, all of which are absent from the Temple decoration as related by biblical descriptions. On the other hand, the latter mention oxen or rather bulls which supported the bronze sea (1 Kings 7:25 || 2 Chr. 4:4), but these are conspicuously rare in the repertoire of Hebrew glyptic (cf. Sass, *supra*, p. 225; GGG: § 119).
2. In historical terms, the Temple of Jerusalem may not be considered to have been the common religious centre of both kingdoms. The major cultic centres of the Northern kingdom were rather situated in Bethel, Samaria, and possibly Dan. Curiously, however, important features of the Israelite and Judaean iconographical repertoire do not parallel their respective sanctuary's symbolism. Winged griffins and sphinxes (the latter being a significant feature in the decoration of the Temple in Jerusalem) are much more prominent on Northern Israelite than on Judaean seals. On the other hand, a bull was the main cultic image in the Israelite state temple of Bethel (Hahn 1981; Schroer 1987a: 84-91), but the only known Hebrew seal on which a bull is represented seems to have belonged to a Judaean individual (*šmʿyhw bn ʿzryhw*).
Considered together, this seems to indicate that the Israelite and Judaean glyptic repertoires were not in general dependent on one country's respective major sanctuary.
3. Avigad's reference to the apotropaic copper serpent obviously serves to make two- or four-winged uraei, so characteristic for the Hebrew glyptic repertoire (Sass, *supra*, pp. 212-213), acceptable to some presumed pre-exilic orthodoxy. However, it is not at all clear whether the copper serpent (the *neḥuštān* of 2 Kings 18:4[75]), whose cult is said to have been suppressed by king Hezekiah, was related to the official state cult of Judah, nor that it stood inside the Temple compound (cf. Schroer 1987a: 108-109).

74. For the latter, see Schroer 1987a: 46-66.71-78.82-84.121-133.

75. Num. 21:6-9 uses the term *sārāf*; and the copper serpent is probably to be understood as an uraeus (cf. GGG: § 161). On the question of historicity, see n. 79.

4. On the whole, the notion of "Ancient Israel" as an "aniconic nation" is erroneous and needs no further refutation. Archaeological evidence for minor arts abounds, and relevant biblical information has been collected by S. Schroer (1987a). Had "Israel" not known images, no veto would ever have been conceived.

Most important with regard to our discussion, it would seem that the so-called biblical "image ban", often referred to as the "second commandment" (Ex. 20:4 || Dtn. 5:8) in spite of its wider attestation outside the decalogue (cf. Ex. 20:23; 34:17; Lev. 19:4; 26:1; Dtn. 4:16ff, 23, 25; 27:15), may be properly understood only on the basis of the relevant biblical texts. These, however, never speak of a ban on images or figurative art in general, but prohibit the production and/or veneration of *cultic* images, and particularly of cultic images of Yahweh. Pictorial designs engraved on seals would not fall under that prohibition anyway, and it seems impossible to understand the growing tendency of aniconism displayed by late Judaean private seals as the result of a direct implementation of the biblical veto on cultic images.

3. An alternative hypothesis

It is relatively easy to refute an erroneous, if commonly-held hypothesis, but can an alternative model be constructed? If the biblical "image ban" concerned cult images alone, and not figurative art in general, is it then possible to relate the two aniconic tendencies, the one attested by the texts, the other by the clear preference of entirely epigraphic private seals in seventh–sixth-century Judah? For methodological reasons, it seems necessary first to consider the two issues separately and in historical perspective.

3.1. The so-called biblical "image ban"

The above-mentioned *texts* prohibiting the production and worship of cultic images have been the focus of several recent critical studies, among them an exegetical thesis entitled "Das Bilderverbot" by Ch. Dohmen (1985).[76] Dohmen's study has shown convincingly that not one single "image ban" text antedates the fall of the Northern kingdom in 722/720 BC.[77] It has always

76. For a detailed discussion, I may refer to my review, published in BiOr 46 (1989) 410-419, of the second edition (1987). Among many studies on "image ban" and "Israelite aniconism", note Mettinger 1979.

77. Only a postulated earlier form of Ex. 20:23 is considered by Dohmen to date to early monarchic times and to have an even earlier, "nomadic" background (Dohmen 1985: 154-180, esp. 171-175, 179). The speculative nature of this reconstruction has been pointed out by L. Schwienhorst-Schönberger (1990: 287-299), who classifies Ex. 20:23 as part of a Deuteronomistic redaction of the Book of the Covenant, to be dated to the sixth century.

been recognized that the contiguity of the "first" and "second commandment" – exclusive worship of Yahweh and "image ban" – is no coincidence. The biblical veto on cultic images seems to have its roots in the growing consciousness of so-called "proto-deuteronomistic" circles in Judah[78] that Yahweh alone was worthy of cultic veneration as the sole Lord of the country. As the worship of other gods and goddesses focused on cultic images, the latter inevitably became objects of abomination to these radically monolatrous Yahwistic circles. Incidentally, it is probable that this opinion on cult and cultic images would not have appeared to be "orthodox" at all to the majority of the Judaean people. The definition of "orthodoxy" is group-related, and its implementation always a matter of power and influence. As is well-known, it was only in the latter days of the Judaean monarchy that the "proto-deuteronomistic" movement was able to exert direct influence on state affairs, as is best exemplified in Josiah's so-called religious reform.[79] This reform, if historical at all, is however not to be understood as a direct implementation of the veto on cultic images in particular, despite the (deuteronomistic) presentation in 2 Kings 22-23, but rather as an attempt to centralize monolatrous worship of Yahweh in Jerusalem.[80]

---

78. These may have ultimate roots in Israel, following a famous extrapolation of A. Alt on the origin of Deuteronomy, but for our present concern with aniconism there is no need to build upon that thesis nor specific evidence to back it, as no aniconic tendencies seem to be attested in Israelite glyptic (see below n. 84) or other areas of figurative art. Note that – the problem of historicity put apart – neither the monolatrous prophetic activities of Elijah nor the so-called purge of Jehu, both intolerant claims for Yahwistic monolatry or rather the radical priority of Yahweh and Yahwistic worship in Israel, are directed specifically against cultic images. It is only in the book of Hosea that the worship of Yahwistic(!) cultic images is explicitly highlighted and criticized. At any rate, aniconic ideology would be rather easily welcomed in Jerusalem where the cult of Yahweh seems to have remained essentially aniconic since the days of Solomon (cf. the empty cherubim throne; one should distinguish between the Temple and its furniture, both amply decorated, and the main deity's worship, which did not center on an iconic representation of Yahweh himself). It is even more probable that it was actually generated there.

79. It is not clear whether the same movement was already influential at the time of Hezekiah. Documentary evidence for Hezekiah's so-called reform (cf. 2 Kings 18:3-5) remains rather elusive. Whether Hezekiah's reform was a powerful precedent to Josiah's, as recently maintained by Lowery (1991: 142-168), Halpern (1991: 25-27, 65-69) and Albertz (1992: 280-290), perhaps even more historical than the latter (the question of political and/or religiousmotivations put aside), or whether its description in 2 Kings 18 is essentially a literary fiction modelled on 2 Kings 23:4ff by a Deuteronomistic editor, the copper serpent incident being the sole historically trustworthy element (so Hoffmann 1980: 146-155; Spieckermann 1982: 170-175), is open to question.

80. This is not to imply that the motives behind Josiah's – or rather, the so-called deuteronomic movement's – reform were exclusively 'religious', but this issue is beyond the

3.2. Aniconism on late Iron Age private name seals

On the other hand, the trend towards aniconism on late Judaean private name seals[81] seems to be influenced by several non-religious factors:[82]

First, if Levy, Reifenberg and others once thought that purely epigraphic seals were a phenomenon restricted to Judah, this is definitely not the case. Particularly Ammonite,[83] but also Moabite and Aramaic glyptic shows a comparable evolution, although on a more limited scale, with an increasing production of aniconic seals towards the later seventh and sixth centuries.[84] One may also mention the well-known seal of *ʿbdʾlʾb bn šbʿt*, a minister of Mitinti II of Ashkelon (ca. 670 BC) which has no iconic decoration, but an elaborate four-line inscription (**fig. 21**). The proliferation of aniconic seals is generally considered a consequence of growing literacy among the seal-owning élite.

---

scope of the present article. For recent assessments, cf. Lowery 1991: 190-209; Albertz 1992: 304-360.

81. This trend may be illustrated by the example of a well-defined group of Judaean bone seals: From the ninth and earlier eighth century BC we know ca. 120 uninscribed items with characteristic squarish shape and stereotyped iconography executed in a very peculiar style (cf. Keel-Leu 1991: 75-78; GGG: §§ 157-159). Towards the seventh century, the group as a whole tends to complete aniconism, at first still retaining the characteristic shape (Bordreuil & Lemaire 1976: no. 5; HD 62; Avigad 1989b: no. 10), then only the material (HD 62, 91-96; Avigad 1989b: no. 6; cf. Lemaire, *supra*, p. 3). Four squarish seals document the transition: one shows a figurative design (a 'worshipper' or greeting man, clearly related to the early group by iconography and execution) with an inscription at its side (cf. Sass, *supra*, fig. 128), three others, still unpublished, are bifacial with an inscription on one and decoration on the other side (Benjamin Sass, personal communication).

82. For the following, see also GGG: §§ 205-207.

83. Hübner (*supra*, p. 134) counts ca. 30 aniconic Ammonite seals among a total of ca. 70, i.e. 43%; cf. CAI 25-27, 36-37, 40, 44, 47, 48(?), 49, 51, 53(?), 56, 67, 70-71, 74-75(?), 86, 90, 100(?)-101, 104, 109, 113, 115, 119-121, 123-125, 130, 139, and the abecedary seals CAI 22 (= 115? B. Sass, private communication), 93.

84. This may be demonstrated by a short look on the public collections in Jerusalem (HD) and Paris (B) taken together, where aniconic seals constitute 72% of the Hebrew, 30% of the Ammonite (but see the preceding note), 15% of the Moabite and 14% of the Aramaic seals (cf. GGG: 408, n. 387). Phoenician glyptic (4%) does not show such an evolution, or rather, only later and to a much more limited extent. With regard to the Hebrew seals counted, ca. 95% of them are to be classified as Judaean on the basis of onomasticon, formal typology (layout etc.) or provenance. 'Ethnic' re-classification may slightly modify these figures, but on the whole, it seems to be a common trait of Phoenician and Israelite glyptic that they did not share the tendency towards aniconism (cf. Parayre 1990a: 286-287). B. Sass remarks that even a rough statistic should also consider material, as the tendency towards aniconism is stronger in soft stone seals of local manufacture (well represented in the collection of the Israel Museum) than in seals made of semi-precious hardstones (which are more frequent in the "gem" collections in Paris).

Moreover, as in any society where non-literate people are the majority, literacy was virtually synonymous with power and authority, and consequently considered a special mark of social prestige (cf. Schousboe & Larsen 1989; Baurain et al. 1991). An aniconic seal may appear somewhat banal to modern iconographers, but the absence of iconic decoration could have rendered a seal just more desirable among inhabitants of seventh-century BC Palestine. We should certainly not underrate the importance of distinctive marks of literacy in a non-literate environment. In my opinion, the need and the want to demonstrate one's literacy might well account for the existence of abecedaries on seals (such as the Ammonite and Ammonito-Aramaean seals CAI 22 (= 115?), 24, 82, 93, 114, two or three of which are aniconic), jars (as in Kuntilet ʿAğrūd, cf. GGG: 276), and other media.

Second, it has to be noted that an important group of aniconic seal impressions antedates the emergence of the "proto-deuteronomistic" movement in Judah by several decades. These are the so-called 'private' seal impressions massively attested on the *lmlk* jar handles, which may be clearly dated to the end of the eighth century (cf. **fig. 22**; Ussishkin 1976; Garfinkel 1984).[85] In this prominent case, aniconism seems to be motivated by three factors at least:

- functional, namely the exclusive use of these 'private' stamps *as seals*, i.e. official markers of some kind of competence (as opposed to amulets); this could have made iconic decoration unnecessary.
- social, namely the prestige factor of ostentatious literacy mentioned above.
- ideological: one may guess that as these 'private seal' impressions appear side by side with the *lmlk* impressions, interference of 'privately-related' iconography with the religious symbols of the Judaean state had to be avoided.[86]

---

85. True, as only the impressions survive, the seals may theoretically have been bifacial (cf. below, n. 91), with an iconic reverse (cf. **fig. 23**). But the ratio of actual bifacial to aniconic seals being only about 3-4:100, this hypothesis has no statistical probability.

86. Purely iconic seal impressions occur alongside *lmlk* type impressions on Judaean jar handles. They represent a lion hunting an ibex (cf. Sass, *supra*, p. 223, fig. 111), a prancing horse (*ibid.*, p. 227, fig. 119; Barkay 1992a), an ibex (Barkay 1992b: 119, no. 35), and perhaps astral symbols (*ibid.*: 119, no. 36; the latters' interpretation as symbols of Sîn, Ishtar and Marduk is open to doubt). Two seal impressions showing a warrior (?) (*ibid.*: 118, nos. 30-31) come from cooking-pots, but this may be accidental. The function of these anepigraphic seal impressions on *lmlk* jars is still to be explained. Barkay considers the designs to be pictographic representations of personal names or family emblems, and refers to the *ʿzryhw hgbh*, *ʿrb nby*, and *ʾnyhw bn myrb* seals (note, however, that each case would need a different explanation for the relationship of name and icon, cf. Sass, *supra*, pp. 217-218 with fig. 93, 218 with fig. 101, 242 with pl. II:12). In light of the so-called 'private name' seal impressions, I

18

19

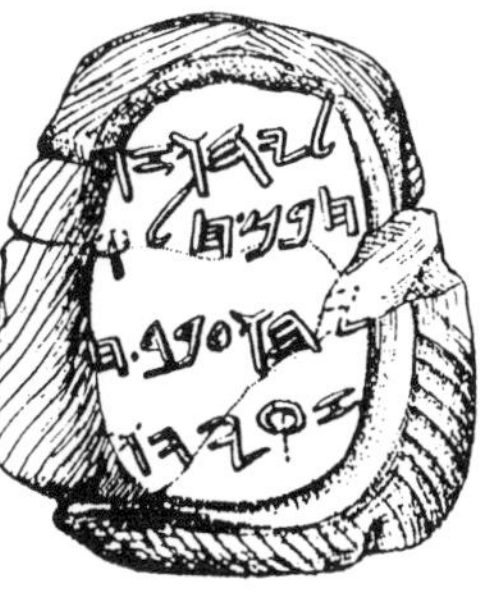
20

21

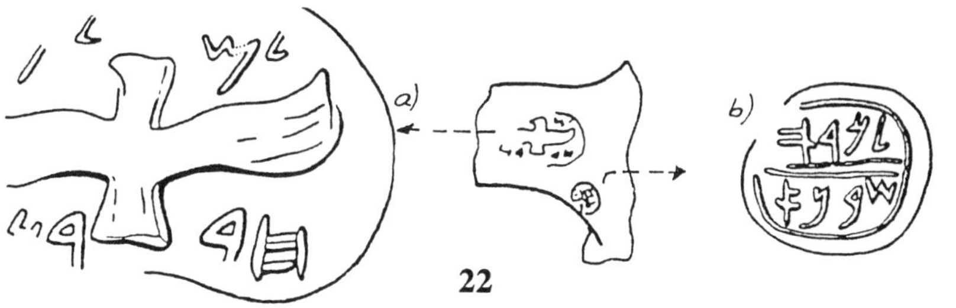

22

In this respect, it is instructive to compare the seals of *ʾbyw* (**fig. 16**), *šbnyw* (**fig. 18**) and *ʾšnʾ* (**fig. 19**),[87] high-ranking officials (*ʿbd*) serving the Judaean kings Uzziah (ca. 773-735?) and Ahaz (ca. 742-726 BC), with the impression of the seal of *yhwzrḥ bn ḥlqyhw* (**fig. 20**),[88] who held the same rank under king Hezekiah (ca. 725-697 BC). While the first three show elaborate solar iconography, the latter is totally aniconic as the seal of Yehozaraḥ's Philistine colleague, but solar symbolism is now displayed by the royal seal impressions (**fig. 22**).[89]

Third, the evolution towards aniconic seals might have been motivated by an increasing distinction of the respective functions of seals and amulets. Bifacial seals which display a figurative design on one side and an inscription on the other (cf. **fig. 23**)[90] may indicate such growing conscience of the

very much doubt that "a high-ranking official of the royal administration" (Barkay 1992a: 128) would use a seal which could cause him to be considered illiterate.

87. Cf. Sass, *supra*, pp. 238-239, 241, figs. 147 and 151.

88. Cf. *ibid.*, p. 202, fig. 22. In passing, one may note the solar implications of the name *yhwzrḥ*, which means "Yahweh has risen" (as the sun, or rather like the sun?).

89. Cf. *ibid.*, pp. 219, fig. 89, and 241, fig. 149.

90. The seal of *ʾḥʾmh (bn) ʿlyhw*, 17.3 x 17.3 x 8 mm, a rectangular plaque of grey-beige limestone, found near the seventh-century necropolis of Beth Shemesh, is mentioned and illustrated here with the kind permission of Sibylle Mähner, whose detailed study on the object is in press (Mähner 1992).

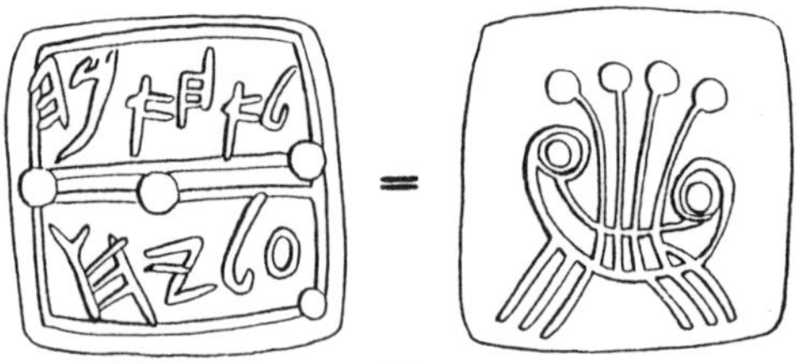

23

distinct functions of picture and inscription, the former being more apt to serve as an amulet, the latter rather as an identifier and competence marker.[91] More significant, Egyptian and Phoenician faïence and glass amulets[92] and scarabs appear to be far more numerous in seventh- and early sixth-century contexts than in earlier periods (see GGG: § 202).[93] These amulets may well have taken over, in part or almost completely, the amuletic, i.e. apotropaic and life-promoting functions of the ealier seal-amulets (see above, pp. 273-274). The appearance of this new fashion at the time of the Egyptian 26th dynasty (664-525 BC) would probably have contributed to make Judaean and Ammonite seal cutters concentrate on a distinct market of their own, i.e. the manufacture of purely epigraphic seals.

---

91. Bifacial seals (21 Hebrew and 15 non-Hebrew items known to this writer) would merit a separate study. Of course one would have to distinguish between the various possible combinations of picture(s) and inscription(s). About half of the seals, Hebrew and non-Hebrew alike, separate picture and text by placing them on either side of the seal, and they could well prove to be diagnostic for several issues discussed here. However, as other layouts and combinations occur (among them text – text), the first reason that seems to have motivated the manufacture of bifacials is probably purely functional, namely that it allowed extension of available surface for engraving (cf. prismatic seals and conoids with engraved sides as further extensions). Note that bifacial plaques are known in anepigraphic seals in the Middle Bronze Age II B, Late Bronze Age, and Iron Age II glyptic (for the latter, cf. Buchanan & Moorey 1988: nos. 2-3, 69, 172, 197, 210, 315, 318-320, 323-325, 341, 347-349, 352, etc.). As no continuity may be demonstrated from the Bronze Age to the Iron Age types, seal-cutters of each period may simply have found the same solution to the same problem.

92. An eagerly awaited corpus of Iron Age amulets excavated in Palestine/Israel is being compiled by Christian Herrmann, a collaborator of the Biblical Institute of the University of Fribourg.

93. Cf. the biblical polemic against amulets, particularly prominent in Ezechiel (Keel 1985: 42-45; Schroer 1987a: 414-419).

24

25

3.3. Synergy after all?

Having observed the two aniconic trends (biblical and glyptic) as separate developments with largely distinct motives, one may speculate about a possible convergence or synergy of the two. As a matter of fact, it has to be acknowledged that the tendency to aniconism is conspicuously stronger in Judaean glyptic than in any other 'national' group. This has to be explained, and as the social, functional or otherwise 'non-religious' factors discussed above should be expected to have had equal impact in Judah and, say, Ammon, they cannot be considered the sole factors responsible for the specific evolution aniconism underwent in Judaean glyptic. I am thus inclined to admit some complementary influence of the growing religious valuation of aniconism on the parallel evolution attested by inscribed seals. In this respect, one may fully agree with Sass (*supra*, pp. 198, 245) that a very typical feature of Judaean glyptic of the later seventh/early sixth century BC, namely the elaborate variations on ornamental register dividers, including vegetal motifs (see p. 203, figs. 35-46), is strongly reminiscent of later Islamic response to the religious veto on representations of humans, animals, or mixed beings.

I would venture even further: Among the Jerusalem bullae published by Avigad (1986) and Shiloh (1986), we find aniconic seal impressions of prominent and influential people,[94] some of which are known to us from the biblical books of Kings and Jeremiah as open partisans or protectors of the "proto-deuteronomistic" milieu and movement (cf. **fig. 24**). The recently published seal of *ḥnn bn ḥlqyhw hkhn*, perhaps the son of the high priest Hilkiah who is said to have found the Torah scroll in the temple (2 Kings 22:8), is equally aniconic (**fig. 25**). It was in this milieu of late-seventh-century

94. Note that at least *at this stage* of the religious history of Judah, aniconic tendencies cannot be plausibly explained by ancient Israel's peripheral location or presumed 'nomadic' background, as has been maintained for earlier periods (cf. Keel 1977: 39-44; Dohmen 1985: 237-244, see note 77). We clearly have to deal with an upper-class phenomenon with complex social and ideological ramifications. For a recent assessment of the social background and milieu of the "deuteronomic" or "proto-deuteronomistic movement", see Albertz 1992: 313-317.

Jerusalem that the deuteronomic and deuteronomistic so-called "name theology" emerged, a new theology which centered around the concept that Yahweh's presence in the Temple was mediated through his *name* only (as against earlier titles of Yahweh as "the one who thrones on the cherubim" or Yahweh Ṣebaoth, cf. Mettinger 1982: 38-79). It is a definitely plausible hypothesis, then (cf. GGG: §§ 207-208), to suspect that this new fervour for God's name might have been influenced by the growing insistence of Judaean seal-cutters and their customers on what could aptly be termed "name-alone" seals.

LIST OF FIGURES

LIST OF CONTRIBUTORS

BIBLIOGRAPHY AND ABBREVIATIONS

INDICES

LIST OF CONTRIBUTORS

BORDREUIL, Pierre, C.N.R.S.; 27, rue des Cordelières, F-75013 Paris, France.

GUBEL, Eric; Palmerston Laan 5, B-1040 Bruxelles, Belgium.

HÜBNER, Ulrich, Universität Heidelberg; Jakob-Steffan-Str. 12, D-6500 Mainz 1, Federal Republic of Germany.

LEMAIRE, André, École Pratique des Hautes Études, Paris; 21bis av. de Stalingrad, F-91120 Palaiseau, France.

ORNAN, Tallay; The Israel Museum, P.O.B. 71117, Jerusalem 91710, Israel.

PARAYRE, Dominique, Université Charles de Gaulle – Lille III; 5 rue Michal, F-75013 Paris, France.

SASS, Benjamin, University of Haifa; Israel Antiquities Authority, P.O.B. 586, Jerusalem 91004, Israel.

TIMM, Stefan, Universität Kiel; Wilhelmplatz 6, D–2300 Kiel, Federal Republic of Germany.

UEHLINGER, Christoph; Biblical Institute, University Miséricorde, CH-1700 Fribourg, Switzerland.

BIBLIOGRAPHY AND ABBREVIATIONS

A = N. Avigad, Hebrew Bullae from the Time of Jeremiah. Remnants of a Burnt Archive, Jerusalem 1986.

Abou Assaf, A., 1980, Untersuchungen zur ammonitischen Rundbildkunst: UF 12, 7-102.

Abu Taleb, M., 1985, The seal of *plṭy bn mʾš* the *mazkīr*: ZDPV 101, 21-29.

ACISFP 1 = Atti del I° Congresso Internazionale di Studi Fenici e Punici (CSF 16/3), Rome 1983.

ACISFP 2 = Atti del II° Congresso Internazionale di Studi Fenici e Punici (CSF 30/II), Rome 1991.

ADPV = Abhandlungen des Deutschen Palästina-Vereins, Wiesbaden.

ÄAT = Ägypten und Altes Testament, Wiesbaden.

Aimé-Giron, N., 1922, Notes épigraphiques: JA XI/19-20, 63-93.

— 1939, Adversaria Semitica: BIFAO 38, 1-63.

AION = Annali dell'Istituto Universitario Orientale di Napoli.

Albertz, R., 1992, Religionsgeschichte Israels in alttestamentlicher Zeit. Teil 1: Von den Anfängen bis zum Ende der Königszeit (Grundrisse zum Alten Testament 8/1), Göttingen.

Albright, W.F., 1938, The Excavation of Tell Beit Mirsim. II: The Bronze Age (AASOR 17), New Haven.

— 1947, Comments on Recently Received Publications: BASOR 105, 12-16.

Amadasi Guzzo, M.G., 1967, Le iscrizioni fenicie e puniche delle colonie in occidente, Rome.

— 1987, Scritture alfabetiche, Rome.

— 1989, Review of Bordreuil 1986a: RSF 17, 147-148.

ʿAmr, A.-J., 1980, A Study of the Clay Figurines and Zoomorphic Vessels of Trans-Jordan during the Iron Age, with Special Reference to their Symbolism and Function, unpubl. Ph.D. thesis, University of London.

ANEP = J.B. Pritchard, The Ancient Near East in Pictures Relating to the Old Testament, 2nd ed. with Supplement, Princeton 1969.

ANET = J.B. Pritchard, Ancient Near Eastern Texts Relating to the Old Testament, Princeton, ^{2}1955.

Anthedon = W.M.F. Petrie & J.C. Ellis, Anthedon, Sinai (BSAE 58), London 1937.

ARAB = D.D. Luckenbill, Ancient Records of Assyria and Babylonia, New York 1926, 1927 (reprint 1975).

Ariel, D.T., 1990, Excavations at the City of David 1978-1985. II: Imported Stamped Amphora Handles, Coins, Worked Bone and Ivory, and Glass (City of David Excavations Final Reports II = Qedem 30), Jerusalem.

Ashdod IV = M. Dothan & Y. Porath, Ashdod IV (ʿAtiqot. English Series 15), Jerusalem 1982.

Aufrecht, W.E., 1989, see CAI.

— 1992, Three Inscribed Seals: EI 23 (1992) 1*-3*.

AUSS = Andrews University Seminary Studies, Berrien Springs, MI.

Avigad, N., 1946, A Seal of a Slave Wife (Amah): PEQ 78, 125-132.

— 1951, Some New Readings of Hebrew Seals: EI 1, 32-34 (Hebrew).

— 1952, An Ammonite Seal: IEJ 2, 163-164.

— 1954a, Three Ornamented Seals: IEJ 4, 236-238.

Avigad, N. (ctd.)
— 1954b, Seven Ancient Hebrew Seals: BIES 18, 147-153 (Hebrew; English summary IV).
— 1957, A New Class of *Yehud* Stamps: IEJ 7, 146-153.
— 1958a, s.v. Seal: Encyclopaedia Biblica, Jerusalem, 67-86 (Hebrew).
— 1958b, An Early Aramaic Seal: IEJ 8, 228-230.
— 1963, A Seal of "Manasseh, son of the King": IEJ 13, 133-136.
— 1964a, Seals and Sealings: IEJ 14, 190-194.
— 1964b, The Seal of Jezebel: IEJ 14, 274-276.
— 1965, Seals of Exiles: IEJ 15, 222-232.
— 1966, Two Phoenician Votive Seals: IEJ 16, 243-251.
— 1968, Notes on Some Inscribed Syro-Phoenician Seals: BASOR 189, 44-49.
— 1969, A Group of Hebrew Seals: EI 9, 1-9 (Hebrew; English summary 134*).
— 1970a, Ammonite and Moabite Seals, in Sanders 1970: 284-295.
— 1970b, Six Ancient Hebrew Seals, in S. Abramsky et al. (eds.), Shemuel Yeivin Festschrift, Jerusalem, 305-308 (Hebrew).
— 1971, An Unpublished Phoenician Seal, in A. Caquot & M. Philonenko (eds.), Hommages à André Dupont-Sommer, Paris, 3-4.
— 1975a, The Priest of Dor: IEJ 25, 101-105.
— 1975b, New Names on Hebrew Seals: EI 12, 66-71 (Hebrew; English summary 120*-121*).
— 1976a, Bullae and Seals from a Post-exilic Judean Archive (Qedem 4), Jerusalem.
— 1976b, New Light on the Naʿar Seals, in F.M. Cross, W.E. Lemke & P.D. Miller (eds.), Magnalia Dei, The Mighty Acts of God. Essays on the Bible and Archaeology in Memory of G.E. Wright, Garden City, NY, 294-300.
— 1977a, Two Ammonite Seals depicting the *Dea Nutrix*: BASOR 230, 67-69.
— 1977b, New Moabite and Ammonite Seals at the Israel Museum: EI 13, 108-110 (Hebrew; English summary 294*).
— 1978a, Gleanings from Unpublished Ancient Seals: BASOR 230, 67-69.
— 1978b, The Seal of Seraiah (Son of) Neriah: EI 14, 86-87 (Hebrew; English summary 125*).
— 1978c, Baruch the Scribe and Jerahmeel the King's Son: IEJ 28, 51-56.
— 1978d, The King's Daughter and the Lyre: IEJ 28, 136-151.
— 1979, A Group of Hebrew Seals from the Hecht Collection, in Festschrift R.R. Hecht, Jerusalem, 119-126.
— 1980a, Discovering Jerusalem, Nashville – Camden – New York.
— 1980b, The Chief of the Corvée: IEJ 30, 170-173.
— 1981, Titles and Symbols on Hebrew Seals: EI 15, 303-305 (Hebrew; English summary 85*).
— 1982, A Hebrew Seal Depicting a Sailing Ship: BASOR 246, 59-61.
— 1985, Some Decorated West Semitic Seals: IEJ 35, 1-7.
— 1986a, see A.
— 1986b, Three Ancient Seals: BA 49, 51-53.
— 1987a, The Contribution of Hebrew Seals to an Understanding of Israelite Religion and Society, in Miller, McCarter & Hanson 1987: 195-208.
— 1987b, On the Identification of Persons Mentioned in Hebrew Epigraphic Sources: EI 19, 235-237 (Hebrew; English summary 79*).
— 1988, Hebrew Seals and Sealings and their Significance for Biblical Research, in J.A.E. Emerton (ed.), Congress Volume, Jerusalem 1986 (VT Suppl. 40), Leiden, 7-16.

Avigad, N. (ctd.)
— 1989a, Another Group of West-Semitic Seals from the Hecht Collection: Michmanim 4, 7-21.
— 1989b, Two Seals of Women and Other Hebrew Seals: EI 20, 90-96 (Hebrew; English summary 197*).
— 1990, The Seal of Mefaᶜah: IEJ 40, 42-43.
— 1992a, A New Bulla of a Moabite Scribe: EI 23, 92-93 (Hebrew; English summary 149*).
— 1992b, A New Seal of a "Son of the King": Michmanim 6, 27*-31*.
— 1992c, A New Seal Depicting a Lion: Michmanim 6, 33*-36*.

B = P. Bordreuil, Catalogue des sceaux ouest-sémitiques inscrits de la Bibliothèque Nationale, du Musée du Louvre et du Musée biblique de Bible et Terre Sainte, Paris 1986.
BAALIM = Bordreuil, P. & Gubel, E., Bulletin d'Antiquités Archéologiques du Levant inédites ou méconnues, I: Syria 60, 1983, 335-341.
— II: Syria 62, 1985, 171-186.
— III: Syria 63, 1986, 417-435.
— IV: Syria 64, 1987, 309-321.
— V: Syria 65, 1988, 437-456.
— VI: Syria 67, 1990, 483-520.
Baqués-Estapé, L., 1976, Escarabeos egipcios y sellos del Museo bíblico del Seminario diocesano de Palma (Mallorca): Boletín de la Asociación Española de los Orientalistas 22, 133-147.
Barag, D., 1985, Phoenician Stone Vessels from the Eighth-Seventh Centuries BCE: EI 18, 215-232 (Hebrew; English summary 72*-73*).
Barkay, G., 1986, Ketef Hinnom. A Treasure Facing Jerusalem's Walls (Israel Museum Catalogue no. 274), Jerusalem.
— 1991, De David à la destruction du temple de Salomon: Les Dossiers de l'Archéologie, 165-166 (Nov.-Dec.), 32-45.
— 1992a, "The Prancing Horse" – An Official Seal Impression from Judah of the 8th Century B.C.E.: Tel Aviv 19, 124-129.
— 1992b, A Group of Stamped Handles from Judah: EI 23, 113-128 (Hebrew; English summary 150*-151*).
Barnett, R.D., 1967a, Layard's Nimrud Bronzes and their Inscriptions: EI 8, 1*-7*.
— 1967b, Recent Acquisitions: British Museum Quarterly 32, 58.
— 1969, ᶜAnath, Baᶜal and Pasargadae: Mémoires de l'Université Saint-Joseph 45 (= Hommages à M. Dunand), 407-422.
— 1982, Ancient Ivories in the Middle East and Adjacent Countries (Qedem 14), Jerusalem.
Barnett, R.D. & Mendleson, C., 1987, Tharros. A Catalogue of Material in the British Museum from Phoenician and other Tombs at Tharros, Sardinia, London.
Bartlett, J.R., 1989, Edom and the Edomites (JSOTS 77 = PEF Monograph Series 1), Sheffield.
Baurain, Cl., Bonnet, C. & Krings, V. (eds.), 1991, Phoinikeia Grammata. Lire et écrire en Méditerranée (Collection d'Études Classiques 6 = StPh XII), Liège – Namur.
Behrens, P., 1984, s.v. Skorpion: LÄ V, 987-989.
Beit-Arieh, I. & Cresson, B., 1985, An Edomite Ostracon from Ḥorvat ᶜUza: Tel Aviv 12, 96-101.
Bennett, C.-M., 1966, Fouilles d'Umm el-Biyara. Rapport préliminaire: RB 73, 372-403.
— 1967-1968, The Excavations at Tawilan nr. Petra: ADAJ 12-13, 53-55.

Bennett, C.-M. (ctd.)
— 1969, [Chronique archéologique] Ṭawilān: RB 76, 386-390.
— 1975, Excavations at Buseirah, Southern Jordan, 1973. Third Preliminary Report: Levant 7, 1-19.
— 1978, Some Reflections on Neo-Assyrian Influence in Transjordan, in P.R.S. Moorey & P.J. Parr (eds.), Archaeology in the Levant. Essays for K.M. Kenyon, Warminster, 165-171.
— 1982, Neo-Assyrian Influence in Transjordan: SHAJ I, 181-187.
— 1983, Excavations at Buseirah (Biblical Bozrah), in J.A. Sawyer & D.J.A. Clines (eds.), Midian, Moab and Edom (JSOTS 24), Sheffield, 9-17.
Benz, F.L., 1972, Personal Names in the Phoenician and Punic Inscriptions (Studia Pohl 8), Rome.
Benzinger, I., 1894, Hebräische Archäologie, Freiburg i.Br. – Leipzig.
— 1907, Hebräische Archäologie (2nd edition), Tübingen.
— 1927, Hebräische Archäologie (3rd edition), Leipzig.
Berger, P., 1907, Intaille à légende hébraïque provenant de Carthage: Revue archéologique 6, 83-84.
Biella, J.C., 1982, Dictionary of Old South Arabic. Sabean Dialect (Harvard Semitic Studies 25), Chico, CA.
Biran, A., 1977, [Notes and News] Tel Dan, 1977: IEJ 27, 242-246.
— 1988, A Mace-Head and the Office of Amadiyahu at Dan: Qadmoniot 21, 11-17 (Hebrew).
Biran, A. & Cohen, R., 1981, Aroer in the Negev: EI 15, 250-273 (Hebrew; English summary 84*).
Bisi, A.M., 1965, Il grifone. Storia di un motivo iconografico nell'antico Oriente mediterraneo (StSem 13), Rome.
— 1988, Antécédents éblaïtes d'un apotropaïon phénico-punique, in H. Waetzoldt – H. Hauptmann (eds.), Wirtschaft und Gesellschaft von Ebla (Heidelberger Studien zum Alten Orient 2), Heidelberg, 21-33.
Bivar, A.D.H., 1961, A "Satrap" of Cyrus the Young: Numismatic Chronicle, 119-127.
Black, J. & Green, A., 1992, Gods, Demons and Symbols of Ancient Mesopotamia. An Illustrated Dictionary, London.
Bleibtreu, E., 1990, s.v. Lotos: RlA VII, 103-106.
Bliss, F.J. & Macalister, R.A.S., 1902, Excavations in Palestine during the Years 1898-1900, London.
BM = The British Museum, London.
BN = Bibliothèque Nationale, Cabinet des Médailles, Paris.
Boardman, J., 1968, Archaic Greek Gems. Schools and Artists in the Sixth and Early Fifth Centuries BC, London.
— 1970, Pyramidal Stamp Seals in the Persian Empire: Iran 8, 19-45.
— 1971, The Danicourt Gems in Péronne: Revue archéologique, 195-214.
— 1990, The Lyre Player Group of Seals, an Encore: Jahrbuch des Deutschen Archäologischen Instituts (Archäologischer Anzeiger) 105, 1-17.
Boardman, J. & Moorey, P.R.S., 1986, The Yunis Cemetery Group: Haematite Scarabs, in Kelly-Buccellati 1986, 35-48.
Börker-Klähn, J., 1971, s.v. Greif: RlA III, 633-639.
— 1982, Altvorderasiatische Bildstelen und vergleichbare Felsreliefs. Mit einem Beitrag von A. Shunnar-Misera (Baghdader Forschungen 4), Mainz.
Börker-Klähn, J. & Röllig, W., 1971, s.v. Granatapfel: RlA III, 616-632.

Bonnet, C., 1988, Melqart. Cultes et mythes de l'Héraclès tyrien en Mediterranée (Bibliothèque de la Faculté de Philosophie et Lettres de Namur 69 = StPh VIII), Leuven & Namur.

— 1989, Le dieu solaire Shamash dans le monde phénico-punique: SEL 6, 97-115.

Bordreuil, P., 1973a, Inscriptions sigillaires ouest-sémitiques, I. Epigraphie ammonite: Syria 50, 181-195.

— 1973b, Une tablette araméenne inédite de 635 av. J.-C.: Semitica 23, 95-102.

— 1981, L'estampille phénicienne d'Ibn Hani: Syria 53, 297-299.

— 1983, Nouveaux apports de l'archéologie et de la glyptique à l'onomastique phénicienne, ACISFP 1, vol. III, 751-755.

— 1985, Inscriptions sigillaires ouest-sémitiques, III. Sceaux de dignitaires et de rois syro-palestiniens du VIIIe et du VIIe siècle avant J.-C.: Syria 62, 21-29.

— 1986a, see B.

— 1986b, Charges et fonctions en Syrie-Palestine d'après quelques sceaux ouest-sémitiques du second et du premier millénaire: CRAIBL (April-June), 290-307.

— 1986c, A Note on the Seal of Peqaḥ the Armor-Bearer, Future King of Israel: BA 49, 54-55.

— 1986d, Les sceaux des grands personnages: Le Monde de la Bible 46, 45.

— 1986e, Sceaux transjordaniens inscrits, in La voie royale. 9000 d'art au royaume de Jordanie, Paris, 128-141.

— 1986f, Un cachet moabite du Musée biblique de Palma de Mallorca: Aula Orientalis 4, 119-120.

— 1986g, Sceau en calcédoine ...: BAALIM III, 429, no. III.5.

— 1987a, Perspectives nouvelles de l'épigraphie sigillaire ammonite et moabite: SHAJ III, 283-286.

— 1987b, Tanit du Liban (Nouveaux documents religieux phéniciens III), in E. Lipiński (ed.), Phoenicia and the East Mediterranean in the First Millenium B.C. (OLA 22 = StPh V), Leuven, 79-85.

— 1988a, A propos d'une tessère de Tamit: BAALIM V, 443, no. III. 4; Gouvernail en bronze à inscription phénicienne: ibid., 443-444, no. III. 5; Sceau d'un Cappadocien habitant dans la Beqaʿa: ibid., 444-445, no. III. 6; Sceau araméen d'un *tartan*:: ibid., 445, no. III. 7.

— 1988b, Notes sur des sceaux à inscriptions sémitiques, in M.-P. Boussac, Sceaux déliens: Revue archéologique, 339-340.

— 1991, Les premiers sceaux royaux phéniciens: ACISFP 2, vol. II, Rome, 463-468.

— 1992, s.v. Sceaux inscrits des pays du Levant: Dictionnaire de la Bible, Supplément vol. XII, fasc. 66, 86-212.

Bordreuil, P. & Lemaire, A., 1976, Nouveaux sceaux hébreux, araméens et ammonites: Semitica 26, 45-63.

— 1979, Nouveau groupe de sceaux hébreux, araméens et ammonites: Semitica 29, 71-84.

— 1982, Nouveaux sceaux hébreux et araméens: Semitica 32, 21-34.

Borowski, E., 1952, Die Sammlung H.A. Layard: Orientalia 21, 168-183.

Bottéro, J., 1958, Les divinités sémitiques anciennes en Mésopotamie, in S. Moscati (ed.), Le antiche divinità semitiche (StSem 1), Rome, 17-63.

Braidwood, R.J., 1940, Report on Two Sondages on the Coast of Syria, South of Tartous: Syria 21, 183-221.

Branden, A. van den & Naster, P., 1981, Un cylindre-sceau d'Abilène: OLP 12, 117-125.

Brandl, B., 1984a, The Restoration of an Engraved Tridacna Shell from Arad: The Israel Museum Journal 3, 76-79.

Brandl, B. (ctd.)
— 1984b, The Engraved Tridacna-Shell Discs: Anatolian Studies 34, 15-41.
Braun-Holzinger, E.A., 1990, s.v. Löwendrache; Löwenmensch: RlA VII: 97-99; 99-102.
BRL² = Biblisches Reallexikon, ed. by K. Galling, 2nd, revised edition (Handbuch zum Alten Testament I/1), Tübingen 1977.
Bron, F., 1979, Recherches sur les inscriptions phéniciennes de Karatepe (Hautes Études Orientales 11), Geneva – Paris.
Brunner-Traut, E., 1980, s.v. Lotos: LÄ III, 1091-1096.
Buchanan, B., 1966, Catalogue of the Ancient Near Eastern Seals in the Ashmolean Museum. I: Cylinder Seals, Oxford.
Buchanan, B. & Moorey, P.R.S., 1988, Catalogue of Near Eastern Seals in the Ashmolean Museum. III: The Iron Age Stamp Seals (c. 1200-350 BC), Oxford.
Buchner, G. & Boardman, J., 1966, Seals from Ischia and the Lyre-Player Group: Jahrbuch des deutschen archäologischen Instituts 81, 1-62.
Bunnens, G., 1989, Review of Bordreuil 1986a : Abr-Nahrain 27, 174-176.

CAI = W.E. Aufrecht, A Corpus of Ammonite Inscriptions (Ancient Near Eastern Texts and Studies 4), Lewiston, NY – Queenston, Ont. – Lampeter, Dyfed (Wales), 1989.
Calmeyer, P., 1975, s.v. "Herr der Tiere"; "Herrin der Tiere": RlA IV, 334-335.
Cantineau, J., 1932, Le nabatéen. II: Choix de textes, Lexique, Paris.
Carchemish III = L. Woolley, Carchemish III, London 1952.
Ciasca, A., 1988, Masken und Protome, in S. Moscati (ed.), Die Phönizier (exhibition catalogue [= I Fenici, Milano 1988]), Munich, 354-369.
CIS = Corpus Inscriptionum Semiticarum, Paris.
Clerc, G., et al., 1976, Fouilles de Kition II. Objets égyptiens et égyptisants: scarabées, amulettes et figurines en pâte de verre et en faïence, vase plastique en faïence. Sites I et II, 1959-1975, Nicosia.
Clercq, J. de, 1903, Collection De Clercq, catalogue méthodique et raisonné. Antiquités assyriennes II: cachets, briques, bronzes, bas-reliefs, etc., Paris.
Clermont-Ganneau, Ch., 1883, Sceaux et cachets israélites, phéniciens et syriens, suivis d'épigraphes phéniciennes inédites ...: JA 8/1, 123-159.506-510; 8/2, 304-305.
— 1885, Les fraudes archéologiques en Palestine, Paris.
— 1890, [Séance du 5 décembre: empreintes de deux anciens sceaux sémitiques du Musée britannique]: CRAIBL, 430-431.
Cogan, M., 1974, Imperialism and Religion: Assyria, Judah and Israel in the Eighth and Seventh Centuries B.C.E. (SBL Monograph Series 19), Missoula, MT.
Collon, D., 1972, The Smiting God: Levant 4, 111-134.
— 1982, The Alalakh Cylinder Seals. A New Catalogue of the Actual Seals Excavated by Sir Leonard Woolley at Tell Atchana, and from Neighbouring Sites on the Syrian-Turkish Border (BAR International Series 132), Oxford.
— 1983, s.v. Kreuzschleife: RlA VI, 240-241.
— 1986a, The Green Jasper Cylinder Seal Workshop, in Kelly-Buccellati 1986, 57-70.
— 1986b, Cylindre en chalcédoine brûlée ...: BAALIM III, 425-426, no. III.3.
— 1987, First Impressions. Cylinder Seals in the Ancient Near East, London.
Contenau, G., 1922, La glyptique syro-hittite, Paris.
Couroyer, B., 1970, Menues trouvailles à Jérusalem: RB 77, 248-252.
Cross, F.M., 1962, An Archaic Inscribed Seal from the Valley of Aijalon: BASOR 168, 12-18.
— 1973, Heshbon Ostracon II: AUSS 11, 126-131.

Cross, F.M. (ctd.)
— 1983, The seal of Miqnêyaw, servant of Yahweh, in Gorelick & Williams-Forte 1983: 55-63.
CSF = Collezione di Studi Fenici, Rome.
Culican, W., 1974, A Phoenician Seal from Khaldeh: Levant 6, 195-198 [= 1986: 385-390].
— 1977, Seals in Bronze Mounts: RSF 5, 1-4 [= 1986: 527-533].
— 1986, Opera Selecta. From Tyre to Tartessos (Studies in Mediterranean Archaeology Pocket-book 40), Gothenburg.
Curtis, J.E. (ed.), 1988, Bronze-working Centres of Western Asia, c. 1000-539 B.C., London.

D = D. Diringer, Le iscrizioni antico-ebraiche palestinesi (Pubblicazioni della R. Università degli Studi di Firenze. Facoltà di lettere e filosofia III/2), Florence 1934.
Dajani, R.W., 1962, A Neo-Babylonian Seal from Amman: ADAJ 6-7, 124-125.
— 1970, A Late Bronze-Iron Age Tomb excavated at Sahab: ADAJ 15, 29-34.
Dalman, G., 1906, Ein neu gefundenes Jahvebild: Palästina-Jahrbuch 2, 44-50.
Dearman, A. (ed.), 1989, Studies in the Mesha Inscription and Moab (ASOR/SBL Archaeology and Biblical Studies 2), Atlanta.
Delaporte, L., 1910, Catalogue des cylindres orientaux et des cachets assyro-babyloniens, perses et syro-cappadociens de la Bibliothèque Nationale, Paris.
— 1920, Catalogue des cylindres, cachets et pierres gravées de style oriental, Musée du Louvre. I: Fouilles et missions, Paris.
— 1923, Catalogue des cylindres, cachets et pierres gravées de style oriental, Musée du Louvre. II: Acquisitions, Paris.
— 1928, Cachets orientaux de la collection de Luynes: Aréthuse 5, 41-65.
Delattre, L. & Berger, P., 1900, Catalogue du Musée Lavigerie de Saint-Louis de Carthage, Paris.
Dessenne, A., 1957, Le Sphinx. Etude iconographique. I: Des origines à la fin du second millénaire, Paris.
Dever, W.G., 1990, Recent Archaeological Discoveries and Biblical Research, Seattle & London.
Dever, W.G. et al., 1986, Gezer IV. The 1969-1971 Seasons in Field VI, the "Acropolis" (Annual of the HUC/Nelson Glueck School of Biblical Archaeology), Jerusalem.
Diehl, E., 1965, Fragmente aus Samos II: Jahrbuch des Deutschen Archäologischen Instituts (Archäologischer Anzeiger) 80, 823-850.
Dion, P.E., 1989, Review of Bordreuil 1986a: BASOR 275, 74-77.
Diringer, D., 1934, see D.
— 1941, On Ancient Hebrew Inscriptions Discovered at Tell ed-Duweir (Lachish). I: PEQ 73, 38-56; II: ibid., 89-106.
Dohmen, Ch., 1985, Das Bilderverbot. Seine Entstehung und seine Entwicklung im Alten Testament (Bonner Biblische Beiträge 62), Frankfurt am Main (^{2}1987).
Driver, G.R., 1945, Seals from ʿAmman and Petra: QDAP 11, 81-82.
— 1957, Aramaic Names in Accadian Texts: RSO 32, 41-57.
Dupont-Sommer, A., 1950, Deux nouvelles inscriptions sémitiques trouvées en Cilicie: Jahrbuch für Kleinasiatische Forschung 1, 43-47.

Ebeling, E., 1928a, s.v. Adad: RlA I, 22-26.
— 1928b, s.v. Baum, heiliger: RlA I, 435.
EI = Eretz-Israel. Archaeological, Historical and Geographical Studies, Jerusalem.

Elayi, J., 1986, Le sceau du prêtre Ḥanan, fils de Ḥilqiyahu: Semitica 36, 43-46.
— 1990, Inscriptions nord-ouest sémitiques inédites: Semitica 38, 101-106.
Ellis, R.S., 1977, 'Lion-Men' in Assyria, in M. deJong Ellis (ed.), Essays on the Ancient Near East in Memory of J.J. Finkelstein (Memoirs of the Connecticut Academy of Arts and Sciences 19), Hamden, CT, 67-78.
En Gedi = B. Mazar, T. Dothan & I. Dunayevsky, En-Gedi, The First and Second Seasons of Excavations 1961-1962 (ʿAtiqot. English Series 5), Jerusalem 1966.
EPRO = Etudes préliminaires aux religions orientales dans l'empire romain, Leiden.
Eretz Israel Museum, 1989, Fakes and Forgeries From Collections in Israel (exhibition catalogue, Tel Aviv.
ESE = M. Lidzbarski, Ephemeris für semitische Epigraphik, I-III (1900-1902, 1902-1907, 1909-1915), Gießen 1902, 1908, 1915.
Euting, J., 1883, Epigraphisches: ZDMG 37, 541-543.

Fales, F.M., 1986, Aramaic Epigraphs on Clay Tablets of the Neo-Assyrian Period (StSem n.s. 2), Rome.
— 1990, Istituzioni a confronto tra mondo semitico occidentale e Assiria nel I° millenio A.C.: il trattato di Sefire, in L. Canfora, M. Liverani & C. Zaccagnini (eds.), I trattati nel mondo antico. Forma, ideologia, funzione, Rome, 149-173.
Falsone, G., 1978, Il simbolo di Tanit a Mozia e nella Sicilia punica: RSF 6, 137-151.
Fowler, J.D., 1988, Theophoric Personal Names in Ancient Hebrew. A Comparative Study (JSOTS 49), Sheffield.
Frankena, R. & Seidl, U., 1971, s.v. Gula: RlA III, 695-697.
Frankfort, H., 1939, Cylinder Seals. A Documentary Essay on the Art and Religion of the Ancient Near East, London.
— 1970, The Art and Architecture of the Ancient Orient, Harmondsworth.
Friedrich, J. & Röllig, W., Phönizisch-punische Grammatik (AnOr 46), Rome ²1970.
Fulco, W.J., 1979, A Seal from Umm el-Qanafīd, Jordan: *gʾlyhw ʿbd hmlk*: Orientalia 48, 107-108.

G = K. Galling, Beschriftete Bildsiegel des ersten Jahrtausends v. Chr. vornehmlich aus Syrien und Palästina. Ein Beitrag zur Geschichte der phönizischen Kunst: ZDPV 64, 1941, 121-202.
Galling, K., 1928, Ein hebräisches Siegel aus der babylonischen Diaspora: ZDPV 51, 234-236.
— 1937, s.v. Siegel, in id., Biblisches Reallexikon (Handbuch zum Alten Testament I/1), Tübingen, 481-490.
— 1941, see G.
— 1967, [Miscellanea Archaeologica] Das Siegel des Jotham von *Tell el-Ḫlēfi*: ZDPV 83, 131-134.
Garbini, G., 1967, Un nuovo sigillo-aramaico-ammonita: AION 17, 251-256.
— 1968, Further Considerations on the Aramaic-Ammonite Seals: AION 18, 453-454.
— 1974, Ammonite Inscriptions: JSS 19, 159-168.
— 1976, Iscrizioni sudarabiche: AION 36, 293-315.
— 1979, Le scritture ebraico-moabitica e ammonitica, in Storia e problemi dell'epigrafia semitica, Naples, 61-64.
— 1982, I sigilli del regno di Israele: OrAnt 21, 163-176.
— 1986, Philistine Seals, in L.T. Geraty & L.G. Herr (eds.), The Archaeology of Jordan and Other Studies Presented to S. Horn, Berrien Springs, MI, 443-448.
— 1987, Review of Avigad 1986a: Henoch 9, 397-399.

Garfinkel, Y., 1984, The Distribution of Identical Seal Impressions and the Settlement Pattern in Judea before Sennacherib's Campaign: Cathedra 32 (July), 35-52 (Hebrew).

Garr, W.R., 1985, Dialect Geography of Syria-Palestine, 1000-586 B.C.E., Philadelphia.

Geertz, C., 1973, The Interpretation of Cultures: Selected Essays, New York.

Genge, H., 1979, Nordsyrisch-südanatolische Reliefs. Eine archäologisch-historische Untersuchung, Datierung und Bestimmung, Copenhagen.

Geraty, L.T., et al., 1988, A Preliminary Report on the Second Season at Tell el-ᶜUmeiri and Vicinity (June 18 to August 6, 1987): AUSS 26, 217-252.

— 1989, Madaba Plains Project 1: The 1984 Season at Tell el-ᶜUmeiri and Vicinity and Subsequent Studies, Berrien Springs, MI.

— 1990, Madaba Plains Project: A Preliminary Report of the 1987 Season at Tell el-ᶜUmeiri and Vicinity, in W.E. Rast (ed.), Preliminary Reports of ASOR-Sponsored Excavations 1983-1987 (BASOR Suppl. 26), Baltimore, 59-88.

Gesenius, W., 1837, Scripturae linguaeque Phoeniciae Monumenta quotquot supersunt, Leipzig.

Geva, Sh., A Fragment of a Tridacna Shell from Shechem: ZDPV 96, 41-47.

Gezer I-III = R.A.S. Macalister, The Excavation of Gezer. 1902-1905 and 1907-1909, I-III, London 1912.

GGG = O. Keel & Ch. Uehlinger, Göttinnen, Götter und Gottessymbole. Neue Erkenntnisse zur Religionsgeschichte Kanaans und Israels aufgrund unerschlossener ikonographischer Quellen (Quaestiones disputatae 134), Freiburg i.Br. – Basle – Vienna 1992.

Gibson, J.C.L., 1975, Textbook of Syrian Semitic Inscriptions. II: Aramaic Inscriptions, Oxford.

— 1982, Textbook of Syrian Semitic Inscriptions. III: Phoenician Inscriptions including inscriptions in the mixed diialect of Arslan Tash, Oxford.

Giveon, R., 1961, Two New Hebrew Seals and their Iconographic Background: PEQ 63, 38-42 [= 1978: 110-116].

— 1978, The Impact of Egypt on Canaan. Iconographical and Related Studies (OBO 20), Fribourg & Göttingen.

— 1985, Egyptian Scarabs from Western Asia from the Collections of the British Museum (OBO.SA 3), Fribourg & Göttingen.

Giveon, R. & Kertesz, T., 1986, Egyptian Scarabs and Seals from Acco. From the Collection of the Israel Department of Antiquities and Museums, Fribourg 1986.

Giveon, R. & Lemaire, A., 1985, Sceau phénicien inscrit d'Akko avec scène religieuse: Semitica 35, 27-32.

Goff, B.L., 1956, The Role of Amulets in Mesopotamian Ritual Texts: Journal of the Warburg and Courtauld Institutes 19, 1-39.

Gorelick, L. & Gwinnet, A.J., 1978, Ancient Seals and Modern Science. Using Scanning Electron Microscope as an Aid in the Study of Ancient Seals: Expedition 20, 38-47.

Gorelick, L. & Williams-Forte, E. (eds.), 1983, Ancient Seals and the Bible (Occasional Papers on the Near East 2/1), Malibu, CA.

Green, A., 1983, Neo-Assyrian Apotropaic Figures: Iraq 45, 87-96.

— 1984, Beneficient Spirits and Malevolent Demons. The Iconography of Good and Evil in Ancient Assyria and Babylonia: Visible Religion 3, 80-105.

— 1986, The Lion-Demon in the Art of Mesopotamia and Neighbouring Regions: Baghdader Mitteilungen 17, 141-254.

Greenfield, J.C., 1972, The Aramean God Rammōn/Rimmōn: IEJ 22, 195-198.

— 1985, A Group of Phoenician City Seals: IEJ 35, 129-134.

Gröndahl, F., 1967, Die Personennamen der Texte aus Ugarit (Studia Pohl 1), Rome.

Grumach-Shirun, I., 1977, s.v. Federn, Federkronen: LÄ II, 142-145.

Gubel, E., 1983, Art in Tyre during the First and Second Iron Age: A Preliminary Survey, in E. Lipiński (ed.), Sauvons Tyr (OLA 15 = StPh I), Leuven, 23-52.

— 1985, Notes on a Phoenician Seal in the Royal Museums for Art and History, Brussels (CGPH 1): OLP 16, 91-110.

— 1987a, 'Syro-Cypriote' Cubical Stamps: The Phoenician Connection (CGPH 2), in E. Lipiński (ed.), Phoenicia and the East Mediterranean in the First Millenium B.C. (OLA 22 = StPh V), Leuven, 195-224.

— 1987b, Phoenician Furniture. A Typology Based on Iron Age Representations with Reference to the Iconographical Context (StPh VII), Leuven.

— 1987c, Scarabée inscrit du Fitzwilliam Museum, Cambridge (E.97.1955): BAALIM IV, 311, no. II.2.

— 1988, Phoenician Seals in the Allard Pierson Museum, Amsterdam (CGPH 3): RSF 16, 145-163.

— 1990a, Le sceau de Menahem et l'iconographie royale sigillaire: Semitica 38, 167-171.

— 1990b, Die phönizische Kunst, in U. Gehrig & H.G. Niemeyer (eds.), Die Phönizier im Zeitalter Homers, Mainz, 75-86.

— 1991a, Notes sur l'iconographie royale sigillaire: ACISFP 2, vol. II, 913-922.

— 1991b, Van Nijl tot Schelde. Du Nil à l'Escaut (exhibition catalogue, Banque Bruxelles Lambert, 5 April - 9 June 1991), Brussels.

Gubel, E. et al., 1986, Les Phéniciens et le monde méditerranéen (exhibition catalogue), Brussels.

Guerrero, V.M., Martín, M. & Roldán, B., 1988, Complemento al estudio de las anforas punicas "Maña-C": RSF 16, 195-205.

H = U. Hübner, Die Ammoniter. Untersuchungen zur Geschichte, Kultur und Religion eines transjordanischen Volkes im 1. Jahrtausend v. Chr. (ADPV), Wiesbaden 1992.

Hadidi, A., 1987, An Ammonite Tomb at Amman: Levant 19, 101-120.

Hahn, J., 1981, Das "Goldene Kalb". Die Jahwe-Verehrung bei Stierbildern in der Geschichte Israels (Europäische Hochschulschriften XXIII/154), Frankfurt a.M. - Berne.

HAL = L. Koehler, W. Baumgartner, J.J. Stamm et al., Hebräisches und Aramäisches Lexikon zum Alten Testament, 3rd edition, I-IV, Leiden 1967-1990.

Hallo, W.W., 1978, "As the Seal upon Thine Arm": Glyptic Metaphors in the Biblical World, in Gorelick & Williams-Forte 1978: 7-17.

Halpern, B., 1991, Jerusalem and the Lineages in the Seventh Century BCE: Kinship and the Rise of Individual Moral Liability, in B.H. & D.W. Hobson (eds.), Law and Ideology in Monarchic Israel (JSOT.S 124), Sheffield, 11-107.

Hamilton, R.W., 1935, Excavations at Tell Abu Hawām: QDAP 4, 1-69.

Harden, D., 1962, The Phoenicians (Ancient Peoples and Places), London.

Harding, G.L., 1937, Some Objects from Transjordan: PEQ 69, 253-255.

— 1950, An Iron-Age Tomb at Meqabelein: QDAP 14, 44-48.

— 1953, The Tomb of Adoni Nur in Amman: PEFA 6, 48-65.

— 1971, An Index and Concordance of Pre-Islamic Arabian Names and Inscriptions, Toronto.

Haussperger, M., 1991, Die Einführungsszene. Entwicklung eines mesopotamischen Motivs von der altakkadischen bis zum Ende der altbabylonischen Zeit (Münchener Uni-

versitäts-Schriften. Philosophische Fakultät 12 = Münchener Vorderasiatische Studien XI), München – Wien.
Hazor II = Y. Yadin et al., Hazor II, Jerusalem 1960.
Hazor III-IV = Y. Yadin et al., Hazor III-IV, Jerusalem, 1961 (Plates); 1989 (Text, ed. A. Ben-Tor et al.).
HD = R. Hestrin & M. Dayagi-Mendels, Inscribed Seals. First Temple Period. Hebrew, Ammonite, Moabite, Phoenician and Aramaic. From the Collections of the Israel Museum and the Israel Department of Antiquities and Museums, Jerusalem 1979.
Heimpel, W. & Boehmer, R.M., 1975, s.v. Held: RlA IV, 287-302.
Heimpel, W. & Seidl, U., 1975, s.v. Hund: RlA IV, 494-497.
Heltzer, M.L., 1981, Inscribed Scaraboid Seals, in O.W. Muscarella (ed.), Ladders to Heaven. Art Treasures from Lands of the Bible, Toronto, 290-293 (= German edition: Länder der Bibel. Archäologische Funde aus dem Vorderen Orient, Mainz, 307-317).
— 1985, An Unpublished Moabite Seal in the Hecht Museum: Michmanim 2, 25-28.
Henig, M. & Whiting, M., 1987, Engraved Gems from Gadara in Jordan, Oxford.
Herr, L.G., 1978, The Scripts of Ancient Northwest Semitic Seals (Harvard Semitic Monographs 18), Missoula, MT.
— 1980a, The Formal Scripts of Iron Age Transjordan, BASOR 238: 21-34.
— 1980b, Palaeography and the Identification of Seal Owners: BASOR 239, 67-70.
— 1985, The Servant of Baalis: BA 48, 169-172.
— 1989, The Inscribed Seal Impression, in Geraty et al. 1989, 369-374.
Herrmann, G., 1986, Ivories from Nimrud (1949-1963) IV. Ivories from Room SW 37, Fort Shalmaneser, London.
— 1989, The Nimrud Ivories, 1. The Flame and Frond School: Iraq 51, 85-109.
— 1992a, Ivories from Nimrud (1949-1963) V. The Small Collections from Fort Shalmaneser, London.
— 1992b, The Nimrud Ivories, 2: A Survey of the Traditions, in B. Hrouda, S. Kroll & P.Z. Spanos (eds.), Von Uruk nach Tuttul (FS Eva Strommenger; Münchener Universitäts-Schriften 12 = Münchener vorderasiatische Studien XII), Munich & Vienna, 65-79.
Hestrin, R., 1983, Hebrew Seals of Officials, in Gorelick & Williams-Forte 1983: 50-54.
— 1987, The Lachish Ewer and the Ashera: IEJ 37, 212-223.
— 1991, Understanding Asherah – Exploring Semitic Iconography: BAR 17/5, 50-59.
Hestrin, R. & Dayagi-Mendels, M., 1974, A Seal Impression of a Servant of King Hezekiah: IEJ 24, 27-29.
— 1979, see HD.
Hoffmann, H.-D., 1980, Reform und Reformen. Untersuchungen zu einem Grundthema der deuteronomistischen Geschichtsschreibung (Abhandlungen zur Theologie des Alten und Neuen Testaments 66), Zurich.
Hofstee, W., 1986, The Interpretation of Religion. Some Remarks on the Work of Clifford Geertz, in H.G. Hubbeling – H.G. Kippenberg (ed.), On Symbolic Representation of Religion, Berlin & New York, 70-83.
Hölbl, G., 1979, Beziehungen der ägyptischen Kultur zu Altitalien, (EPRO 62), Leiden.
— 1986, Ägyptisches Kulturgut im phönikischen und punischen Sardinien (EPRO 102), Leiden.
— 1989, Ägyptische Kunstelemente im phönizischen Kulturkreis des 1. Jahrtausends v. Chr. Zur Methodik ihrer Verwendung: Orientalia 58, 318-325.
Hogarth, D.G., 1920, Hittite Seals with Particular Reference to the Ashmolean Collection, Oxford.

Holladay, J.S., 1987, Religion in Israel and Judah under the Monarchy: An Explicitly Archaeological Approach, in Miller, McCarter & Hanson 1987: 249-299.

Homès-Frédéricq, D., 1987, Possible Phoenician Influence in Jordan in the Iron Age: SHAJ III, 89-96.

Horn, S.H., 1971, Three Seals from Sahab Tomb "C": ADAJ 16, 103-106.

Hornung, E. & Staehelin, E., 1976, Skarabäen und andere Siegelamulette aus Basler Sammlungen (Ägyptische Denkmäler in der Schweiz 1), Mainz.

HU = Hebrew University, Jerusalem.

HUC = Hebrew Union College, Cincinnati & Jerusalem.

Hübner, U., 1989a, Schweine, Schweineknochen und ein Speiseverbot im alten Israel: VT 39, 225-236.

— 1989b, Fälschungen ammonitischer Siegel: UF 21, 217-226.

— 1989c, Das Fragment einer Tonfigurine vom *Tell el-Milḥ*. Überlegungen zur Funktion der sog. Pfeilerfigurinen in der israelitischen Volksreligion: ZDPV 105, 47-55.

— 1992a, see H.

— 1992b, ʿAmman before the Hellenistic Period, in A.E. Northedge (ed.), Studies on Roman and Islamic ʿAmman. The Excavations of Mrs C.-M. Bennett and other Investigations. I: The Site and its Architecture (British Institute at Amman for Archaeology and History, British Academy Monographs in Archaeology 3), London [in press].

— 1992c, Supplementa ammonitica I: BN 65 [in press].

Hübner, U. & Knauf, E.A., 1992, Review of Aufrecht 1989: ZDPV 108 [in press].

Hulot, J. & Fougères, G., 1910, Sélinonte, Paris.

IAA = Israel Antiquities Authority, Jerusalem.

Ibrahim, M.M., 1983, Siegel und Siegelabdrücke aus *Saḥāb*: ZDPV 99, 43-53.

IMJ = Israel Museum, Jerusalem.

IR = Inscriptions Reveal. Documents from the Time of the Bible, the Mishna and the Talmud (Israel Museum Catalogue no. 100), Jerusalem 1973.

Israel, F., 1979a, The Language of the Ammonites: OLP 10, 143-159.

— 1979b, Miscellanea Idumea: Rivista Biblica Italiana 27, 171-203.

— 1984, Geographic Linguistics and Canaanite Dialects, in J. Bynon (ed.), Current Progress in Afro-Asiatic Linguistics. Papers of the Third International Hamito-Semitic Congress (Amsterdam Studies in the Theory and History of Linguistic Science IV/28), Amsterdam – Philadelphia, 363-387.

— 1986, Observations on Northwest Semitic Seals (review of Herr 1978): Orientalia 55, 70-77.

— 1987a, Les sceaux ammonites: Syria 64, 141-146.

— 1987b, Studi moabiti I: Rassegna di epigrafia moabita e i sigilli, in G. Bernini & V. Brugnatelli (eds.), Atti della 4ª giornata di Studi Camito-Semitici e Indeuropei, Milan, 101-138.

— 1987c, Studi moabiti II: Da Kamiš à K'môš: Studi e Materiali Storico-Religiosi 53, 5-39.

— 1987d, Supplementum Idumeum: Rivista Biblica Italiana 35, 337-356.

— 1988, Review of Bordreuil 1986a: Orientalia 57, 93-96.

— 1989, Note ammonite I. Gli arabismi nella documentazione onomastica ammonita: SEL 6, 91-96.

— 1990, Note ammonite II: La religione degli Ammoniti attraverso le fonti epigrafiche: Studi e Materiali Storico-Religiosi 56, 307-337.

Israel, F. (ctd.)
— 1991a, Note ammonite III: Problemi di epigrafia sigillare ammonita, in Baurain, Bonnet & Krings 1991: 215-242.
— 1991b, Note di onomastica semitica 7/I: Rassegna critico-bibliografica su alcune onomastiche palestinesi: Israele e Giuda, la regione filistea: SEL 8 (1991) 119-140 [part II forthcoming in SEL 9 (1992)].
— 1992, Note di onomastica semitica 6: L'apporto della glittica all'onomastica aramaica: Vicino Oriente 8/2 (1992) [in press].

Jackson, K.P., 1983a, The Ammonite Language of the Iron Age (Harvard Semitic Monographs 27), Chico, CA.
— 1983b, Ammonite Personal Names in the Context of the West Semitic Onomasticon, in C.L. Meyers & M. O'Connor (eds.), The Word of the Lord Shall Go Forth. Essays in Honor of D.N. Freedman ... (ASOR Special Volume Series 1), Winona Lake, IN, 507-521.
Jakob-Rost, L., 1975, Die Stempelsiegel im Vorderasiatischen Museum, Berlin.
Jamieson-Drake, D.W., 1991, Scribes and Schools in Monarchic Judah. A Socio-Archeological Approach (JSOTS 109 = SWBA 9), Sheffield & Decatur, GA.
Jaroš, K., 1976, Des Mose "strahlende Haut": Eine Notiz zu Ex 34:29.30.35: ZAW 88, 275-288.
Jericho II = K.M. Kenyon, Excavations at Jericho II, London 1965.
Jones, M. (ed.), 1990, Fake? The Art of Deception, London.
JSOTS = Journal for the Study of the Old Testament, Supplements, Sheffield.

Känel, F. von, 1984, s.v. Selqet: LÄ V, 830-833.
KAI = H. Donner & W. Röllig, Kanaanäische und aramäische Inschriften, Wiesbaden ^{3}1973.
Kaufmann, S.A., 1970, Si'gabbar, Priest of Shahr in Nerab: JAOS 90, 270-271.
Keel, O., 1977, Jahwe-Visionen und Siegelkunst. Eine neue Deutung der Majestätsschilderungen in Jes 6, Ez 1 und 10 und Sach 4 (Stuttgarter Bibelstudien 84-85), Stuttgart.
— 1978, The Symbolism of the Biblical World: Ancient Near Eastern Iconography and the Book of Psalms, New York [= English edition of next].
— ^{3}1980, ^{4}1984, Die Welt der altorientalischen Bildsymbolik und das Alte Testament. Am Beispiel der Psalmen, Zurich – Einsiedeln – Cologne & Neukirchen-Vluyn.
— 1980, Das Böcklein in der Milch seiner Mutter und Verwandtes. Im Lichte eines altorientalischen Bildmotivs (OBO 33), Fribourg & Göttingen.
— 1982, Der Pharao als "vollkommene Sonne": Ein neuer ägypto-palästinischer Skarabäentyp, in S. Israelit-Groll (ed.), Egyptological Studies (Scripta Hierosolymitana 28), Jerusalem, 406-529.
— 1984, Deine Blicke sind Tauben. Zur Metaphorik des Hohen Liedes (Stuttgarter Bibelstudien 114-115), Stuttgart.
— 1985, Bildträger aus Palästina/Israel und die besondere Bedeutung der Miniaturkunst, in id. & S. Schroer, Studien zu den Stempelsiegeln aus Palästina/Israel [I] (OBO 67), Fribourg & Göttingen, 7-47.
— 1986a, Das Hohelied (Zürcher Bibelkommentare AT 18), Zurich.
— 1986b, A Stamp Seal Research Project and a Group of Scarabs with Raised Relief: Akkadica 49, 1-16.
— 1989a, Die Jaspis-Skarabäen-Gruppe. Eine vorderasiatische Skarabäenwerkstatt des 17. Jahrhunderts v.Chr., in Keel, Keel-Leu & Schroer 1989: 211-242.

Keel, O. (ctd.)

— 1989b, Zur Identifikation des Falkenköpfigen auf den Skarabäen der ausgehenden 13. und der 15. Dynastie, ibid. 243-280.

— 1990a, Berichtigungen und Nachträge zu den Beiträgen II-IV, in Keel, Shuval & Uehlinger 1990: 261-321.

— 1990b, Früheisenzeitliche Glyptik in Palästina/Israel, ibid. 331-421.

— 1990c, Aramäisch inspirierte Ikonographie aus Palästina (unpublished lecture manuscript, Lyon, Nov. 1990; an updated version is to appear in Studien zu den Stempelsiegeln aus Palästina/Israel, IV, 1993).

— 1992a, s.v. Iconography and the Bible, in D.N. Freedman (ed.), The Anchor Bible Dictionary, vol. 3, New York, 358-374.

— 1992b, Das Recht der Bilder, gesehen zu werden. Drei Fallstudien zur Methode der Interpretation altorientalischer Bilder (OBO 122), Fribourg & Göttingen.

Keel, O., Keel-Leu, H. & Schroer, S., 1989, Studien zu den Stempelsiegeln aus Palästina/ Israel II (OBO 88), Fribourg & Göttingen.

Keel, O., Shuval, M. & Uehlinger, Ch., 1990, Studien zu den Stempelsiegeln aus Palästina/Israel III: Die Frühe Eisenzeit. Ein Workshop (OBO 100), Fribourg & Göttingen.

Keel, O. & Uehlinger, Ch., 1990, Altorientalische Miniaturkunst. Die ältesten visuellen Massenkommunikationsmittel. Ein Blick in die Sammlungen des Biblischen Instituts der Universität Freiburg Schweiz, Mainz.

— 1992, see GGG.

Keel, O. & Winter, U., 1977, Vögel als Boten. Studien zu Ps 68,12-14, Gen 8,6-12, Koh 10,20 und dem Aussenden von Botenvögeln in Ägypten. Mit einem Beitrag von U.W. zu Ps 56,1 und zur Ikonographie der Göttin mit der Taube (OBO 14), Fribourg & Göttingen.

Keel-Leu, H., 1991, Vorderasiatische Stempelsiegel (OBO 110), Fribourg & Göttingen.

Kelly-Buccellati, M. (ed.), 1986, Insight through Images. Studies in Honor of Edith Porada (Bibliotheca Mesopotamica 21), Malibu, CA.

Kenna, V.E.G., 1973, A Late Bronze Stamp Seal from Jordan: ADAJ 18, 79.

Kienast, B., 1984, Das altassyrische Kaufvertragsrecht, Stuttgart.

Knauf, E.A., 1988a, Midian. Untersuchungen zur Geschichte Palästinas und Nordarabiens am Ende des 2. Jahrtausends v. Chr. (ADPV), Wiesbaden.

— 1988b, Zur Herkunft und Sozialgeschichte Israels. "Das Böcklein in der Milch seiner Mutter": Biblica 69, 153-169.

— ^{2}1989, Ismael. Untersuchungen zur Geschichte Palästinas und Nordarabiens im 1. Jahrtausend v. Chr. (ADPV), Wiesbaden.

Knauf, E.A. & Maʿani, S., 1987, On the Phonemes of Fringe Canaanite: The Cases of Zerah-Uḏruḥ and "Kamâsḫaltā": UF 19, 91-94.

Koch, K., 1979, Zur Entstehung der Baʿal-Verehrung: UF 11, 465-475 [= Studien zur alttestamentlichen und zur altorientalischen Religionsgeschichte (ed. E. Otto), Göttingen 1988, 189-205].

Königsweg, see Voie royale.

Kooij, G. van der, 1987, The Identity of Trans-Jordanian Alphabetic Writing in the Iron Age: SHAJ II, 107-121.

Kornfeld W., 1978, Onomastica Aramaica aus Ägypten (SÖAW.PH 333), Vienna.

Lachish III = O. Tufnell, Lachish III (Tell ed-Duweir). The Iron Age, London 1953.

Lachish IV = O. Tufnell, Lachish IV (Tell ed-Duweir). The Bronze Age, London 1958.

LÄ = Lexikon der Ägyptologie, Wiesbaden.

Lajard, F., 1847, Introduction à l'étude du culte public et des mystères de Mithra en Orient et en Occident, Paris.
— 1867, Recherches sur le culte public et les mystères de Mithra en Orient et en Occident, Paris.
Lambert, W.G., 1979, Near Eastern Seals in the Gulbenkian Museum of Oriental Art, University of Durham: Iraq 41, 1-45.
— 1985, Trees, Snakes and Gods in Ancient Syria and Anatolia: Bulletin of the School of Oriental and African Studies 48, 435-451.
Lambert, W.G. & Frantz-Szabo, G., 1980, s.v. Išḫara: RlA V, 176-180.
Lancel, S., 1991, Un bracelet en argent doré de la nécropole de Byrsa, à Carthage: ACISFP 2, vol. II, 969-976.
Layard, A.H., 1853, Discoveries in the Ruins of Nineveh and Babylon, London.
Layton, S.C., 1991, A New Interpretation of an Edomite Seal Impression: JNES 50, 37-43.
Lemaire, A., 1975, Note on an Edomite Seal-Impression from Buseirah: Levant 7, 18.
— 1976, Milkiram, nouveau roi phénicien de Tyr?: Syria 53, 83-93.
— 1977a, Essai sur cinq sceaux phéniciens: Semitica 27, 29-40.
— 1977b, Review of Avigad 1976a: Syria 54, 129-131.
— 1978a, Abécédaires et exercices d'écolier en épigraphie nord-ouest sémitique: JA 266, 221-235.
— 1978b, Le sceau CIS, II, 74 et sa signification historique: Semitica 28, 11-14.
— 1979, Nouveaux sceaux nord-ouest sémitiques avec un lion rugissant: Semitica 29, 67-69.
— 1980, Review of Hestrin & Dayagi-Mendels 1979: Syria 57, 496-497.
— 1981, Classification des estampilles royales judéennes: EI 15, 54*-60*.
— 1983, Nouveaux sceaux nord-ouest sémitiques: Semitica 33, 17-31.
— 1984, Date et origine des inscriptions paléo-hébraïques et phéniciennes de Kuntillet ʿAjrud: SEL 1, 131-143.
— 1985a, Sept sceaux nord-ouest sémitiques inscrits: EI 18, 29-32.
— 1985b, Notes d'épigraphie nord-ouest sémitique: Syria 62, 31-47.
— 1986, Nouveaux sceaux nord-ouest sémitiques: Syria 63, 305-325.
— 1987a, Notes d'épigraphie nord-ouest sémitique: Semitica 37, 47-55.
— 1987b, Ammon, Moab, Edom: l'époque du Fer en Jordanie, in La Jordanie de l'âge de la pierre à l'époque byzantine (Rencontres de l'École du Louvre), Paris, 47-74.
— 1988, Recherches actuelles sur les sceaux nord-ouest sémitiques: VT 38, 220-230.
— 1989, Les inscriptions palestiniennes d'époque perse: un bilan provisoire: Transeuphratène 1, 87-105.
— 1990a, Trois sceaux inscrits inédits avec lion rugissant: Semitica 39, 13-21.
— 1990b, Cinq nouveaux sceaux inscrits ouest-sémitiques: SEL 7, 97-109.
— 1990c: ʾBŠʿL: anthroponyme hébreu fantôme?: ZAH 3, 212-213.
— 1990d, Populations et territoires de la Palestine à l'époque perse: Transeuphratène 3, 31-74.
— 1990e, Aux origines d'Israël: la montagne d'Ephraïm et le territoire de Manassé (XIII-XIe siècle av. J.-C.), in E.M. Laperrousaz (ed.), La protohistoire d'Israël. De l'exode à la monarchie, Paris, 183-292.
— 1991a, Épigraphie: Transeuphratène 4, 113-118.
— 1991b, L'écriture phénicienne en Cilicie et la diffusion des écritures alphabétiques, in Baurain, Bonnet & Krings 1991: 133-146.
— 1991c, Notes d'épigraphie nord-ouest sémitique: Semitica 40, 39-54.
— forthcoming, Sceau "De Clercq 2505": araméen ou plutôt lydien?: Kadmos.

Levy, M.A., 1869, Siegel und Gemmen mit aramäischen, phönizischen, althebräischen, himjarischen, nabathäischen und altsyrischen Inschriften, Breslau.
Lidzbarski, M., 1898, Handbuch der nordsemitischen Epigraphik, I, Weimar.
Lipiński, E., 1975, Nordsemitische Texte aus dem 1. Jt. v. Chr., in W. Beyerlin (ed.), Religionsgeschichtliches Textbuch zum Alten Testament (Das Alte Testament Deutsch. Ergänzungsreihe 1), Göttingen, 245-283.
— 1985, Review of W.D. Davies et al., The Cambridge History of Judaism I, Cambridge 1984: BiOr 42, 161-168.
— 1986, Review of Jackson 1983: BiOr 43, 448-450.
Lloyd, S., 1954, Sultantepe: Anatolian Studies 4, 101-110.
Loon, M. van, 1986, The Drooping Lotus Flower, in Kelly-Buccellati 1986, 245-252.
Lowery, R.H., The Reforming Kings. Cults and Society in First Temple Judah (JSOT.S 120), Sheffield.
Lux, U.-M., 1961, Beiträge zur Darstellung des "Herrn der Tiere" im griechischen, etruskischen und römischen Bereich vom 8. Jh. v. Chr. unpublished Ph.D. thesis, Bonn.

M = S. Moscati, L'epigrafia ebraica antica, 1935-1950 (Biblica et Orientalia 15), Rome 1951.
Mähner, S., 1992, Ein Namens- und Bildsiegel aus *ʿĒn Šems* (Beth Schemesch): ZDPV 108 [in press].
Mallowan, M.E.L., 1966, Nimrud and Its Remains, I-III, London.
Manfredi, L.I., 1986, Bolli anforici da Tharros: RSF 14, 101-107.
Maraqten, M., 1988, Die semitischen Personennamen in den alt- und reichsaramäischen Inschriften aus Vorderasien (Texte und Studien zur Orientalistik 5), Hildesheim.
Markoe, G., 1985, Phoenician Bronze and Silver Bowls from Cyprus and the Mediterranean (University of California Publications. Classical Studies 26), Berkeley – Los Angeles – London.
Martin, G.T., 1968, A New Mayor of Byblos?: JNES 27, 141-142.
— 1971, Egyptian Administrative and Private-Name Seals. Principally of the Middle Kingdom and Second Intermediate Period, Oxford.
Masson, O., 1986, Un scarabée de Cambridge à inscription chypriote syllabique: Kadmos 25, 162-163.
Matthews, D.M., 1990, Principles of Composition in Near Eastern Glyptic of the Later Second Millennium B.C. (OBO.SA 8), Fribourg & Göttingen.
Mattingly, G., Moabite Religion, in Dearman 1989: 211-238.
Mayer-Opificius, R., 1984, Himmels- und Regendarstellungen im alten Vorderasien: UF 16, 189-236.
Mazar, B., 1951, The Excavations at Tell Qasîle: Preliminary Report, III: IEJ 1, 194-218.
McGovern, P.E. et al., 1986, The Late Bronze and Early Iron Ages of Central Transjordan: The Baqʿah Valley Project, 1977-1981 (UMM 65), Philadelphia.
— 1989, The Baqʿah Valley Project 1987: Khirbet Umm ad-Dananir and al-Qeṣir: ADAJ 33, 123-136.
Meeks, D., 1977, s.v. Harpokrates: LÄ II, 1003-1011.
Megiddo I = R.S. Lamon & G.M. Shipton, Megiddo I. Seasons of 1925-34. Strata I-V (OIP 42), Chicago 1939.
Megiddo II = G. Loud, Megiddo II. Seasons of 1935-1939 (OIP 62), Chicago 1948.
Merhav, R. (ed.), 1991, Urartu - A Metalworking Center in the First Millennium (Israel Museum Catalogue no. 324), Jerusalem.
Merrillees, P.H., 1992, Cylinder and Stamp Seals in Australian Collections (Victoria College Archaeology Research Unit, Occasional Papers No. 3), Malvern Victoria.

Mettinger, T.N.D., 1979, The Veto on Images and the Aniconic God in Ancient Israel, in H. Biezais (ed.), Religious Symbols and their Functions (Scripta Instituti Donneriani Aboensis 10), Stockholm, 15-29.
— 1982, The Dethronement of Sabaoth. Studies in the Shem and Kabod Theologies (Coniectanea Biblica. Old Testament Series 18), Lund.
Milik, J.T., 1958, Nouvelles inscriptions sémitiques et grecques du pays de Moab: LA 9, 330-358.
Millard, A.R., 1972/1983a, The Practice of Writing in Ancient Israel: BA 35, 98-111 [= The Biblical Archaeologist Reader IV, Sheffield 1983, 181-195].
— 1983b, Assyrians and Arameans: Iraq 45, 101-108.
— 1988, Inscribed Seals, in Buchanan & Moorey 1988: 44-59.
— 1991, Writing in Jordan: From Cuneiform to Arabic, in P. Bienkowski (ed.), The Art of Jordan, Liverpool, 133-149.
Miller, P.D., McCarter, P.K. & Hanson, P.D. (eds.), Ancient Israelite Religion. Essays in Honor of F.M. Cross, Philadelphia.
Moorey, P.R.S., 1978, The Iconography of an Achaemenid Stamp-Seal Acquired in the Lebanon: Iran 16, 143-154.
— 1980, Cemeteries of the First Millennium B.C. at Deve Hüyük, near Carchemish, salvaged by T.E. Lawrence and C.L. Woolley in 1913 (with a catalogue raisonné of the objects in Berlin, Cambridge, Liverpool, London and Oxford) (BAR International Series 87), Oxford.
Moortgat, A., 1940, Vorderasiatische Rollsiegel. Ein Beitrag zur Geschichte der Steinschneidekunst, Berlin (reprint 1988).
Moortgat-Correns, U., 1971, s.v. Glyptik: RlA III, 440-462.
Morenz, S. & Schubert, J., 1954, Der Gott auf der Blume. Eine ägyptische Kosmogonie und ihre weltweite Bildwirkung (Artibus Asiae, Supplementum 12), Ascona.
Morton, W.H., 1989, A Summary of the 1955, 1956 and 1965 Excavations at Diban, in Dearman 1989: 239-346.
Moscati, S., 1951, see M.
— 1966, Die Phöniker. Von 1200 vor Christus bis zum Untergang Karthagos (Kindlers Kulturgeschichte), Zurich [= German edition of next].
— 1968, The World of the Phoenicians, London.
— 1987, Le officine di Tharros, Rome.
Moscati, S. & Costa, A.M., 1982, L'origine degli scarabei in diaspro: RSF 10, 203-210.
Müller, M., 1903, Eine phönizische Gemme: OLZ 7, 304-305.
Mussel, M.-L., 1989, The Seal Impression from Dhiban, in Dearman 1989: 247-252.
Mutesellim II = C. Watzinger, Tell el-Mutesellim. II: Die Funde, Leipzig 1929.

NAAG 1987 = Ancient Art of the Mediterranean World. Public auction, Friday 20th November 1987 (Numismatic Art & Ancient Coins, Catalogue no. 5), Zurich.
— 1991 = Ancient Art of the Mediterranean World and Ancient Coins. Public auction, Thursday, 11th April 1991 (Numismatic and Ancient Art Gallery, Catalogue no. 7), Zurich.
Na'aman, N. & Zadok, R., 1988, Sargon II's Deportations to Israel and Philistia (716-708 B.C.): JCS 40, 36-46.
Naṣbeh I = Ch.Ch. McCown, Tell en-Naṣbeh. Excavated under the Direction of the Late William Frederic Badè. I: Archaeological and Historical Results, Berkeley – New Haven 1947.
Naveh, J., 1966, The Scripts of Two Ostraca from Elath: BASOR 183, 27-30.

Naveh, J. (ctd.)
— 1970a, The Development of the Aramaic Script (Proceedings of the Israel Academy of Sciences and Humanities 5), Jerusalem.
— 1970b, The Scripts in Palestine and Transjordan in the Iron Age, in Sanders 1970: 277-283.
— 1979, The Aramaic Ostraca from Tel Beer-Sheba (Season 1971-1976): Tel Aviv 6, 182-188.
— 1980, Review of Herr 1978: BASOR 239, 75-76.
— 1982, The Early History of the Alphabet, Jerusalem & Leiden.
— 1985, Writing and Scripts in Seventh-Century B.C.E. Philistia: The New Evidence from Tell Jemmeh: IEJ 35, 8-21.
— 1988, Review of Bordreuil 1986a: JSS 33, 115-116.
Naveh, J. & Tadmor, H., 1968, Some Doubtful Aramaic Seals: AION 18, 448-452.
Newberry, P.E., 1933, A Statue and a Scarab: JEA 19, 53-54.

Oakeshott, M.F., 1978, A Study of the Iron Age II Pottery of East Jordan with Special References to Unpublished Material from Edom, unpublished Ph.D. thesis, London.
OBO.SA = Orbis Biblicus et Orientalis, Series Archaelogica, Fribourg & Göttingen.
OLB = O. Keel, M. Küchler & Ch. Uehlinger, Orte und Landschaften der Bibel. Ein Handbuch und Studien-Reiseführer zum Heiligen Land. 1: Geographisch-geschichtliche Landeskunde; 2: Der Süden, Zurich – Einsiedeln – Cologne & Göttingen 1984, 1982 respectively.
Ornan, T. & Sass, B., 1992, A Product of Cultural Interaction: The Seal of Nergal-Sallim: Israel Museum Journal 10, 63-66.
Orthmann, W., 1971, Untersuchungen zur späthethitischen Kunst (Saarbrücker Beiträge zur Altertumskunde 8), Bonn.
Osten, H.H. von der, 1934, Ancient Oriental Seals in the Collection of Mr. Edward T. Newell (OIP 22), Chicago.

Parayre, D., 1987, Carchemish entre Anatolie et Syrie à travers l'image du disque solaire ailé (ca 1800-717 av. J.-C.): Hethitica 8, 319-360.
— 1990a, Les cachets ouest-sémitiques à travers l'image du disque solaire ailé (perspective iconographique): Syria 67, 269-301.
— 1990b, Deux chapiteaux hathoriques à Amathonte: étude des disques solaires ailés: Bulletin de Correspondance Hellénique 114, 215-240.
Parker, B., 1949, Cylinder Seals of Palestine: Iraq 11, 1-42.
— 1955, Excavations at Nimrud 1949-1953. Seals and Impressions: Iraq 17, 93-125.
— 1962, Seals and Seal Impressions from the Nimrud Excavations 1955-1958: Iraq 24, 26-40.
Parrot, A., Chéhab, M.H. & Moscati, S., 1975, Les Phéniciens, Paris.
Peckham, J.B., 1968, The Development of the Late Phoenician Scripts, Cambridge.
Pecorella, P.M., 1980, Dieci sigilli cilindrici del Vicino Oriente: Studi micenei ed egeo-anatolici 22, 328-330.
Pernigotti, S., 1983, Una rappresentazione religiosa egiziana su uno scarabeo con iscrizione fenicia: ACISFP 1, vol. II, 583-587.
Perrot, G. & Chipiez, C., 1885, History of Art in Phoenicia and its Dependencies, London.
Persepolis II = E.F. Schmidt, Persepolis II. Contents of the Treasury and Other Discoveries (OIP 69), Chicago 1957.
Petrie, W.M.F., 1928, Gerar (BSAE 43), London.

Pisano, G., 1978, Dieci scarabei da Tharros: RSF 6, 37-56.
Pomponio, F., 1978, Nabû. Il culto e la figura di un dio del pantheon babilonese ed assiro (StSem 51), Rome.
Porada, E., 1947, Suggestions for the Classification of Neo-Babylonian Cylinder Seals: Orientalia 16, 145-165.
— 1948, Corpus of Ancient Near Eastern Seals in North American Collections. I: The Collection of the Pierpont Morgan Library (The Bollingen Series XIV), Washington D.C.
— 1961, Review of Persepolis II: JNES 20, 66-71.
— 1975-1976, The Cylinder Seal from Tomb 66 at Ruweise: Berytus 26, 27-33.
— 1989, Two Cylinder Seals from ʿUmeiri, nos. 49 and 363, in Geraty et al. 1989, 381-384.
Prideaux, W.F., 1877, On an Aramean Seal: TSBA 5, 456-458.
Pritchard, J.B, 1961, The Water System of Gibeon (UMM), Philadelphia.
— 1985, Tell es-Saʿidiyeh. Excavations on the Tell, 1964-1966 (UMM 60), Philadelphia.
Puech, E., 1976, Deux nouveaux sceaux ammonites: RB 83, 59-62.
— 1977, Documents épigraphiques de Buseirah: Levant 9, 11-20.
— 1989, Review of Bordreuil 1986a: RB 96, 588-592.
— 1991, Approches paléographiques de l'inscription sur plâtre de Deir ʿAlla, in J. Hoftijzer & G. Van der Kooij (eds.), The Balaam Text from Deir ʿAlla Re-evaluated, Leiden, 221-238.

Rahmani, L.Y., 1964, Two Syrian Seals: IEJ 14, 180-184.
Rakob, F., 1990, Ein punisches Heiligtum in Karthago und sein römischer Nachfolgebau. Erster Bericht. Mit einem Beitrag von T. Redissi: Mitteilungen des Deutschen Archäologischen Instituts, Römische Abteilung 98, 33-80.
Ramat Raḥel II = Y. Aharoni et al., Excavations at Ramat Raḥel. Seasons 1961 and 1962, (StSem. Serie Archeologica 6), Rome 1964.
Reade, J.E., 1979, Assyrian Architectural Decoration: Techniques and Subject-Matter: Baghdader Mitteilungen 10, 17-49.
Reese, D.S., 1988, A New Engraved Tridacna Shell from Kish: JNES 47, 35-41.
Reifenberg, A., 1938, Some Ancient Hebrew Seals: PEQ 71, 113-116.
— 1945-1946, Two Moabite Seals: BJPES 12, 45-46 (Hebrew).
— 1950, Ancient Hebrew Seals, London.
Reisner, G.A., Fisher, C.A. & Lyon, D.G., 1924, Harvard Excavations at Samaria 1908-1910, Cambridge, MA.
Renan, E., 1864-1874, Mission en Phénicie, Paris.
RES = Répertoire d'épigraphie sémitique, Paris.
Rice, K.A., 1980, Geertz and Culture (Anthropology Series: Studies in Cultural Analysis), Ann Arbor, MI.
Ridder, A. de, 1911, Collection De Clercq. Catalogue. VII: Les bijoux et les pierres gravées. 2: Les pierres gravées, Paris.
Riis, P.J. & Buhl, M.-L. (eds.), 1990, Hama. Fouilles et Recherches de la Fondation Carlsberg 1931-1938. II,2: Les objects de la période dite syro-hittite (âge du fer), Copenhagen.
RlA = Reallexikon der Assyriologie, Berlin – New York.
Röllig, W., 1988, Review of Bordreuil 1986a: Die Welt des Orients 19, 194-197.
Rowe, A., 1936, A Catalogue of Egyptian Scarabs, Scaraboids, Seals and Amulets in the Palestine Archaeological Museum, Cairo.

Rüterswörden, U., 1985, Die Beamten der israelitischen Königszeit. Eine Studie zu *śr* und verwandten Begriffen (Beiträge zur Wissenschaft vom Alten und Neuen Testament VI/17 = 117), Stuttgart.

Sachau, E., 1896, Aramäische Inschriften: SPAW 1896, 1051-1064.
Sachs, A.J., 1953, The Late Assyrian Royal Seal Type: Iraq 15, 167-170.
Saidah, R., 1986, Nouveaux éléments de datation de la céramique de l'Age du Fer au Levant: ACISFP 1, vol. II, 213-216.
Saller, S., 1965-1966, Iron Age Tombs at Nebo: LA 16, 165-298.
Samaria-Sebaste 2 = J.W. Crowfoot, G.M. Crowfoot & E.L. Sukenik, Samaria-Sebaste 2: Early Ivories from Samaria, London 1938.
Samaria-Sebaste 3 = J.W. Crowfoot, G.M. Crowfoot & K.M. Kenyon, Samaria-Sebaste 3: The Objects from Samaria, London 1957.
Samter, A., 1897, s.v. Caduceus: PWRE V, 1170-1171.
Sanders, J.A. (ed.), 1970, Near Eastern Archaeology in the Twentieth Century: Essays in Honor of N. Glueck, Garden City, NY.
Sass, B., 1983, The Revadim Seal and its Archaic Phoenician Inscription: Anatolian Studies 33, 169-175.
— 1988, The Genesis of the Alphabet and its Development in the Second Millennium B.C. (ÄAT 13), Wiesbaden.
— 1991, Studia Alphabetica. On the Origin and Early History of the Northwest Semitic, South Semitic and Greek Alphabets (OBO 102), Fribourg & Göttingen.
— forthcoming: Two Scarabs and a Scaraboid, in R. Reich, Excavations in the Mamilla Area, Jerusalem (ʿAtiqot. English Series), Jerusalem.
Schmid, H.H., 1968, Gerechtigkeit als Weltordnung (Beiträge zur historischen Theologie 40), Tübingen.
Schneider, T., 1988, Azaryahu son of Hilkiahu (High Priest?) on a City of David Bulla?: IEJ 38, 139-141.
— 1991, Six Biblical Signatures. Seals and Seal Impressions of Six Biblical Personages Recovered: BAR 17/4, 26-33.
Schousboe, K. & Larsen, M.T. (eds.), 1989, Literacy and Society, Copenhagen.
Schroeder, P., 1880, Phönicische Miszellen 3: Drei Siegelsteine mit phönicischen Aufschriften: ZDMG 34, 681-684.764-766.
Schroer S., 1987a, In Israel gab es Bilder. Nachrichten von darstellender Kunst im Alten Testament (OBO 74), Fribourg & Göttingen.
— 1987b, Die Zweiggöttin in Palästina/Israel von der Mittelbronze II B-Zeit bis zu Jesus Sirach, in M. Küchler & Ch. Uehlinger (eds.), Jerusalem. Texte – Bilder – Steine (Festshrift H. & O. Keel-Leu = Novum Testamentum et Orbis Antiquus 6), Fribourg & Göttingen, 201-225.
— 1989, Die Göttin auf den Stempelsiegeln aus Palästina/Israel, in Keel, Keel-Leu & Schroer 1989: 89-207.
Schwienhorst-Schönberger, L., Das Bundesbuch (Ex 20,22-23,33). Studien zu seiner Entstehung und Theologie (Beihefte zur Zeitschrift füer die Alttestamentliche Wissenschaft 188), Berlin & New York.
Seidl, U., 1989, Die babylonischen Kudurru-Reliefs. Symbole mesopotamischer Gottheiten (OBO 87), Fribourg & Göttingen.
Seidl, U., Hrouda, B. & Krecher, J., 1971, s.v. Göttersymbole und -attribute: RlA III, 483-498.
SEL = Studi epigrafici e linguistici sul Vicino Oriente antico, Verona.
Sellers, O.R., 1968, The 1957 Excavation at Beth-Zur (AASOR 38), Cambridge, MA.

Sendschirli V = F. von Luschan & W. Andrae, Ausgrabungen in Sendschirli V: Die Kleinfunde von Sendschirli (Mitteilungen aus den orientalischen Sammlungen 15), Berlin 1943.

Seyrig, H., 1955, Quelques cylindres orientaux: Syria 37, 29-48.

— 1960, Antiquités Syriennes, 78. Les dieux de Hiérapolis: Syria 37, 233-252.

SHAJ = Studies in the History and Archaeology of Jordan, Amman.

Shiloh, Y., 1986, A Group of Hebrew Bullae from the City of David: IEJ 36, 16-38.

Shiloh, Y. & Tarler, D., 1986, Bullae from the City of David. A Hoard of Seal Impressions from the Israelite Period: BA 49, 196-209.

Shuval, M., 1990, A Catalogue of Early Iron Stamp Seals from Israel, in Keel, Shuval & Uehlinger 1990: 67-161.

Silverman, M.H., 1969, Aramaean Name-Types in the Elephantine Documents: JAOS 89, 691-709.

Silverman, M.H. (ctd.)

— 1970, Hebrew Name-Types in the Elephantine Documents: Orientalia 39, 465-491.

Simons, J., 1943, Enkele opmerkingen over 'Palestijnsche zegels' en de bestudeering daarvan: JEOL II/8, 683-689.

SÖAW.PH = Sitzungsberichte der Österreichischen Akademie der Wissenschaften, Philosophisch-historische Klasse, Wien.

Sommerfeld, W., Kammenhuber, A. & Rittig, D., 1990, s.v. Marduk: RIA VII, 360-374.

SPAW = Sitzungsberichte der Preussischen Akademie der Wissenschaften, Berlin.

Speleers, L., 1943, Catalogue des intailles et empreintes orientales des Musées Royaux d'Art et d'Histoire, Supplément, Brussels.

Spieckermann, H., 1982, Juda unter Assur in der Sargonidenzeit (Forschungen zur Religion und Literatur des Alten und Neuen Testaments 129), Göttingen.

Spijkerman, A., 1978, The Coins of the Decapolis and Provincia Arabia (SFB.CMa 25), Jerusalem.

Spycket, A., 1973, Le culte du dieu-lune à Tell Keisan: RB 80, 383-395.

— 1974, Nouveaux documents pour illustrer le culte du dieu-lune: RB 81, 258-259.

Stamm, J.J., 1981, Der Name Zedekia, in M. Carrez, J. Doré & P. Grelot (eds.), Mélanges H. Cazelles, Paris, 227-235.

Stark, J.K., Personal Names in Palmyrene Inscriptions, Oxford 1971.

StPh = Studia Phoenicia, Leuven (& Namur).

StSem = Studi Semitici, Rome.

Stucky, R.A., 1974, The Engraved Tridacna Shells (Dédalo X/19), Sao Paolo..

Sukenik, E.L., 1928, An Israelite Gem from Samaria: PEFQS 60, 51.

— 1941, A Note on the Seal of the Servant of Ahaz: BASOR 84, 17-18.

— 1942a, A Further Note on Hebrew Seals: Kedem 1, 46 (Hebrew).

— 1942b, Gleanings: A. A Seal of the Servant of King Ahaz; B. A Hebrew Seal from Ezion-Geber: Kedem 1, 94-95 (Hebrew).

— 1945, Three Ancient Seals: Kedem 2, 8-10 (Hebrew).

Swan Hall, V., 1986, The Pharaoh Smites his Enemies. A Comparative Study (Münchener ägyptologische Studien 44), Berlin.

SWBA = The Social World of Biblical Antiquity Series, Sheffield & Decatur, GA.

Sznycer, M., 1969, Note sur le dieu Ṣid et le dieu Ḥoron d'après les nouvelles inscriptions puniques d'Antas (Sardaigne): Carthago 15, 69-74.

Tadmor, H. & M., 1967, The Seal of Bēlu-ašarēdu, Majordomo: BIES 31, 68-79 (Hebrew).

Tallqvist, K.L., 1914, Assyrian Personal Names (Annales academiae scientiarum Fennicae 43/1), Helsinki.
Teissier, B., 1984, Ancient Near Eastern Cylinder Seals from the Marcopoli Collection, Berkeley – Los Angeles – London.
Thompson, H.O., 1972, The 1972 Excavation of Khirbet al-Hajjar: ADAJ 17, 47-72 [= 1989: 73-104].
— 1987, A Tyrian Coin in Jordan: BA 50, 101-104 [= 1989: 105-112].
— 1989, Archaeology in Jordan (American University Studies IX/55), New York.
Thomsen, P., 1951, Review of Reifenberg 1950: BiOr 8, 150.
Thureau-Dangin, F., 1936, Til Barsip (Bibliothèque Archéologique et Historique XXIII), Paris.
Tigay, J.H., 1986, You Shall Have No Other Gods. Israelite Religion in the Light of Hebrew Inscriptions (Harvard Semitic Studies 31), Atlanta.
— 1987, Israelite Religion: The Onomastic and Epigraphic Evidence, in Miller, McCarter & Hanson 1987: 157-194.
Timm, S., 1989a, Moab zwischen den Mächten. Studien zu historischen Denkmälern und Texten (ÄAT 17), Wiesbaden.
— 1989b, Anmerkungen zu vier neuen hebräischen Namen: ZAH 2, 188-198.
Tournay R., 1967, Un cylindre babylonien découvert en Transjordanie: RB 74, 248-254.
Tufnell, O., 1984, Studies on Scarab Seals II: Scarab Seals and their Contribution to the History of the Early Second Millenium B.C., Warminster.
Tushingham A.D., 1970, A Royal Israelite Seal(?) and the Royal Jar Handle Stamps (part one): BASOR 200, 71-78.
— 1971, A Royal Israelite Seal(?) and the Royal Jar Handle Stamps (part two): BASOR 201, 23-35.
— 1985, A Selection of Scarabs and Scaraboids, in J.N. Tubb (ed.), Palestine in the Bronze und Iron Ages. Papers in Honour of O. Tufnell (University of London, Institute of Archaeology, Occasional Publications, 11), London, 197-212.

Uberti, M.L., 1977, Gli scarabei in steatite e in pasta, in E. Acquaro, S. Moscati & M.L. Uberti, La collezione Biggio. Antichità puniche a Sant'Antioco (CSF 9), Rome, 37-43.
— 1978, Horon ad Antas e Astarte a Mozia: AION 38, 315-319.
Uehlinger, Ch., 1990, [Nachträge zu "La glyptique de Tell Keisan"] Ein *ʿnḫ*-ähnliches Astralkultsymbol auf Stempelsiegeln des 8./7. Jhs., in Keel, Shuval & Uehlinger 1990: 322-330.
UMM = University Museum Monographs, Philadelphia.
Unger E., 1938a, s.v. Dämonenbilder: RlA II, 113-115.
— 1938b, s.v. Drachen und Drachenkampf: RlA II, 231-235.
Ussishkin, D., 1976, Royal Judean Storage Jars and Private Seal Impressions: BASOR 223, 2-13.

Vercoutter, J., 1945, Les objets égyptiens et égyptisants du mobilier funéraire carthaginois (Bibliothèque Archéologique et Historique 40), Paris.
Vitelli, G. (ed.), 1917, Papiri graeci e latini, vol. IV (Pubblicazioni della Società Italiana per la ricercha dei papyri graeci e latini in Egitto), Florence.
Vogüé, M. de, 1868, Mélanges d'archéologie orientale, Paris.
La Voie royale. 9000 ans d'art au royaume de Jordanie, Paris 1986 (exhibition catalogue; German edition: Der Königsweg. 9000 Jahre Kunst und Kultur in Jordanien und Palästina (exhibition catalogue), Mainz 1987].

Vollenweider, M.-L., 1967, Musée d'Art et d'Histoire de Genève. Catalogue raisonné des sceaux, cylindres et intailles. I, Geneva.
— 1983, Musée d'Art et d'Histoire de Genève. Catalogue raisonné des sceaux, cylindres, intailles et camées. III: La collection du Révérend Dr. V.E.G. Kenna et d'autres acquisitions et dons récents, Mainz.
VSA = F. Vattioni, I sigilli aramaici: Augustinianum 11, 1971, 47-87.
VSE = F. Vattioni, I sigilli ebraici [I]: Biblica 50, 1969, 357-388; II: Augustinianum 11, 1971, 454-474; III: AION 38, 1978, 227-254.
VSF = F. Vattioni, I sigilli fenici: AION 31, 1981, 177-193.

Wagner, P., 1980, Der ägyptische Einfluß auf die phönizische Architektur, Bonn.
Walters, H.B., 1926, Catalogue of the Engraved Gems and Cameos, Greek, Etruscan and Roman in the British Museum, London.
Ward, W.A., 1964, Cylinders and Scarabs from the Late Bronze Temple at ᶜAmman: ADAJ 8-9, 47-55.
— 1966, Scarabs, Seals and Cylinders from two Tombs at Amman: ADAJ 11, 5-18.
— 1968, The Four-Winged Serpent on Hebrew Seals: RSO 43, 135-143.
— 1976, Some Personal Names of the Hyksos Period Rulers and Notes on the Epigraphy of their Scarabs: UF 8, 353-369.
— 1978, Studies on Scarab Seals I. Pre-12th Dynasty Scarab Amulets, Warminster.
Weber, O., 1920, Altorientalische Siegelbilder, Leipzig.
Weippert, H., 1978, Siegel mit Mondsichelstandarten aus Palästina: Biblische Notizen 5, 43-58.
— 1988, Palästina in vorhellenistischer Zeit (Handbuch der Archäologie. Vorderasien II/1), Munich.
Weippert, M., 1961, Gott und Stier: ZDPV 77, 93-117.
— 1979, Ein Siegel vom *Tell Ṣāfūt*: ZDPV 95, 173-177.
— 1980, Berichtigung: ZDPV 96, 100.
— 1987, The Relations of the States East of the Jordan with the Mesopotamian Powers during the First Millenium B.C.: SHAJ III, 97-105.
Welten, P., 1969, Die Königs-Stempel. Ein Beitrag zur Militärpolitik Judas unter Hiskia und Josia (ADPV), Wiesbaden.
— 1977a, s.v. Götterbild, männliches: BRL^2, 99-111.
— 1977b, s.v. Mischwesen: BRL^2, 224-227.
— 1977c, s.v. Siegel und Stempel: BRL^2, 299-306.
Wiggermann, F.A.M., 1992, Mesopotamian Protective Spirits. The Ritual Texts (Cuneiform Monographs 1), Groningen.
Wilcke, C. & Seidl, U., 1980, s.v. Inanna/Ištar (Mesopotamien): RlA V, 74-89.
Wildung, S., 1977, s.v. Flügelsonne: LÄ II, 277-279.
Wimmer, D.H., 1987, The Excavations at Tell Safut, SHAJ III, 279-282.
Winter, I.J., 1976, Phoenician and North Syrian Ivory Carving in Historical Context: Questions of Style and Distribution: Iraq 38, 1-26.
— 1981, Is there a South Syrian Style of Ivory Carving in the Early First Millenium B.C.?: Iraq 43, 101-130.
— 1982, Art as Evidence for Interaction: Relations between the Assyrian Empire and North Syria, in H.-J. Nissen & J. Renger (eds.), Mesopotamien und seine Nachbarn. Politische und kulturelle Wechselbeziehungen im Alten Vorderasien vom 4. bis 1. Jahrtausend v. Chr. (XXVe Rencontre Assyriologique Internationale = Berliner Beiträge zum Vorderen Orient 1), Berlin, 355-382.
— 1983, Carchemish *ša kišad puratti*: Anatolian Studies 33, 177-197.

Winter, I.J. (ctd.)

— 1989, North Syrian Ivories and Tell Halaf Reliefs: The Impact of Luxury Goods upon 'Major' Arts, in A. Leonard & B.B. Williams (eds.), Essays in Ancient Civilization Presented to H.J. Kantor (Studies in Ancient Oriental Civilization 47), Chicago, 321-332.

— 1992, Review of Herrmann 1986: JNES 51, 135-141.

Winter, U., 1983, Frau und Göttin. Exegetische und ikonographische Studien zum weiblichen Gottesbild im Alten Israel und in dessen Umwelt (OBO 53), Fribourg & Göttingen (^{2}1987).

— 1986, Der "Lebensbaum" in der altorientalischen Bildsymbolik, in H. Schweizer (ed.), "... Bäume braucht man doch!" Das Symbol des Baumes zwischen Hoffnung und Zerstörung, Sigmaringen, 57-88.

Wiseman, D.J., 1958, Cylinder Seals of Western Asia, London.

Wolfe, L.A. & Sternberg, F., 1989, Objects with Semitic Inscriptions, 1100 B.C. - A.D. 700. Jewish, Early Christian and Byzantine Antiquities. Auction XXIII, Monday 20 November 1989, Zurich.

— 1990, Antiquities of the Phoenician World – Ancient Inscriptions, in Antike Münzen, Griechen – Römer – Byzantiner. Phönizische Kleinkunst – Objekte mit antiken Inschriften. Geschnittene Steine und Schmuck der Antike .... Auction XXIV, 19-20 November 1990, Zurich, 63-111.

— 1991, Ancient Inscriptions – Seals of the Phoenician World, in Antike Münzen, Griechen – Römer – Byzantinische Münzen und Bleisiegel. Renaissance Medaillen. Geschnittene Steine und Schmuck der Antike .... Auction XXV, 25-26 November 1991, Zurich, 87-92.

Worschech, U., 1990, Die Beziehungen Moabs zu Israel und Ägypten in der Eisenzeit. Siedlungsarchäologische und siedlungshistorische Untersuchungen im Kernland Moabs (*Arḍ el-Kerak*) (ÄAT 18), Wiesbaden.

Wozak H., 1966, Herr und Herrin der Tiere in Vorderasien, unpublished Ph.D. thesis, Vienna.

Wright, G.E., 1965, Shechem. The Biography of a Biblical City, New York – Toronto.

Wyatt, N., 1991, Of Calves and Kings: the Canaanite Dimension in the Religion of Israel: Scandinavian Journal of the Old Testament 6, 68-91.

Xella, P., 1988, D'Ugarit à la Phénicie: sur les traces de Rashap, Horon, Eshmun: Die Welt des Orients 19, 45-64.

— 1990, KAI 78 e il pantheon di Carthagine: RSF 18, 209-217.

Yassine, Kh., 1988, Ammonite Seals from Tell El-Mazar, in id., Archaeology of Jordan: Essays and Reports, Amman, 143-155.

York, H., 1975, s.v. Heiliger Baum: RlA IV, 269-282.

Younker, R.W., 1985, Israel, Judah, and Ammon and the Motifs on the Baalis Seal from Tell el-ʿUmeiri: BA 48, 173-180.

— 1989, Historical Background and Motifs of a Royal Seal Impression, in Geraty et al. 1989: 375-380.

— 1990, The Joint Madaba Plains Project: A Preliminary Report of the 1989 Season, including the Regional Survey and Excavations at el-Dreijat, Tell Jawa, and Tell el-ʿUmeiri (1989): AUSS 28, 5-52.

Zadok, R., 1988, The Pre-Hellenistic Israelite Anthroponymy and Prosopography (OLA 28), Leuven.

ZAH = Zeitschrift für Althebraistik, Stuttgart.

Zayadine, F., 1977-1978, Excavations on the Upper Citadel of Amman, Area A (1975 and 1977): ADAJ 22, 20-56.

— 1985a, [Chronique archéologique] Fouilles de Djebel Akhdar: Syria 62, 152.

— 1985b, [Chronique archéologique] Une tombe du fer II à Umm Udheinah: Syria 62, 155-158.

Zazoff, P. (ed.), 1975, Antike Gemmen in deutschen Sammlungen. IV: Hannover, Kestner-Museum; Hamburg, Museum für Kunst und Gewerbe, Wiesbaden.

Zettler, R.L., 1979, On the Chronological Range of Neo-Babylonian and Achaemenid Seals: JNES 38, 257-270.

Zuckerman, B. (ed.), 1987, Puzzling out the Past: Making Sense on Ancient Inscriptions from Biblical Times. An Exhibition of Ancient Inscriptions from Biblical Times, Dubin Wolf Exhibition Center, Wilshire Boulevard Temple, April 5th - November 15th, 1987.

Zyl, A.H. van, 1960, The Moabites (Pretoria Oriental Series 3), Leiden.

INDEX

(A. General, B. Northwest Semitic letters and words,
C. Names of seal owners and other legends or personal names)

A. General

B. Northwest Semitic letters and words

C. Names of seal owners and other legends or personal names

PN: names other than those of seal owners.
DN: divine names contained in theophoric personal names but discussed separately.
CS: cylinder seals.
Not specified: stamp seal.

yḥzq 7, 24 (fig. 14)
yḥmlyhw mʿšyhw 146
yḥn 204[19], 231[85], 259[10]
yḥṣ 53, 66 (fig. 55), 68, 185[40], 262[24]
yklʾ 58, 59 (fig. 21), 145, 236
ylʾ 53, 67 (fig. 63), 68, 71, 146, 185[40], 186[42], 262[24]
ynḥm 137, 158 (fig. 15)
yʿ... 138, 167
yʿdrʾl 88, 89 (fig. 20), 139, 221, 266[36]
ypʿhd mpšr (CS) 80-82, 81 (fig. 8), 262[22], 266[35]
yqmyhw 107 (+ fig. 12), 222[66], 226, 227 (fig. 122), 228, 233 (fig. 129)
yqmyhw bn nḥm 53, 68, 69 (fig. 67), 200, 202 (fig. 20), 204, 229, 231, 233 (fig. 133), 263[29]
yrʾ 164
yrḥmʾl bn hmlk 199
yrḥʿzr (PN) 146, 147
yrm zmryhw 211 (fig. 71), 212
yrmyhw 274f (+ fig. 9)
yrpʾl br hdʿdr (CS) 93 (fig. 33), 94, 266[35]
yšdʾ 118-121, 119 (fig. 44), 146, 230
yšʿʾl 137, 138
yšʿyhw bn ḥml 206, 207 (fig. 49)
ytm XVI

klbydšmš 53, 56, 63, 65 (fig. 37), 262[22]
klkl (PN) 172[18]
klkl mnḥm 6, 172[18]
klklyhw (PN) 172[18]
km... 53, 67 (fig. 56), 68, 162-163[2], 181[35], 183, 232[88], 240[115], 262[24], 263, 264 (fig. 1)
kmš 146, 165, 167-169, 171, 183, 184, 186, 187, 192 (fig. 5)
kmšdn 145, 166-169, 171, 173-175, 187, 189, 192 (fig. 4)
kmšḥsd hspr 163[2]
kmšyḥy 32, 34, 43 (fig. 14), 163f, 165, 168, 170, 171, 181, 182[38], 188, 192 (fig. 1)
kmšmʾš 164f, 168, 169, 171, 174[25], 182, 183, 186, 192 (fig. 2)
kmšntn 18, 162, 163, 168, 169, 187
kmšʿz hspr 163[2]
kmšʿm kmšʾl hspr 161, 163, 168
kmšplṭ (PN) 185[40]
kmšṣdq 165f, 168-171, 175, 177-180, 188, 192 (fig. 3), 208[31], 268[42]
knbw 60, 61 (fig. 23), 262[22]
kpr 68, 69 (fig. 69), 87[17], 231[85], 262[24], 263[29]
kpr (CS) 87
krzy 142

lʾl 112
lmlk, see *mlk*

mʾš (PN) 164[7], 174[25]
mʾš (worshipper) 64, 66 (fig. 49), 68[21], 180[34], 182, 193 (fig. 16), 262[24], 263[29]
mʾš (griffin) 174, 189, 192 (fig. 10)
mʾš bn mnḥ hspr 164[7], 174[25]
mbn 217[57]
mḥsʾ 233 (fig. 144), 237
mḥsyhw nby 223 (fig. 116), 224
mypʿh 123, 125 (fig. 64), 172[18], 178-180, 185[40], 188, 193 (fig. 13)
mky yqmyh 200, 203 (fig. 33), 204, 205
mkmʾl 134
mksp 118-121, 119 (fig. 51)
(l)mlk (unspecified) 284[+86]
(l)mlk (winged sun) XVIII[29], 31, 43 (fig. 10), 197[6], 200, 202 (fig. 21), 204, 220, 238f, 241 (fig. 149), 243, 285 (fig. 22)
(l)mlk (beetle) XVIII[29], 140, 197[6], 216, 219 (fig. 89), 220, 238, 243
(l)mlk (?) (dockets) 237
mlkḥrm(?) 32, 34, 43 (fig. 16)
mlkyhw ḥlq 218, 219 (fig. 94)
mlkyʿzr 32, 34, 43 (fig. 15), 188
mlklbʿ ʿbd hmlk 12[9]
mlkm (DN) 10[5]
mlkmʾwr ʿbd bʿlyšʿ 139, 140, 147, 158 (fig. 16)
mlkmgd 56, 84[12], 135, 140, 144, 146, 148, 158 (fig. 17), 166
mlkrm 196, 204, 208[31], 211 (fig. 61), 213, pl. I:4
mmh 178
mngʾnrt brk lmlkm 9, 21, 25 (fig. 16), 53, 54[+3], 55 (fig. 1), 68, 69 (fig 71), 134, 140, 141, 151, 158 (fig. 18), 262[22], 263[28]
mnḥm (PN) 13
mnḥm (B 108) 17, 53, 63, 65 (fig. 41), 144, 262[22]
mnḥm bn brkʾl 137
mnḥm bn ynḥm 139, 147, 159 (fig. 19)

šʾʿl (šʾʿn?) 56, 57 (figs. 12, 13), 60, 97 (fig. 39), 99, 262[22]
šʾgbr (PN) 99[32]
šbʾl 56, 57 (fig. 8), 58, 59 (fig. 17), 134, 145, 262[22]
šbʾl bn ʾlyšʿ 18
šbnʾ 35, 45 (fig. 27)
šbnyhw 200, 202 (fig. 24), 207 (fig. 55), 208
šbnyw/šbnyw ʿbd ʿzyw 35, 44 (fig. 23), 53, 68, 69 (fig. 68), 86[14], 198-200, 201 (fig. 13), 202 (fig. 23), 204, 229, 231, 233 (fig. 132), 239, 241 (fig. 151), 262[24], 263f[29], 285 (+ fig. 18)
šbʿ yḥmlyhw 200, 203 (fig. 39), 204, 205
šgʾdd 58, 59 (fig. 19)
šdh/šrh (CS) 81 (fig. 9), 82, 262[22], 266[35]
šwḥr hnss 139, 140, 147, 159 (fig. 23)
šḥr bn gdy 197, 201 (fig. 3), 206, 207 (fig. 51)
šḥr bn gdyhw 211 (fig. 69), 212
šḥrḥr bn ṣpnyhw 20
škr 53, 67 (fig. 60), 68, 262[24]
šlm (PN) 13
šlm (HD 81) 220
šlm (G 100) 231[86], 245[121]
šlm bn mnḥm 19
šlmʾl 17, 18, 234, 264 (+ fig. 6)
šlmt(?) 118-121, 120 (fig. 52)
šmʿ (HD 98) 17[18]
šmʿ (B 21) 118-121, 119 (fig. 46)
šmʿ (G 3) 175[27]
šmʿ bn ywstr 6
šmʿ ʿbd yrbʿm 87[16], 198, 221f, 223 (fig. 109)
šmʿʾl 11, 167
šmʿyhw... 200, 202 (fig. 26)
šmʿyhw bn ʿzryhw 199, 225, 227 (fig. 118), 272[56], 278[70], 280
šmʿl bn plṭw 13[11]
šmr... 200, 201 (fig. 9), 204, 214, 215 (fig. 83)
šmryhw bn pdyhw 6, 24 (fig. 9)
šmryw 111, 112 (fig. 20)
šmšʿdry 12, 63, 62 (fig. 30), 93 (fig. 35), 95f
šmšʿzr ʿbdšhr 12, 97 (fig. 37), 98, 240[114]
šnʾb (šmʾb) 76[+2], 77 (fig. 4), 139
šnḥṣr 57 (fig. 10), 58, 68, 76, 77 (fig. 3), 146, 262[22]
šnyw(?) 224[68], 228[77]
šnsrṣr 62 (fig. 32), 63, 64, 65 (fig. 45), 66 (fig. 54), 262[22]
šʿl bn ʾlyšʿ 18[19], 137, 146, 159 (fig. 24)
šʿly 84[11]
šʿnp (šʿnf) bn nby 197[5]
špṭ XX[42], 200, 201 (fig. 12), 202 (fig. 25), 212
špṭyhw ʿšyhw 200, 202 (fig. 18), 204, 211 (fig. 75), 212
šṣry (or *mṣry*) (CS) 16[13]
šr (worshipper) 53, 68, 70 (fig. 75), 142, 262[24], 263[29]
šr (soldier and captive) 237f, 241 (fig. 145)
šrhʿr 67 (fig. 66), 68, 71, 237f, 241 (fig. 146), 273
štʾl 124, 125 (fig. 70), 145

tbly mn ʾblnh (CS) 64[17], 82[8], 93 (fig. 34), 94f, 266[35]
tmkʾl (CAI 84) 144
tmkʾl bn ḥgt 139
tmkʾ bn mqnmlk 137, 159 (fig. 25)
tmkʾl br mlkm 10, 12, 13, 25 (fig. 18), 135, 137, 140, 146, 147, 152, 159 (fig. 26)
tnʾl 221
tsmr 76[4]
trtn (CS?) 76

...ʾbndb šndr lʿšt bṣdn tbrkh 8[4]
...ʾlḥnn 139, 147
...yhw bn ʿmlyhw 220, 223 (fig. 104)
...bn gdyhw 200, 201 (fig. 15), 204, 223 (fig. 115), 224
...ṣpnyhw (smk? ṣpnyhw) 213, 215 (fig. 79), 243, pl. I:3
...ḥm(?)*...bʿ* 218, 219 (fig. 98), 244

ORBIS BIBLICUS ET ORIENTALIS

Bd. 1 OTTO RICKENBACHER: *Weisheitsperikopen bei Ben Sira.* X–214–15* Seiten. 1973. Vergriffen.

Bd. 2 FRANZ SCHNIDER: *Jesus der Prophet.* 298 Seiten. 1973. Vergriffen.

Bd. 3 PAUL ZINGG: *Das Wachsen der Kirche.* Beiträge zur Frage der lukanischen Redaktion und Theologie. 345 Seiten. 1974. Vergriffen.

Bd. 4 KARL JAROŠ: *Die Stellung des Elohisten zur kanaanäischen Religion.* 294 Seiten, 12 Abbildungen. 1982. 2. verbesserte und überarbeitete Auflage.

Bd. 5 OTHMAR KEEL: *Wirkmächtige Siegeszeichen im Alten Testament.* Ikonographische Studien zu Jos 8, 18–26; Ex 17, 8–13; 2 Kön 13, 14–19 und 1 Kön 22, 11. 232 Seiten, 78 Abbildungen. 1974. Vergriffen.

Bd. 6 VITUS HUONDER: *Israel Sohn Gottes.* Zur Deutung eines alttestamentlichen Themas in der jüdischen Exegese des Mittelalters. 231 Seiten. 1975.

Bd. 7 RAINER SCHMITT: *Exodus und Passa. Ihr Zusammenhang im Alten Testament.* 124 Seiten. 1982. 2. neubearbeitete Auflage.

Bd. 8 ADRIAN SCHENKER: *Hexaplarische Psalmenbruchstücke.* Die hexaplarischen Psalmenfragmente der Handschriften Vaticanus graecus 752 und Canonicianus graecus 62. Einleitung, Ausgabe, Erläuterung. XXVIII–446 Seiten. 1975.

Bd. 9 BEAT ZUBER: *Vier Studien zu den Ursprüngen Israels.* Die Sinaifrage und Probleme der Volks- und Traditionsbildung. 152 Seiten. 1976. Vergriffen.

Bd. 10 EDUARDO ARENS: *The* ΗΛΘΟΝ-*Sayings in the Synoptic Tradition.* A Historico-critical Investigation. 370 Seiten. 1976.

Bd. 11 KARL JAROŠ: *Sichem.* Eine archäologische und religionsgeschichtliche Studie, mit besonderer Berücksichtigung von Jos 24. 280 Seiten, 193 Abbildungen. 1976.

Bd. 11a KARL JAROŠ/BRIGITTE DECKERT: *Studien zur Sichem-Area.* 81 Seiten, 23 Abbildungen. 1977.

Bd. 12 WALTER BÜHLMANN: *Vom rechten Reden und Schweigen.* Studien zu Proverbien 10–31. 371 Seiten. 1976. Vergriffen.

Bd. 13 IVO MEYER: *Jeremia und die falschen Propheten.* 155 Seiten. 1977. Vergriffen.

Bd. 14 OTHMAR KEEL: *Vögel als Boten.* Studien zu Ps 68, 12–14, Gen 8, 6–12, Koh 10, 20 und dem Aussenden von Botenvögeln in Ägypten. – Mit einem Beitrag von Urs Winter zu Ps 56, 1 und zur Ikonographie der Göttin mit der Taube. 164 Seiten, 44 Abbildungen. 1977. Vergriffen.

Bd. 15 MARIE-LOUISE GUBLER: *Die frühesten Deutungen des Todes Jesu.* Eine motivgeschichtliche Darstellung aufgrund der neueren exegetischen Forschung. XVI–424 Seiten. 1977. Vergriffen.

Bd. 16 JEAN ZUMSTEIN: *La condition du croyant dans l'Evangile selon Matthieu.* 467 pages. 1977. Epuisé.

Bd. 17 FRANZ SCHNIDER: *Die verlorenen Söhne.* Strukturanalytische und historisch-kritische Untersuchungen zu Lk 15. 105 Seiten. 1977.

Bd. 18 HEINRICH VALENTIN: *Aaron.* Eine Studie zur vor-priesterschriftlichen Aaron-Überlieferung. VIII–441 Seiten. 1978.

Bd. 19 MASSÉO CALOZ: *Etude sur la LXX origénienne du Psautier.* Les relations entre les leçons des Psaumes du Manuscrit Coislin 44, les Fragments des Hexaples et le texte du Psautier Gallican. 480 pages. 1978.

Bd. 20 RAPHAEL GIVEON: *The Impact of Egypt on Canaan.* Iconographical and Related Studies. 156 Seiten, 73 Abbildungen. 1978.

Bd. 21 DOMINIQUE BARTHÉLEMY: *Etudes d'histoire du texte de l'Ancien Testament.* XXV–419 pages. 1978. Epuisé.

Bd. 22/1 CESLAS SPICQ: *Notes de Lexicographie néo-testamentaire.* Tome I: p. 1–524. 1978. Epuisé.

Bd. 22/2 CESLAS SPICQ: *Notes de Lexicographie néo-testamentaire.* Tome II: p. 525–980. 1978. Epuisé.

Bd. 22/3 CESLAS SPICQ: *Notes de Lexicographie néo-testamentaire.* Supplément. 698 pages. 1982.

Bd. 23 BRIAN M. NOLAN: *The Royal Son of God.* The Christology of Matthew 1–2 in the Setting of the Gospel. 282 Seiten. 1979. Out of print.

Bd. 24 KLAUS KIESOW: *Exodustexte im Jesajabuch.* Literarkritische und motivgeschichtliche Analysen. 221 Seiten. 1979. Vergriffen.

Bd. 25/1 MICHAEL LATTKE: *Die Oden Salomos in ihrer Bedeutung für Neues Testament und Gnosis.* Band I. Ausführliche Handschriftenbeschreibung. Edition mit deutscher Parallel-Übersetzung. Hermeneutischer Anhang zur gnostischen Interpretation der Oden Salomos in der Pistis Sophia. XI–237 Seiten. 1979.

Bd. 25/1a MICHAEL LATTKE: *Die Oden Salomos in ihrer Bedeutung für Neues Testament und Gnosis.* Band Ia. Der syrische Text der Edition in Estrangela Faksimile des griechischen Papyrus Bodmer XI. 68 Seiten. 1980.

Bd. 25/2 MICHAEL LATTKE: *Die Oden Salomos in ihrer Bedeutung für Neues Testament und Gnosis.* Band II. Vollständige Wortkonkordanz zur handschriftlichen, griechischen, koptischen, lateinischen und syrischen Überlieferung der Oden Salomos. Mit einem Faksimile des Kodex N. XVI–201 Seiten. 1979.

Bd. 25/3 MICHAEL LATTKE: *Die Oden Salomos in ihrer Bedeutung für Neues Testament und Gnosis.* Band III. XXXIV–478 Seiten. 1986.

Bd. 26 MAX KÜCHLER: *Frühjüdische Weisheitstraditionen.* Zum Fortgang weisheitlichen Denkens im Bereich des frühjüdischen Jahweglaubens. 703 Seiten. 1979. Vergriffen.

Bd. 27 JOSEF M. OESCH: *Petucha und Setuma.* Untersuchungen zu einer überlieferten Gliederung im hebräischen Text des Alten Testaments. XX–392–37* Seiten. 1979.

Bd. 28 ERIK HORNUNG/OTHMAR KEEL (Herausgeber): *Studien zu altägyptischen Lebenslehren.* 394 Seiten. 1979.

Bd. 29 HERMANN ALEXANDER SCHLÖGL: *Der Gott Tatenen.* Nach Texten und Bildern des Neuen Reiches. 216 Seiten, 14 Abbildungen. 1980.

Bd. 30 JOHANN JAKOB STAMM: *Beiträge zur Hebräischen und Altorientalischen Namenkunde.* XVI–264 Seiten. 1980.

Bd. 31 HELMUT UTZSCHNEIDER: *Hosea - Prophet vor dem Ende.* Zum Verhältnis von Geschichte und Institution in der alttestamentlichen Prophetie. 260 Seiten. 1980.

Bd. 32 PETER WEIMAR: *Die Berufung des Mose.* Literaturwissenschaftliche Analyse von Exodus 2, 23–5, 5. 402 Seiten. 1980.

Bd. 33 OTHMAR KEEL: *Das Böcklein in der Milch seiner Mutter und Verwandtes.* Im Lichte eines altorientalischen Bildmotivs. 163 Seiten, 141 Abbildungen. 1980.

Bd. 34 PIERRE AUFFRET: *Hymnes d'Egypte et d'Israël.* Etudes de structures littéraires. 316 pages, 1 illustration. 1981.

Bd. 35 ARIE VAN DER KOOIJ: *Die alten Textzeugen des Jesajabuches.* Ein Beitrag zur Textgeschichte des Alten Testaments. 388 Seiten. 1981.

Bd. 36 CARMEL McCARTHY: *The Tiqqune Sopherim and Other Theological Corrections in the Masoretic Text of the Old Testament.* 280 Seiten. 1981.

Bd. 37 BARBARA L. BEGELSBACHER-FISCHER: *Untersuchungen zur Götterwelt des Alten Reiches im Spiegel der Privatgräber der IV. und V. Dynastie.* 336 Seiten. 1981.

Bd. 38 MÉLANGES DOMINIQUE BARTHÉLEMY. *Etudes bibliques offertes à l'occasion de son 60e anniversaire.* Edités par Pierre Casetti, Othmar Keel et Adrian Schenker. 724 pages, 31 illustrations. 1981.

Bd. 39 ANDRÉ LEMAIRE: *Les écoles et la formation de la Bible dans l'ancien Israël.* 142 pages, 14 illustrations. 1981.

Bd. 40 JOSEPH HENNINGER: *Arabica Sacra.* Aufsätze zur Religionsgeschichte Arabiens und seiner Randgebiete. Contributions à l'histoire religieuse de l'Arabie et de ses régions limitrophes. 347 Seiten. 1981.

Bd. 41 DANIEL VON ALLMEN: *La famille de Dieu.* La symbolique familiale dans le paulinisme. LXVII–330 pages, 27 planches. 1981.

Bd. 42 ADRIAN SCHENKER: *Der Mächtige im Schmelzofen des Mitleids.* Eine Interpretation von 2 Sam 24. 92 Seiten. 1982.

Bd. 43 PAUL DESELAERS: *Das Buch Tobit.* Studien zu seiner Entstehung, Komposition und Theologie. 532 Seiten + Übersetzung 16 Seiten. 1982.

Bd. 44 PIERRE CASETTI: *Gibt es ein Leben vor dem Tod?* Eine Auslegung von Psalm 49. 315 Seiten. 1982.

Bd. 45 FRANK-LOTHAR HOSSFELD: *Der Dekalog.* Seine späten Fassungen, die originale Komposition und seine Vorstufen. 308 Seiten. 1982. Vergriffen.

Bd. 46 ERIK HORNUNG: *Der ägyptische Mythos von der Himmelskuh.* Eine Ätiologie des Unvollkommenen. Unter Mitarbeit von Andreas Brodbeck, Hermann Schlögl und Elisabeth Staehelin und mit einem Beitrag von Gerhard Fecht. XII–129 Seiten, 10 Abbildungen. 1991. 2. ergänzte Auflage.

Bd. 47 PIERRE CHERIX: *Le Concept de Notre Grande Puissance (CG VI, 4).* Texte, remarques philologiques, traduction et notes. XIV–95 pages. 1982.

Bd. 48 JAN ASSMANN/WALTER BURKERT/FRITZ STOLZ: *Funktionen und Leistungen des Mythos.* Drei altorientalische Beispiele. 118 Seiten, 17 Abbildungen. 1982. Vergriffen.

Bd. 49 PIERRE AUFFRET: *La sagesse a bâti sa maison.* Etudes de structures littéraires dans l'Ancien Testament et spécialement dans les psaumes. 580 pages. 1982.

Bd. 50/1 DOMINIQUE BARTHÉLEMY: *Critique textuelle de l'Ancien Testament.* 1. Josué, Juges, Ruth, Samuel, Rois, Chroniques, Esdras, Néhémie, Esther. Rapport final du Comité pour l'analyse textuelle de l'Ancien Testament hébreu institué par l'Alliance Biblique Universelle, établi en coopération avec Alexander R. Hulst †, Norbert Lohfink, William D. McHardy, H. Peter Rüger, coéditeur, James A. Sanders, coéditeur. 812 pages. 1982.

Bd. 50/2 DOMINIQUE BARTHÉLEMY: *Critique textuelle de l'Ancien Testament.* 2. Isaïe, Jérémie, Lamentations. Rapport final du Comité pour l'analyse textuelle de l'Ancien Testament hébreu institué par l'Alliance Biblique Universelle, établi en coopération avec Alexander R. Hulst †, Norbert Lohfink, William D. McHardy, H. Peter Rüger, coéditeur, James A. Sanders, coéditeur. 1112 pages. 1986.

Bd. 50/3 DOMINIQUE BARTHÉLEMY: *Critique textuelle de l'Ancien Testament.* Tome 3. Ézéchiel, Daniel et les 12 Prophètes. Rapport final du Comité pour l'analyse textuelle de l'Ancien Testament hébreu institué par l'Alliance Biblique Universelle, établi en coopération avec Alexander R. Hulst†, Norbert Lohfink, William D. McHardy, H. Peter Rüger, coéditeur†, James A. Sanders, coéditeur. 1424 pages. 1992.

Bd. 51 JAN ASSMANN: *Re und Amun.* Die Krise des polytheistischen Weltbilds im Ägypten der 18.–20. Dynastie. XII–309 Seiten. 1983.

Bd. 52 MIRIAM LICHTHEIM: *Late Egyptian Wisdom Literature in the International Context.* A Study of Demotic Instructions. X–240 Seiten. 1983.

Bd. 53 URS WINTER: *Frau und Göttin.* Exegetische und ikonographische Studien zum weiblichen Gottesbild im Alten Israel und in dessen Umwelt. XVIII–928 Seiten, 520 Abbildungen. 1987. 2. Auflage. Mit einem Nachwort zur 2. Auflage.

Bd. 54 PAUL MAIBERGER: *Topographische und historische Untersuchungen zum Sinaiproblem.* Worauf beruht die Identifizierung des Ǧabal Mūsā mit dem Sinai? 189 Seiten, 13 Tafeln. 1984.

Bd. 55 PETER FREI/KLAUS KOCH: *Reichsidee und Reichsorganisation im Perserreich.* 119 Seiten, 17 Abbildungen. 1984. Vergriffen. Neuauflage in Vorbereitung

Bd. 56 HANS-PETER MÜLLER: *Vergleich und Metapher im Hohenlied.* 59 Seiten. 1984.

Bd. 57 STEPHEN PISANO: *Additions or Omissions in the Books of Samuel.* The Significant Pluses and Minuses in the Massoretic, LXX and Qumran Texts. XIV–295 Seiten. 1984.

Bd. 58 ODO CAMPONOVO: *Königtum, Königsherrschaft und Reich Gottes in den Frühjüdischen Schriften.* XVI–492 Seiten. 1984.

Bd. 59 JAMES KARL HOFFMEIER: *Sacred in the Vocabulary of Ancient Egypt.* The Term *DSR,* with Special Reference to Dynasties I–XX. XXIV–281 Seiten, 24 Figures. 1985.

Bd. 60 CHRISTIAN HERRMANN: *Formen für ägyptische Fayencen.* Katalog der Sammlung des Biblischen Instituts der Universität Freiburg Schweiz und einer Privatsammlung. XXVIII-199 Seiten. Mit zahlreichen Abbildungen im Text und 30 Tafeln. 1985.

Bd. 61 HELMUT ENGEL: *Die Susanna-Erzählung.* Einleitung, Übersetzung und Kommentar zum Septuaginta-Text und zur Theodition-Bearbeitung. 205 Seiten + Anhang 11 Seiten. 1985.

Bd. 62 ERNST KUTSCH: *Die chronologischen Daten des Ezechielbuches.* 82 Seiten. 1985.

Bd. 63 MANFRED HUTTER: *Altorientalische Vorstellungen von der Unterwelt.* Literar- und religionsgeschichtliche Überlegungen zu «Nergal und Ereškigal». VIII–187 Seiten. 1985.

Bd. 64 HELGA WEIPPERT/KLAUS SEYBOLD/MANFRED WEIPPERT: *Beiträge zur prophetischen Bildsprache in Israel und Assyrien.* IX–93 Seiten. 1985.

Bd. 65 ABDEL-AZIZ FAHMY SADEK: *Contribution à l'étude de l'Amdouat.* Les variantes tardives du Livre de l'Amdouat dans les papyrus du Musée du Caire. XVI–400 pages, 175 illustrations. 1985.

Bd. 66 HANS-PETER STÄHLI: *Solare Elemente im Jahweglauben des Alten Testamentes.* X–60 Seiten. 1985.

Bd. 67 OTHMAR KEEL / SILVIA SCHROER: *Studien zu den Stempelsiegeln aus Palästina/Israel.* Band I. 115 Seiten, 103 Abbildungen. 1985.

Bd. 68 WALTER BEYERLIN: *Weisheitliche Vergewisserung mit Bezug auf den Zionskult.* Studien zum 125. Psalm. 96 Seiten. 1985.

Bd. 69 RAPHAEL VENTURA: *Living in a City of the Dead.* A Selection of Topographical and Administrative Terms in the Documents of the Theban Necropolis. XII–232 Seiten. 1986.

Bd. 70 CLEMENS LOCHER: *Die Ehre einer Frau in Israel.* Exegetische und rechtsvergleichende Studien zu Dtn 22, 13–21. XVIII–464 Seiten. 1986.

Bd. 71 HANS-PETER MATHYS: *Liebe deinen Nächsten wie dich selbst.* Untersuchungen zum alttestamentlichen Gebot der Nächstenliebe (Lev 19,18). XII–204 Seiten. 1990. 2. verbesserte Auflage.

Bd. 72 FRIEDRICH ABITZ: *Ramses III. in den Gräbern seiner Söhne.* 156 Seiten, 31 Abbildungen. 1986.

Bd. 73 DOMINIQUE BARTHÉLEMY/DAVID W. GOODING/JOHAN LUST/EMANUEL TOV: *The Story of David and Goliath.* 160 Seiten. 1986.

Bd. 74 SILVIA SCHROER: *In Israel gab es Bilder.* Nachrichten von darstellender Kunst im Alten Testament. XVI–553 Seiten, 146 Abbildungen. 1987.

Bd. 75 ALAN R. SCHULMAN: *Ceremonial Execution and Public Rewards.* Some Historical Scenes on New Kingdom Private Stelae. 296 Seiten, 41 Abbildungen. 1987.

Bd. 76 JOŽE KRAŠOVEC: *La justice (Ṣdq) de Dieu dans la Bible hébraïque et l'interprétation juive et chrétienne.* 456 pages. 1988.

Bd. 77 HELMUT UTZSCHNEIDER: *Das Heiligtum und das Gesetz.* Studien zur Bedeutung der sinaitischen Heiligtumstexte (Ez 25–40; Lev 8–9). XIV–326 Seiten. 1988.

Bd. 78 BERNARD GOSSE: *Isaie 13,1-14,23.* Dans la tradition littéraire du livre d'Isaïe et dans la tradition des oracles contre les nations. 308 pages. 1988.

Bd. 79 INKE W. SCHUMACHER: *Der Gott Sopdu - Der Herr der Fremdländer.* XVI–364 Seiten, 6 Abbildungen. 1988.

Bd. 80 HELLMUT BRUNNER: *Das hörende Herz.* Kleine Schriften zur Religions- und Geistesgeschichte Ägyptens. Herausgegeben von Wolfgang Röllig. 449 Seiten, 55 Abbildungen. 1988.

Bd. 81 WALTER BEYERLIN: *Bleilot, Brecheisen oder was sonst?* Revision einer Amos-Vision. 68 Seiten. 1988.

Bd. 82 MANFRED HUTTER: *Behexung, Entsühnung und Heilung.* Das Ritual der Tunnawiya für ein Königspaar aus mittelhethitischer Zeit (KBo XXI 1 – KUB IX 34 – KBo XXI 6). 186 Seiten. 1988.

Bd. 83 RAPHAEL GIVEON: *Scarabs from Recent Excavations in Israel.* 114 Seiten. Mit zahlreichen Abbildungen im Text und 9 Tafeln. 1988.

Bd. 84 MIRIAM LICHTHEIM: *Ancient Egyptian Autobiographies chiefly of the Middle Kingdom.* A Study and an Anthology. 200 Seiten, 10 Seiten Abbildungen. 1988.

Bd. 85 ECKART OTTO: *Rechtsgeschichte der Redaktionen im Kodex Ešnunna und im «Bundesbuch».* Eine redaktionsgeschichtliche und rechtsvergleichende Studie zu altbabylonischen und altisraelitischen Rechtsüberlieferungen. 220 Seiten. 1989.

Bd. 86 ANDRZEJ NIWIŃSKI: *Studies on the Illustrated Theban Funerary Papyri of the 11th and 10th Centuries B.C.* 488 Seiten, 80 Seiten Tafeln. 1989.

Bd. 87 URSULA SEIDL: *Die babylonischen Kudurru-Reliefs.* Symbole mesopotamischer Gottheiten. 236 Seiten, 33 Tafeln und 2 Tabellen. 1989.

Bd. 88 OTHMAR KEEL/HILDI KEEL-LEU/SILVIA SCHROER: *Studien zu den Stempelsiegeln aus Palästina/Israel.* Band II. 364 Seiten, 652 Abbildungen. 1989.

Bd. 89 FRIEDRICH ABITZ: *Baugeschichte und Dekoration des Grabes Ramses' VI.* 202 Seiten, 39 Abbildungen. 1989.

Bd. 90 JOSEPH HENNINGER SVD: *Arabica varia.* Aufsätze zur Kulturgeschichte Arabiens und seiner Randgebiete. Contributions à l'histoire culturelle de l'Arabie et de ses régions limitrophes. 504 Seiten. 1989.

Bd. 91 GEORG FISCHER: *Jahwe unser Gott.* Sprache, Aufbau und Erzähltechnik in der Berufung des Mose (Ex. 3–4). 276 Seiten. 1989.

Bd. 92 MARK A. O'BRIEN: *The Deuteronomistic History Hypothesis:* A Reassessment. 340 Seiten. 1989.

Bd. 93 WALTER BEYERLIN: *Reflexe der Amosvisionen im Jeremiabuch.* 120 Seiten. 1989.

Bd. 94 ENZO CORTESE: *Josua 13–21.* Ein priesterschriftlicher Abschnitt im deuteronomistischen Geschichtswerk. 136 Seiten. 1990.

Bd. 95 ERIK HORNUNG (Herausgeber): *Zum Bild Ägyptens im Mittelalter und in der Renaissance. Comment se représente-t-on l'Egypte au Moyen Age et à la Renaissance.* 268 Seiten. 1990.

Bd. 96 ANDRÉ WIESE: *Zum Bild des Königs auf ägyptischen Siegelamuletten.* 264 Seiten. Mit zahlreichen Abbildungen im Text und 32 Tafeln. 1990.

Bd. 97 WOLFGANG ZWICKEL: *Räucherkult und Räuchergeräte.* Exegetische und archäologische Studien zum Räucheropfer im Alten Testament. 372 Seiten. Mit zahlreichen Abbildungen im Text. 1990.

Bd. 98 AARON SCHART: *Mose und Israel im Konflikt.* Eine redaktionsgeschichtliche Studie zu den Wüstenerzählungen. 296 Seiten. 1990.

Bd. 99 THOMAS RÖMER: *Israels Väter.* Untersuchungen zur Väterthematik im Deuteronomium und in der deuteronomistischen Tradition. 664 Seiten. 1990.

Bd. 100 OTHMAR KEEL/MENAKHEM SHUVAL/CHRISTOPH UEHLINGER: *Studien zu den Stempelsiegeln aus Palästina/Israel.* Band III. Die Frühe Eisenzeit. Ein Workshop. XIV–456 Seiten. Mit zahlreichen Abbildungen im Text und 22 Tafeln. 1990.

Bd. 101 CHRISTOPH UEHLINGER: *Weltreich und «eine Rede».* Eine neue Deutung der sogenannten Turmbauerzählung (Gen 11,1–9). XVI–654 Seiten. 1990.

Bd. 102 BENJAMIN SASS: *Studia Alphabetica.* On the Origin and Early History of the Northwest Semitic, South Semitic and Greek Alphabets. X–120 Seiten. 16 Seiten Abbildungen. 2 Tabellen. 1991.

Bd. 103 ADRIAN SCHENKER: *Text und Sinn im Alten Testament.* Textgeschichtliche und bibeltheologische Studien. VIII–312 Seiten. 1991.

Bd. 104 DANIEL BODI: *The Book of Ezekiel and the Poem of Erra.* IV–332 Seiten. 1991.

Bd. 105 YUICHI OSUMI: *Die Kompositionsgeschichte des Bundesbuches Exodus 20,22b–23,33.* XII–284 Seiten. 1991.

Bd. 106 RUDOLF WERNER: *Kleine Einführung ins Hieroglyphen-Luwische.* XII–112 Seiten. 1991.

Bd. 107 THOMAS STAUBLI: *Das Image der Nomaden im Alten Israel und in der Ikonographie seiner sesshaften Nachbarn.* XII–408 Seiten. 145 Abb. und 3 Falttafeln. 1991.

Bd. 108 MOSHÉ ANBAR: *Les tribus amurrites de Mari.* VIII–256 Seiten. 1991.

Bd. 109 GÉRARD J. NORTON/STEPHEN PISANO (eds.): *Tradition of the Text.* Studies offered to Dominique Barthélemy in Celebration of his 70th Birthday. 336 Seiten. 1991.

Bd. 110 HILDI KEEL-LEU: *Vorderasiatische Stempelsiegel.* Die Sammlung des Biblischen Instituts der Universität Freiburg Schweiz. 180 Seiten. 24 Tafeln. 1991.

Bd. 111 NORBERT LOHFINK: *Die Väter Israels im Deuteronomium.* Mit einer Stellungnahme von Thomas Römer. 152 Seiten. 1991.

Bd. 112 EDMUND HERMSEN: *Die zwei Wege des Jenseits.* Das altägyptische Zweiwegebuch und seine Topographie. XII–282 Seiten, 1 mehrfarbige und 19 Schwarz-weiss-Abbildungen. 1992.

Bd. 113 CHARLES MAYSTRE: *Les grands prêtres de Ptah de Memphis.* XIV–474 pages, 2 planches. 1992.

Bd. 114 THOMAS SCHNEIDER: *Asiatische Personennamen in ägyptischen Quellen des Neuen Reiches.* 480 Seiten. 1992.

Bd. 115 ECKHARD VON NORDHEIM: *Die Selbstbehauptung Israels in der Welt des Alten Orients.* Religionsgeschichtlicher Vergleich anhand von Gen 15/22/28, dem Aufenthalt Israels in Ägypten, 2 Sam 7, 1 Kön 19 und Psalm 104. 240 Seiten. 1992.

Bd. 116 DONALD M. MATTHEWS: *The Kassite Glyptic of Nippur.* 208 Seiten. 210 Abbildungen. 1992.

Bd. 117 FIONA V. RICHARDS: *Scarab Seals from a Middle to Late Bronze Age Tomb at Pella in Jordan.* XII–152 Seiten, 16 Tafeln. 1992.

Bd. 118 YOHANAN GOLDMAN: *Prophétie et royauté au retour de l'exil. Les origines littéraires de la forme massorétique du livre de Jérémie.* XIV–270 pages. 1992.

Bd. 119 THOMAS M. KRAPF: *Die Priesterschrift und die vorexilische Zeit. Yehezkel Kaufmanns vernachlässigter Beitrag zur Geschichte der biblischen Religion.* XX-364 Seiten. 1992.

Bd. 120 MIRIAM LICHTHEIM: *Maat in Egyptian Autobiographies and Related Studies.* 236 Seiten, 8 Tafeln. 1992.

Bd. 121 ULRICH HÜBNER: *Spiele und Spielzeug im antiken Palästina.* 256 Seiten. 58 Abbildungen. 1992.

Bd. 122 OTHMAR KEEL: *Das Recht der Bilder, gesehen zu werden. Drei Fallstudien zur Methode der Interpretation altorientalischer Bilder.* 332 Seiten, 286 Abbildungen. 1992.

Bd. 123 WOLFGANG ZWICKEL (Hrsg.): *Biblische Welten. Festschrift für Martin Metzger zu seinem 65. Geburtstag.* 268 Seiten, 19 Abbildungen. 1993.

Bd. 124 AHMED FERJAOUI: *Recherches sur les relations entre l'Orient phénicien et Carthage.* 528 pages, 57 planches. 1993.

Bd. 125 BENJAMIN SASS/CHRISTOPH UEHLINGER (eds): *Studies in the Iconography of Northwest Semitic Inscribed Seals. Proceedings of a symposium held in Fribourg on April 17-20, 1991.* 368 pages. 1993.

Sonderband PASCAL ATTINGER: *Eléments de linguistique sumérienne. La construction de du_{11}/e/di «dire».* 816 pages. 1993.

UNIVERSITY PRESS FRIBOURG SWITZERLAND

English Summary

Hundreds of Northwest Semitic inscribed seals combine on a single artifact image and script. Both the pictures and the inscriptions are instrumental for our understanding of the cultural and religious history of Syria and Palestine. But while the seals' inscriptions have been the focus of studies since the 19th century, their figurative decoration has only rarely been approached in a systematic way.

The present volume contains revised versions of papers read at a symposium held at the University of Fribourg (Switzerland) on April 17-20, 1991. Designed as a stimulus for further research in a much neglected area, it offers methodological discussions relating to the classification of seals into ethnic or national corpora, and studies on some specific iconographical motifs such as the winged disk or Mesopotamian-inspired scenes of worship. Five articles discuss the iconographical repertoires of Phoenician, Aramaean, Ammonite, Moabite, and Hebrew inscribed seals. A final contribution offers preliminary conclusions, issues for future glyptic and religio-historical research, and an inquiry into the apparent contradiction between decorated Hebrew seals on the one hand, and ancient Israel's supposed aniconism and the biblical image ban on the other.